JavaServer Faces
Programming

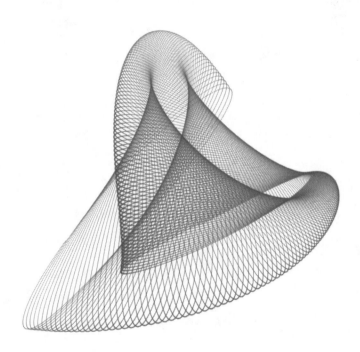

About the Author

Budi Kurniawan is an IT consultant specializing in Internet and object-oriented programming, and has taught both Java and Microsoft technologies. Budi is also the developer of the most popular Java Upload bean from BrainySoftware.com, which is licensed by Commerce One and used by major corporations.

Budi has written several computer programming books, among which is *Java for the Web with Servlets, JSP, and EJB: A Developer's Guide to J2EE Solutions* (New Riders, 2002), and has published articles for more than ten publications, including prestigious Java magazines, such as *Java-Pro*, *JavaWorld*, *JavaReport*, and O'Reilly's www.onjava.com. He is now the weekly contributor for the servlets/JSP section of the online version of JavaPro.

JavaServer Faces Programming

Budi Kurniawan

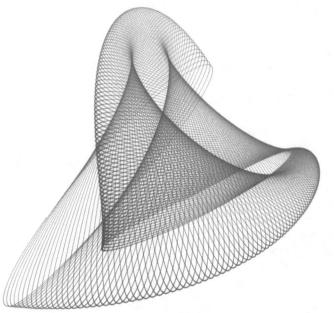

McGraw-Hill/Osborne

New York   Chicago   San Francisco
Lisbon   London   Madrid   Mexico City   Milan
New Delhi   San Juan   Seoul   Singapore   Sydney   Toronto

The McGraw-Hill Companies

McGraw-Hill/Osborne
2100 Powell Street, 10th Floor
Emeryville, California 94608
U.S.A.

To arrange bulk purchase discounts for sales promotions, premiums, or fund-raisers, please contact **McGraw-Hill**/Osborne at the above address. For information on translations or book distributors outside the U.S.A., please see the International Contact Information page immediately following the index of this book.

JavaServer Faces Programming

234567890 CUS CUS 01987654

ISBN 0-07-222983-7

Publisher	Brandon A. Nordin
Vice President & Associate Publisher	Scott Rogers
Acquisitions Editor	Nancy Maragioglio
Project Editor	Lisa Wolters-Broder
Acquisitions Coordinator	Athena Honore
Technical Editor	James Holmes
Copy Editor	Marilyn Smith
Proofreader	Emily Hsuan
Indexer	Irv Hershman
Composition	John Patrus, Dick Schwartz
Illustrators	Kathleen Edwards, Melinda Lytle, Michael Mueller, Lyssa Wald
Series Design	Roberta Steele
Cover Series Design	Greg Scott
Cover Illustration	Akira Inoue/Photonica

This book was composed with Corel VENTURA™ Publisher.

Contents at a Glance

Contents

Introduction

JavaServer Faces (JSF) is a new technology for building Web applications in Java whose specification was developed by the JSR-127 expert group under the Java Community Process. Based on the Servlet and JavaServer Pages (JSP) technologies, JSF makes the development process more rapid by providing the following features that solve practical problems in Web development:

▶ **Ready-to-use and extensible user interface (UI) components**   JSF programmers can use UI components that are rendered as HTML tags in the client browser, rather than spending time outputting these tags themselves. Better still, these components are extensible.

▶ **Easy page navigation**   Any serious Web application consists of more than one page. JSF enables page navigation through easily configurable navigation rules and cases.

▶ **Input validators**   One of the time-consuming tasks in developing Web applications is writing code to validate user input. JSF solves this problem by providing standard input validators that are ready to use. More importantly, if you can't find one that suits your need, you can extend an existing component to create a custom input validator.

▶ **JavaBeans management**   JSF automatically manages JavaBeans instances for different scopes for use from inside your pages.

▶ **Event handling**   JSF is event-driven. Those familiar with Swing will find similarity between Swing and JSF. Event-driven-ness supports maximum code reusability and easier code maintenance.

▶ **Easy error handling**   JSF provides a sophisticated mechanism for error handling.

▶ **Support for internationalization**   JSF supports internationalization and localization of your Web applications, making it possible to build sites that cater for audience from different countries and backgrounds.

NOTE

JSF is also designed to work with other technologies, such as Portlet. However, this book focuses on how to use JSF to build Web applications.

Sun Microsystems proposed JSF to be the ultimate technology for building Java Web applications. It is easy to predict that JSF will soon be the preferred framework because of its support for rapid development and easy code maintenance. There will also be new industries that cater to the needs of JSF programmers, such as those making JSF components and tools that assist in JSF application development.

NOTE

The official JSF web site is `http://java.sun.com/j2ee/javaserverfaces/`. *An open source version of the JSF implementation is available from* `http://sourceforge` `.net/projects/myfaces/`.

Who Should Read This Book?

This book discusses all aspects of Web development using JSF. You need this book if you are one of the following:

▶ A JSF page author who needs to design JSF pages that employs JSF UI components.

▶ A JSF application developer who is responsible for writing business logic for JSF applications.

▶ A component writer who would like to create reusable components.

▶ A J2EE architect who is looking for the best technology to build scalable Java Web-based applications.

▶ IT managers who need to be informed of new and exciting Java technologies for possible use in their own organizations.

Required Software

JSF applications are servlet applications. They need a Web container to host them. Basically, you can use any Servlet 2.3 and Servlet 2.4 compliant container, such as Tomcat from the Apache Software Foundation (`http://jakarta.apache.org/tomcat/`). For your JSF application to work, you need the JSF reference implementation that is included in the Java Web Services Developer Pack (currently at version 1.3) (`http://java.sun.com/` `webservices/downloads/webservicespack.html`). Once you download and install it, you will find a directory called `jsf`. Inside `jsf`, there is a directory called `lib` that contains all the .jar files needed by a JSF application. You need to copy these files to the `WEB-INF/lib` directory of your Web application. Here is the list of the jar files.

▶ `jsf-api.jar`   Contains the Faces servlet and related classes in the `javax.faces` package

▶ `jfs-ri.jar`   The reference implementation of JSF

▶ `jstl.jar` and `standard.jar` Required to use JSP Standard Tag Library (JSTL) tags and referenced by JFS reference implementation classes

In addition, a JSF application will need the following libraries that are part of the Apache Jakarta project.

▶ `commons-beanutils.jar` Utilities for defining and accessing JavaBeans component properties

▶ `commons-digester.jar` The library containing the Apache Common Digester classes

▶ `commons-logging.jar` A general purpose, flexible logging facility

This release of JavaServer Faces has been tested with various configurations with the Java 2 SDK, Standard Edition version 1.3.1_04, 1.4, and 1.4.1 on the following platforms and browsers:

▶ Solaris 2.8

▶ Solaris 2.9

▶ Windows 2000

▶ Windows XP

▶ RedHat Linux 7.2

▶ Netscape 6.x

▶ Internet Explorer 6

Sample Applications and Code Listings

All JSF applications and code listings used in this book can be downloaded from the author's Web site `http://www.brainysoftware.com`. To easily test an application that accompanies a chapter, simply copy the application to your Web container. Each application is named after the chapter. For example, the JSFCh01 is the application for Chapter 1, JSFCh05 for Chapter 5, etc. Chapter 2 presented three sample applications, and the applications are named JSFCh02a, JSFCh02b, and JSFCh02c.

The required JSF libraries are not included, however, and must be downloaded separately from the Java Web Services Developer Pack. Once you get the library files, copy them to the `WEB-INF/lib` directory of each sample application.

All applications offered in this book are based on JSF version 1.0 Early Access 4. Any update and errata will also be available from the author's site.

James Holmes, the technical editor for this book, has written a nice Swing application that can help you manage your JSF applications. You can download this tool from his Web site at `http://www.jamesholmes.com/JavaServerFaces/`.

Overview of All Chapters

The following is the overview of how this book is organized.

Chapter 1: Underlying Technologies

This chapter is meant as a refresher for those of you who need to brush up your servlet and JSP programming skills. It presents the Servlet and JSP technologies as well as the introduction to JavaBeans, custom tags, and the Model 2 architecture. You will need to understand the topics here to be able to understand the rest of the book.

Chapter 2: Introduction to JavaServer Faces

This chapter gently introduces the JavaServer Faces technology. More importantly, it teaches you how to write your first JSF application to get a feel for how this great technology works. In addition to the sample chapters, this chapter prepares you for what you should expect in the next chapters. The JSF Application Programming Interface (API) is also briefly discussed here. In addition, it also covers the Application Configuration file that you can use to configure your JSF application.

Chapter 3: Objects for Request Processing

As a servlet/JSP programmer, you must be familiar with the `ServletRequest` and `ServletResponse` objects as well as the `ServletContext` and `ServletConfig` objects. In JSF, you don't normally access these objects directly. All these are encapsulated in the `FacesContext` object, which is the highlight of this chapter. Apart from `FacesContext`, you can also find the discussion of some basic objects such as `ExternalContext`, `Tree`, and `Application`. Understanding these objects is key to writing effective code for your JSF applications.

Chapter 4: JSF UI Component Model

JSF comes with ready-to-use UI components. This chapter explains the members of the `javax.faces.component` package that represents UI components. Of particular interest is the `UIComponent` interface, the interface that all UI components must implement. You'll also find discussions on `UIForm`, `UICommand`, `UIOutput`, `UIInput`, `UIPanel`, etc.

Chapter 5: Using Simple Components

This chapter and Chapter 6 show how to use JSF UI components through custom tags in JSP pages. This chapter presents the easier components, such as `UIForm`, `UICommand`, `UIOutput`, and `UIInput`. Other more advanced components are discussed in Chapter 6.

Chapter 6: Using Advanced Components

This chapter is the continuation of Chapter 5 and covers the use of custom tags that represents the UI components such as `UIPanel` and `UISelectItem`, `UISelectItems`, `UISelectMany`, and `UISelectOne`.

Chapter 7: Event Handling

JSF is event-driven, therefore building JSF applications means spending a big fraction of the development time writing event handlers. This chapter shows you how you can capture events in JSF and handle them.

Chapter 8: Page Navigation

This chapter shows how you can easily manage page navigation in JSF by using the navigation-rule element in the Application Configuration file. The chapter basically covers all aspects of page navigation, starting from the simple to conditional navigation.

Chapter 9: Validators

One of the most useful features that JSF provides is validators. As the name implies, you use validators to validate the values input by the user. This chapter teaches you how to use the standard validators as well as how to write custom validators just in case the existing ones do not suit your needs.

Chapter 10: Converters

Data conversion is an advanced topic that needs special attention. Actually data conversion happens automatically during the request processing lifecycle. This chapter brings data converters to your attention. In this chapter you will find the technique to write custom converters.

Chapter 11: Internationalization and Localization

JSF supports internationalization and localization. This chapter explains how to create multilingual sites and how to make full use of JSF internationalization and localization supports.

Chapter 12: Renderers

The UI components created for a page need to be rendered, which means its state needs to be presented to the client. In a Web application this means sending HTML tags to the browser. There are two programming models available with regard to rendering: direct implementation and delegated implementation. This chapter discusses these two models and explains how to create your own renderers.

Chapter 13: Custom Components

Chapter 13 offers the complete guide to writing your own UI components. This is an advanced topic, but this chapter starts from the simplest component to smooth the learning process. In addition to explaining the related classes, there are some more advanced custom components presented.

Chapter 14: An Online Store Application

This chapter discusses a project called BuyDirect, an online store that is built using the JSF technology. Even though not a complete solution, the project presented here offers basic functionality of an online store, such as searching, browsing, shopping cart, etc. This chapter shows how JSF can be used in real-world applications.

Chapter 15: Application Configuration File

JSF applications can be easily configured using the Application Configuration file. This chapter presents all the elements that can be present in the Application Configuration.

Chapter 16: Summing Up: How JSF Works

Chapter 2 discussed how JSF works briefly. Now, after getting familiar with all the features in JSF, you can learn how JSF works in much more technical depth. This chapter is for the curious.

Chapter 17: Expression Language in JSP 2.0

This chapter presents the new features in JSP 2.0 that can greatly improve your JSF application: the expression language (EL). This chapter discusses the EL in great detail and shows how you can use it in conjunction with the JSF custom tags.

Chapter 18: JSTL Library for Formatting

Seasoned JSP programmers use JSTL to rapidly author JSP pages. This chapter discusses a small fraction of JSTL that can help in writing JSF pages.

Appendix A: Tomcat 5 Installation

To run, JSF needs to be hosted in a Servlet 2.3 compliant servlet container, such as Tomcat. In fact, Tomcat is the most popular servlet container which is free and open-source, the reason why it was chosen to be the container for all JSF sample application in this book. This appendix shows how to easily install and configure Tomcat 5.

Appendix B: Web Deployment Descriptor

A JSF application is a servlet application. As such, it also utilizes the deployment descriptor (web.xml file) to set different settings for the application. This appendix presents the Web deployment descriptor for Servlet 2.3.

Overview of Java Web Technologies

IN THIS CHAPTER:

Servlets

JavaServer Pages (JSP)

JSP and JavaBeans

Custom Tags

Model 2 Architecture

Summary

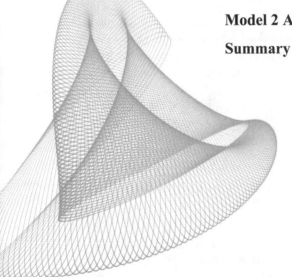

J avaServer Faces (JSF) applications are servlet/JavaServer Pages (JSP) applications based on the Model 2 architecture. Therefore, writing JSF applications requires you to be familiar with the servlet and JSP technologies, as well as the related technologies of JavaBeans and custom tags, plus the Model 2 architecture. This book assumes that you already have some servlet/JSP programming experience. However, to quickly refresh your memory, this chapter presents a brief overview of those technologies, focusing on topics directly related to writing JSF applications.

Servlets

Servlets are Java classes that run on a special Web server called a servlet/JSP container or Web container. In servlet programming, you use the classes and interfaces from two packages:

▶   `javax.servlet`, which contains basic types for servlet programming

▶   `javax.servlet.http`, which contains interfaces and classes that extend those from the `javax.servlet` package

The most important type in these two packages is the `javax.servlet.Servlet` interface, which all servlets must implement (or extend a class that does). We'll begin our review of servlets by taking a look at the `Servlet` interface.

Using the Servlet Interface

The `javax.servlet.Servlet` interface defines the three lifecycle methods: `init`, `service`, and `destroy`. The servlet container calls these methods during the life of a servlet.

NOTE

The alternative to implementing the `Servlet` *interface directly is to extend the* `javax.servlet .GenericServlet` *class or the* `javax.servlet.http.HttpServlet` *class.*

The init Method

The `init` method is called the first time the servlet is invoked. It is called exactly once to indicate to the servlet that the servlet is being placed into service. You override this method to write initialization code that needs to be executed only once, such as initializing values, loading database drivers, and so on.

The following is the method's signature:

```
public void init(ServletConfig config) throws ServletException
```

The service Method

The `service` method is called by the servlet container each time the servlet is invoked. For each incoming HTTP request, the servlet container creates a request object (that

implements `javax.servlet.ServletRequest` or `javax.servlet.http`
`.HttpServletRequest`) and a response object (that implements `javax.servlet`
`.ServletResponse` or `javax.servlet.http.HttpServletResponse`)
and passes both objects to the servlet's `service` method. The request object encapsulates
information parsed from the HTTP request that the servlet can use, such as the request URI,
request headers and cookies, and request parameters. The servlet uses the response object to
send responses to the Web client.

The `service` method has the following signature:

```
public void service(ServletRequest request, ServletResponse response)
   throws ServletException, java.io.IOException
```

TIP

*If you're interested in knowing how a servlet container creates request and response objects, or how it works
in general, read How Tomcat Works, available from www.brainysoftware.com.*

The destroy Method

The servlet container calls the `destroy` method before removing a servlet instance from
service. This normally happens when the servlet container is shut down or the servlet
container needs some free memory. You use this method to clean up any resources (such
as memory, file handles, and threads) that are being held and make sure that any persistent
state is synchronized with the servlet's current state in memory.

The following is the `destroy` method's signature:

```
public void destroy()
```

Creating a Servlet Directory Structure

To run your servlet applications, you need a servlet container. One such container is Tomcat,
the most popular container, which is an open-source project. The code in this book was tested
using Tomcat, but you can use any Servlet 2.3-compliant servlet container to run it.

NOTE

*JSF is currently based on the Servlet 2.3 specification, but this may change. The release version may be
based on the Servlet 2.4 specification (to be released soon also).*

When you first install Tomcat (Appendix A provides step-by-step instruction on installing
and configuring Tomcat), several directories are created under the directory in which you
install Tomcat. Tomcat's directory structure is shown in Figure 1-1.

In Figure 1-1, Tomcat is installed in the `tomcat5` directory. This directory is also known
as `%CATALINA_HOME%`. One of the subdirectories is `webapps`. This is the parent directory
of every Web application that will be run under this Tomcat installation.

When you first install Tomcat, a number of sample applications are also created: `jsp-`
`examples`, `ROOT`, `servlets-examples`, and `tomcat-docs`. Therefore, a directory
under `webapps` is called an application directory, and it contains the resources for a

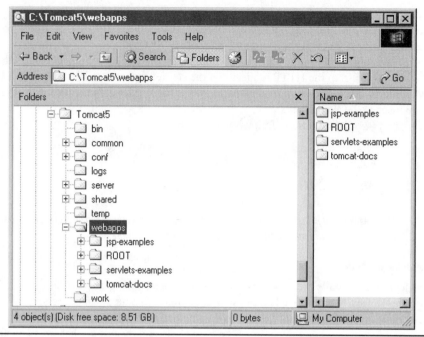

Figure 1-1   *Tomcat's directory structure.*

particular application. For an example of an application directory structure, look at the
jsp-examples application directory.

   Directly beneath an application directory is a directory called WEB-INF, which has
special significance in a Web application. Under WEB-INF, you can have a classes
directory and a lib directory. The classes directory contains all servlet classes and
other Java classes used by the Web application. The directory structure under classes
must represent the fully qualified name of the Java class. For example, if you have a
servlet class called ch01.MyServlet, you must create a ch01 directory under
classes and put the MyServlet.class file in classes/ch01. The lib directory,
if one exists, contains all libraries (.jar files) referenced by any resource in the Web
application.

   All static resources and JSP files are stored directly under the application directory.
For better organization, you can create subdirectories under the application directory.
For example, you may want to create a jsp directory for all JSP pages and an images
directory for all your image files. A Web client can access anything you put under the
application directory, except those under WEB-INF, because WEB-INF is a special
directory.

   A Web application normally has a deployment descriptor, which is an XML file called
web.xml containing the description of the application. You store the web.xml file under
WEB-INF. We'll take a look at the deployment descriptor in the next section.

Reviewing Deployment Descriptors

A deployment descriptor is an XML file, so you can edit it using a text editor. The deployment descriptor for an application compliant with the Servlet 2.3 specification starts with the following:

```
<?xml version="1.0" encoding="ISO-8859-1"?>
<!DOCTYPE web-app
  PUBLIC "-//Sun Microsystems, Inc.//DTD Web Application 2.3//EN"
  "http://java.sun.com/dtd/web-app_2_3.dtd">
```

These headers indicate that the document type definition (DTD) for this deployment descriptor can be downloaded from `http://java.sun.com/dtd/web-app_2_3.dtd`. If you open the DTD file, you can see that the root element of a deployment descriptor is `web-app`. The `web-app` element can have up to 23 kinds of subelements, as shown here:

```
<!ELEMENT web-app (icon?, display-name?, description?,
distributable?, context-param*, filter*, filter-mapping*,
listener*, servlet*, servlet-mapping*, session-config?,
mime-mapping*, welcome-file-list?, error-page*, taglib*,
resource-env-ref*, resource-ref*, security-constraint*,
login-config?, security-role*, env-entry*, ejb-ref*,
ejb-local-ref*)>
```

All of these subelements are optional, so you are not required to include any of them. The subelements preceding a question mark (?) can appear only once. Those followed by an asterisk (*) can appear many times. Additionally, some of these subelements can have subelements.

Note that in Servlet 2.4, a deployment descriptor is validated against a schema, not a DTD file. However, the elements under `web-app` are pretty much the same.

Servlet Mapping

Before you can access a servlet from a Web browser, you must map the servlet to a path in your deployment descriptor. For example, the deployment descriptor in Listing 1-1 creates the servlet name `MyServlet` and maps it to `/aUrl`.

Listing 1-1   *The Deployment Descriptor Mapping*

```
<?xml version="1.0" encoding="ISO-8859-1"?>
<!DOCTYPE web-app
  PUBLIC "-//Sun Microsystems, Inc.//DTD Web Application 2.3//EN"
  "http://java.sun.com/dtd/web-app_2_3.dtd">

<web-app>
```

```
<servlet>
  <servlet-name>MyServlet</servlet-name>
  <servlet-class>ch01.MyServlet</servlet-class>
</servlet>
<!-- mapping -->
<servlet-mapping>
  <servlet-name>MyServlet</servlet-name>
  <url-pattern>/aUrl</url-pattern>
</servlet-mapping>
</web-app>
```

This enables your users to access the servlet using the following URL:

```
http://localhost:8080/appName/aUrl
```

Defining Context Parameters

In a deployment descriptor (the web.xml file), you can define settings for the application the deployment descriptor describes. This allows you to define context initial parameters that are available to all servlets/JSP pages in that application, register servlets, register listeners, map resources to URLs, and so on. This section explains how you can define context parameters.

Using context parameters can save you from needing to hard-code certain information in the servlet code. This way, if you want to change the information, you will not need to recompile the servlet.

You can specify context parameter name/value pairs that will be available to all servlets/JSP pages in that application using the context-param element. For example, Listing 1-2 shows a deployment descriptor that contains a servlet called MyServlet, which has two initial parameter name/value pairs: userName/budi and password/secret.

Listing 1-2 *The Deployment Descriptor Initial Parameter Name/Value Pairs*

```
<?xml version="1.0" encoding="ISO-8859-1"?>
<!DOCTYPE web-app
  PUBLIC "-//Sun Microsystems, Inc.//DTD Web Application 2.3//EN"
  "http://java.sun.com/dtd/web-app_2_3.dtd">
<web-app>
  <context-param>
    <param-name>userName</param-name>
    <param-value>budi</param-value>
  </context-param>
  <context-param>
    <param-name>password</param-name>
    <param-value>secret</param-value>
  </context-param>
</web-app>
```

Retrieving Context Parameters

To retrieve a context parameter name and value defined in the deployment descriptor, you first need to obtain the ServletContext object using the getServletContext method of the ServletConfig object. You then call two methods of the ServletContext interface:

▶ The getInitParameterNames method, which does not take an argument and returns a java.util.Enumeration containing all the context parameter names.

▶ The getInitParameter method, which takes a String argument containing the parameter name and returns a String containing the value of the parameter.

The code in Listing 1-3 is an init method of a servlet called ContextParamDemoServlet. It loops through the Enumeration object called parameters, which is returned from the getInitParameterNames method. For each parameter, it outputs the parameter name and value. The parameter value is retrieved using the getInitParameter method.

Listing 1-3   *Retrieving Context Parameters*

```
public void init(ServletConfig config) throws ServletException {
  ServletContext servletContext = servletConfig.getServletContext();
Enumeration parameters = servletContext.getInitParameterNames();
  while (parameters.hasMoreElements()) {
    String parameter = (String) parameters.nextElement();
    System.out.println("Parameter name : " + parameter);
    System.out.println("Parameter value : " +
      config.getInitParameter(parameter));
  }
}
```

The output of the code in the console is as follows:

```
Parameter name  : userName
Parameter value : budi
Parameter name  : password
Parameter value : secret
```

Listening to Application Events

The Servlet 2.3 and 2.4 specifications allow you to write listener classes for servlet contexts, session objects, and request objects (only in Servlet 2.4). In this section, we're interested in the listener classes for a servlet context.

The `javax.servlet` package provides two listener interfaces that support event notifications for state changes in the `ServletContext` object: the `ServletContext Listener` interface and the `ServletContextAttributesListener` interface. We'll examine the `ServletContextListener` interface here, because it's directly related to writing JSF applications.

You use the `ServletContextListener` interface to listen to the `ServletContext` lifecycle events. `ServletContextListener` provides two methods:

▶ The `contextInitialized` method is called when the Web application is ready to service requests. The method is called automatically by the servlet container when its own initialization process is finished. You can write code that needs to be executed when the application initializes, such as loading a JDBC driver, creating a database `Connection` object, or assigning initialization values to global variables.

▶ The `contextDestroyed` method is invoked when the servlet context is about to be shut down. You can use this method to write code that needs to run when the application shuts down, such as closing a database connection or writing to the log.

The signatures of `contextInitialized` and `contextDestroyed` are as follows:

```
public void contextInitialized(ServletContextEvent sce)
public void contextDestroyed(ServletContextEvent sce)
```

As an example, the code in Listing 1-4 is a listener class called `ApplicationListener`. It listens to the lifecycle events of the `ServletContext`. It simply prints the string "Application initialized" when the `ServletContext` is initialized and "Application destroyed" when the `ServletContext` is destroyed.

Listing 1-4   *The ApplicationListener Class*

```
import javax.servlet.ServletContextListener;
import javax.servlet.ServletContextEvent;
public class ApplicationListener implements ServletContextListener {
  public void contextInitialized(ServletContextEvent cse) {
    System.out.println("Application initialized");
  }
  public void contextDestroyed(ServletContextEvent cse) {
    System.out.println("Application shut down");
  }
}
```

For the `ApplicationListener` class to work, you must register it in the deployment descriptor, such as the one in Listing 1-5.

Listing 1-5   *The Deployment Descriptor for the ApplicationListener Class*

```xml
<?xml version="1.0" encoding="ISO-8859-1"?>
<!DOCTYPE web-app
  PUBLIC "-//Sun Microsystems, Inc.//DTD Web Application 2.3//EN"
  "http://java.sun.com/dtd/web-app_2_3.dtd">
<web-app>
  <listener>
    <listener-class>ApplicationListener</listener-class>
  </listener>
</web-app>
```

Now, every time your application starts (the first time a servlet or JSP page is invoked), you will see the string "Application initialized" at the console. And before your application is taken out of service, it will display "Application shut down."

Packaging and Deploying a Web Application

You can deploy an application to a production machine by just copying the application directory and all of its contents to that machine. Alternatively, you can package your application into a Web archive (WAR) file. A WAR file has a .war extension. A WAR file is basically a Java archive (JAR) file you create using the `jar` program. The WAR filename is usually the same as the application's name, but you can use a different name if you desire.

To deploy an application packaged in a WAR file, copy the WAR file into the `webapps` directory. You then can access your application just as you would access an unpackaged application. The name used for your packaged application is the .war filename. For example, if you package an application called `myApp` into a WAR file called `aWarApp.war`, when deployed, the application name is `aWarApp`, not `myApp`. This is because the application name is not included in the WAR file when you package your application.

JavaServer Pages (JSP)

Sun introduced servlets in 1996, and this technology soon became popular as a faster solution than the Common Gateway Interface (CGI) technology, which was the first technology for writing Web applications. However, Sun realized that writing servlets could be very cumbersome, especially if you need to send a long HTML page with little code. Take the following servlet as an example:

```java
import javax.servlet.*;
import javax.servlet.http.*;
import java.io.*;
import java.util.*;
```

```
public class MyLongServlet extends HttpServlet {
  //Process the HTTP GET request
  public void doGet(HttpServletRequest request,
    HttpServletResponse response)
    throws ServletException, IOException {
    doPost(request, response);
  }
  //Process the HTTP POST request
  public void doPost(HttpServletRequest request,
    HttpServletResponse response)
    throws ServletException, IOException {
    response.setContentType("text/html");
    PrintWriter out = response.getWriter();
    out.println("<HTML>");
    out.println("<HEAD><TITLE>Using Servlets</TITLE></HEAD>");
    out.println("<BODY BGCOLOR=#123123>");
    //Get parameter names
    Enumeration parameters = request.getParameterNames();
    String param = null;
    while (parameters.hasMoreElements()) {
      param = (String) parameters.nextElement();
      out.println(param + ":" + request.getParameter(param) +
        "<BR>");
    }
    out.println("</BODY>");
    out.println("</HTML>");
    out.close();
  } //End of doPost method
} //End of class
```

Half of the content sent from the `doPost` method is static HTML. However, each HTML tag must be embedded in a `String` and sent using the `println` method of the `PrintWriter` object. It is a tedious chore. Worse still, every single change, even the change to a color code in an HTML tag, requires you to recompile the servlet.

Sun's solution to this problem is JSP. According to Sun's Web site, "JSP technology is an extension of the servlet technology created to support authoring of HTML and XML pages." Combining fixed or static template data with dynamic content is easier with JSP. JSP makes development more rapid than using servlets alone because it allows HTML tags to intersperse with Java code. No compilation is necessary. The first time a JSP page is invoked, the servlet/JSP container compiles it automatically. The `MyLongServlet` in the previous example can be rewritten in a JSP page like this:

```
<%@ page import="java.util.Enumeration" %>
<HTML>
<HEAD><TITLE>Using JSP</TITLE></HEAD>
```

```
<BODY BGCOLOR=#DADADA>
<%
  //Get parameter names
  Enumeration parameters = request.getParameterNames();
  String param = null;
  while (parameters.hasMoreElements()) {
    param = (String) parameters.nextElement();
    out.println(param + ":" + request.getParameter(param) +
      "<BR>");
  }
  out.close();
%>
</BODY>
</HTML>
```

However, note that JSP did *not* make servlets obsolete. In fact, JSP pages and servlets coexist in many Java Web applications. And, bear in mind that JSP is an extension of servlets.

Inside the JSP container is a special servlet called the *page compiler*. The servlet container is configured to forward to this page compiler all HTTP requests with URLs that match the .jsp file extension. This page compiler turns a servlet container into a JSP container. When a JSP page is first called, the page compiler parses and compiles the JSP page into a servlet class. If the compilation is successful, the JSP servlet class is loaded into memory.

On subsequent calls, the servlet class for that JSP page is already in memory; however, it could have been updated. Therefore, the page compiler servlet will always compare the timestamp of the JSP servlet with the JSP page. If the JSP page is more current, recompilation is necessary. With this process, once deployed, JSP pages go through the time-consuming compilation process only once.

You may be thinking that after the deployment, the first user requests for a JSP page will experience unusually slow response, due to the time spent compiling the .jsp file into a JSP servlet. That scenario was anticipated, and to avoid this unpleasant situation, a mechanism in JSP allows the JSP pages to be precompiled before any user request for them is received. Alternatively, you can automatically load a JSP page by using the <load-on-startup> element under the <servlet> element in the deployment descriptor.

JSP and JavaBeans

Although you can easily write JSP pages by interweaving HTML tags and Java code, there are at least two disadvantages to this approach. First, the resulting page lacks readability. Second, there is no separation of the presentation and business rule implementation. To write a JSP page this way, a JSP author must master both Java and page design. This is difficult because not many people are conversant in both graphic design and Java programming.

A separation of labor between a graphic designer and a Java programmer is needed to expedite the development of JSP applications. This is possible through the use of JavaBeans. In this approach, the Java programmer writes and compiles JavaBeans that incorporate all the functionality needed in an application. While the programmer is doing this, the graphic designer can work with the page design. When the JavaBeans are ready, the page designer uses tags similar to HTML to call methods and properties of the beans from the JSP page.

In fact, using beans is a common practice in JSP application development. This approach is popular because using JavaBeans introduces reusability. Rather than building your own piece of code, you can simply use what other people have written. For example, you can purchase a bean for file upload and start uploading files within 30 seconds.

NOTE

When you are designing a JavaBean for your JSP page, reusability and modularity are of utmost importance. Therefore, it is uncommon to use a bean to send HTML tags to the Web browser, because this makes the bean customized for that page. If you need to send HTML tags customized for a page, you can use custom tags instead, as explained later in this chapter.

Really, a JavaBean is just a Java class. You do not need to extend any base class or implement any interface to create a JavaBean. To be a bean, however, a Java class must follow certain rules specified by the JavaBeans specification. For example, the bean class must have a no-argument constructor. If a Java class does not contain a constructor, the compiler will create a no-argument constructor.

Setting and Getting JavaBean Properties

Optionally, a bean can have a public method that can be used to set the value of a property. This method is called a *setter* method or a *mutator*. The method does not return any value, and its name starts with set, followed by the name of the property. A setter method has the following signature:

```
public void setPropertyName (PropertyType value)
```

For example, the setter method for the property name operand must be named setOperand. Notice that the letter case for the property name is different. A property name starts with a lowercase letter, but the name of the setter uses an uppercase letter after set.

Optionally, a bean can also have a public method that can be called to obtain the value of a property. This method is called a *getter* method or a *accessor*, and its return type is the same as the property type. Its name must begin with get, followed by the name of the property. A getter method has the following signature:

```
public propertyType getPropertyName();
```

For example, the getter method for the property named operand is getOperand. As with the setter method syntax, the property name begins with an uppercase letter within the getter method syntax.

Both setter and getter methods are known as *access methods*. In JSP, the jsp:getProperty and jsp:setProperty action elements are used to invoke a getter and a setter method, respectively. You can call these methods the same way you call an ordinary method, as described in the "Accessing Bean Properties" section later in this chapter.

Calling a Bean from a JSP Page

Before you can use a bean in your JSP page, you must make the bean available, using the `jsp:useBean` action element. This element has attributes that you can use to set the bean's properties. The syntax for the `jsp:useBean` element has two forms:

```
<jsp:useBean (attribute="value")*/>
```

```
<jsp:useBean (attribute="value")*>
  initialization code
</jsp:useBean>
```

You use the first form if you do not need to write any initialization code, and the second form if you do. The `(attribute="value")*` part of the code means that one or more attributes must be present. The five attributes that can be used in a `jsp:useBean` action element are as follows:

▶ The `id` attribute defines a unique identifier for the bean. This identifier can be used throughout the page and can be thought of as the object reference for the bean. The value for the `id` attribute has the same requirements as a valid variable name in the current scripting language.

▶ The `class` attribute specifies the fully qualified name for the `JavaBean` class. A fully qualified name is not required if the bean's package is imported using the `page` directive, however.

▶ If the `type` attribute is present in a `jsp:useBean` element, it specifies the type of the JavaBean class. The type of the bean could be the type of the class itself, the type of its superclass, or an interface the bean class implements. Normally, this attribute isn't often used and you use the `class` attribute instead.

▶ The `scope` attribute defines the accessibility and the life span of the bean. This attribute can take one of the following values: `page`, `request`, `session`, or `application`. The default value of the scope attribute is `page`. The scope attribute values control how long the bean will continue to exist, as follows:

    ▶ **page**   The bean is available only in the current page after the point where the `jsp:useBean` action element is used. A new instance of the bean will be instantiated every time the page is requested. The bean will be automatically destroyed after the JSP page loses its scope; that is, when the control moves to another page. If you use the `jsp:include` or `jsp:forward` tags, the bean will not be accessible from the included or forwarded page.

    ▶ **request**   The accessibility of the bean is extended to the forwarded or included page referenced by a `jsp:forward` or `jsp:include` action element. The forwarded or included page can use the bean without a `jsp:useBean` action element. For example, from a forwarded or included page, you can use the `jsp:getProperty` and `jsp:setProperty` action elements that reference the bean instantiated in the original page.

▶ **session** The bean scope applies to the user's session object. The instance of the bean will continue to exist as long as the user's session object exists. In other words, the bean's accessibility extends to other pages. Because the bean's instance is put in the session object, you cannot use this scope if the page on which the bean is instantiated does not participate in the JSP container's session management.

▶ **application** This scope lives throughout the life of the JSP container itself. The bean is available from any resource in the application.

▶ The beanName attribute represents a name for the bean that the instantiate method of the java.beans.Beans class expects.

Either the class attribute or the type attribute must be present.

For example, here is how you use the jsp:useBean element to instantiate a bean called ch01.LongBean:

```
<jsp:useBean id="theBean" class="ch01.LongBean"/>
```

Alternatively, you can import the package ch01 using a page directive and refer to the class using its name, as follows:

```
<%@ page import="ch01" %>
<jsp:useBean id="theBean" class="LongBean"/>
```

NOTE

The bean is available in the page after the jsp:useBean action element. It is not available before that point.

As an example, lets go through the process of using a simple bean on a JSP page. Listing 1-6 shows a Java class called ch01.AdderBean.

Listing 1-6 *The ch01.AdderBean Class*

```
package ch01;
public class AdderBean {
  public int add(int a, int b) {
    return (a + b);
  }
}
```

After you create the AdderBean, you need to compile it to obtain the AdderBean.class file. Then you need to copy the bean class file to the classes directory under WEB-INF under your application directory. The deployment must take into account the package name. In this case, you need to create a directory called ch01. Copy your AdderBean.class file to this ch01 directory. Once you have a JavaBean ready and its class file stored in the proper directory, you can use it from a JSP page. Now, you can create a JSP page that calls the bean, as shown in Listing 1-7.

Listing 1-7   *Calling a Bean from a JSP Page (`callBean.jsp`)*

```
<jsp:useBean id="theBean" class="ch01.AdderBean"/>
<html>
<head></head>
<body>
<%
  int x = 4;
  int y = 5;
  int result = theBean.add(x, y);
  out.print("4+5=" + result);
%>
</body>
</html>
```

After you create the JSP page, start or restart Tomcat and direct your browser to the URL and to the JSP page you just wrote. Your browser should display the following string:

```
4+5=9
```

NOTE

You can also use a JAR for your JavaBean. In this case, you must copy the .jar file into the `lib` directory under the `WEB-INF` directory of your application directory to make it available to JSP pages in your application.

Accessing Bean Properties

To access a property in a bean, use the `jsp:getProperty` and `jsp:setProperty` action elements. The `jsp:getProperty` element obtains the value of an internal variable, and the bean must provide a getter method. A `jsp:getProperty` element returns the property value converted into `String`. The return value is then automatically fed into an `out.print` method, so it will be displayed in the current JSP page. The syntax of the `jsp:getProperty` element is as follows:

```
<jsp:getProperty name="Bean Name" property="propertyName"/>
```

The `name` attribute must be assigned the name of the bean instance from which the property value will be obtained. The `property` attribute must be assigned the name of the property.

The `jsp:setProperty` action element sets the value of a property. Its syntax has four forms:

```
<jsp:setProperty name="Bean Name" property="PropertyName"  value="value"/>
<jsp:setProperty name="Bean Name" property="PropertyName"/>
```

```
<jsp:setProperty name="Bean Name" property="PropertyName" param="parameterName"/>
<jsp:setProperty name="Bean Name" property="*"/>
```

In this book, you will learn about and use only the first form. The `name` attribute is assigned the name of the bean instance available in the current JSP page. In the first form of the syntax, the `property` attribute is assigned the name of the property whose value is to be set, and the `value` attribute is assigned the value of the property.

The following example demonstrates the use of the `jsp:getProperty` and `jsp:setProperty` action elements.

Listing 1-8 shows a variation of the `AdderBean` used in the previous example. It has a private integer called `memory`. (Note that the variable name starts with a lowercase *m*.) It also has a getter method called `getMemory` and a setter method named `setMemory`. (Note that in both access methods, memory is spelled using an uppercase *M*.)

Listing 1-8   *The AdderBean with Access Methods*

```java
package ch01;
public class AdderBean {
  private int memory;
  public void setMemory(int number) {
    memory = number;
  }

  public int getMemory() {
    return memory;
  }
  public int add(int x, int y) {
    return (x + y);
  }
}
```

Using the `jsp:setProperty` and `jsp:getProperty` action elements, you can set and obtain the value of `memory`, as demonstrated in the JSP page in Listing 1-9.

Listing 1-9   *Accessing a Bean Property Using jsp:setProperty and jsp:getProperty*

```
<jsp:useBean id="theBean" class="ch01.AdderBean"/>
<jsp:setProperty name="theBean" property="memory" value="169"/>
The value of memory is <jsp:getProperty name="theBean" property="memory"/>
```

NOTE

For more information about JavaBeans, see
http://java.sun.com/docs/books/tutorial/javabeans/index.html.

Custom Tags

Using JavaBeans allows you to separate the presentation part of a JSP page from the Java code. However, only three action elements—jsp:useBean, jsp:getProperty, and jsp:setProperty—are available for accessing a bean. Therefore in some situations, we need to resort to using code in a JSP page. In other words, in many cases, JavaBeans do not offer complete separation of presentation and business rule implementation.

Also, JavaBeans are designed with reusability in mind, meaning that using a bean to output HTML tags directly is not recommended. Outputting HTML tags from a bean makes the bean usable only from a certain page.

In recognition of the imperfection of JavaBeans as a solution to separation of presentation and business rule implementation, JSP 1.1 defined a new feature: custom tags that can be used to perform custom actions. For example, the following JSP page uses custom tags:

```
<%@ taglib uri="/myTLD" prefix="c"%>
<html>
<head>
<title>Using custom tags</title>
</head>
<body>
<c:myTag/>
</body>
</html>
```

As you can see, the JSP page above is free from Java code. On the first line, you declare that you are using a custom tag in the JSP page, and on the seventh line, you use the custom tag itself. The result output by the <c:myTag/> tag depends on the Java class associated with the custom tag.

Understanding how to use and develop custom tags is important in developing JSF applications, because, in fact, JSF uses custom tags extensively.

To use custom tags, you must develop a custom tag library. We will examine the process of creating custom tag libraries and using them from JSP pages in detail. But first, we'll take a look at the differences between JavaBeans and custom tags.

Comparing Custom Tags with JavaBeans

Compared to JavaBeans, custom tags offer some advantages:

▶ Custom tags have access to all the objects available to JSP pages.

▶ Custom tags can be customized using attributes.

However, custom tags have the disadvantage of being slightly harder to build and use than JavaBeans. Sometimes, JavaBeans are preferable because of their reusability. There is no hard-and-fast rule governing whether to use JavaBeans or custom tags. You often need to decide which one to use based on the particular project's specifications.

Developing and Using Custom Tag Libraries

Developing a custom tag library consists of three main steps:

▶ **Write a tag handler.**   A *tag handler* is a Java class that contains the logic for your custom tag. Every time a JSP page encounters a custom tag, the JSP container finds the associated tag handler of the custom tag and executes it. Listing 1-10 shows an example of a tag handler called MyTagHandler.

▶ **Write a tag library descriptor (TLD).**   A TLD is an XML file that defines a tag library and its tags. Listing 1-11 shows an example of a TLD file called myTaglib.tld.

▶ **Edit your Web application's deployment descriptor (web.xml file).**   To use custom tags, you must specify a taglib element in the deployment descriptor. Listing 1-12 shows a deployment descriptor with this element.

▶ **Write a JSP page that includes the taglib directive.**   To use a custom tag in a JSP page, you need to use the taglib directive to identify the TLD and tag. Listing 1-13 shows an example of a .jsp that uses a custom tag.

Before we go into the details of each of these steps, let's use the examples in Listings 1-10 through 1-13 to demonstrate how custom tags work. First, write the tag handler in Listing 1-10 and compile it to obtain the MySimpleTag.class file. Next, write the TLD file in Listing 1-11. Then edit the application's deployment descriptor as shown in Listing 1-12. Finally, create the customTagExample.jsp file in Listing 1-13 to use the custom tag.

Listing 1-10   *The Tag Handler: MyTagHandler.java*

```
package ch01;
import javax.servlet.jsp.tagext.TagSupport;
import javax.servlet.jsp.JspException;
import javax.servlet.jsp.JspWriter;

public class MyTagHandler extends TagSupport {
  public int doEndTag() throws JspException {
    JspWriter out = pageContext.getOut();
    try {
      out.print("This is the output from the custom tag.");
```

```
    }
    catch (Exception e) {
      System.out.println(e.toString());
    }
    return super.doEndTag();
  }
}
```

Listing 1-11   *The Tag Library Descriptor: myTaglib.tld*

```
<?xml version="1.0" encoding="ISO-8859-1" ?>
<!DOCTYPE taglib
  PUBLIC "-//Sun Microsystems, Inc.//DTD JSP Tag Library 1.2//EN"
  "http://java.sun.com/dtd/web-jsptaglibrary_1_2.dtd">

<taglib>
  <tlib-version>1.0</tlib-version>
  <jsp-version>1.2</jsp-version>
  <short-name></short-name>
  <tag>
    <name>myTag</name>
    <tag-class>ch01.MyTagHandler</tag-class>
  </tag>
</taglib>
```

Listing 1-12   *The Deployment Descriptor (web.xml)*

```
<?xml version="1.0" encoding="ISO-8859-1"?>
<!DOCTYPE web-app
  PUBLIC "-//Sun Microsystems, Inc.//DTD Web Application 2.3//EN"
  "http://java.sun.com/dtd/web-app_2_3.dtd">

<web-app>
  <display-name>Custom Tag</display-name>
  <taglib>
    <taglib-uri>/myTLD</taglib-uri>
    <taglib-location>/WEB-INF/myTaglib.tld</taglib-location>
  </taglib>
</web-app>
```

Listing 1-13   *The JSP Page: customTagExample.jsp*

```
<%@ taglib uri="/myTLD" prefix="c"%>
<html>
<head>
<title>Using custom tags</title>
</head>
<body>
<c:myTag/>
</body>
</html>
```

NOTE

Tomcat reports an error if your tag handler belongs to the default package.

To compile the `MyTagHandler.java`, you need the `servlet-api.jar` file in your class path. In Tomcat 5, the `servlet-api.jar` can be found in the `common/lib` directory under `%CATALINA_HOME%`. If you copy the `servlet-api.jar` file to the directory where subdirectory `ch01` resides, here is the command to compile the source code:

```
javac -classpath ./servlet-api.jar ch01/MyTagHandler.java
```

The directory structure for deployment is shown in Figure 1-2. The application name is JSFCh01.

Now, start Tomcat and direct your browser to the following URL:

```
http://localhost:8080/JSFCh01/customTagExample.jsp
```

You will see the result shown in Figure 1-3.

When the JSP container encounters the `taglib` element in the JSP page, it looks up the deployment descriptor for the location of the `taglib` where the URI is `/myTLD` and gets the path to the TLD file. This path is stored in memory for later use. When the custom tag

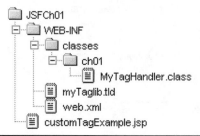

Figure 1-2   *The directory structure for the application that uses the custom tag*

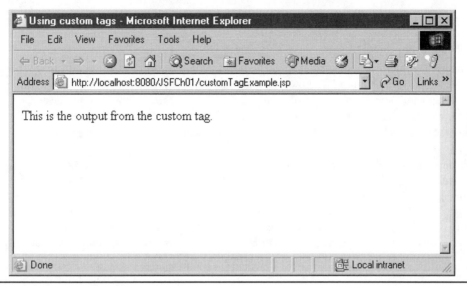

Figure 1-3   *Output from the custom tag*

<myTag> is encountered, the JSP container reads the TLD file and finds the fully qualified name of the tag handler. The JSP container then loads the tag handler and processes it. Figure 1-4 illustrates this process.

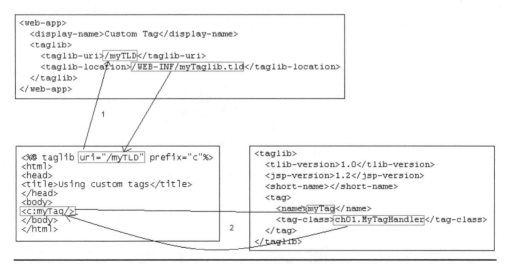

Figure 1-4   *The relationship between the deployment descriptor, the JSP page, and the TLD file*

The following sections discuss the steps for developing and using a custom tag library in detail.

Writing a Tag Handler

You use the interfaces and classes in the `javax.servlet.jsp.tagext` package to write tag handlers. Figure 1-5 shows the main members of this package.

A tag handler must implement the `Tag`, `IterationTag`, or `BodyTag` interface, or extend a class that implements one of these interfaces. We will look at each of these interfaces, as well as the classes in the `javax.servlet.jsp.tagext` package.

The Tag Interface   The `Tag` interface has the following methods: `doStartTag`, `doEndTag`, `getParent`, `setParent`, `setPageContext`, and `release`. The JSP container interacts with the `Tag` interface as follows:

1. The JSP container instantiates the tag handler or obtains an instance from a pool and calls its `setPageContext` method, passing a `PageContext` object representing the JSP page where the custom tag is found.

2. The JSP container calls the `setParent` method, passing a tag object that represents the closest tag enclosing the current tag handler. If there is no enclosing tag, a `null` object reference is passed.

3. The JSP container sets all the attributes in the custom tag, if any. Attributes are handled like properties in a JavaBean, by using the getter and setter methods. For example, if the custom tag has an attribute named `rate`, the getter method is called `getRate` and

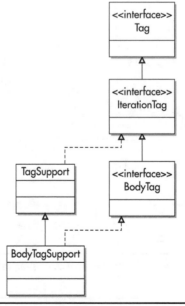

Figure 1-5   *The main members of the javax.servlet.jsp.tagext package*

the setter method is called `setRate`. The JSP container calls all the available setter methods to set attribute values.

4. The JSP container calls the `doStartTag`. The `doStartTag` method can return either `Tag.SKIP_BODY` or `Tag.EVAL_BODY_INCLUDE`. If it returns `Tag.SKIP_BODY`, the JSP container will not process the tag's body contents, if any. If it returns `Tag.EVAL_BODY_INCLUDE`, the body contents, if any, will be processed.

5. Regardless of the return value of the `doStartTag` method, the JSP container next calls the `doEndTag` method. This method returns either `Tag.SKIP_PAGE` or `Tag.EVAL_PAGE`. If it returns `Tag.SKIP_PAGE`, the JSP container will not process the remainder of the JSP page. If it returns `Tag.EVAL_PAGE`, the JSP container processes the rest of the JSP page as normal.

6. The JSP container calls the `release` method. You can write cleanup code in this method's implementation.

7. The JSP container returns the instance of the tag handler to a pool for future use.

The IterationTag Interface   The `IterationTag` interface extends the `Tag` interface and has an extra method called `doAfterBody` and a static final integer `EVAL_BODY_AGAIN`. The JSP container invokes the `doAfterBody` method implementation of a tag handler, implementing `IterationTag` after it calls the `doStartTag` method. The `doAfterBody` method returns either `Tag.SKIP_BODY` or `IterationTag.EVAL_BODY_AGAIN`. If the latter is returned, the `doAfterBody` method is called again. If the return value is `Tag.SKIP_BODY`, the body will be skipped and the JSP container will call the `doEndTag` method.

The BodyTag Interface   Implementing the `Tag` or `IterationTag` interface does not give you access to the body content of a custom tag. If you want to manipulate the body content, you must implement the `BodyTag` interface. The `BodyTag` interface extends `IterationTag` and adds two methods, `doInitBody` and `setBodyContent`, as well as two static final integers, `EVAL_BODY_BUFFERED` and `EVAL_BODY_TAG`. The JSP container calls the `setBodyContent` method after the `doStartTag`. The `doInitBody` method is called after the `doStartTag` method is called.

The `doStartTag` method of a tag handler implementing the `BodyTag` interface can return `SKIP_BODY`, `EVAL_BODY_INCLUDE`, or `EVAL_BODY_BUFFERED`. If the method returns `EVAL_BODY_INCLUDE`, the body is evaluated as it is in `IterationTag`. If the method returns `EVAL_BODY_BUFFERED`, a `BodyContent` object is created that represents the custom tag's body content.

The `doInitBody` method can be used to prepare for evaluation of the body. Normally, this method is called by the JSP container after the `setBodyContent` method. This method will not be called, however, if the custom tag does not have a body content or the `doStartTag` method returns `SKIP_BODY` or `EVAL_BODY_INCLUDE`.

The BodyContext Class   The `BodyContent` class is an abstract class that extends the `javax.servlet.jsp.JspWriter` class. The `BodyContent` class represents the body content of the custom tag, if any. You obtain the body content from the `setBodyContent` method in the `BodyTag` interface.

The TagSupport and BodyTagSupportClasses   The `javax.servlet.jsp.tagext` package also provides support classes that you can extend to create a tag handler. The benefit of extending these classes instead of implementing an interface is that you need to provide only the method implementation of the methods you want to override. As a result, you have shorter code. The `TagSupport` class implements the `IterationTag` interface, and the `BodyTagSupport` implements the `BodyTag` interface.

Writing a Tag Library Descriptor (TLD)

A TLD is an XML document that describes a tag library. A TLD is validated against a DTD file. Currently, the latest version of the DTD is 1.2. A TLD must begin with the following header:

```
<?xml version="1.0" encoding="ISO-8859-1" ?>
<!DOCTYPE taglib PUBLIC "-//Sun Microsystems, Inc.//DTD JSP Tag
Library 1.2//EN"
"http://java.sun.com/dtd/web-jsptaglibrary_1_2.dtd">
```

The root element of a TLD file is `<taglib>`. The subelements for the `taglib` element are as follows:

```
<!ELEMENT taglib (tlib-version, jsp-version, short-name, uri?,
display-name?, small-icon?, large-icon?, description?, validator?,
listener*, tag+) >
```

A `taglib` element must have the following elements:

▶ The `tlib-version` element specifies the version of the tag library implementation.

▶ The `jsp-version` element defines the JSP version that the tag library can work with.

▶ The `short-name` element encloses a unique name for the tag library.

▶ The `tag` element specifies a custom tag in the library. Its subelements are as follows:

```
<!ELEMENT tag (name, tag-class, tei-class?, body-content?,
display-name?, small-icon?, large-icon?, description?, variable*,
attribute*, example?) >
```

The other subelements are optional. You can read the description of each element in the DTD file downloadable from `http://java.sun.com/dtd/web-jsptaglibarary_1_2.dtd`.

Using a Custom Tag in a JSP Page

To use a custom tag in a JSP page, you need to be familiar with the `taglib` directive in JSP. A `taglib` directive has the following syntax:

```
<%@ taglib uri="tagLibraryURI" prefix="tagPrefix" %>
```

The `uri` attribute specifies an absolute or relative URI that uniquely identifies the TLD associated with this prefix. The `prefix` attribute defines a string that will become the prefix to distinguish a custom action.

With a `taglib` directive, you can use a custom tag of the following format for a custom tag that does not have a content body:

```
<prefix:tagName/>
```

Or, you can use the following format for a custom tag that has a content body:

```
<prefix:tagName>body</prefix:tagName>
```

You can pass attributes to the tag handler by specifying the attributes in the custom tag, each with the following format:

```
attributeName="attributeValue"
```

The following example is a custom tag whose prefix is m and whose name is `myTag`. The tag has two attributes: `number`, with a value of 12, and `power`, with a value of 13.

```
<m:myTag number="12" power="13"/>
```

Note that an attribute value must be enclosed in quotation marks.

Model 2 Architecture

Java Web application can be designed based on Model 1 or Model 2. Model 1 is for very small applications that will never grow more complex and consists of JSP pages only. Each JSP page references another JSP page, making maintenance very hard as the application grows bigger. The Model 2 architecture is the recommended design model for medium sized and large applications, and is based on the Model-View-Controller (MVC) pattern. A Model 2 architecture is indicated by the presence of a controller servlet between the client browser and the JSP pages (or the servlets that present the content). See Figure 1-6. The controller servlet dispatches HTTP requests to the corresponding presentation JSP pages—based on the request URL, input parameters, and application state. In this model, presentation parts (JSP pages or servlets) are isolated from each other.

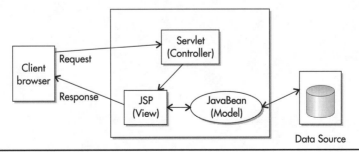

Figure 1-6   *Model 2 Architecture*

Model 2 applications are more flexible and easier to maintain, and to extend, because views do not reference each other directly. The Model 2 controller servlet provides a single point of control for security and logging, and often encapsulates incoming data into a form usable by the back-end MVC model.

JSF is based on the Model 2 architecture, in which there is one controller servlet and multiple JSP pages. The controller servlet is called Faces Servlet and is already provided by the JSF implementation. The development of a JSF application focuses on the authoring of JSP pages and the writing of other components.

Summary

To start developing JSF applications, you need to be familiar with servlets and JSP technologies and related technologies, especially JavaBeans and custom tag libraries. It is also helpful if you are familiar with the Model 2 architecture as JSF is based on this design model. This chapter provided a brief review of the four technologies as well as the Model 2 architecture. For more details on these technologies you should consult a servlet/JSP book, such as my own "Java Web Development with Servlets, JSP, and EJB, Second Edition" (Sams Publishing, 2004).

Introduction to JavaServer Faces (JSF)

AJSF application looks like any other servlet/JSP application. It has a deployment descriptor, JSP pages, custom tag libraries, static resources, and so on. The user interface of a JSF application is one or many JSP pages that host JSF components such as forms, input boxes, and buttons. These components are represented by JSF custom tags and can hold data. A component can be nested inside another component, and it is possible to draw a tree of components. In fact, a JSP page in a JSF application is represented by a component tree. Just as in normal servlet/JSP applications, you use JavaBeans to store the data the user entered.

In this chapter, you will get an overview of how JSF works and the steps to writing a simple JSF application. Then you will put this knowledge to use by working through three examples. Finally, you will be introduced to the JSF Application Programming Interface (API).

How Does JSF Work?

A JSF application works by processing events triggered by the JSF components on the pages. These events are caused by user actions. For example, when the user clicks a button, the button triggers an event. You, the JSF programmer, decide what the JSF application will do when a particular event is fired. You do this by writing event listeners. In other words, a JSF application is event-driven. Figure 2-1 illustrates the processing of a JSF application.

When an event occurs (say, when the user clicks a button), the event notification is sent via HTTP to the server. On the server is a special servlet called the `FacesServlet`. Each JSF application in the Web container has its own `FacesServlet`.

In the background, three things happen for each JSF request, as illustrated in Figure 2-2.

For JSF requests to be processed, they must be directed to a servlet called `FacesServlet`. The redirection is accomplished by using the following `servlet` and `servlet-mapping` tags in the deployment descriptor:

```
<!-- Faces Servlet -->
<servlet>
  <servlet-name>Faces Servlet</servlet-name>
  <servlet-class>javax.faces.webapp.FacesServlet</servlet-class>
  <load-on-startup>1</load-on-startup>
</servlet>
<!-- Faces Servlet Mapping -->
<servlet-mapping>
  <servlet-name>Faces Servlet</servlet-name>
  <url-pattern>/faces/*</url-pattern>
</servlet-mapping>
```

This means that the URL of every request must contain the `/faces/` pattern, as specified in the `url-pattern` element under the `servlet-mapping` element.

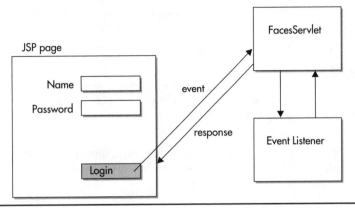

Figure 2-1   *JSF applications are event-driven.*

NOTE

You can specify a context parameter `saveStateInClient` *with a value of* `true` *to force JSF to save state in the client as opposed to saving it in the server. If you choose to do so, you must add the following* `context-param` *element before the* `servlet` *element in your deployment descriptor.*

```
<context-param>
  <param-name>saveStateInClient</param-name>
  <param-value>false</param-value>
</context-param>
```

`FacesServlet` creates an object called `FacesContext`, which contains information necessary for request processing. To be more precise, `FacesContext` contains the `ServletContext`, `ServletRequest`, and `ServletResponse` objects that are passed to the `service` method of `FacesServlet` by the Web container. During processing, `FacesContext` is the object that is modified.

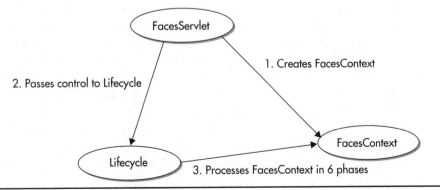

Figure 2-2   *How JSF works in a nutshell*

Next is the processing. The processor is an object called `Lifecycle`. The `FacesServlet` servlet hands over control to the `Lifecycle` object. The `Lifecycle` object processes the `FacesContext` object in six phases, which we will look at next.

NOTE

The series of actions necessary for JSF request processing by the Lifecycle object is referred to as the request processing lifecycle. You will encounter this term throughout this book.

JSF also allows you to configure a JSF application via an application configuration file. After discussing the `Lifecycle` object phases, we will discuss how to use this configuration file to register JavaBeans.

Understanding the Request Processing Lifecycle Phases

The `Lifecycle` object processes a JSF request (encapsulated in the `FacesContext` object; the `FacesContext` is the object that is read and modified by `Lifecycle` during processing) in six phases, executed in the following order:

▶ **Reconstitute Component Tree**   A JSP page in a JSF application is represented by a component tree. This phase starts the `Lifecycle` request processing by constructing this tree. Each component tree has an identifier that is unique throughout the application. The identifier of a component tree is the path information portion of the request URI. For a request with the URI `/faces/index.jsp`, for instance, the tree identifier is `/index.jsp`. The constructed component tree is then saved in the `FacesContext` object for processing by the following request processing phases.

▶ **Apply Request Values**   In this phase, the local value of each component in the component tree is updated from the current request. A value can come from a request parameter, a header, a cookie, and so on. During this phase, a component may queue events. These events will be processed during the process event steps in the request processing lifecycle.

▶ **Process Validations**   After the local value of each component is updated, in the Process Validations phase, the `Lifecycle` object will validate those values if necessary. A component that requires validation must provide implementation of the validation logic. Alternatively, a JSF programmer can register zero or more validators with the component. If one or more external validators are found, the local value of each component will be validated using the validation logic in these external validators.

▶ **Update Model Values**   This phase can be reached only if the local values of all components in the tree are valid. In this phase, the `Lifecycle` object updates the application's model data. During this phase, a component may again queue events.

▶ **Invoke Application**   During this phase, the JSF implementation handles any application level events, such as submitting a form or linking to another page.

▶ **Render Response**   In this phase, the JSF implementation renders the response to the client.

The Apply Request Values, Process Validations, Update Model Values, and Invoke Application phases in the request processing lifecycle may queue events in the `FacesContext` instance associated with the current request. Therefore, the JSF implementation must handle these events after these phases.

Between two phases, the `Lifecycle` object checks any event listener that needs to be called. When writing an event listener, you can choose after which phase the listener should be executed. Alternatively, you can write an event listener that is called after various phases.

Figure 2-3 illustrates the processing of a JSF request through these phases. The smaller boxes that are labeled "Process Events" indicate the steps that the `Lifecycle` object takes to execute event listeners.

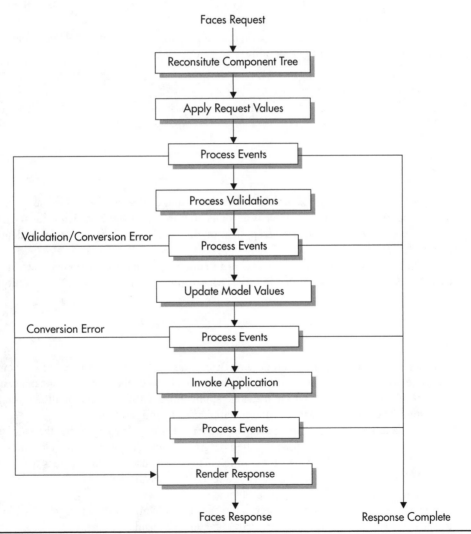

Figure 2-3   *The phases of the request processing lifecycle*

Note that an event listener can change the course of the processing flow by indicating to the `Lifecycle` object that the processing should jump to the last phase or be terminated immediately after the current event processing.

Using an Application Configuration File to Register JavaBeans

You can easily configure a JSF application via an application configuration file. In this file, you can register JavaBeans used in the application, define the program-control flow by specifying page-navigation rules, register custom components, and perform other configuration tasks.

The application configuration file is an XML file and can be declared in several places. The easiest way to use this file is to put it in the `WEB-INF` directory and call it `faces-config.xml`.

The root element of an application configuration file is `faces-config`. Here is the skeleton of an application configuration file:

```
<?xml version="1.0"?>
<!DOCTYPE faces-config PUBLIC
   "-//Sun Microsystems, Inc.//DTD JavaServer Faces Config 1.0//EN"
   "http://java.sun.com/dtd/web-facesconfig_1_0.dtd">


<faces-config>
</faces-config>
```

There are a number of aspects of a JSF application that can be configured in the application configuration file. Here, we will focus on how to register JavaBeans (as used in the examples later in this chapter). The application configuration file is explained in detail in Chapter 15.

In a JSP page, you can use the `jsp:useBean` action to tell the JSP container that you are using the JavaBean class specified in the `class` attribute of the `jsp:useBean` action, such as the following:

```
<jsp:useBean id="numberBean" class="ch02.NumberBean"
  scope="session" />
```

This tells the Web container to load the JavaBean class and create an instance of it when the JSP page is called. The `jsp:useBean` action needs to be declared in only one page, and it will be usable in all the JSP pages in the same application. A JSF application allows you to do this instead of registering a JavaBean in the application configuration file.

However, there is a drawback when using `<jsp:useBean>`. If a page other than the one containing the `jsp:useBean` action is called before the page that does use the element is called, the Web container will throw an exception. This is because the other page is trying to use a JavaBean that has not been created. If you register the JavaBean in the application configuration file, you will not have this problem.

For each JavaBean you want to register in the application configuration file, you use the `managed-bean` tag inside the `faces-config` element. Inside the `managed-bean` element, you have the following subelements:

▶ The `managed-bean-name` tag defines a name to refer to the JavaBean from a JSP page.

▶ The `managed-bean-class` element specifies the JavaBean class.

▶ The `managed-bean-scope` element defines the scope of the JavaBean.

Here is an example of a `managed-bean` element:

```
<managed-bean>
  <managed-bean-name>myBean</managed-bean-name>
  <managed-bean-class>myPackage.MyBean</managed-bean-class>
  <managed-bean-scope>session</managed-bean-scope>
</managed-bean>
```

The `managed-bean` element in this example is of type `myPackage.MyBean` and can be referred to as `MyBean` from any JSP page in the JSF application. The scope of the bean is `session`, meaning that an instance of this bean is created at the beginning of a user session. The `managed-bean` element will be explained further in Chapter 3.

Later in this chapter, in the "Creating the Page Navigation Example" section, you will see how to use an application configuration file to define page-navigation rules in a JSF application with many pages.

Writing a JSF Application

Building a JSF application requires the following three steps:

▶ Author JSP pages, using custom tags representing JSF components that will be rendered as HTML elements.

▶ Write JavaBeans as the state holder of the user input and components' data. A component can be bound with a JavaBean. In this case, the component's local value will be copied to the JavaBean's property if the local value is valid.

▶ Write an event listener that determines what should happen when an event occurs, such as when the user clicks a button or submits a form. JSF supports two events: `ActionEvent` and `ValueChangedEvent`. `ActionEvent` is fired when the user submits a form or clicks a button, and `ValueChangedEvent` is triggered when a value in a JSF component changes.

NOTE

The JSF implementation also provides a default event listener for page navigation that can be configured easily. You should not write an event listener that tampers with page navigation.

These steps do not need to happen in a particular order. In fact, they can occur simultaneously in a project with a clear separation of labor. Now, let's take a closer look at each of these three steps.

Authoring JSP Pages

Authoring a JSP page requires you to be familiar with the standard JSF components. JSF components are discussed in detail in Chapters 4 and 5. The following components are used in the examples in this chapter:

▶ The `UIForm` component is rendered as an HTML form.

▶ The `UIInput` component is rendered as an input field to accept user input.

▶ The `UIOutput` component is rendered as normal HTML text and is used for displaying output.

▶ The `UICommand` component is rendered as a button.

In a JSP page, you use custom tags that represent JSF components. These custom tags are part of two custom tag libraries, HTML and Core, and are included in the `WEB-INF/lib` directory of the application directory (as discussed in the "Introduction" to this book). The tag library descriptors (TLD files) for these libraries have also been included in the .jar files, so you do not need to worry about them.

To use the custom tags that represent JSF components, you need the following two `taglib` directives on top of every JSP page in the JSF application:

```
<%@ taglib uri="http://java.sun.com/jsf/html" prefix="h" %>
<%@ taglib uri="http://java.sun.com/jsf/core" prefix="f" %>
```

All custom tags representing the component must be enclosed in the `use_faces` tags of the Core custom tag library:

```
<f:use_faces>
<%-- custom tags representing JSF components here --%>
</f:use_faces>
```

The custom tags representing JSF components are discussed in Chapters 4 and 5. The following are some of the custom tags used in the examples in this chapter:

▶ `<h:form>` represents a `UIForm` component.

▶ `<h:input_text>` represents a `UIInput` component that accepts any text.

▶ `<h:input_number>` represents a `UIInput` component that accepts a number.

▶ `<h:output_text>` represents a `UIOutput` component that displays any text.

▶ `<h:output_number>` represents a `UIOutput` component that displays a number.

▶ `<h:output_errors>` represents a `UIOutput` component that displays error messages that occurred during the request processing.

▶ `<h:command_button>` represents a `UICommand` component.

▶ `<f:action_listener>` represents an `ActionListener`.

▶ `<f:valuechanged_listener>` represents a `ValueChangedListener`.

▶ `<f:validator>` represents a validator.

Writing JavaBeans

As noted earlier, you can bind a component to a JavaBean. In this case, the component's local value will be copied to the JavaBean's property if the local value is valid. To bind a component to a JavaBean's property, you use the `valueRef` attribute in the custom tag representing the component. For example, to bind a `UIOutput` component so that it can retrieve its value from the `result` property of a JavaBean called `testingBean`, use the following:

```
<h:output_text valueRef="testingBean.result"/>
```

Writing Event Listeners

Because JSF applications are event-driven, you need to write event listeners to determine how your applications will behave. You need to register any event listener that you want to be notified when an event is triggered by a component. To register an `ActionListener` with a component such as a `UICommand`, use the `action_listener` tag of the Core custom tag library inside the custom tag representing the component:

```
<h:command_button id="submitButton" label="Add"
  commandName="submit" >
  <f:action_listener type="ch02a.MyActionListener" />
</h:command_button>
```

You must also write your listener class by implementing the `javax.faces.event.ActionListener` interface or the `javax.faces.event.ValueChangedListener` interfaces.

Events and listeners are discussed in more detail in Chapter 7.

Creating the Event Listener and Component Tree Example

The example presented in this section illustrates the process of developing a simple JSF application. It demonstrates how to write a JSF application with an event listener that is executed when the user clicks a button. The event listener simply prints the names of the components in the component tree.

The application consists of a JSP page that has a form with two input fields to accept two numbers and print the result of the addition of the two numbers. There is also a button that, when clicked, fires an `ActionEvent` and causes an event listener to be executed.

The page has five user interface (UI) components: a `UIForm` component, two `UIInput` components, a `UIOutput` component, and a `UICommand` component (these are described in the previous section). The UIInput components and the UIOutput component are bound to a JavaBean that stores the two input values and contains the logic of the addition.

As explained earlier in this chapter, the request processing lifecycle always begins with the Reconstitute Component Tree phase. In this phase, the Lifecycle object builds the component tree representing the requested page. This example shows how a component tree looks conceptually. To be able to draw the tree, you need to create an event listener that will be called during one of the process event steps in the request processing lifecycle.

The application consists of the following:

▶ A JSP page named adder.jsp

▶ A NumberBean JavaBean for storing user data

▶ An action listener called MyActionListener

▶ A deployment descriptor (web.xml)

▶ An application configuration file for registering the JavaBean

For your JSF application to work, it needs a set of .jar files containing the JSF reference implementation and other libraries. See the "Introduction" of this book for the list of all libraries you need to include in your JSF application.

NOTE

Don't worry if you don't fully understand the code used in the application examples in this chapter. The code will be explained in later chapters.

Creating the Directory Structure for the Listener and Component Tree Example

As the first step, you need to create a directory structure for your JSF application. In Tomcat, you create this under webapps. The directory structure for your application, called JSFCh02a, is depicted in Figure 2-4. The directory contains all the required components that you will build in this example.

First, note that you must copy the .jar files containing the JSF implementation into the WEB-INF/lib directory. Then, in the WEB-INF/classes directory, you have the JavaBean class. In the WEB-INF directory, you have the deployment descriptor (web.xml) and the application configuration file (faces-config.xml). Lastly, the adder.jsp page is in the application directory itself.

Writing the Deployment Descriptor for the Listener and Component Tree Example

Just like any other servlet/JSP application, this JSF application needs a deployment descriptor. Listing 2-1 presents the deployment descriptor for this application.

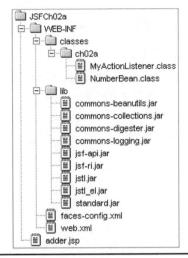

Figure 2-4   *The directory structure of the listener and component tree example*

Listing 2-1   *The Deployment Descriptor (web.xml)*

```xml
<?xml version="1.0"?>
<!DOCTYPE web-app PUBLIC
  "-//Sun Microsystems, Inc.//DTD Web Application 2.3//EN"
  "http://java.sun.com/dtd/web-app_2_3.dtd">

<web-app>
  <!-- Faces Servlet -->
  <servlet>
    <servlet-name>Faces Servlet</servlet-name>
    <servlet-class>javax.faces.webapp.FacesServlet</servlet-class>
    <load-on-startup> 1 </load-on-startup>
  </servlet>

  <!-- Faces Servlet Mapping -->
  <servlet-mapping>
    <servlet-name>Faces Servlet</servlet-name>
    <url-pattern>/faces/*</url-pattern>
  </servlet-mapping>
</web-app>
```

There are two sections in the deployment descriptor. The `servlet` element registers the `FacesServlet`, and the `servlet-mapping` element states that any request containing the pattern `/faces/` in the URL must be passed to the `FacesServlet`.

Writing the Object Model for the Listener and Component Tree Example

For this application, you need a JavaBean to store the two numbers to add and the result of the addition. Listing 2-2 presents the JavaBean called NumberBean.

Listing 2-2   *The NumberBean JavaBean*

```
package ch02a;
public class NumberBean {
  int firstNumber = 0;
  int secondNumber = 0;
  public NumberBean () {
    System.out.println("Creating NumberBean");
  }
  public void setFirstNumber(int number) {
    firstNumber = number;
    System.out.println("setFirstNumber: " + number);
  }
  public int getFirstNumber() {
    System.out.println("getFirstNumber: " + firstNumber);
    return firstNumber;
  }
  public void setSecondNumber(int number) {
    secondNumber = number;
    System.out.println("setSecondNumber: " + number);
  }
  public int getSecondNumber() {
    System.out.println("getSecondNumber: " + secondNumber);
    return secondNumber;
  }
  public int getResult() {
    System.out.println("getResult " + (firstNumber + secondNumber));
    return firstNumber + secondNumber;
  }
}
```

Writing the Application Configuration File for the Listener and Component Tree Example

As explained earlier in the chapter, the best way to make the JavaBean available to the JSF application is to register it in the application configuration file. Listing 2-3 shows the application configuration file (faces-config.xml) needed by the application.

Listing 2-3	*The Application Configuration File (faces-config.xml) for the Listener and Component Tree Example*

```xml
<?xml version="1.0"?>
<!DOCTYPE faces-config PUBLIC
  "-//Sun Microsystems, Inc.//DTD JavaServer Faces Config 1.0//EN"
  "http://java.sun.com/dtd/web-facesconfig_1_0.dtd">

<faces-config>
  <managed-bean>
    <managed-bean-name>numberBean</managed-bean-name>
    <managed-bean-class>ch02a.NumberBean</managed-bean-class>
    <managed-bean-scope>session</managed-bean-scope>
  </managed-bean>
</faces-config>
```

Authoring the JSP Page for the Listener and Component Tree Example

For the user interface, you need a JSP page called adder.jsp, which is shown in Listing 2-4.

Listing 2-4	*The adder.jsp Page*

```jsp
<%@ taglib uri="http://java.sun.com/jsf/html" prefix="h" %>
<%@ taglib uri="http://java.sun.com/jsf/core" prefix="f" %>
<html>
<head>
<title>Add 2 numbers</title>
</head>
<body>
<f:use_faces>
<h:form formName="addForm" >
  <br/>First Number:
  <h:input_number id="firstNumber"
    valueRef="numberBean.firstNumber"/>
  <br/>Second Number:
  <h:input_number id="secondNumber"
    valueRef="numberBean.secondNumber"/>
  <br/>Result:
  <h:output_number id="output" valueRef="NumberBean.result"/>
  <br/>
  <h:command_button id="submitButton" label="Add"
    commandName="submit" >
    <f:action_listener type="ch02a.MyActionListener" />
```

```
     </h:command_button>
  </h:form>
</f:use_faces>
</body>
</html>
```

First, you define two `taglib` directives to use the two JSF tag libraries: HTML and Core. The tag library descriptors for these two libraries can be found in the `jsf-ri.jar` file, so you do not need to worry about them. The prefix for the HTML tag library is `h`, and the prefix for the Core tag library is `f`.

```
<%@ taglib uri="http://java.sun.com/jsf/html" prefix="h" %>
<%@ taglib uri="http://java.sun.com/jsf/core" prefix="f" %>
```

Next are the JSF controls. Note that JSF controls must be enclosed in the `<f:use_faces>` opening and closing elements:

```
<f:use_faces>
...
</f:use_faces>
```

Inside these elements, you have a form:

```
<h:form formName="addForm">
...
</h:form>
```

Nested inside the form are two `input_number` controls, an `output_number` control, and a `command_button` control.

```
  <br/>First Number:
  <h:input_number id="firstNumber"
    valueRef="numberBean.firstNumber"/>
  <br/>Second Number:
  <h:input_number id="secondNumber"
    valueRef="numberBean.secondNumber"/>
  <br/>Result:
  <h:output_number id="output" valueRef="NumberBean.result"/>
  <br/>
  <h:command_button id="submitButton" label="Add"
    commandName="submit" >
    <f:action_listener type="ch02a.MyActionListener" />
  </h:command_button>
```

Notice the `ActionListener` for the command button.

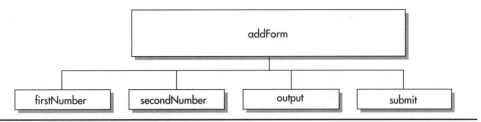

Figure 2-5   *The component tree of the adder.jsp page*

Conceptually, the component tree for this JSP page is depicted in Figure 2-5, with the root omitted. The main component is the form, and the form has four child components.

Writing the ActionListener for the Listener and Component Tree Example

The `ActionListener` for the command button is the most interesting part of this JSF application. It demonstrates how an event causes a listener to be executed. The listener simply prints messages to the console. However, it shows important information such as the hierarchy of the component tree of the JSP page from which the event was fired and the component that triggered the event. The `ActionListener` is shown in Listing 2-5.

Listing 2-5   *The ActionListener for the Command Button (MyActionListener.java)*

```
package ch02a;

import java.util.Iterator;
import javax.faces.component.UIComponent;
import javax.faces.context.FacesContext;
import javax.faces.event.ActionEvent;
import javax.faces.event.ActionListener;
import javax.faces.event.PhaseId;
import javax.faces.tree.Tree;

public class MyActionListener implements ActionListener {

  public PhaseId getPhaseId() {
    System.out.println("getPhaseId called");
    return PhaseId.APPLY_REQUEST_VALUES;
  }

  public void processAction(ActionEvent event) {
    System.out.println("processAction called");
```

```java
        // the component that triggered the action event
        UIComponent component = event.getComponent();
        System.out.println(
          "The id of the component that fired the action event: "
          + component.getComponentId());
        // the action command
        String actionCommand = event.getActionCommand();
        System.out.println("Action command: " + actionCommand);

        FacesContext facesContext = FacesContext.getCurrentInstance();
        Tree tree = facesContext.getTree();
        UIComponent root = tree.getRoot();
        System.out.println("----------- Component Tree -------------");
        navigateComponentTree(root, 0);
        System.out.println("---------------------------------------");
    }

  private void navigateComponentTree(
    UIComponent component, int level) {
    // indent
    for (int i=0; i<level; i++)
      System.out.print("  ");
    // print component id
    System.out.println(component.getComponentId());
    Iterator children = component.getChildren();
    // navigate children
    while (children.hasNext()) {
      UIComponent child = (UIComponent) children.next();
      navigateComponentTree(child, level + 1);
    }
  }
}
```

An `ActionListener` must implement the `javax.faces.event.ActionListener` interface. It provides the implementations for the `getPhaseId` and `processAction` methods. The `getPhaseId` method must return a `javax.faces.event.PhaseId`, and its return value determines in which process event step of the request processing lifecycle the listener will be executed. The `getPhaseId` method in the `ActionListener` in Listing 2-5 returns `PhaseId.APPLY_REQUEST_VALUES`. This will make the `ActionListener`'s `processAction` method be called after the Apply Request Values phase of the request processing lifecycle.

The `processAction` method accepts the `javax.faces.event.ActionEvent` object from the `Lifecycle` object. In the `ActionListener` in Listing 2-5, the `processAction` method first obtains the component that triggered the event by calling the getComponent method of the ActionEvent class, and then it prints the component identifier.

```
UIComponent component = event.getComponent();
System.out.println(
    "The id of the component that fired the action event: "
    + component.getComponentId());
```

It then prints the action command of the ActionEvent object.

```
// the action command
String actionCommand = event.getActionCommand();
System.out.println("Action command: " + actionCommand);
```

Next, it obtains the instance of the current FacesContext and calls its getTree method to acquire the component tree (an instance of javax.faces.tree.Tree class) representing the request page.

```
FacesContext facesContext = FacesContext.getCurrentInstance();
Tree tree = facesContext.getTree();
```

To get the root of the component tree, it calls the getRoot method of the Tree class.

```
UIComponent root = tree.getRoot();
```

Next, it passes the root to the private method navigateComponentTree, which draws the component tree hierarchy.

```
navigateComponentTree(root, 0);
```

The navigateComponentTree method is called recursively. It first prints the identifier of the component passed in to it. The identifier is indented by a number of blank spaces proportionate to the level argument. The level argument determines the number of spaces before the component name. The indention gives the effect of a hierarchy. When called from the processAction method, the navigateComponentTree method is passed 0 as the level argument.

```
for (int i=0; i<level; i++)
    System.out.print("  ");
// print component id
System.out.println(component.getComponentId());
```

The navigateComponentTree method then obtains the children of the passed in component by calling the getChildren method of the UIComponent interface. The getChildren method returns an Iterator containing all children of the component.

```
Iterator children = component.getChildren();
```

Next, it iterates all the children and calls the navigateComponentTree method for each of the component's children.

```
    // navigate children
  while (children.hasNext()) {
    UIComponent child = (UIComponent) children.next();
    navigateComponentTree(child, level + 1);
  }
}
```

NOTE

All the applications for this book can be downloaded from the book's web site on http://www.brainysoftware.com. Applications are named after the chapters, thus JSFCh01 for Chapter 1, JSFCh10 for Chapter 10, and so on. Because Chapter 2 has three applications, they are named JSFCh02a, JSFCh02b, and JSFCh02c, respectively. You simply need to copy these applications to the webapps directory under %CATALINA_HOME%. All .java files are located under the WEB-INF/classes directory. Also, you must copy the jar files to the WEB-INF/lib directory of each application, as explained in the "Introduction."

Compiling and Running the Listener and Component Tree Example

To compile the application, change to the JSFCh02a/WEB-INF/classes directory. If you are using Windows, type the following command:

```
javac -classpath ../lib/jsf-api.jar;../lib/jsf-
ri.jar;../../../../common/lib/servlet-api.jar ch02a/*.java
```

Note that to compile the source files, you need two library files in the lib directory and the servlet-api.jar file. In Tomcat 5, the servlet-api.jar file can be found in the common/lib directory of Tomcat's home directory.

If you are using Linux/Unix, use colons (rather than semicolons) to separate the library files:

```
javac -classpath ../lib/jsf-api.jar:../lib/jsf-
ri.jar:../../../../common/lib/servlet-api.jar ch02a/*.java
```

Then run Tomcat. You can then direct your browser to the following URL:

```
http://localhost:8080/JSFCh02a/faces/adder.jsp
```

Note that you use the /faces/ pattern before the JSP page name. You will see something similar to Figure 2-6 in your browser.

And, in the console, you will see the following message:

```
Model Object Created
getFirstNumber: 0
getSecondNumber: 0
getResult: 0
getPhaseId called
```

Viewing the source, you can see the following HTML tags:

```
<html>
<head>
<title>Add 2 numbers</title>
</head>
<body>

<form method="post"
action="/JSFCh02a/faces/adder.jsp;jsessionid=
1EF862DDA5B0B99F69E73A32F417552B">
  <br/>First Number:
  <input type="text" name="firstNumber"
    id="firstNumber" value="0"/>
  <br/>Second Number:
  <input type="text" name="secondNumber"
    id="secondNumber" value="0"/>
  <br/>Result:
  0
  <br/>
  <input type="submit" name="submitButton"
    value="  Add  "/>


</form>

</body>
</html>
```

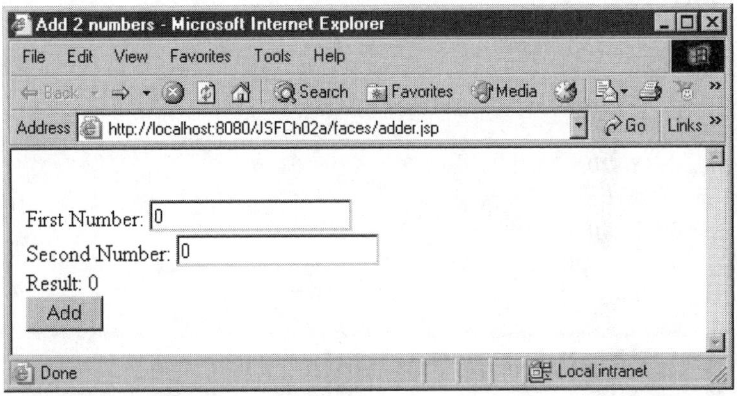

Figure 2-6   *Running the application*

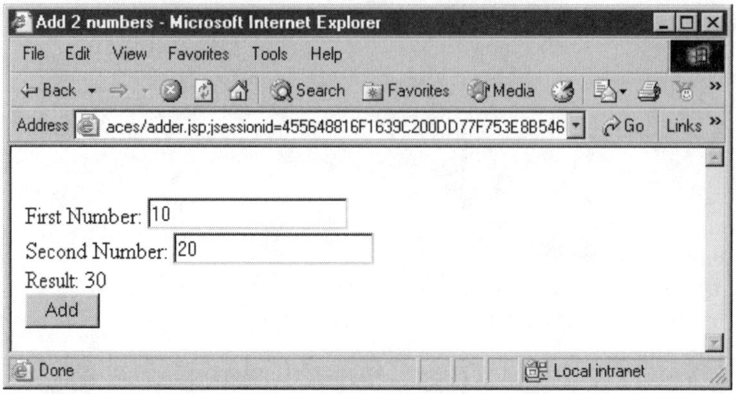

Figure 2-7 *The result of the addition*

Now, type two numbers into the input boxes and click the Add button. You can see the browser now displays the result of the addition, as shown in Figure 2-7.

More informative is the message that is displayed in the console:

```
getFirstNumber: 0
getSecondNumber: 0
processAction called
The id of the component that fired the action event: submitButton
Action command: submit
----------- Component Tree -------------
null
  addForm
    firstNumber
    secondNumber
    output
    submitButton
-----------------------------------------
setFirstNumber: 10
setSecondNumber: 20
getFirstNumber: 10
getSecondNumber: 20
getResult: 30
```

Creating the Validator Example

The example presented in this section demonstrates how you can validate user input very easily in JSF. This application is even simpler than the one presented in the previous section. It consists of only one JSP page, and it does not require a JavaBean or an application configuration file. However, you will still need a directory structure for the application and the deployment descriptor. The deployment descriptor is the same as the one in Listing 2-1. Here, we will look at the directory structure and JSP page.

Creating the Directory Structure for the Validator Example

The directory structure for your application, called JSFCh02b, is depicted in Figure 2-8. In Tomcat, you create this under webapps. The directory contains all the required components that you will build in this example.

Again, you must copy the .jar files containing the JSF implementation into the WEB-INF/lib directory. Then, in the application directory, you have the validatorTest.jsp page.

Authoring the JSP Page for the Validator Example

The JSP page is the only component in this application. It is called validatorTest.jsp and is shown in Listing 2-6.

Listing 2-6   *The validatorTest.jsp Page*

```
<%@ taglib uri="http://java.sun.com/jsf/html" prefix="h" %>
<%@ taglib uri="http://java.sun.com/jsf/core" prefix="f" %>
<html>
<head>
<title>Validator Test</title>
</head>
<body>
<f:use_faces>
<h:form formName="myForm">
Enter a minimum of 6 characters here:
   <h:input_text>
     <f:validate_length minimum="6"/>
   </h:input_text>
   <br/>
   <h:command_button label="Submit" commandName="submit"/>
   <br/>
   <h:output_errors/>
</h:form>
</f:use_faces>
</body>
</html>
```

The validatorTest.jsp page contains a form with a UIInput component represented by the input_text custom tag. The form also contains a command_button tag representing a UICommand, as well as an output_errors tag for displaying any

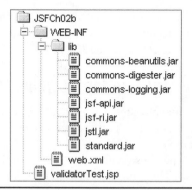

Figure 2-8   *The directory structure for the validator example*

error that occurs during processing. The most important part is the `validate_length` tag inside the `input_text` tag.

```
<h:input_text>
  <f:validate_length minimum="6"/>
</h:input_text>
```

The `validate_length` tag represents one of the standard validators in JSF. It checks for the length of the input and makes sure that it has a minimum of six characters. Any input shorter than six characters will generate an error that will be displayed by the `output_errors` tag.

Running the Validator Example

To run the application, you need to restart Tomcat. Then, use the following URL to invoke the `validatorTest.jsp` page:

```
http://localhost:8080/JSFCh02b/faces/validatorTest.jsp
```

Figure 2-9 shows the error message displayed for an input value shorter than six characters.

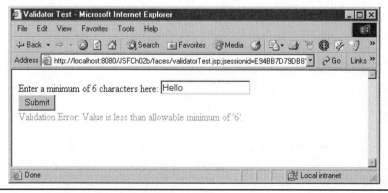

Figure 2-9   *The validator example in action*

Creating the Page Navigation Example

This section presents another sample application, which features an online survey application with two JSP pages. What makes it different from the previous two examples is that this application has multiple pages. Its main purpose is to demonstrate how to navigate from one JSP page to another.

Like the first two applications, this application is simple. The first page displays a form that takes two input boxes, where you enter your favorite singer and favorite band. After you submit the form, the second JSP page is displayed. The second JSP page displays the values you entered into the form in the first page. It also allows you to go back to the first page by clicking a button. A JavaBean called SurveyBean is used to store the user's data.

This application requires a directory structure, deployment descriptor (the same as the ones for the previous examples, shown in Listing 2-1), a JavaBean, an application configuration file, and two JSP pages.

Creating the Directory Structure for the Page Navigation Example

You need to create a directory called JSPCh02c for this application. In Tomcat, you create the directory under the webapps directory. The directory structure for this application is shown in Figure 2-10. Notice that it has two JSP pages: page1.jsp and page2.jsp. Also, the SurveyBean class resides under the WEB-INF/classes directory. As usual, you must copy all required libraries to the WEB-INF/lib directory.

Creating the SurveyBean

Your application needs a JavaBean to store data. This bean is called SurveyBean, and it can be found in the SurveyBean.java file in the ch02c package. It is shown in Listing 2-7.

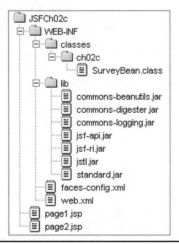

Figure 2-10   *The directory structure of the page navigation example*

Listing 2-7   *The SurveyBean*

```
package ch02c;
public class SurveyBean {
  String favSinger = null;
  String favBand = null;
  public void setFavSinger(String favSinger) {
    this.favSinger = favSinger;
  }
  public String getFavSinger() {
    return favSinger;
  }
  public void setFavBand(String favBand) {
    this.favBand = favBand;
  }
  public String getFavBand() {
    return favBand;
  }
}
```

There is nothing special in the SurveyBean class. It has two properties, favSinger and favBand, and accessors and mutators (get and set methods) for the properties.

Writing the JSP Files for the Page Navigation Example

This application has two JSP pages (page1.jsp and page2.jsp) as the user interface. The page1.jsp page is shown in Listing 2-8, and the page2.jsp page is shown in Listing 2-9.

Listing 2-8   *The page1.jsp File*

```
<%@ taglib uri="http://java.sun.com/jsf/html" prefix="h" %>
<%@ taglib uri="http://java.sun.com/jsf/core" prefix="f" %>
<html>
<head>
<title>Online Survey</title>
</head>
<body>
<h2>Online Survey</h2>
<f:use_faces>
<h:form formName="surveyForm" >
  <br/>Favorite Singer:
  <h:input_text id="favSinger" valueRef="surveyBean.favSinger"/>
```

```
   <br/>Favorite Band:
   <h:input_text id="favBand" valueRef="surveyBean.favBand"/>
   <br/>
   <h:command_button id="submit" label="Submit"
   commandName="submit" />
</h:form>
</f:use_faces>
</body>
</html>
```

Listing 2-9   *The page2.jsp File*

```
<%@ taglib uri="http://java.sun.com/jsf/html" prefix="h" %>
<%@ taglib uri="http://java.sun.com/jsf/core" prefix="f" %>
<html>
<head>
<title>Thank You</title>
</head>
<body>
<h2>Thank you for your feedback.</h2>
<f:use_faces>
<h:form formName="thankYouForm" >
   Your favorite singer is
   <h:output_text id="favSinger" valueRef="surveyBean.favSinger"/>
   and your favorite band is
   <h:output_text id="favBand" valueRef="surveyBean.favBand"/>
   <br/>Now, click the button to go back to the previous page.
   <br/>
   <h:command_button id="goBack" label="Go Back"
      commandName="goBack" />
</h:form>
</f:use_faces>
</body>
</html>
```

In both pages, you use the same UI components you used in the previous examples. In the page1.jsp file, you use a form containing two UIInput components for the user's favorite singer and favorite band. Both UIInput components are bound to the SurveyBean's properties.

In the page2.jsp page, you use two UIOutput components to display the values entered by the user. The UIOutput components are also bound to the SurveyBean's properties, from which the components get their values.

Creating the Application Configuration File for the Page Navigation Example

In JSF, page navigation is controlled using one or more navigation rules in the application configuration file. Each rule specifies a page of origin and one or more possible targets. A page is represented by its tree identifier, and each possible target is represented by a navigation case. You need to specify a navigation rule for each page from which the user can navigate to another page. You also need to register the SurveyBean in the application configuration file. The application configuration file is shown in Listing 2-10.

Listing 2-10   *The Application Configuration File for the Page Navigation Example*

```
<?xml version="1.0"?>
<!DOCTYPE faces-config PUBLIC
   "-//Sun Microsystems, Inc.//DTD JavaServer Faces Config 1.0//EN"
   "http://java.sun.com/dtd/web-facesconfig_1_0.dtd">

<faces-config>
  <managed-bean>
    <managed-bean-name>surveyBean</managed-bean-name>
    <managed-bean-class>ch02c.SurveyBean</managed-bean-class>
    <managed-bean-scope>session</managed-bean-scope>
  </managed-bean>

  <navigation-rule>
    <from-tree-id>/page1.jsp</from-tree-id>
    <navigation-case>
      <to-tree-id>/page2.jsp</to-tree-id>
    </navigation-case>
  </navigation-rule>
  <navigation-rule>
    <from-tree-id>/page2.jsp</from-tree-id>
    <navigation-case>
      <to-tree-id>/page1.jsp</to-tree-id>
    </navigation-case>
  </navigation-rule>
</faces-config>
```

A navigation rule is defined by the navigation-rule element in the application configuration file. For this application, each navigation-rule element needs to contain the from-tree-id element and navigation-case subelements. The from-tree-id subelement is the tree identifier of the page of origin. The navigation-case subelement represents a possible target. A navigation-rule element can have zero or several navigation-case subelements. Each navigation-case element specifies the target page for a particular outcome of the from-tree-id processing. For this application, the navigation-case element simply contains a to-tree-id subelement that specifies the destination page.

To specify which page to navigate to from the page1.jsp page, you use the following navigation-rule element:

```
<navigation-rule>
   <from-tree-id>/page1.jsp</from-tree-id>
   <navigation-case>
     <to-tree-id>/page2.jsp</to-tree-id>
   </navigation-case>
</navigation-rule>
```

To specify which page to navigate to from the page2.jsp page, you use the following navigation-rule element:

```
<navigation-rule>
   <from-tree-id>/page2.jsp</from-tree-id>
   <navigation-case>
     <to-tree-id>/page1.jsp</to-tree-id>
   </navigation-case>
</navigation-rule>
```

Compiling and Running the Page Navigation Example

To compile the application, change to the JSFCh02c/WEB-INF/classes directory. If you are using Windows, type the following command:

```
javac -classpath ../lib/jsf-api.jar;../lib/jsf-
ri.jar;../../../../common/lib/servlet-api.jar ch02c/*.java
```

Note that you need two library files in the lib directory and the servlet-api.jar file. In Tomcat 5, the servlet-api.jar file can be found in the common/lib directory of Tomcat's home directory.

If you are using Linux/Unix, replace the semicolons that separate library files with colons:

```
javac -classpath ../lib/jsf-api.jar:../lib/jsf-
ri.jar:../../../../common/lib/servlet-api.jar ch02c/*.java
```

To run the application, direct your browser to the following URL:

```
http://localhost:8080/JSFCh02c/faces/page1.jsp
```

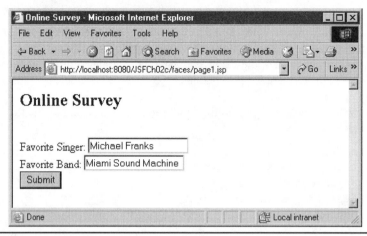

Figure 2-11 *The survey page*

You will see something similar to Figure 2-11.

Type something in both input boxes and click Submit. You will see a result similar to Figure 2-12 in your browser.

If you click the Go Back button in the second page (page2.jsp), you will go back to the first page.

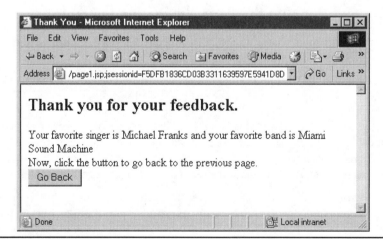

Figure 2-12 *The response page*

Introducing the JSF Application Programming Interface (API)

The JSF implementation consists of various interfaces and classes that you can use to write event listeners, validators, custom components, and so on. These interfaces and classes are grouped into the following packages:

- ► `javax.faces`
- ► `javax.faces.application`
- ► `javax.faces.component`
- ► `javax.faces.context`
- ► `javax.faces.convert`
- ► `javax.faces.el`
- ► `javax.faces.event`
- ► `javax.faces.lifecycle`
- ► `javax.faces.render`
- ► `javax.faces.tree`
- ► `javax.faces.validator`
- ► `javax.faces.webapp`

Each package is briefly described in the following sections. Bear in mind that this is only a general introduction to the classes and interfaces in the packages. You will get more details about using these packages in the upcoming chapters, which discuss specific topics related to the classes and interfaces.

The javax.faces Package

The `javax.faces` package contains the `FactoryFinder` and `FacesException` classes. The `FactoryFinder` is responsible for discovering all factory objects specified in the JSF API. An example of a factory object is the `javax.faces.context.FacesContextFactory` object, which is responsible for creating `FacesContext` instances. You probably will never need to use the `FactoryFinder` class during your career as a JSF programmer.

On the other hand, the `FacesException` class, which is a subclass of `java.lang.RuntimeException`, encapsulates general JSF exceptions. You will often need to throw an instance of this class in your JSF classes.

The javax.faces.application Package

The `javax.faces.application` package contains important classes such as `Action`, `NavigationHandler`, and `Application`, as well as the `Message` interface. The `Action` class represents an object that performs a task and can return a `String`. The `NavigationHandler` class handles page navigation.

The `Application` class represents a per-Web-application singleton object to which JSF can register objects that provide functionality required by JSF. As an example, the default `NavigationHandler` object that manages page navigation is registered with the `Application` object.

The `Message` interface represents a validation or other message. For example, a validator will add a `Message` object to the `FacesContext` if the validation of the local value of a component fails. The `javax.faces.application.MessageImpl` class is the concrete implementation of the `Message` interface.

The javax.faces.component Package

The `javax.faces.component` package provides interfaces and classes that represent the standard UI components in JSF. The most notable member of this package is the `UIComponent` interface, which every UI component must implement. A convenience base class that implements this interface is `UIComponentBase`. Then there are other classes that represent UI components, such as `UIForm`, `UICommand`, `UIGraphic`, `UIInput`, `UIOutput`, `UIPanel`, and `UISelectItem`. These components are discussed in Chapters 4 and 5.

The javax.faces.context Package

The `javax.faces.context` package contains classes and interfaces that define per-request state information. The `FacesContext` class represents all of the per-request state information that is needed by the `Lifecycle` object during the request processing lifecycle. A `FacesContext` contains many other important objects, such as the component tree and the `ExternalContext` class.

The `ExternalContext` class, also a member of this package, is there so that JSF does not need to depend on any particular container. Thanks to this class, JSF can run in either a servlet or a portlet. In a servlet environment, you can get information contained in the `ServletContext`, `ServletRequest`, and `ServletResponse` objects through the instance of `ExternalContext`.

Other important members of this package are `FacesContextFactory` and `MessageResources`. `FacesContextFactory` is responsible for the creation of `FacesContext` objects. The `MessageResources` class represents a collection of message templates that help in constructing localized messages. Chapter 11 discusses how you can achieve internationalization and localization of your JSF applications.

The javax.faces.convert Package

Data conversion happens naturally during the request processing lifecycle. User input, always in `String` form, is converted into corresponding formats such as numeric and date formats. The `javax.faces.convert` package contains one interface (`Converter`) and one `Exception` class (`ConverterException`). You use the `Converter` interface if you want to write a custom converter, and the `ConverterException` is thrown for each failed data conversion. Converters are discussed in detail in Chapter 10.

The javax.faces.el Package

The `javax.faces.el` package contains classes that are useful in evaluating and processing expressions encountered in JSP pages in a JSF application. The `el` stands for expression language. One of the classes you may want to get familiar with is `ValueBinding`. This class is used for accessing the property represented by an action or value reference expression.

The javax.faces.event Package

The `javax.faces.event` package contains classes and interfaces useful for event processing. The `FacesEvent` class, for example, extends the `java.util.EventObject` class and is the base class for any event that can be emitted in a JSF application. This class has two subclasses that are also members of the `javax.faces.event` package: `ActionEvent` and `ValueChangedEvent`. These are the only events that can be fired in a JSF application. `ActionEvent` represents the activation of a UI component, such as the clicking of a button. `ValueChangedEvent` is trigged when the local value of a component has been changed.

The `javax.faces.event` package also provides three interfaces: `FacesListener`, `ActionListener`, and `ValueChangedListener`. The `FacesListener` interface is the base interface that must be implemented by any event listener in JSF. The `FacesListener` interface is also the superinterface of the `ActionListener` and `ValueChangedListener`. You implement the `ActionListener` interface to write a listener that can receive `ActionEvents`. Implement the `ValueChangedListener` interface if you want to receive `ValueChangedEvents`.

Another member of the `javax.faces.event` package is the `PhaseId` class. This class encapsulates type-safe enumeration of possible values used to indicate after which phase in the request processing lifecycle an event listener will be executed. The `FacesListener` interface has the `getPhaseId` method, which returns a `PhaseId`. The request processing lifecycle calls the `getPhaseId` method of all registered listeners to find out when to execute the listener. If a listener's `getPhaseId` returns `PhaseId.APPLY_REQUEST_VALUES`, for example, the listener will be executed in the process event step after the Apply Request Values phase.

The `AbortProcessingException` class in the `javax.faces.event` package may be thrown by event listeners to terminate the processing of the current event.

The javax.faces.lifecycle Package

The `javax.faces.lifecycle` package contains classes and an interface that have something to do with the request processing lifecycle. There are two classes in this package: `Lifecycle` and `LifecycleFactory`. As explained earlier in this chapter, the `Lifecycle` object is the object that processes a JSF request. The `Lifecycle` object is represented by the `javax.faces.lifecycle.Lifecycle` class. The `LifecycleFactory` class is responsible for creating a `Lifecycle` instance.

The only interface in this package is `ViewHandler`. This interface defines a mechanism by which the Render Response phase of the request processing lifecycle can support different response-generation technologies.

The javax.faces.render Package

The `javax.faces.render` package contains three classes: `Renderer`, `RenderKit`, and `RenderKitFactory`. A `Renderer` is responsible for converting the internal representation of a UI component into something that is understood by the JSF client. When JSF is used in a Web application, a `Renderer` sends HTML tags to the browser as the representation of a UI component's state. A `Renderer` normally can render one UI component, so there are always many `Renderer` objects for the various standard UI components used in a JSF application.

A `RenderKit` represents a collection of `Renderer` instances. The JSF implementation comes with the default `RenderKit`.The `RenderKitFactory` is a factory object that returns a `RenderKit` instance.

Renderers are discussed in Chapter 12.

The javax.faces.tree Package

The `javax.faces.tree` package contains the `Tree` and `TreeFactory` classes. The `Tree` class represents a component tree. The `TreeFactory` is responsible for creating `Tree` instances.

The javax.faces.validator Package

The `javax.faces.validator` package contains the `Validator` interface that you implement to write your custom validator. It also contains a number of standard validator classes: `DoubleRangeValidator`, `LengthValidator`, `LongRangeValidator`, `RequiredValidator`, and `StringRangeValidator`. Validators and input validation are discussed in Chapter 9.

The javax.faces.webapp Package

The members of the `javax.faces.webapp` package are classes that are required for integrating JSF into Web applications. The most important class in this package is the `FacesServlet` class. An instance of this class is required by each JSF application to manage the request processing lifecycle. Its job description includes obtaining a `FacesContext` instance and passing it to the `Lifecycle` object for processing.

Another member, `UIComponentTag`, is a base class that you need to extend to create a tag handler that handles a JSP custom action that is related to a UI component. You can see this class used in Chapters 12 and 13.

Summary

This chapter provided a gentle introduction to JSF. Its main objective was to give you the experience of running your first JSF applications. You got an idea of how JSF works, without going into all of the details yet. You will learn more about JSF processing in later chapters.

In this chapter, you learned the most important characteristic of JSF applications that makes them different from other servlet/JSP applications: their event-driven nature. You also built three simple JSF applications that illustrate the component tree, event processing, input validation, and page navigation. The last section of this chapter offered a general overview of the JSF API, which you will be using to develop JSF components in the next chapters.

Objects for Request Processing

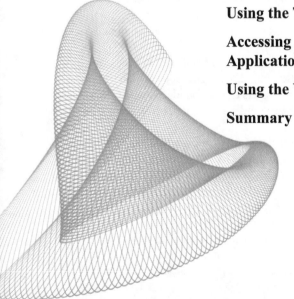

T his chapter describes five basic classes that are useful for programming JSF components:

▶ `javax.faces.context.FacesContext`

▶ `javax.faces.context.ExternalContext`

▶ `javax.faces.tree.Tree`

▶ `javax.faces.application.Application`

▶ `javax.faces.el.ValueBinding`

The `FacesContext`, `ExternalContext`, and `Tree` classes will be discussed in detail, because you were introduced to them in Chapter 2. The `Application` and `ValueBinding` classes will be explained briefly here, and described in more detail when we use them in later chapters.

This chapter includes examples of how to use the methods of each of the five classes covered here. You will find the code snippets especially useful when you are writing event listeners.

Why Are These Classes Important?

Coming from servlet/JSP programming background, you are familiar with the `ServletRequest` and `ServletResponse` objects, the two most widely accessed objects. From a `ServletRequest` object, you can get an input field value by calling its `getParameter` method, get the value of a request header by invoking its `getHeader` method, and so on. For the `ServletResponse` object, you normally call its `getWriter` method to obtain its `PrintWriter`, which you can then use to write to the client browser.

In addition to `ServletRequest` and `ServletResponse`, in servlet programming you also occasionally access the `ServletContext` object, from which you can obtain context initial parameters and other information about the Web context.

In JSF applications, it's a totally different playing field. You do not normally access the `ServletRequest`, `ServletResponse`, and `ServletContext` objects directly. Instead, the information normally contained in those objects can be found in two JSF objects: `javax.faces.context.FacesContext` and `javax.faces.context.ExternalContext`.

Another important difference between JSF and servlet programming is that in JSF, you use JSF UI components as the user interface, as opposed to the HTML elements used in servlet programming. So, think differently. In JSF, you do not often deal with parameter values to obtain the value of an input field. Instead, you deal with UI components. In fact, each JSP page in a JSF application is represented by a component tree. A component tree is represented by the `javax.faces.tree.Tree` class.

As in servlet/JSP programming, you employ JavaBeans to store values and encapsulate business logic. However, in JSF you do not access a JavaBean by using a `jsp:useBean` action element. Instead, you use two classes: `javax.faces.application.Application` and `javax.faces.el.ValueBinding`. (The `Application` class also has other functions, but those will be explained in other chapters.)

Now that you know why the classes we will cover in this chapter are important, let's start with how to use the `FacesContext` class.

Using the FacesContext Class

As mentioned in Chapter 2, the `FacesServlet` object acquires an instance of the `javax .faces.context.FacesContext` class for each JSF request. The `FacesServlet` object does this by passing the following three objects that it receives from the Web container to the `getFacesContext` method of the `javax.faces.context.FacesContextFactory` object:

▶ `javax.servlet.ServletContext`

▶ `javax.servlet.ServletRequest`

▶ `javax.servlet.ServletResponse`

This means that the `FacesContext` instance contains all per-request state information used for processing the JSF request. Figure 3-1 shows other objects that a `FacesContext` instance encapsulates.

Getting the Current Instance

One method you will use frequently is the static `getCurrentInstance` method, which returns the current instance of `FacesContext`. The signature of this method is as follows:

```
public static FacesContext getCurrentInstance()
```

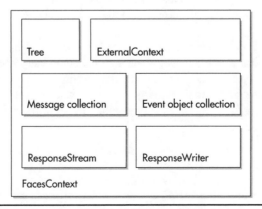

Figure 3-1   *The FacesContext instance and the objects it encapsulates*

As an example, the following code obtains the current instance of FacesContext:

```
FacesContext facesContext = FacesContext.getCurrentInstance();
```

Getting and Modifying the Component Tree

The most important element inside the FacesContext instance is the component tree of the request page. A component tree is represented by the javax.faces.tree.Tree class (discussed in the "Using the Tree Class" section later in this chapter). The Tree object is represented by the tree property of the FacesContext instance.

To obtain and modify the Tree object, you use the property's accessor and mutator:

```
public abstract Tree getTree()
public abstract void setTree(Tree tree)
```

Adding and Getting Messages

During the request processing lifecycle, a component may encounter an error. For example, an input validation performed by a validator may fail because the user entered an incorrect value. A UI component may fail to convert an input value to the type required by the model object bound to the component. Any error must be saved into the FacesContext instance for further processing. You may even want to display the error message in the page, so that the user knows how to correct the problem.

An error message is represented by the javax.faces.application.Message interface (discussed in detail in Chapter 11). You can add a Message object to the FacesContext instance by using the addMessage method of the FacesContext class. The signature of this method is as follows:

```
public abstract void addMessage(
  UIComponent component, Message message)
```

The appended Message is associated with the UIComponent, if *component* is not null. Otherwise, the Message is assumed to not be associated with any specific component instance.

As an example, a validator that fails to validate the value of a component may call the FacesContext's addMessage method, passing the component whose value is invalid and a new Message object containing a specific error message.

Any Message object added to the FacesContext instance is appended to a collection. You can obtain the Message objects added by calling either of the two overloads of the getMessages method:

```
public abstract Iterator getMessages()
public abstract Iterator getMessages(UIComponent component)
```

The first overload returns all Message objects in an Iterator. The second overload returns only Message objects associated with the given UIComponent.

Adding and Getting Request Processing Events

A UIComponent may emit a FacesEvent object. For example, a UICommand component that is clicked will trigger an ActionEvent object (the ActionEvent class is a subclass of FacesEvent). This FacesEvent object must be saved in the FacesContext instance for processing in the next process events step during the request processing lifecycle.

You can add a FacesEvent object to the FacesContext instance using the addFacesEvent method of the FacesContext class. The signature of this method is as follows:

```
public abstract void addFacesEvent(FacesEvent event)
```

You can retrieve all of the added FacesEvent objects by calling the getFacesEvents method:

```
public abstract Iterator getFacesEvents()
```

The FacesEvent objects are returned in the order they were queued.

Writing to Response Objects

For writing to the Response objects, the FacesContext class provides two properties of types javax.faces.context.ResponseStream and javax.faces.context .ResponseWriter. You use the ResponseStream object to write binary output, and you use the ResponseWriter object to send characters to the user. The accessors and mutators for these properties are as follows:

```
public abstract ResponseStream getResponseStream()
public abstract void setResponseStream(ResponseStream responseStream)
public abstract ResponseWriter getResponseWriter()
public abstract void setResponseWriter(ResponseWriter responseWriter)
```

Getting and Setting the Locale

JSF supports internationalization and localization, as discussed in detail in Chapter 11. This means that you can send responses to the user based on the user's locale. The locale property contains the Locale object used for this processing.

Initially, the value of the locale property is the same as the locale specified by the Web browser. However, you can change this value so that the locale used for sending output is independent of the one used by the browser. The accessor and mutator for this property are as follows:

```
public abstract Locale getLocale()
public abstract void setLocale(Locale locale)
```

Manipulating the Request Processing Lifecycle

The FacesContext class also provides two methods to interfere with the request processing lifecycle:

▶ You call the renderResponse method to tell the JSF implementation that control should be passed to the Render Response phase when the current phase of the request processing lifecycle has been completed. This means that all other phases between the current phase and the Render Response phase will not be executed.

▶ You invoke the responseComplete method to indicate to the JSF implementation that the HTTP response for this request has been generated (such as in the case of HTTP redirect), and therefore the request processing lifecycle must be terminated when the current phase is completed.

The signatures of these methods are as follows:

```
public abstract void renderResponse()
public abstract void responseComplete()
```

Getting Other Request State Information

Other per-request state information is encapsulated in the ExternalContext object that you can retrieve by using the getExternalContext method:

```
public abstract ExternalContext getExternalContext()
```

The ExternalContext class is discussed in the next section.

Using the ExternalContext Class

The methods in the ExternalContext class allow you to retrieve the ServletContext, ServletRequest, and ServletResponse objects used to construct the FacesContext instance. In addition, the ExternalContext instance provides wrapper methods that you can use to obtain information that otherwise is available by calling the methods in the ServletContext, ServletRequest, and ServletResponse objects.

Getting the ServletContext, ServletRequest, and ServletResponse Objects

You can use the following methods to get servlet information:

▶ getContext This method retrieves the ServletContext object for the Web application associated with this request. Its signature is as follows:

```
public abstract Object getContext()
```

▶   getRequest   This method retrieves the ServletRequest object representing the current request being processed. Its signature is as follows:

```
public abstract Object getRequest()
```

▶   getResponse   This method retrieves the ServletResponse object representing the current response being rendered. Its signature is as follows:

```
public abstract Object getResponse()
```

These methods return a java.lang.Object, not a Servlet-specific type, so that the JSF implementation can remain independent of its containing environment. For example, JSF can be used in a Web container as well as another container, such as a portlet.

Getting ServletContext Attributes

The getApplicationMap method returns a Map object containing all attribute name/value pairs in the ServletContext object. Here is the signature of this method:

```
public abstract java.util.Map getApplicationMap()
```

As an example, the following code retrieves an attribute named databaseUtility:

```
Object contextAttribute = null;
FacesContext facesContext = FacesContext.getCurrentInstance();
ExternalContext externalContext = facesContext.getExternalContext();
Map contextMap = externalContext.getApplicationMap();
if (contextMap!=null)
   contextAttribute = contextMap.get("databaseUtility");
```

Getting the Session Object and Its Attributes

The ExternalContext object allows you to access the Session object associated with the current request. The getSession method retrieves the javax.servlet.http .HttpSession object for the current user. It creates one if you pass true as its argument and there is currently no Session object for this user. Otherwise, if you pass false and there is no Session object for this user, the getSession method returns null. Here is the signature of the getSession method:

```
public abstract Object getSession(boolean create)
```

This method is the wrapper for the getSession method of the javax.servlet.http .HttpServletRequest interface.

The getSessionMap method returns a Map object containing the attribute name/value pairs of the Session object associated with the current request. Here is the signature of the getSessionMap method:

```
public abstract java.util.Map getSessionMap()
```

To retrieve an attribute in the `Session` object, you call the `get` method of the `Map` class, passing the name of the attribute you want to retrieve. The documentation does not specify whether the method returns a `null` or an empty `Map` object if no `Session` object exists for the request. Therefore, you should check whether the return value is `null` before calling the `get` method on the `Map`. Here is how you can retrieve a `Session` attribute in your code:

```
Object sessionAttribute = null;
FacesContext facesContext = FacesContext.getCurrentInstance();
ExternalContext externalContext = facesContext.getExternalContext();
Map sessionMap = externalContext.getSessionMap();
if (sessionMap!=null)
  sessionAttribute = sessionMap.get(key);
```

On the last line, *key* is a `String` containing the attribute name.

Getting the Initial Parameters of the ServletContext Object

The `getInitParameter` method is the wrapper for the `getInitParameter` method of the `ServletContext` object. You use this method to retrieve an initial parameter value that you specify using the `context-init` element in the deployment descriptor (`web.xml` file). The signature of this method is as follows:

```
public abstract String getInitParameter(String parameterName)
```

For example, suppose you declared the following `context-init` element in your deployment descriptor:

```
<context-param>
  <param-name>contactPerson</param-name>
  <param-value>Scott Jobim</param-value>
</context-param>
```

The `initParam String` variable in the following code will have the value Scott Jobim.

```
FacesContext facesContext = FacesContext.getCurrentInstance();
ExternalContext externalContext = facesContext.getExternalContext();
String initParam = externalContext.getInitParameter("contactPerson");
```

The `getInitParameterMap` method returns a `Map` object containing all of the initial parameters in the `ServletContext` object. Its signature is as follows:

```
public abstract java.util.Map getInitParameterMap()
```

To retrieve the value of an initial parameter, you use the `get` method on the `Map` object, passing the initial parameter name. As an example, the following code prints to the console the value of the initial parameter `databaseName`.

```
FacesContext facesContext = FacesContext.getCurrentInstance();
ExternalContext externalContext = facesContext.getExternalContext();
```

```
Map paramMap = externalContext.getInitParameterMap();
if (paramMap!=null) {
  System.out.println(paramMap.get("databaseName"));
}
```

Getting Request Object Attributes

The getRequestMap method returns a Map object containing attribute name/value pairs in the current Request object. The signature of this method is as follows:

```
public abstract java.util.Map getRequestMap()
```

As an example, here is the code that you can use to retrieve an attribute in the Request object:

```
Object requestAttribute = null;
FacesContext facesContext = FacesContext.getCurrentInstance();
ExternalContext externalContext = facesContext.getExternalContext();
Map requestMap = externalContext.getRequestMap();
if (requestMap!=null)
  requestAttribute = requestMap.get(key);
```

In the last line, *key* is a String containing the name of the attribute to be retrieved.

Accessing Parameter Names and Values in Request Objects

The getRequestParameterMap, getRequestParameterNames, and getRequestParameterValuesMap methods are used to access the parameter names and values in the Request object.

The getRequestParameterMap method returns a Map object containing all of the parameter name/value pairs in the Request object. Its signature is as follows:

```
public abstract java.util.Map getRequestParameterMap()
```

As an example, here is the code to retrieve the value of the request parameter named id:

```
String id = null;
FacesContext facesContext = FacesContext.getCurrentInstance();
ExternalContext externalContext = facesContext.getExternalContext();
Map requestParameterMap = externalContext.getRequestParameterMap();
if (requestParameterMap!=null)
  id = (String) requestParameterMap.get("id");
```

The getRequestParameterNames method returns an Iterator of all request parameter names. This method acts as the wrapper for ServletRequest .getParameterNames. However, instead of returning a java.util.Enumeration, the getRequestParameterNames method of the ExternalContext class returns an Iterator. The signature of this method is as follows:

```
public abstract java.util.Iterator getRequestParameterNames()
```

As an example, the following code prints all request parameter name/value pairs to the console.

```
FacesContext facesContext = FacesContext.getCurrentInstance();
ExternalContext externalContext = facesContext.getExternalContext();
Map requestParameterMap = externalContext.getRequestParameterMap();
Iterator parameterNames = externalContext.getRequestParameterNames();
while (parameterNames.hasNext()) {
  String parameterName = (String) parameterNames.next();
  String parameterValue =
    (String) requestParameterMap.get(parameterName);
  System.out.println(parameterName + " : " + parameterValue);
}
```

The getRequestParameterValuesMap method returns a Map object containing all the parameter name/value pairs in the Request object. This method is similar to the getRequestParameterMap method, but getRequestParameterValuesMap returns all values having the same parameter name. Calling the get(*key*) method on the Map object obtained from this method is the same as getting the ServletRequest for this request and calling getParameterValues(key) on it; that is, the Map object returns an array of String values.The signature of the getRequestParameterValuesMap method is as follows:

```
public abstract java.util.Map getRequestParameterValuesMap()
```

As an example, here is the code to print to the console all values of the request parameter named id.

```
String[] id = null;
FacesContext facesContext = FacesContext.getCurrentInstance();
ExternalContext externalContext = facesContext.getExternalContext();
Map requestParameterValuesMap = externalContext.getRequestParameterValuesMap();
if (requestParameterValuesMap!=null) {
  id = (String[]) requestParameterValuesMap.get("id");
  // print all values of id
  for (int i=0; i<id.length; i++) {
    System.out.println(id[i]);
  }
}
```

Getting Request Header Names and Values

The `getRequestHeaderMap` method returns a `Map` object containing all the header name/value pairs in the current request. The signature of this method is as follows:

```
public abstract java.util.Map getRequestHeaderMap()
```

As an example, the following code retrieves the value of the `host` header:

```
String host = null;
FacesContext facesContext = FacesContext.getCurrentInstance();
ExternalContext externalContext = facesContext.getExternalContext();
Map headerMap = externalContext.getRequestHeaderMap();
if (headerMap!=null) {
  host = (String) headerMap.get("host");
  System.out.println(host);
}
```

NOTE

Header names are case-insensitive. For example, passing host, Host, or HOST to the get method of the Map object returned by the getRequestHeaderMap method returns the same value.

The `getRequestHeaderValuesMap` method is similar to the `getRequestHeaderMap` method. However, calling the `get` method on the `Map` object returned by `getRequestHeaderValuesMap` gives you an array of `String` values. The `getRequestHeaderValuesMap` method's signature is as the following.

```
public abstract java.util.Map getRequestHeaderValuesMap()
```

Calling the `get` method on the `Map` object returned by the `getRequestHeaderValuesMap` method returns a `java.util.Enumeration` value.

The following code uses the `getRequestHeaderValuesMap` method to get a `Map` object containing all the header name/value pairs. It then calls the `get` method of the `Map` object returned to get all of the values of the `Accept-Encoding` header and prints these values to the console.

```
FacesContext facesContext = FacesContext.getCurrentInstance();
ExternalContext externalContext = facesContext.getExternalContext();
Map headerValuesMap = externalContext.getRequestHeaderValuesMap();
if (headerValuesMap!=null) {
  Enumeration headers =
    (Enumeration) headerValuesMap.get("Accept-Encoding");
  while (headers.hasMoreElements()) {
    String value = (String) headers.nextElement();
```

```
    System.out.println(value);
  }
}
```

Getting Cookies

The getRequestCookies method is the wrapper for HttpServletRequest
.getCookies and returns an array of javax.servlet.http.Cookie objects
found in the current Request object. The signature of this method is as follows:

```
public abstract Cookie[] getRequestCookies()
```

For instance, the following code returns all Cookie objects in the current request and
iterates the cookie names and values.

```
FacesContext facesContext = FacesContext.getCurrentInstance();
ExternalContext externalContext = facesContext.getExternalContext();
Cookie[] cookies = externalContext.getRequestCookies();
for (int i=0; i<cookies.length; i++) {
  Cookie cookie = cookies[i];
  String cookieName = cookie.getName();
  String cookieValue = cookie.getValue();
  System.out.println(cookieName + " : " + cookieValue);
}
```

The getRequestCookieMap method returns a Map object containing all of the cookies
in the current request, with the cookie names as keys. Calling the get method on the Map
object obtained from this method returns a javax.servlet.http.Cookie object. Here
is the signature of the getRequestCookieMap method:

```
public abstract java.util.Map getRequestCookieMap()
```

As an example, the following code gets the Cookie object whose name is password
and prints its value to the console.

```
FacesContext facesContext = FacesContext.getCurrentInstance();
ExternalContext externalContext = facesContext.getExternalContext();
Map cookieMap = externalContext.getRequestCookieMap();
if (cookieMap!=null) {
  Cookie cookie = (Cookie) cookieMap.get("password");
  if (cookie!=null)
    System.out.println("Value:" + cookie.getValue());
}
```

NOTE

Cookie names are case-sensitive.

Getting the Locale

The `getRequestLocale` method is the wrapper for `ServletRequest.getLocale` and returns the `Locale` object in the `Request` object. The signature for this method is as follows:

```
public abstract java.util.Locale getRequestLocale()
```

For example, the following code retrieves the user locale and prints the display language and the display country of the locale.

```
FacesContext facesContext = FacesContext.getCurrentInstance();
ExternalContext externalContext = facesContext.getExternalContext();
Locale locale = externalContext.getRequestLocale();
System.out.println("Language:" + locale.getDisplayLanguage());
System.out.println("Country:" + locale.getDisplayCountry());
```

Getting the Context Path

The `getRequestContextPath` method is the wrapper for `HttpServletRequest` `.getContextPath` and returns the context path portion of the request URI that indicates the context of the request. The signature of this method is as follows:

```
public abstract String getRequestContextPath()
```

The following is a code snippet that prints the context path of the request URI to the console:

```
FacesContext facesContext = FacesContext.getCurrentInstance();
ExternalContext externalContext = facesContext.getExternalContext();
System.out.println("Context path:" +
  externalContext.getRequestContextPath());
```

For the URL http://localhost:8080/JSFCh03/faces/test.jsp, the return value of the `getRequestContextPath` method is /JSFCh03.

The `getRequestPathInfo` method is the wrapper for `HttpServletRequest` `.getPathInfo` and returns the extra path information associated with the URL the client sent when it made this request. The extra path information follows the servlet path but precedes the query string. The signature of this method is as follows:

```
public abstract String getRequestPathInfo()
```

For example, the following code prints the path information of the request URL.

```
FacesContext facesContext = FacesContext.getCurrentInstance();
ExternalContext externalContext = facesContext.getExternalContext();
System.out.println("Path info:" +
  externalContext.getRequestPathInfo());
```

For the URL http://localhost:8080/JSFCh03/faces/test.jsp, the return value of the getRequestPathInfo method is /test.jsp.

Getting Resource Paths

The getResourcePaths method is the wrapper for ServletContext .getResourcePaths and returns a Set containing the paths to resources within the Web application whose longest subpath matches the supplied path argument. Paths indicating subdirectory paths are terminated with a /. The returned paths are relative to the root of the Web application and have a leading /. The signature of this method is as follows:

```
public abstract java.util.Set getResourcePaths(String path)
```

For example, consider the following code:

```
FacesContext facesContext = FacesContext.getCurrentInstance();
ExternalContext externalContext = facesContext.getExternalContext();
Set resourcePaths = externalContext.getResourcePaths("/");

Iterator iterator = resourcePaths.iterator();
while (iterator.hasNext()) {
  String path = (String) iterator.next();
  System.out.println(path);
}

System.out.println("----------------------------");
resourcePaths = externalContext.getResourcePaths("/WEB-INF");
iterator = resourcePaths.iterator();
while (iterator.hasNext()) {
  String path = (String) iterator.next();
  System.out.println(path);
}
```

The code calls the getResourcePaths method twice, the first time by passing / and the second time by passing "/WEB-INF". Now, suppose you run the code in a Web application with a directory structure similar to Figure 3-2.

The first Set will return the following paths:

```
/order.jsp
/index.jsp
/Styles.css
/images/
/details.jsp
/WEB-INF/
/checkOut.jsp
```

```
/browse.jsp
/shoppingCart.jsp
/search.jsp
/menu.jsp
```

The second Set returns the following paths:

```
/WEB-INF/faces-config.xml
/WEB-INF/web.xml
/WEB-INF/classes/
/WEB-INF/lib/
```

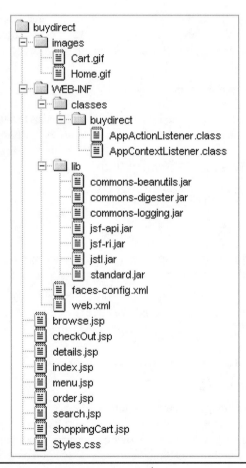

Figure 3-2   *Directory structure to test getResourcesPath*

The getResourceAsStream method is the wrapper for ServletContext .getResourceAsStream and returns the resource located at the named path as a java.io.InputStream object. The signature of this method is as follows:

```
public abstract java.io.InputStream getResourceAsStream(String path)
```

Encoding URLs

The encodeURL method is the wrapper for HttpServletResponse.encodeURL and encodes the specified URL by including the session ID in it, or, if encoding is not needed, returns the URL unchanged. The signature of this method is as follows:

```
public abstract String encodeURL(String url)
```

The encodeActionURL and encodeResourceURL methods are useful when you are using JSF inside a portlet. The encodeActionURL method forces the URL passed as the argument that causes an action to work within a portal/portlet. The signature of this method is as follows:

```
public abstract String encodeActionURL(String sb)
```

The encodeResourceURL method forces the URL passed as the argument that references a resource to work within a portal/portlet. The method causes the URL to have the required redirection for the specific portal to be included. In reality, it simply returns an absolute URL. Here is the signature of the encodeResourceURL method:

```
public abstract String encodeResourceURL(String sb)
```

Dispatching Requests

The dispatchMessage method dispatches a request to the appropriate context. In the case of servlets, this is done via forward, but for portlets, it must use include. The method has the following signature:

```
public abstract void dispatchMessage(String requestURI)
  throws java.io.IOException, FacesException
```

Using the Tree Class

Each JSF request is represented by a component tree. The javax.faces.tree.Tree abstract class represents a component tree. For each request, the JSF implementation constructs a component tree and stores it in the FacesContext instance associated with the request. You can obtain the Tree object by calling the getTree method on the FacesContext instance.

The `Tree` class has four methods:

► `getTreeId`   This method returns the identifier of the `Tree` object. For a `Tree` object representing a JSP page called `index.jsp`, the tree identifier will be `/index.jsp`. The signature of `getTreeId` is as follows:

```
public abstract String getTreeId()
```

► `getRoot`   This method returns the root component of the `Tree` object. Once you get the root component, you can traverse all of its children. The signature of `getRoot` is as follows:

```
public abstract UIComponent getRoot()
```

► `getRenderKitId`   This method is used to access the identifier of the `RenderKit` object associated with this `Tree` object.

► `setRenderKitId`   This method is used to change the identifier of the `RenderKit` object associated with this `Tree` object.

The `UIComponent` interface is a member of the `javax.faces.component` package and will be explained in detail in Chapters 4 and 5. `RenderKit` will be explained in more detail in Chapters 12 and 13.

Accessing JavaBeans through the Application Class

The `javax.faces.application.Application` class represents a singleton object that is available for every JSF-based Web application. Each JSF application has one instance of this class, and the instance is available from any point in the JSF application. There are many uses of the `Application` object; however, what you need to know at this stage is that you can use the `Application` instance to get access to the JavaBeans instantiated in the Web application. This means that you can change the property value of a JavaBean, as well as call the methods on it.

NOTE

The Singleton design pattern is a pattern that allows your class to have only one instance. For more information, read the "Singleton Pattern" at http://www.brainysoftware.com.

Getting a Reference to an Application Instance

The first step to making use of the `Application` instance is to get a reference to it. You accomplish this by using the `getApplication` method of the `ApplicationFactory` object. You obtain the `javax.faces.application.ApplicationFactory` object by using the `getFactory` static method of the `javax.faces.FactoryFinder` class. You can use the following code to get the `Application` instance.

```
ApplicationFactory factory = (ApplicationFactory)
  FactoryFinder.getFactory(FactoryFinder.APPLICATION_FACTORY);
Application application = factory.getApplication();
```

You will learn more about the `ApplicationFactory` and `FactoryFinder` classes in Chapter 16.

Getting an Application's ValueBinding Object

Once you get a reference to the `Application` instance, use its `getValueBinding` method to obtain a `javax.faces.el.ValueBinding` object, passing the value reference. The `getValueBinding` method has the following signature:

```
public abstract ValueBinding getValueBinding(String valueRef)
  throws javax.faces.el.ReferenceSyntaxException
```

One of the uses of `ValueBinding` is to access the property of a JavaBean. For example, here is the code to obtain a `ValueBinding` object representing the JavaBean called `ShoppingCartBean` (assuming that `ShoppingCartBean` has been registered in the application configuration file):

```
ApplicationFactory factory = (ApplicationFactory)
  FactoryFinder.getFactory(FactoryFinder.APPLICATION_FACTORY);
Application application = factory.getApplication();
ValueBinding valueBinding =
  application.getValueBinding("ShoppingCartBean");
```

The following is the code to obtain a `ValueBinding` object that represents the `shoppingItems` property of the `ShoppingCartBean` JavaBean:

```
ApplicationFactory factory = (ApplicationFactory)
  FactoryFinder.getFactory(FactoryFinder.APPLICATION_FACTORY);
Application application = factory.getApplication();
ValueBinding valueBinding =
  application.getValueBinding("ShoppingCartBean.shoppingItems");
```

Interestingly, a `ValueBinding` object can represent a JavaBean instance or a property in it. In fact, it can also represent other types of objects. The `ValueBinding` class is explained in the next section.

Using the ValueBinding Class

The `javax.faces.el.ValueBinding` class represents an object you can use to access the property represented by an action or by a value reference expression. You get a

ValueBinding instance by calling the getValueBinding method of the
javax.faces.application.Application class and passing the value reference.

The ValueBinding class has four methods: getType, getValue, setValue, and
isReadOnly. These methods are discussed in the following sections.

Getting the Type of the Object Represented by ValueBinding

When you call the getValueBinding method of the Application class, you pass a
value reference. The return value can be a JavaBean, a JavaBean property, or another object.
The getType method returns the type of the object represented by the ValueBinding.
The following is the signature of the getType method:

```
public abstract Class getType(FacesContext facesContext)
   throws javax.faces.el.PropertyNotFoundException;
```

For example, suppose that you have the following managed-bean tag in your
application configuration file.

```
<managed-bean>
  <managed-bean-name>shoppingCartBean</managed-bean-name>
  <managed-bean-class>
    buydirect.ShoppingCartBean
  </managed-bean-class>
  <managed-bean-scope>session</managed-bean-scope>
</managed-bean>
```

Using the following code, you can print on the console the name of the class representing
ShoppingCartBean, which is buydirect.ShoppingCartBean.

```
FacesContext facesContext = FacesContext.getCurrentInstance();
ApplicationFactory factory = (ApplicationFactory)
   FactoryFinder.getFactory(FactoryFinder.APPLICATION_FACTORY);
Application application = factory.getApplication();
ValueBinding valueBinding =
   application.getValueBinding("shoppingCartBean");
System.out.println(valueBinding.getType(facesContext).getName());
```

Getting and Setting ValueBinding Object Properties

You use the getValue method to obtain the value of the property represented by the
ValueBinding object. This method has the following signature:

```
public abstract Object getValue(FacesContext facesContext)
   throws javax.faces.el.PropertyNotFoundException
```

As an example, the following code retrieves the ShoppingCartBean object represented by a ValueBinding:

```
FacesContext facesContext = FacesContext.getCurrentInstance();
ApplicationFactory factory = (ApplicationFactory)
  FactoryFinder.getFactory(FactoryFinder.APPLICATION_FACTORY);
Application application = factory.getApplication();
ValueBinding valueBinding =
  application.getValueBinding("shoppingCartBean");
ShoppingCartBean bean =
 (ShoppingCartBean) valueBinding.getValue(facesContext);
```

The setValue method is used to change the value of the property represented by the ValueBinding object. The signature of the setValue method is as follows:

```
public abstract void setValue
  (FacesContext facesContext, Object value)
   throws javax.faces.el.PropertyNotFoundException
```

As an example, suppose the ShoppingCartBean has a property called purchaseId, which is declared as follows:

```
private String purchaseId;
public String getPurchaseId() {
  return purchaseId;
}
public void setPurchaseId(String purchaseId) {
  this.purchaseId = purchaseId;
}
```

The following code retrieves the purchaseId property of the ShoppingCartBean object and sets its value to 12345.

```
FacesContext facesContext = FacesContext.getCurrentInstance();
ApplicationFactory factory = (ApplicationFactory)
  FactoryFinder.getFactory(FactoryFinder.APPLICATION_FACTORY);
Application application = factory.getApplication();
ValueBinding valueBinding =
  application.getValueBinding("ShoppingCartBean.purchaseId");
valueBinding.setValue(facesContext, "12345");
// print the current value
System.out.println("Purchase Id:" +
  valueBinding.getValue(facesContext));
```

The code will print the following text on the console:

```
Purchase Id: 12345
```

Checking Whether a ValueBinding Property Is Writable

The isReadOnly method returns a boolean value that indicates whether or not the property represented by the current ValueBinding object can be changed. The isReadOnly method has the following signature:

```
public abstract boolean isReadOnly(FacesContext facesContext)
  throws javax.faces.el.PropertyNotFoundException
```

For example, the following code checks if the purchaseId property of the ShoppingCartBean is writable before changing its value.

```
FacesContext facesContext = FacesContext.getCurrentInstance();
ApplicationFactory factory = (ApplicationFactory)
  FactoryFinder.getFactory(FactoryFinder.APPLICATION_FACTORY);
Application application = factory.getApplication();
ValueBinding valueBinding =
  application.getValueBinding("shoppingCartBean.purchaseId");
if (!valueBinding.isReadOnly(facesContext))
  valueBinding.setValue(facesContext, "12345");
```

Summary

In this chapter, you learned about five classes that you will find useful in writing code for your JSF components: FacesContext, ExternalContext, Tree, Application, and ValueBinding. The FacesContext and ExternalContext classes are important because they encapsulate the information from the ServletContext, ServletRequest, and ServletResponse objects.

The Tree class is important because it represents the component tree that represents a JSP page. The Application class is important because, among other things, it allows you to retrieve the ValueBinding object representing a property that represents an action or a value reference expression. The ValueBinding class is important because you can use it to access a JavaBean or another object and read or change its value.

The User Interface Component Model

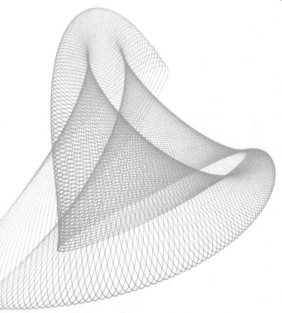

J SF provides a set of standard user interface (UI) components that you can use in your JSP pages. Understanding these components and how they work is a crucial part of developing JSF applications.

This chapter will introduce the UIComponent interface, explain how to use UI components from JSP pages, and describe the components represented by each of the UI component classes. Finally, it will discuss binding UIInput and UIOutput components to a model object, which allows you to store the local value of a component in a JavaBean and retrieve it for later use.

NOTE

Because of the depth of the discussion of the object model, you may find this chapter looks more like a reference, rather than a tutorial. Therefore, feel free to read this chapter once without bothering to understand it completely, and then come back here again after reading Chapters 5 and 6.

Introducing the UIComponent Interface

The UIComponent interface defines the contract between a UI component and the JSF implementation. In fact, it is the very foundation of the JSF technology, and every UI component must implement this interface either directly or indirectly. Figure 4-1 shows the standard components in JSF, all of which implement the UIComponent interface and are part of the javax.faces.component package.

The UIComponent interface is the central type in the javax.faces.component package. A convenience base class, javax.faces.component.UIComponentBase, is provided for all of the other component classes to extend. It's recommended that you extend the UIComponentBase class, rather than implement the UIComponent interface directly, to minimize the impact of any future changes to the UIComponent interface to your applications.

The UIComponent interface is a complex interface, which provides methods that cater to features such as input validation, data conversion, event handling, and so on. In fact, all of the topics discussed in this book relate to the UIComponent interface in one way or another. Here, we will cover some of the more basic methods. Other methods are discussed throughout this book.

Identifying Components with Identifiers

A JSF request is represented by the component tree constructed from state information in the request. To identify a component in the component tree, each component must have an identifier that is used by the JSF implementation during processing. There are two identifiers in a component: the client identifier and component identifier.

Component Identifiers

The component identifier is the name that is given by the user. The user can give a component an identifier by using the id attribute in the tag that represents the UI component. For example, if you write the following tag in your JSP page:

```
<h:input_text id="firstName" valueRef="testingBean.name"/>
```

Then, the component identifier is firstName.

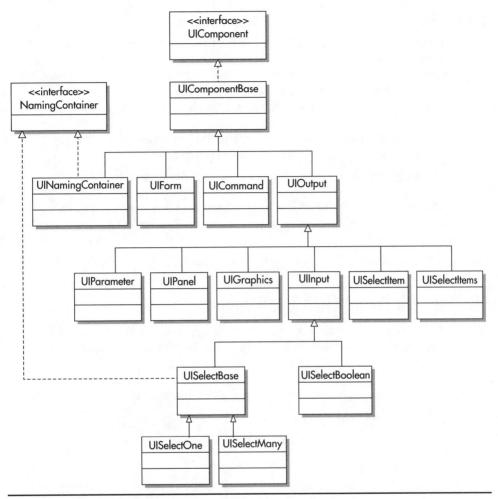

Figure 4-1 *The standard UI components in JSF*

A component identifier should be as short as possible, to minimize the size of the response generated by the JSF implementation. In addition, a component identifier must conform to the following rules:

► Start with a letter

► Be composed of only letters (*a–z, A–Z*), digits (0–9), dashes (-), and underscores (_)

The UIComponent interface provides the getComponentId and setComponentId methods to obtain or change the component identifier. Their signatures are as follows:

```
public String getComponentId();
public void setComponentId(String componentId);
```

Client Identifiers

The client identifier is the name used by the JSF implementation to identify the component. If the component identifier is present (i.e., the user gives the component a name), the client identifier is the same as the component identifier. If no component identifier is present, the client identifier is generated automatically.

A client identifier is used by the JSF implementation for the following purposes:

▶ As the name of a request parameter, so that the JSF implementation will recognize value input into this parameter in a subsequent request

▶ As the anchor for client-side scripting code or accessibility labels

You can retrieve the client identifier of a component from that component by calling the getClientId method of the UIComponent interface. The getClientId method has the following signature:

```
public String getClientId(FacesContext context);
```

Working with Parent-Child Relationships

All components reside in a component tree; this is, components live in a parent-child relationship, in which the root is at the top of the hierarchy. You can manage parent and children components as follows:

▶ To get the parent of a component, use the getParent method:

```
public UIComponent getParent();
```

▶ To assign a parent for a component, use the setParent method:

```
public void setParent(UIComponent parent);
```

▶ To retrieve all children in a component, use the getChildren method, which returns an Iterator containing all child components:

```
public Iterator getChildren();
```

▶ To obtain a child at a position, use the getChild method (the index is zero-based, so the first child is denoted by 0):

```
public UIComponent getChild(int index)
```

▶ To get the number of children a component has, use the getChildCount method:

```
public int getChildCount();
```

▶ If you want to know whether a component is a child of another component, use the containsChild method, which returns true if the component passed is a child of the current component:

```
public boolean containsChild(UIComponent child);
```

▶ To add a child to a component and append it to the end of the list of children, use this addChild method:

```
public void addChild(UIComponent child);
```

▶ To add a child to a component and insert the child into the list at the position specified by the index, use this addChild method:

```
public void addChild(int index, UIComponent child);
```

▶ To remove a child when you have a reference to the child component, use this removeChild method:

```
public void removeChild(UIComponent child);
```

▶ To remove a child when you know the index position of the child component in the collection, use this method:

```
public void removeChild(int index);
```

▶ To remove all child components, use the clearChildren method:

```
public void clearChildren();
```

Creating a Subordinate Component with Facets

Two components can also have a relationship that is not a parent-child relationship. A component can become a subordinate of another component by becoming a *facet* of the owning component. This way, you can have a complex component made up of other components, but without those subordinate components needing to become child components of the main component. Technically, facets are a named collection of subordinate (non-child) components that are related to the current component.

To add a facet to a component, use the addFacet method of the UIComponent interface, as in this example:

```
public void addFacet(String facetName, UIComponent facet);
```

If a facet known by facetName has already been added, it will be replaced by the newly added facet.

You can retrieve the names of all of the facets in a component by calling the getFacetNames method:

```
public Iterator getFacetNames();
```

This method returns an Iterator containing the names.

The getFacetsAndChildren method returns an Iterator containing all of the facets and children in the current component:

```
public Iterator getFacetsAndChildren();
```

To obtain and remove a facet, pass the facet name to the `getFacet` and `removeFacet` methods:

```
public UIComponent getFacet(String facetName);
public void removeFacet(String facetName);
```

Rendering Components

A UI component needs to be rendered to the JSF client. In terms of using JSF to develop Web applications, this means rendering the component to HTML tags. A UI component can choose to perform rendering itself or delegate this task to an outside renderer. All standard UI components that come with JSF delegate the rendering to an outside renderer.

Renderers have `decode`, `encodeBegin`, `encodeChildren`, and `encodeEnd` methods, which the JSF implementation calls during the request processing lifecycle. It calls the `decode` method during the Apply Request Values phase, to obtain the current state of the `UIComponent` from the request in the `FacesContext` instance. JSF attempts to convert this state information into the local value of the component. The JSF implementation calls the `encodeBegin`, `encodeChildren`, and `encodeEnd` methods during the Render Response phase of the request processing lifecycle to complete the rendering of the UI component.

Because the standard UI components have external renderers, they do not need to provide implementations for their `decode`, `encodeBegin`, `encodeChildren`, and `encodeEnd` methods. If a UI component is to do the rendering itself, its `rendererType` property should have `null` as its value, and it needs to provide implementations for its `decode`, `encodeBegin`, `encodeChildren`, and `encodeEnd` methods.

Chapters 12 and 13 discuss renderers in detail. In Chapter 12, you will learn how you can replace the default renderer of a standard component with a custom renderer. In Chapter 13, you will learn how to write a custom component that performs its own rendering.

Managing the Lifecycle

The component tree is the object that is manipulated by the six phases of the request processing lifecycle. Each phase performs its task by calling a specific method of the root of the component tree, which in turns calls the same method in every component in the tree.

The methods that are called during the request processing lifecycle phases are `processReconstitutes`, `processDecodes`, `processValidators`, and `processUpdate`. These methods are discussed in Chapter 16.

Using Validators

A UI component can opt to have its local value validated by providing an implementation of its `validate` method. For example, if an input component is designed to accept a number, it should not accept a non-numeric string. The `validate` method will be called by the JSF implementation during the Process Validations phase of the request processing lifecycle. The signature of this method is as follows:

```
public void validate(FacesContext context)
```

When calling this method, the JSF implementation will pass the `FacesContext` instance associated with the current method. This `FacesContext` instance is necessary because if the validation fails, the `validate` method should add a `javax.faces.application.Message` object to the `FacesContext`. Also, if the validation fails, the `valid` property of the current component should be set to `false`.

In addition, you can plug external validators into a UI component. The `getValidators` method returns an `Iterator` containing all validators registered with the current component. The signature of the `getValidators` method is as follows:

```
public java.util.Iterator getValidators();
```

Validators are discussed in detail in Chapter 9.

Using UI Components from JSP Pages

As you have learned in Chapter 2, you author JSP pages simply by putting custom tags on those pages. To create a `UIInput` component, for example, you can use the following tag:

```
<h:input_text/>
```

Here, we will look at the roles of the tag handler and component properties. Then we will examine each of the UI component classes.

Creating UI Components with Custom Tags

You do not need to do any programming to instantiate the UI components used in your pages. The tag handler mapped to the custom tag does this for you. Among other tasks, the tag handler does the following:

▶ Locates the component (in the component tree) corresponding to this tag, creating a new one if necessary.

▶ Overrides the component's properties with values set in the corresponding custom tag attributes. The property values are overridden only if values for the corresponding attributes are *not* already set on the component.

Therefore, it's important that you use the attributes in your custom tag properly. The list of attributes belonging to a custom tag can be found in the tag library descriptor (TLD) of the tag. You need to know the properties in the component class.For example, the `UIInput` component has the `value` and `valueRef` properties. From a custom tag representing the `UIInput` component, such as `input_text`, you can use the corresponding attributes (having the same names) to initialize the property values, such as in the following examples:

```
<h:input_text value="Hello"/>
<h:input_text valueRef="TestingBean.value"/>
```

A UI component may be associated with more than one custom tag. The difference between two custom tags representing the same UI component lies in the attributes they have. In addition, different custom tags use different renderers to render the same UI components, generating different HTML tags on the browser.

For the JSF implementation to recognize and process the custom tags representing UI components, all tag handlers for those custom tags must extend the `javax.faces.webapp.UIComponentTag` class. This class will be discussed in Chapters 12 and 13.

Introducing the UI Component Classes

The UI component classes include the following:

▶ `UIForm`, which represents an input form

▶ `UICommand`, which represents a command component that can perform an action when activated

▶ `UIOutput`, which represents a component that displays a value

▶ `UIGraphic`, which represents a component that displays an image

▶ `UIInput`, which represents a component that gets and displays user input

▶ `UIParameter`, for configuring parameter values for parent components

▶ `UIPanel`, which represents a panel (container) component

▶ `UISelectItem`, which represents a single select item for select components

▶ `UISelectItems`, which represents multiple select items for select components

▶ `UISelectBoolean`, which represents a component that have a boolean value

▶ `UISelectOne`, which represents a component that allows the user to select zero or one value from a set of values

▶ `UISelectMany`, which represents a component that allows the user to select zero or more values from a set of values

Here, we will focus on the render-independent properties of each type of component, because this will tell you how to use the corresponding attributes in the tag whose handler creates the component. *Render-independent properties* refer to properties that do not affect how the component will be rendered on the client.

NOTE

If you do not understand the properties covered here, do not despair! The next chapters will explain just how these properties are used.

All of the IO component classes, except for the `UIForm` and `UICommand` classes, have the two render-independent properties listed in Table 4-1.

The UIForm Class

The `UIForm` class represents an input form that can contain input fields. The class extends `UIComponentBase` and adds one property, `formName`, which is the name used by the JSF implementation to identify the form.

Property	Access	Type	Description
value	Read-write	Object	The current local value or literal value of the component
valueRef	Read-write	String	The value reference expression that points to the location which the value of this component is to be stored to or retrieved from

Table 4-1   *Common Render-Independent Properties of UI Components (Except UIForm and UICommand)*

The UICommand Class

The UICommand class represents a UI component that the user can activate to trigger an action or a command. This component is rendered as a button or a hyperlink. The render-independent properties of this class are listed in Table 4-2.

On activation, a UICommand component can emit a javax.faces.event .ActionEvent object. This type of event can be captured by a javax.faces.event .ActionListener. Therefore, the UICommand component provides two methods for registering and deregistering an ActionListener: addActionListener and removeActionListener. The signatures of these methods are as follows:

```
public void addActionListener(ActionListener actionListener);
public void removeActionListener(ActionListener actionListener);
```

In addition, the fireActionEvent method is provided to queue an ActionEvent in the current instance of FacesContext. The signature of this method is as follows:

```
public void fireActionEvent(FacesContext facesContext);
```

Events and listeners are discussed in Chapter 7.

The UIOutput Class

The UIOutput class represents a UI component that can display a value to the user. The user cannot change the value of this component. The render-independent properties of this component are value and valueRef (see Table 4-1).

For the value property, the UIOutput class provides the getValue and setValue methods. The getValue method returns the value of the value property. However, the

Property	Access	Type	Description
action	Read-write	String	The literal outcome value returned when the UICommand component is activated
actionRef	Read-write	String	A value reference expression that points to an object of type javax.faces.application.Action
commandName	Read-write	String	The logical name of the command, to be included in the ActionEvent object fired when this command is activated

Table 4-2   *The Render-Independent Properties of UICommand*

UIOutput class also has a currentValue method, which is different from getValue. If the value of the value property is not null, the currentValue method returns the value property's value. Therefore, the return value is the same as that of the getValue method. If the value property's value is null, however, the currentValue method retrieves the value pointed at by the valueRef property.

The UIGraphic Class

The UIGraphic class is a subclass of the UIOutput class and represents a UI component for displaying a graphical image. In a Web application, this class is rendered as <img>.

Along with the value and valueRef properties (see Table 4-1), this class has the url render-independent property, a read-write property of type String. This property is the URL of the image to be displayed. If the URL starts with a / character, the URL is assumed to be relative to the context path of the current Web application.

The UIInput Class

The UIInput class extends UIOutput and represents a UI component that can accept a value from the user as well as display the value.

Along with the value and valueRef properties (see Table 4-1), this class has the previous render-independent property, a read-write property of type Object. This property is the previous local value of this component, which is needed so that the component knows when to emit a ValueChangedEvent when a user enters a new value.

The UIInput component can emit a javax.faces.event.ValueChangedEvent if the user enters a new value that is different from the previous value. For registering and deregistering a ValueChangedEvent, the UIInput class provides the addValueChangedListener and removeValueChangedListener methods. The signatures of these methods are as follows:

```
public void addValueChangedListener(ValueChangedListener listener);
public void removeValueChangedListener(
    ValueChangedListener listener);
```

In addition, the UIInput class has the fireValueChangedEvent method to queue a ValueChangedEvent to the FacesContext instance of the current request. The signature of this method is as follows:

```
public void fireValueChangedEvent(FacesContext facesContext,
    Object oldValue, Object newValue);
```

The UIInput class can override the validate method to ensure the correctness of the user input. This method will be called by the JSF implementation during the Perform Validations phase of the request processing lifecycle. Overriding this method allows you to define logic to validate the user input.

The `UIInput` also overrides the `updateModel` method to assign the local value of this component to the corresponding model object.

The UIParameter Class

The `UIParameter` class extends `UIOutput` and represents a UI component with no visible rendering behavior. It provides a mechanism for configuring parameter values to a parent component. For example, you can use the `UIParameter` class to add request parameters to a generated hyperlink.

Along with the `value` and `valueRef` properties (see Table 4-1), this class has the name render-independent property, a read-write property of type `String`. This property is the optional name for this parameter.

The UIPanel Class

The `UIPanel` class extends `UIOutput` and represents a UI component that is used mainly as a container for its child components. The default implementation of this class has no rendering behavior and sets its `rendersChildren` property to `true`.

The `UIPanel` class's render-independent properties are `value` and `valueRef` (see Table 4-1.)

The UISelectItem Class

The `UISelectItem` class extends `UIOutput` and represents a single select item for select components. The `UISelectItem` component can be nested inside a `UISelectOne` or `UISelectMany` component.

A select item is represented by the `javax.faces.component.SelectItem` class. This class implements `java.io.Serializable` and contains three `String` read-only properties: `label`, `value`, and `description`. The properties are initialized through the class's constructor:

```
public SelectItem(String value, String label, String description);
```

Three `get` methods are provided to access the properties: `getLabel`, `getValue`, and `getDescription`.

In a Web browser, a select item is rendered as an option tag for a select element, such as this:

```
<option value="[value]">[text]</option>
```

The `value` property is rendered as the `value` attribute's value. The `label` property is for the text of the option.

The `UISelectItem` class provides render-independent properties to access the properties of the `SelectItem` instance it represents, as well as the properties that it must have as a `UIOutput` object. These properties are listed in Table 4-3.

Property	Access	Type	Description
itemDescription	Read-write	String	The description of this select item, an optional property
itemLabel	Read-write	String	The localized label that will be displayed to the user
itemValue	Read-write	String	The value that will be submitted to the server if the user selects this select item
value	Read-write	Object	The literal value of this select item
valueRef	Read-write	String	The value reference expression that points to the location from which the value of this component is to be retrieved

Table 4-3   *The Render-Independent Properties of UISelectItem*

The UISelectItems Class

The UISelectItems class extends UIOutput and represents a set of select items for select components. The UISelectItems component can be nested inside a UISelectOne or UISelectMany component. The value of this component must be one of the following types:

▶   SelectItem instance

▶   Array of SelectItem instances

▶   Collection of SelectItem instances

▶   Map, with the keys of the Map containing labels and the values of the Map as values of the UISelectItems instance

The UISelectBoolean Class

The UISelectBoolean class extends UIInput and represents a UI component that can have a boolean value and is most commonly rendered as a check box.

Along with the value and valueRef properties (see Table 4-1), UISelectBoolean has the selected render-independent property. This is a read-write property of type boolean, which represents the current state of this component.

The UISelectOne Class

The UISelectOne class extends UIInput and represents a UI component that allows the user to select no items or one item from a set of available options.

The UISelectOne class has the render-independent properties value and valueRef (see Table 4-1), as well as the selectedValue property. selectedValue is a read-write property of type Object, which holds the value of the currently selected item.

The UISelectMany Class

The UISelectMany class extends UIInput and represents a UI component that allows the user to select no items or multiple items from a set of available options.

The `UISelectMany` class has the render-independent properties `value` and `valueRef` (see Table 4-1), as well as the `selectedValues` property. This is a read-write property of type `Object`, which holds the values of the currently selected items.

Binding a Component to a Model Object

A UI component can store data locally. However, a UI component is destroyed (or recycled) after the JSP page in which it resides goes out of scope. In most cases, you want the data to stay longer, so that it will be available from other JSP pages. For example, in an online store application, users may enter the quantity of an item they want to put in their shopping cart in a `buy.jsp` page. This number must still be available when the `buy.jsp` page goes out of scope, such as when control is passed to another page that calculates the total purchase of that user.

JSF allows you to bind a component data to a model object (a JavaBean). Since the JavaBean can have a session or application scope, the bound component data lives longer than the component itself. Any `UIInput` or `UIOutput` component can be bound to a model object. However, you cannot bind a `form` or a `command_button` component to a model object, because they are not `UIInput` or `UIOutput` components.

When a `UIInput` component's data is bound to a model object, the data will be copied to the model object when the form containing the `UIInput` component is submitted. If the flow goes back to the original JSP page (because the business logic dictates or if there is an error during processing), by default, the previous value is redisplayed in the `UIInput` component.

When a `UIOutput` component's data is bound to a model object, the data in the model object will be copied to the component before the component is displayed.

Meeting Binding Requirements

Because binding means copying data from one Java object to another (from the UI component to the JavaBean and vice versa), the component data and the JavaBean's property the component is bound to must have matching data types. This is to say, you can bind an `input_number` tag to a JavaBean's property that has a numeric data type (such as a `Long`, `int`, `float`, and so on), but not to a `Date`.

You use the `valueRef` attribute of the tag representing a component to bind a component data to a model object. You assign the name of the JavaBean's property that is supposed to store the value to the `valueRef` attribute.

The `valueRef` attribute uses a reference expression to refer to the model object property that holds the component data. The part of the expression before the first dot (`.`) must match the name defined in the `useBean` action element or by the `managed-bean-name` element corresponding to the proper `managed-bean` declaration in the application configuration file. The part of the expression after the first dot must match the name defined by the `property-name` element corresponding to the proper `managed-bean` declaration.

In addition, you can also bind a `UIInput` or `UIOutput` component to an implicit object's property to display the value of the property. We'll discuss the `valueRef` attribute and implicit objects in the next sections.

Evaluating Value Reference Expressions

The UIOutput and UIInput component classes support the value and valueRef properties. The value property represents the literal value to be manipulated for a UIOutput or UIInput component, and the valueRef property indirectly references a value to be retrieved from (or stored to) some location.

The Render Response phase of the request processing lifecycle retrieves the value and valueRef properties in both UIOutput and UIInput components. If the component has a non-null value property, the component's or an associated renderer's encodeBegin, encodeChildren, and encodeEnd methods will render the corresponding data. If the value property is null, but the valueRef property is not null, the component or the associated renderer will retrieve the data pointed to by the valueRef property.

During the Update Model Values phase of the request processing lifecycle, if the valueRef property of a UIInput component in not null, the JSF implementation will copy the current value property to the location pointed to by the valueRef property, and the local value property will be cleared. The JSF implementation will also perform any necessary conversion of the value property to a format acceptable by the resource referenced by the valueRef property. If conversion is not possible, an exception will be thrown.

How the value reference expression is evaluated is important, because you will use it a lot for the valueRef and actionRef properties of your components. A value reference expression follows ECMAScript (the standard script language that originated from JavaScript), in that the . and [] operators are considered equivalent. This means that expression-a.identifier-b is the same as a["identifier-b"]; in other words, the identifier identifier-b is used to construct a literal whose value is the identifier, and then the [] brackets are used with that value.

Value reference expression can be evaluated in one of two modes:

▶ **Lvalue mode**   During the Update Model Values phase of the request processing lifecycle, the value reference expression is treated as an *lvalue*, meaning that the value pointed to by the rightmost identifier or literal will be replaced by the local value of the component that contains this reference. Figure 4-2 illustrates the process of evaluating expr-a[expr-b] in the lvalue mode.

▶ **Rvalue mode**   During the Render Response phase of the request processing lifecycle, the value reference expression is treated as an *rvalue*, which means the value pointed to by the rightmost identifier or literal is the result of the expression evaluation. Figure 4-3 illustrates the process of evaluating expr-a[expr-b] in the rvalue mode.

The identifiers that are implicit objects, such as applicationScope and cookie, and the objects they return, are described in the next section.

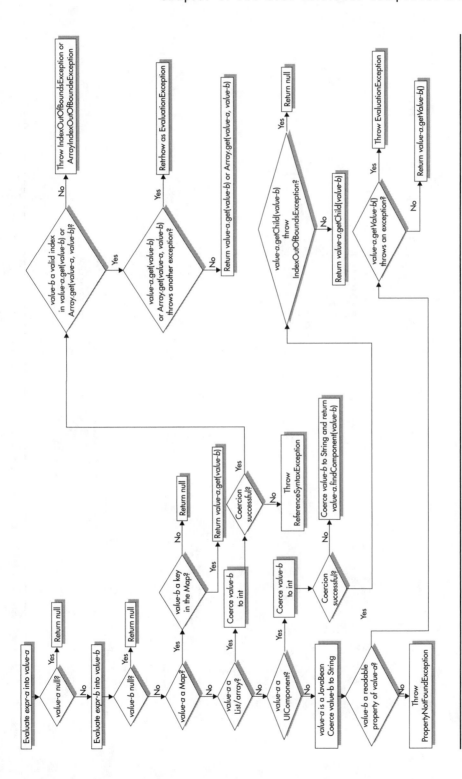

Figure 4-2 *Evaluating expr-a[expr-b] in the lvalue mode*

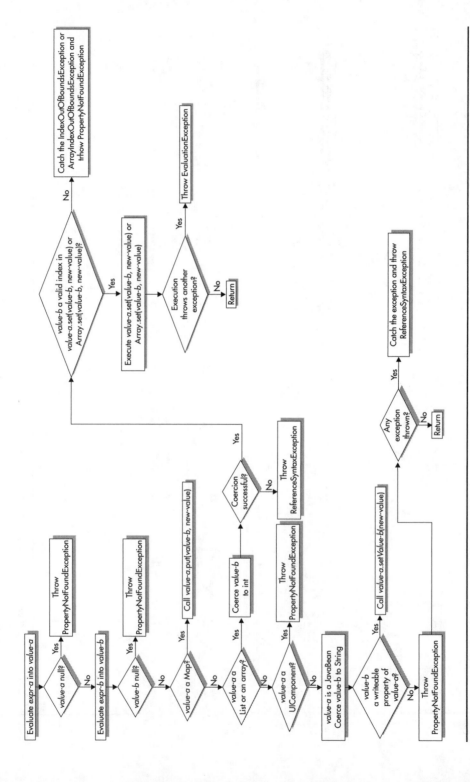

Figure 4-3 Evaluating expr-a[expr-b] in the rvalue mode

Retrieving Information with Implicit Objects

In JSF programming, you often need to retrieve information from both the `ServletRequest` and `ServletContext` objects. When writing a Java class, such as an event listener, this should not be a problem, because you can obtain the `FacesContext` instance for the current processing, which encapsulates the information (as described in Chapter 2). But, how do you obtain the same information from a JSP page? JSF provides implicit objects that you can use for this purpose. For example, to retrieve an HTTP request header, you use the implicit object `header`. To retrieve cookies, use `cookie`. Table 4-4 lists the JSF implicit objects.

For example, the following references the host header of the `Request` object:

```
header.host
```

And, the following is the expression that references the `contactName` initial parameter.

```
initParam.contactName
```

Using Value Reference Expressions to Get Values

This section presents examples of how to use value reference expressions to obtain values from a JavaBean called `TestingBean`, shown in Listing 4-1. This JavaBean has several properties of different types: a `String`, a `Map`, an array, a `List`, and another JavaBean named `AddressBean`.

Implicit Object	Description
applicationScope	A Map containing the application scope attribute values. The attribute names are the keys of the Map.
cookie	A Map containing the cookie values for the current request. The cookie names are the keys of the Map.
facesContext	The FacesContext instance of the current request.
header	A Map containing the HTTP headers. The header names are the keys of the Map. Only the first value for each header name is included.
headerValues	A Map of String arrays containing all of the header values for HTTP headers in the current request. The header names are the keys of the Map.
initParam	A Map of the context initialization parameters for this Web application. The initial parameter names are the keys of the Map.
param	A Map containing the parameter values of the current request. The parameter names are the keys of the Map.
paramValues	A Map of String arrays containing all of the parameter values for request parameters in the current request. The parameter names are the keys of the Map.
requestScope	A Map containing the request scope attribute values. The attribute names are the keys of the Map.
sessionScope	A Map containing the session scope attribute values. The attribute names are the keys of the Map.
tree	The root UIComponent in the current component tree.

Table 4-4   *The JSF Implicit Objects*

Listing 4-1 *The TestingBean Class*

```java
package ch04;

import java.util.ArrayList;
import java.util.HashMap;
import java.util.List;
import java.util.Map;

public class TestingBean {
  String name = "Jonathan";
  Map capitals = new HashMap();
  String[] countries =
     {"Australia", "Brazil", "China", "Denmark", "Egypt"};
  List cities = new ArrayList();
  AddressBean address = new AddressBean();

  public TestingBean() {
    capitals.put("Australia", "Canberra");
    capitals.put("UK", "London");
    capitals.put("China", "Beijing");
    cities.add("Chicago");
    cities.add("New York");
    cities.add("San Francisco");
    address.setStreet("45 Foyer Street");
    address.setCity("Straighton");
    address.setZipCode("34534");
    address.setCountry("USA");
  }
  public Map getCapitals() {
    return capitals;
  }
  public void setCapitals(Map capitals) {
    this.capitals = capitals;
  }
  public String getName() {
    return name;
  }
  public void setName(String name) {
    this.name = name;
  }
  public String[] getCountries() {
    return countries;
  }
```

```
public void setCountries(String[] countries) {
  this.countries = countries;
}
public List getCities() {
  return cities;
}
public void setCities(List cities) {
  this.cities = cities;
}
public AddressBean getAddress() {
  return address;
}
public void setAddress(AddressBean address) {
  this.address = address;
}
}
```

As you can see in Listing 4-1, all properties are initialized either in the variable declaration or in the constructor.

The AddressBean class referenced from inside the TestingBean class is presented in Listing 4-2.

Listing 4-2   *The AddressBean Class*

```
package ch04;
public class AddressBean {
  private String street;
  private String city;
  private String zipCode;
  private String country;

  public String getStreet() {
    return street;
  }
  public void setStreet(String street) {
    this.street = street;
  }
  public String getCity() {
    return city;
  }
  public void setCity(String city) {
    this.city = city;
  }
```

```
  public String getZipCode() {
    return zipCode;
  }
  public void setZipCode(String zipCode) {
    this.zipCode = zipCode;
  }
  public String getCountry() {
    return country;
  }
  public void setCountry(String country) {
    this.country = country;
  }
}
```

To use the TestingBean from a JSF application, you need to register it in the application configuration file, in the JSFCh04 application, as shown in Listing 4-3. (The fully qualified class name for TestingBean is ch04.TestingBean.)

Listing 4-3   *The TestingBean Registration in the Application Configuration File*

```xml
<?xml version="1.0"?>
<!DOCTYPE faces-config PUBLIC
  "-//Sun Microsystems, Inc.//DTD JavaServer Faces Config 1.0//EN"
  "http://java.sun.com/dtd/web-facesconfig_1_0.dtd">

<faces-config>
  <managed-bean>
    <managed-bean-name>testingBean</managed-bean-name>
    <managed-bean-class>ch04.TestingBean</managed-bean-class>
    <managed-bean-scope>session</managed-bean-scope>
  </managed-bean>
</faces-config>
```

The simplest property in TestingBean is the name property, which is a String. To bind a UIComponent with this property, you need to write the following expression:

```
testingBean.name
```

For example, the following line of code shows how to bind a UIOutput component represented by the output_text tag with the name property of the TestingBean.

```
My name is <h:output_text valueRef="testingBean.name"/>
```

The `capitals` property in the `TestingBean` is a `java.util.Map`. The value reference expression to refer to this property is as follows:

```
testingBean.capitals
```

To bind a `UIComponent` to a value in the `Map`, you specify the key using a `.` or `[]`. The following two `UIOutput` components are bound to the `Map` values whose keys are 'Australia' and 'China', using both forms of accessing the values.

```
<h:output_text valueRef="testingBean.capitals['Australia']"/>
<h:output_text valueRef="testingBean.capitals.China"/>
```

The `countries` property of the `TestingBean` is an array of `String`. You use the following code to reference this property:

```
testingBean.countries
```

To access the member of this array, use its index. For instance, here is a `UIOutput` component that is bound to the first member of the `countries` array:

```
<h:output_text valueRef="testingBean.countries[0]"/>
```

The `cities` property is a `java.util.List`. Use the following expression to reference the `cities` property:

```
testingBean.cities
```

To reference to the members of the `cities` `List`, you pass the index number in square brackets. The following lines of code present `UIOutput` components that are bound to the first, second, and third members of the `List`, respectively.

```
<h:output_text valueRef="testingBean.cities[0]"/>
<h:output_text valueRef="testingBean.cities[1]"/>
<h:output_text valueRef="testingBean.cities[2]"/>
```

The last property in the `TestingBean` is `address`, which is an `AddressBean`. To reference the `address` property, use the following expression:

```
testingBean.address
```

For example, the following lines show `UIOutput` components bound to properties in the `AddressBean`.

```
<h:output_text valueRef="testingBean.address.street"/>
<h:output_text valueRef="testingBean.address.city"/>
<h:output_text valueRef="testingBean.address.zipCode"/>
<h:output_text valueRef="testingBean.address.country"/>
```

The `test.jsp` page, shown in Listing 4-4, shows examples of using value reference expressions.

Listing 4-4   *The test.jsp Page for Testing Value Reference Expressions*

```
<%@ taglib uri="http://java.sun.com/jsf/html" prefix="h" %>
<%@ taglib uri="http://java.sun.com/jsf/core" prefix="f" %>
<html>
<head>
<title>Testing</title>
</head>
<body>
<f:use_faces>
<h:form formName="myForm" >

  <%-- Testing String property --%>
  My name is <h:output_text valueRef="testingBean.name"/>
  <br>
  <br>
  <%-- Testing Map property --%>
  The capital of Australia is
  <h:output_text valueRef="testingBean.capitals['Australia']"/>
  <br>
  The capital of China is
  <h:output_text valueRef="testingBean.capitals.China"/>
  <br>
  <br>
  <%-- Testing Array property --%>
  The first country in the list is
  <h:output_text valueRef="testingBean.countries[0]"/>
  <br>
  <br>
  <%-- Testing List property --%>
  <br>The list of cities:
  <br><h:output_text valueRef="testingBean.cities[0]"/>
  <br><h:output_text valueRef="testingBean.cities[1]"/>
  <br><h:output_text valueRef="testingBean.cities[2]"/>
  <br>
  <%-- Testing JavaBean property --%>
  <br>My Address:
  <br><h:output_text valueRef="testingBean.address.street"/>
  <br><h:output_text valueRef="testingBean.address.city"/>
  <br><h:output_text valueRef="testingBean.address.zipCode"/>
  <br><h:output_text valueRef="TestingBean.address.country"/>
  <br>
  <br>Contact Name: <h:output_text valueRef="initParam.contactName"/>
```

```
  </h:form>
  </f:use_faces>
  </body>
  </html>
```

The last h:output_text tag is bound to a context initial parameter called contactName. It is assumed that your deployment descriptor (web.xml file) contains the following element:

```
<context-param>
  <param-name>contactName</param-name>
  <param-value>John Sutton</param-value>
</context-param>
```

To run the page, use the following URL from your browser:

```
http://localhost:8080/JSFCh04/faces/test.jsp
```

The result is shown in Figure 4-4.

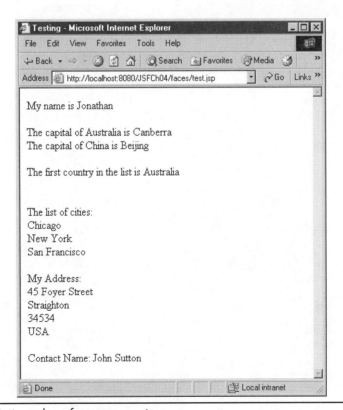

Figure 4-4   *Testing value reference expressions*

Summary

In this chapter, you learned about the object model of the UI components that come with the standard JSF implementation. As you learned in this chapter, JSF is founded on the `UIComponent` interface, which every UI component must implement directly or indirectly.

You also learned how to bind `UIInput` and `UIOutput` components to various types of model objects. Binding lets you store component values in a JavaBean, so you can retrieve those values later.

The next chapter explains the use of the custom tags representing the UI components.

CHAPTER 5

JSF Simple Components

IN THIS CHAPTER:

Using Custom Tag Libraries in JSP Pages

Introducing the HTML Custom Tag Library

Using Custom Tags

Summary

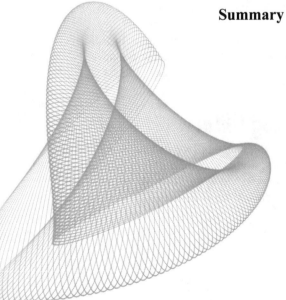

J SF provides two custom tag libraries to help you rapidly write Web applications: HTML and Core. The HTML custom tag library defines tags that represent user interface (UI) components. The Core custom tag library defines core actions for registering event handlers, using validators with components, and so on. You use the tags from both libraries in the JSP pages in your JSF applications. Therefore, you need to understand these tags to be able to lay out UI components, use validators, and connect events to event listeners.

This chapter provides an introduction to using the HTML custom tag library in JSP pages. It presents an overview of all the tags associated with the UI components, and then focuses on the tags for the more basic components. The next chapter continues with the advanced component tags.

Using Custom Tag Libraries in JSP Pages

To use the HTML and Core custom tag libraries in a JSP page, you must include the following `taglib` directives in the JSP page:

```
<%@ taglib uri="http://java.sun.com/jsf/html/" prefix="h" %>
<%@ taglib uri="http://java.sun.com/jsf/core/" prefix="f" %>
```

The `prefix` attribute values can be anything. However, by convention, you normally use h and f.

The HTML and Core custom tag libraries are described in the `html_basic.tld` file and `jsf_core.tld` file, respectively. Both TLD files are included in the `jsf-ri.jar` file that contains the JSF reference implementation and must be present in the `WEB-INF/lib` directory of your JSF application. Therefore, you do not need to worry about deploying these TLD files, because they are automatically included when you copy the `.jar` files into the `WEB-INF/lib` directory.

Writing the JSP pages in a JSF application is the responsibility of the page author. In addition to laying out components, this responsibility includes binding the components to model object data and adding core tags (such as event listeners and validators) to component tags.

Introducing the HTML Custom Tag Library

There are 33 tags in the HTML custom tag library. Each component is rendered as an HTML element. You may be wondering why there are 33 tags, while the number of HTML elements is much less than 33. The reason is that many tags are rendered as the same HTML element. Table 5-1 lists the UI components and the tags that represent the components.

UI Component	Tag	Description
UIForm	form	Represents a form
UIGraphic	graphic_image	Displays an image
UICommand	command_button	Represents a button to submit a form to the server
	command_hyperlink	Represents a hyperlink to navigate to another page or a location on a page
UIInput	input_date	Represents an input box that accepts a date
	input_datetime	Represents an input box that accepts a date and time
	input_hidden	Represents a hidden element
	input_number	Represents an input box that accepts a number
	input_secret	Represents a password box
	input_text	Represents an input box that accepts a string
	input_textarea	Represents a text area that accepts a multiline string
	input_time	Represents an input box that accepts a time
UIOutput	output_date	Displays a formatted date
	output_datetime	Displays a formatted date and time
	output_errors	Displays error messages
	output_label	Displays text
	output_message	Displays a localized message
	output_number	Displays a formatted number
	output_text	Displays a line of text
	output_time	Displays a formatted time
UISelectBoolean	selectboolean_checkbox	Represents a check box
UIPanel	panel_data	Iterates over a collection of data
	panel_grid	Displays a table
	panel_group	Groups a set of components

Table 5-1   *UI Components and Their Tags*

UI Component	Tag	Description
	`panel_list`	Displays a table of data from a collection, an array, an iterator, or a map
`UISelectItem`	`selectitem`	Represents a select item
`UISelectItems`	`selectitems`	Represents a list of items
`UISelectMany`	`selectmany_checkboxlist`	Displays a set of check boxes from which the user can select multiple values
	`selectmany_listbox`	Represents a select box from which a user can select multiple items
	`selectmany_menu`	Represents a list of items from which a user can select multiple items
`UISelectOne`	`selectone_listbox`	Represents a select box from which a user can select one item
	`selectone_menu`	Represents a list of items from which a user can select one item
	`selectone_radio`	Represents a set of radio buttons

Table 5-1 *UI Components and Their Tags* (continued)

Using Custom Tags

In this section, you will learn how to use the custom tags associated with the `UIForm`, `UIGraphic`, `UICommand`, `UIInput`, `UIOutput`, and `UISelectBoolean` components. The next chapter covers custom tags representing the `UIPanel`, `UISelectItem`, `UISelectItems`, `UISelectMany`, and `UISelectOne` components. First, we will discuss how to use tag attributes, and then we will create a bean for testing the tags. Finally, we will look at the tags.

Applying Tag Attributes

Each tag can have attributes, and there are two categories of attributes: the HTML 4.0 attributes and the attributes that are associated with the properties of the underlying component. The HTML 4.0 attributes are rendered as they are, not processed on the server. For example, the `input_number` tag, rendered as an HTML `<input type=text>` in the browser, has the attributes of an HTML input element, such as `value`, `size`, `maxLength`, and so on. In addition, the `input_number` tag has attributes that are associated with the properties of the component, such as `valueRef`, `numberStyle`, `formatPattern`, and so on.

All of the UI component tags defined in the HTML custom tag library have an optional `id` attribute. This attribute corresponds to the identifier of the component object represented by this tag. If you do not specify an `id` attribute for a component, JSF will generate one for you. You must include this attribute if you need to reference the component from other tags.

Creating the MyBean JavaBean for Tag Tests

Some of the examples in this chapter use the MyBean shown in Listing 5-1. MyBean is a simple JavaBean that has properties with various data types.

Listing 5-1   *The MyBean Used by Some Examples in This Chapter*

```java
package ch05;
import java.util.Date;

public class MyBean {
  private boolean discounted;
  private int quantity;
  private float price;
  private Date today;
  private String value;

  public boolean getDiscounted() {
    return discounted;
  }
  public void setDiscounted(boolean discounted) {
    this.discounted = discounted;
  }
  public int getQuantity() {
    return quantity;
  }
  public void setQuantity(int quantity) {
    this.quantity = quantity;
  }
  public float getPrice() {
    return price;
  }
  public void setPrice(float price) {
    this.price = price;
  }
  public Date getToday() {
    return new Date(System.currentTimeMillis());
  }
  public void setToday (Date today) {
    this.today = today;
  }
  public String getValue() {
    return value;
  }
```

```
public void setValue(String value) {
    this.value = value;
  }
}
```

You need to register `MyBean` in the application configuration file, as shown in Listing 5-2, so that you can use it from any JSP page without the `jsp:useBean` action element.

Listing 5-2   *MyBean Registration in the Application Configuration File*

```
<?xml version="1.0"?>
<!DOCTYPE faces-config PUBLIC
  "-//Sun Microsystems, Inc.//DTD JavaServer Faces Config 1.0//EN"
  "http://java.sun.com/dtd/web-facesconfig_1_0.dtd">

<faces-config>
  <managed-bean>
    <managed-bean-name>myBean</managed-bean-name>
    <managed-bean-class>ch05.MyBean</managed-bean-class>
    <managed-bean-scope>session</managed-bean-scope>
  </managed-bean>
</faces-config>(2)Introducing the Custom Tags
```

Now that we have the `MyBean` ready for some of the examples, we can see how the tags in the HTML custom tag library work. Here, we will cover the custom tags that represent the `UIForm`, `UIGraphic`, `UICommand`, `UIInput`, `UIOutput`, and `UISelectBoolean` components.

The form Tag

The `form` tag represents an input form for the user to enter data and submit it to the server. This tag nests tags that represent the other components, such as `input_number`, `output_text`, `command_button`, and so on.

The following is an example of the `form` tag in a JSP page:

```
<f:use_faces>
<h:form formName="myForm" >
  <%-- other components --%>
</h:form>
</f:use_faces>
```

Note that the `formName` attribute must be present in a `form` tag.

The command_button Tag

The command_button tag is rendered as a submit button in the browser. A command_button tag must have the commandName attribute and either the key attribute or the label attribute. The commandName attribute refers to the name of the command generated by the event of clicking the button.

Here is an example of the command_button tag:

```
<h:command_button label="Submit" commandName="submit"/>
```

This tag is discussed in more detail in Chapter 7, which covers event handling.

The command_hyperlink Tag

The command_hyperlink tag is rendered as an <a> link in the browser. You can use it to either submit an ActionEvent to the server or to navigate to another URL. We will discuss using the tag with events in Chapter 7. Here, you will see how to use the command_hyperlink tag to navigate to another URL.

To use the command_hyperlink tag to navigate to a URL, the tag must contain the href attribute, which indicates the relative or absolute destination URL. If the href attribute references an absolute URL, it must be assigned a full URL, such as http://www.brainysoftware.com, rather than www.brainysoftware.com. The tag must also contain a label or image attribute.

The label attribute specifies the clickable text on the browser:

```
<h:command_hyperlink href="shop.html" label="Start Shopping"/>
```

This tag will be rendered as the following HTML <a> element:

```
<a href="shop.html">Start Shopping</a>
```

The image attribute specifies an image to click:

```
<h:command_hyperlink href="http://www.yahoo.com"
  image="images/promo.gif"/>
This tag will be rendered as the following HTML <a> element:<a
href="http://www.yahoo.com"><img src="images/promo.gif"></a>
```

With the command_hyperlink tag, you can also pass query strings by using the parameter tags from the Core custom tag libraries. For example, the following command_hyperlink tag passes two parameters: firstName, with the value of Austin, and lastName, with the value of Powers.

```
<h:command_hyperlink href="login.jsp" label="Identify yourself">
  <f:parameter name="firstName" value="Austin"/>
  <f:parameter name="lastName" value="Powers"/>
</h:command_hyperlink>
```

It will be rendered as the following <a> element:

```
<a href="login.jsp?firstName=Austin&lastName=Powers">
  Identify yourself</a>
```

The graphic_image Tag

The `graphic_image` tag displays an image. You use its `url` attribute to specify the source of the image. Here is an example of the `graphic_image` tag:

```
<h:graphic_image url="images/promo.gif" width="120" height="35"/>
```

The tag is rendered as the following <img> element in the browser:

```
<img id="id0" src="images/promo.gif">
```

The input_text and output_text Tags

Use the `input_text` tag to allow the user to enter a single-line string. In the browser, this tag is rendered as <input type=text>. You can use the `size` attribute in an `input_text` tag to manage the width of the input box and the `maxLength` attribute to determine how many characters can be entered into the input box.

The `output_text` tag displays a one-line string and is rendered as normal text in the browser. Even though you can display data of types other than `String`, such as numeric and date types, it's better to use the corresponding output tags for those data types, such as the `output_number` and `output_date` tags, because they provide more suitable formatting.

The `input_text` and `output_text` tags are used in the `textTest.jsp` page, shown in Listing 5-3.

Listing 5-3   *The textTest.jsp Page*

```
<%@ taglib uri="http://java.sun.com/jsf/html" prefix="h" %>
<%@ taglib uri="http://java.sun.com/jsf/core" prefix="f" %>
<html>
<head>
<title>Entering and Displaying A String</title>
</head>
<body>
<f:use_faces>

<h:form formName="myForm">
  <br>Value: <h:input_text valueRef="myBean.value"/>
  <br>Displayed using output_text:
    <h:output_text valueRef="myBean.value"/>
  <br><h:output_errors/>
  <br><h:command_button label="Submit" commandName="submit"/>
</h:form>
```

```
</f:use_faces>
</body>
</html>
```

As you can see in Listing 5-3, the `input_text` and `output_text` tags are bound to the `MyBean`'s `value` property. This property has the type `String`.

You can invoke the `textTest.jsp` page using the following URL:

```
http://localhost:8080/JSFCh05/faces/textTest.jsp
```

Figure 5-1 displays the result after the user types in some text.

The input_number and output_number Tags

The `input_number` tag represents a text field component that accepts a number from the user. In the browser, it is rendered as `<input type=text>`. If you type a nonnumeric value into this component, an error is thrown. The `output_number` tag displays a number as normal text in the browser.

The `numberStyle` and `formatPattern` attributes are important attributes in the `input_number` and `output_number` tags because they determine what the acceptable format is that the user can enter to a UIInput component and how the number is displayed in a UIOutput component.

NOTE

The input_number and output_number tags can be bound to a JavaBean property of a primitive data type or its wrappers (Byte, Integer, Long, Short, and any subclass of java.lang.Number).

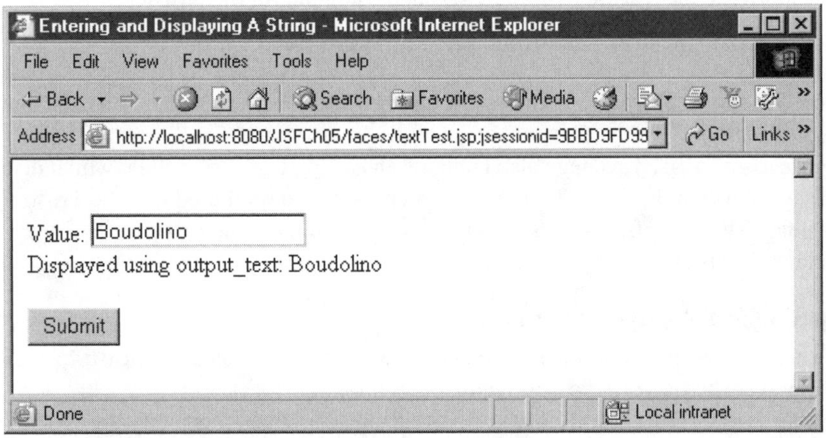

Figure 5-1   *Using the input_text and output_text tags*

You can use the numberTest.jsp page, shown in Listing 5-4, to test the input_number and output_number tags. This example uses the valueRef attribute in both tags to bind the components to the MyBean's quantity property.

Listing 5-4   *The numberTest.jsp Page*

```
<%@ taglib uri="http://java.sun.com/jsf/html" prefix="h" %>
<%@ taglib uri="http://java.sun.com/jsf/core" prefix="f" %>
<html>
<head>
<title>Entering and Displaying A Number</title>
</head>
<body>
<f:use_faces>
<h:form formName="myForm">
  <br>Quantity: <h:input_number valueRef="myBean.quantity"/>
  <br>Displayed using output_number:
    <h:output_number valueRef="myBean.quantity"/>
  <br>
  <br><h:output_errors/>
  <br><h:command_button label="Submit" commandName="submit"/>
</h:form>
</f:use_faces>
</body>
</html>
```

You can invoke the numberTest.jsp page using the following URL:

http://localhost:8080/JSFCh05/faces/numberTest.jsp

Figure 5-2 shows the result of entering a number into the input_number tag and clicking the button.

The numberTest.jsp page also contains an output_errors tag, which displays the message shown in Figure 5-3 when a nonnumeric value is entered into the input_number tag. The output_errors tag is discussed in the "The output_errors Tag" section later in this chapter.

The input_date and output_date Tags

The input_date tag allows the user to enter a date. It is rendered as <input type=text> in the browser. The output_date tag displays a Date as text.

Both the input_date and output_date tags allow you to specify the style of the date using the dateStyle attribute. The possible values of the dateStyle attribute are "short", "medium" (the default for both input_date and output_date tags),

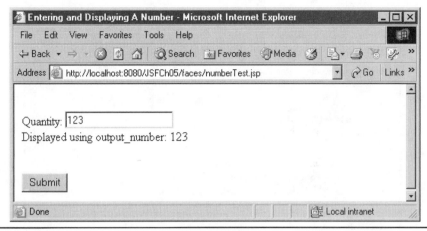

Figure 5-2   *Entering a number into an input_number tag*

"long", and "full". See Figure 5-4 for examples of the style produced by each value. The input_date and output_date tags also support the timezone attribute.

The dateTest.jsp page, shown in Listing 5-5, uses an input_date tag and a few output_date tags, employing the different values for the dateStyle attribute for the display.

NOTE

The input_date, output_date, input_time, output_time, input_datetime, and output_datetime tags can be bound to a java.util.Date object.

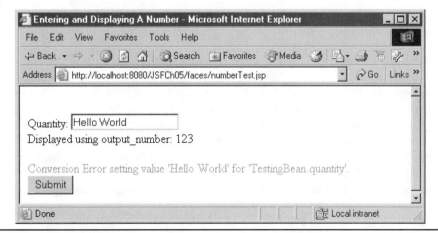

Figure 5-3   *Entering a nonnumeric value into an input_number tag*

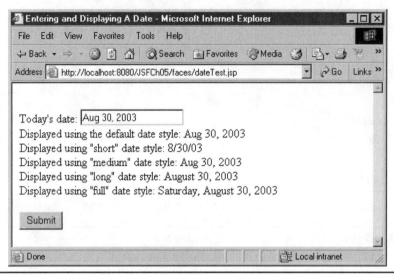

Figure 5-4   *Using the input_date and output_date tags*

Listing 5-5   *The dateTest.jsp Page*

```
<%@ taglib uri="http://java.sun.com/jsf/html" prefix="h" %>
<%@ taglib uri="http://java.sun.com/jsf/core" prefix="f" %>
<html>
<head>
<title>Entering and Displaying A Date</title>
</head>
<body>
<f:use_faces>
<h:form formName="myForm">
  <br>Today's date: <h:input_date valueRef="myBean.today"/>
  <br>Displayed using the default date style:
    <h:output_date valueRef="myBean.today"/>
  <br>Displayed using "short" date style:
    <h:output_date dateStyle="short" valueRef="myBean.today"/>
  <br>Displayed using "medium" date style:
    <h:output_date dateStyle="medium" valueRef="myBean.today"/>
  <br>Displayed using "long" date style:
    <h:output_date dateStyle="long" valueRef="myBean.today"/>
  <br>Displayed using "full" date style:
    <h:output_date dateStyle="full" valueRef="myBean.today"/>
  <br><h:output_errors/>
  <br><h:command_button label="Submit" commandName="submit"/>
```

```
  </h:form>
  </f:use_faces>
  </body>
  </html>
```

You can invoke the `dateTest.jsp` page using the following URL:

```
http://localhost:8080/JSFCh05/faces/dateTest.jsp
```

Figure 5-4 shows the result of entering a date in the `dateTest.jsp` page.

The input_time and output_time Tags

Use the `input_time` tag to accept a time. This tag is rendered as an `<input type=text>` HTML element. The `output_time` tag displays a time.

Both `input_time` and `output_time` have the `timeStyle` and `timezone` attributes. The possible values for the `timeStyle` attribute are "`short`" (the default for both the `input_time` and `output_time` tags), "`medium`", "`long`", and "`full`". See Figure 5-5 for examples of the style produced by each value.

Listing 5-6 shows the `timeTest.jsp` page, which demonstrates the use of the `input_time` and `output_time` tags. It includes several `output_time` tags with different `timeStyle` attribute values.

Listing 5-6   *The timeTest.jsp Page*

```
<%@ taglib uri="http://java.sun.com/jsf/html" prefix="h" %>
<%@ taglib uri="http://java.sun.com/jsf/core" prefix="f" %>
<html>
<head>
<title>Entering and Displaying A Time</title>
</head>
<body>
<f:use_faces>
<h:form formName="myForm">
  <br>Current time: <h:input_time valueRef="myBean.today"/>
  <br>Displayed using the default time style:
    <h:output_time valueRef="myBean.today"/>
  <br>Displayed using "short" time style:
    <h:output_time timeStyle="short" valueRef="myBean.today"/>
  <br>Displayed using "medium" time style:
    <h:output_time timeStyle="medium" valueRef="myBean.today"/>
  <br>Displayed using "long" time style:
    <h:output_time timeStyle="long" valueRef="myBean.today"/>
  <br>Displayed using "full" time style:
    <h:output_time timeStyle="full" valueRef="myBean.today"/>
```

```
    <br><h:output_errors/>
    <br><h:command_button label="Submit" commandName="submit"/>
</h:form>
</f:use_faces>
</body>
</html>
```

You can invoke the `timeTest.jsp` page using the following URL:

`http://localhost:8080/JSFCh05/faces/timeTest.jsp`

Figure 5-5 shows the result of typing a time into the component represented by the `input_time` tag and clicking the button. Notice that the `short` and `medium` time styles display the same value, and so do the `long` and `full` time styles.

The input_datetime and output_datetime Tags

The `input_datetime` tag accepts a date and time from the user. The `output_datetime` tag displays a date and time. Both tags have the `dateStyle`, `timeStyle`, `timezone`, and `formatPattern` attributes. The first three attributes are the same as those described for other tags described in the previous sections. The `formatPattern` attribute allows you to specify a pattern for a date and time. You can use the `dateStyle`, `timeStyle`, and `timezone` attributes in the same tag simultaneously or separately. Alternatively, you can use the `formatPattern` attribute without the other three attributes.

The `dateTimeTest.jsp` page, shown in Listing 5-7, uses an `input_datetime` tag and a number of `output_datetime` tags with various attribute values. The last one has a custom format pattern.

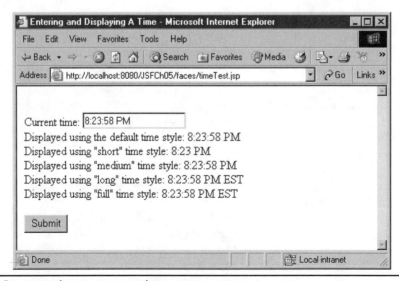

Figure 5-5   *Using the input_time and output_time tags*

Listing 5-7 *The dateTimeTest.jsp Page*

```
<%@ taglib uri="http://java.sun.com/jsf/html" prefix="h" %>
<%@ taglib uri="http://java.sun.com/jsf/core" prefix="f" %>
<html>
<head>
<title>Entering and Displaying A DateTime</title>
</head>
<body>
<f:use_faces>
<h:form formName="myForm">
  <br>Current date/time:
  <h:input_datetime valueRef="myBean.today"/>
  <br>Displayed using the default date/time styles:
    <b><h:output_datetime valueRef="myBean.today"/></b>
  <br>Displayed using "short" date style and "short" time style:
    <b><h:output_datetime dateStyle="short" timeStyle="short"
      valueRef="myBean.today"/></b>
  <br>Displayed using "medium" date style and "medium" time style:
    <b><h:output_datetime dateStyle="medium" timeStyle="medium"
      valueRef="myBean.today"/></b>
  <br>Displayed using "long" date style and "long" time style:
    <b><h:output_datetime dateStyle="long" timeStyle="long"
      valueRef="myBean.today"/></b>
  <br>Displayed using "full" date style and "full" time style:
    <b><h:output_datetime dateStyle="full" timeStyle="full"
      valueRef="myBean.today"/></b>
  <br>Displayed using the "MM/dd/yyyy hh:mm" pattern:
    <b><h:output_datetime formatPattern="MM/dd/yyyy hh:mm"
      valueRef="myBean.today"/></b>
  <br>Displayed using the "EEEEEEE, d-MM-yyyy hh:mm" pattern:
    <b><h:output_datetime formatPattern="EEEEEEE, d-MM-yyyy hh:mm"
      valueRef="myBean.today"/></b>
  <br><h:output_errors/>
  <br><h:command_button label="Submit" commandName="submit"/>
</h:form>
</f:use_faces>
</body>
</html>
```

You can invoke the dateTimeTest.jsp page using the following URL:

http://localhost:8080/JSFCh05/faces/dateTimeTest.jsp

Figure 5-6 shows the result of typing a time into the component represented by the input_time tag and clicking the button.

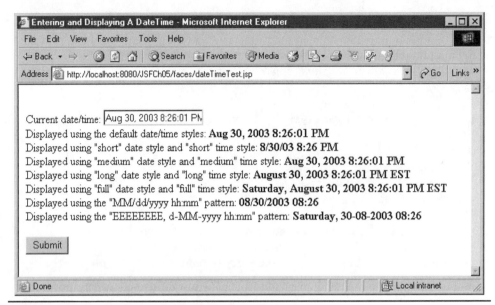

Figure 5-6   *Using the input_datetime and output_datetime tags*

The input_hidden Tag

The input_hidden tag is rendered as an <input type=hidden> element in the browser. You use it as a hidden element.

The input_secret Tag

The input_secret tag is rendered as an <input type=password> element in the browser. Each character typed into this box is displayed as an asterisk. The input_secret tag has the redisplay attribute, which, by default, has the value of "false". If the redisplay attribute is set to "true", the value will be redisplayed after the form containing the input_secret tag is submitted (and the JSP page is redisplayed). If the redisplay attribute value is "false" (the default), the value will not be redisplayed.

Listing 5-8 shows the secretTest.jsp page, which uses an input_secret tag.

Listing 5-8   *The secretTest.jsp Page*

```
<%@ taglib uri="http://java.sun.com/jsf/html" prefix="h" %>
<%@ taglib uri="http://java.sun.com/jsf/core" prefix="f" %>
<html>
<head>
```

```
<title>Entering A Secret String</title>
</head>
<body>
<f:use_faces>
<h:form formName="myForm">
  <br>Your secret word: <h:input_secret redisplay="true"
    valueRef="myBean.value"/>
  <br>Displayed using output_text:
    <h:output_text valueRef="myBean.value"/>
  <br><h:output_errors/>
  <br><h:command_button label="Submit" commandName="submit"/>
</h:form>
</f:use_faces>
</body>
</html>
```

You can invoke the `secretTest.jsp` page using the following URL:

`http://localhost:8080/JSFCh05/faces/secretTest.jsp`

The `input_secret` tag in the `secretTest.jsp` page has its `redisplay` attribute value set to "true". Therefore, if you type in a string and submit the form, the input box will show the string you entered as asterisks. Figure 5-7 shows the `secretTest.jsp` page in action.

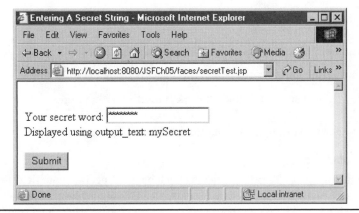

Figure 5-7   *The input_secret tag in action*

The input_textarea Tag

The input_textarea tag accepts multiline string input from the user. It is rendered as a <textarea> element in the browser. The input_textarea tag can have rows and cols attributes to control the number of rows in the display area and the number of characters per line. The textAreaTest.jsp page, shown in Listing 5-9, demonstrates the use of this tag.

Listing 5-9   *The textAreaTest.jsp Page*

```
<%@ taglib uri="http://java.sun.com/jsf/html" prefix="h" %>
<%@ taglib uri="http://java.sun.com/jsf/core" prefix="f" %>
<html>
<head>
<title>Testing input_textarea</title>
</head>
<body>
<f:use_faces>
<h:form formName="myForm">
  <br>Address: <h:input_textarea cols="40" rows="5"
  valueRef="myBean.value"/>
  <br>Displayed using output_text:
    <h:output_text valueRef="myBean.value"/>
  <br><h:output_errors/>
  <br><h:command_button label="Submit" commandName="submit"/>
</h:form>
</f:use_faces>
</body>
</html>
```

You can invoke the textAreaTest.jsp page by using the following URL:

```
http://localhost:8080/JSFCh05/faces/textAreaTest.jsp
```

Figure 5-8 shows an example of using textAreaTest.jsp.

The output_label Tag

You can use the output_label tag to attach a label to a specific input field so that it can be seen more easily by visually-impaired people. This tag is rendered as a <label> element in the browser. Listing 5-10 presents the labelTest.jsp page, which uses an output_label tag.

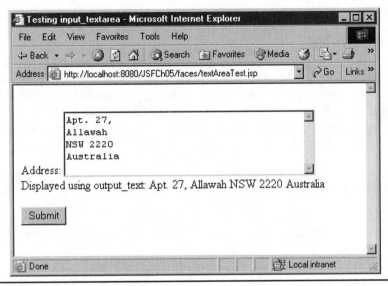

Figure 5-8   *Using the input_textarea tag*

Listing 5-10   *The labelTest.jsp Page*

```
<%@ taglib uri="http://java.sun.com/jsf/html" prefix="h" %>
<%@ taglib uri="http://java.sun.com/jsf/core" prefix="f" %>
<html>
<head>
<title>Entering and Displaying A String</title>
</head>
<body>
<f:use_faces>
<h:form formName="myForm">
  <h:output_label for="userName">
    <h:output_text id="userNameLabel" value="User Name"/>
  </h:output_label>
  <h:input_text id="userName" valueRef="myBean.value"/>
  <br><h:command_button label="Submit" commandName="submit"/>
</h:form>
</f:use_faces>
</body>
</html>
```

You can use the following URL to test the `labelTest.jsp` page.

`http://localhost:8080/JSFCh05/faces/labelTest.jsp`

However, in a typical browser, there is no apparent visual effect, as shown in Figure 5-9.

The output_errors Tag

The output_errors tag is used to display error messages that occur during page processing. The output_errors tag can have the for attribute. If this attribute is present, you assign the identifier of a component that the output_errors tag should watch. The output_errors tag will then display only the error message from the watched component.

Listing 5-11 shows an example, the errorsTest.jsp page, which uses an output_errors tag without the for attribute and input_number tags.

Listing 5-11   *The errorsTest.jsp Page*

```
<%@ taglib uri="http://java.sun.com/jsf/html" prefix="h" %>
<%@ taglib uri="http://java.sun.com/jsf/core" prefix="f" %>
<html>
<head>
<title>Testing output_errors</title>
</head>
<body>
<f:use_faces>
<h:form formName="myForm">
  <br>Quantity: <h:input_number valueRef="myBean.quantity"/>
  <br>Price: <h:input_number valueRef="myBean.price"/>
  <br><h:output_errors/>
  <br><h:command_button label="Submit" commandName="submit"/>
</h:form>
</f:use_faces>
</body>
</html>
```

Figure 5-9   *Using the output_label tag*

To test the `errorsTest.jsp` page, use the following URL:

`http://localhost:8080/JSFCh05/faces/errorsTest.jsp`

When you enter nonnumeric values in the boxes, you get the result shown in Figure 5-10.

Listing 5-12 shows another example, the `forAttributeTest.jsp` page, which uses the `output_errors` tag with the `for` attribute. Notice that for an input field to be watched, the tag representing the field must have an `id` attribute.

Listing 5-12 *The forAttributeTest.jsp Page*

```
<%@ taglib uri="http://java.sun.com/jsf/html" prefix="h" %>
<%@ taglib uri="http://java.sun.com/jsf/core" prefix="f" %>
<html>
<head>
<title>Testing output_errors</title>
</head>
<body>
<f:use_faces>
<h:form formName="myForm">
  <br>Quantity: <h:input_number id="quantity"
    valueRef="myBean.quantity"/>
  <br>Price: <h:input_number id="price" valueRef="myBean.price"/>
  <br><h:output_errors for="quantity"/>
  <br><h:command_button label="Submit" commandName="submit"/>
</h:form>
</f:use_faces>
</body>
</html>
```

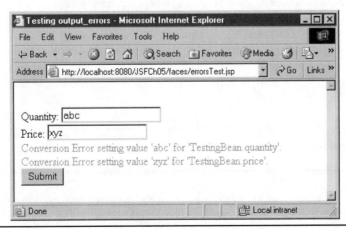

Figure 5-10 *Using the output_errors tag without the for attribute*

To test the forAttributeTest.jsp page, use this URL:

```
http://localhost:8080/JSFCh05/faces/forAttributeTest.jsp
```

Again, enter nonnumeric values in the boxes. This time, only the error message from the first input_number tag is displayed, as shown in Figure 5-11.

The output_message Tag

With the output_message tag, you can display concatenated messages. Listing 5-13 shows the messageTest.jsp page, which illustrates the use of this tag.

Listing 5-13   *The messageTest.jsp Page*

```
<%@ taglib uri="http://java.sun.com/jsf/html" prefix="h" %>
<%@ taglib uri="http://java.sun.com/jsf/core" prefix="f" %>
<html>
<head>
<title>Testing output_message</title>
</head>
<body>
<f:use_faces>
<h:form formName="myForm">
  <br>Quantity: <h:input_number valueRef="myBean.quantity"/>
  <br>Price: <h:input_number valueRef="myBean.price"/>
  <br><h:output_errors/>
  <br><h:command_button label="Submit" commandName="submit"/>
  <hr>
  <br>
  <h:output_message
  value="You have purchased {0} item(s) at the price of ${1}">
    <f:parameter id="param1" valueRef="myBean.quantity"/>
    <f:parameter id="param2" valueRef="myBean.price"/>
  </h:output_message>
</h:form>
</f:use_faces>
</body>
</html>
```

To invoke the messageTest.jsp page, use this URL:

```
http://localhost:8080/JSFCh05/faces/messageTest.jsp
```

Figure 5-12 shows the result of calling the messageTest.jsp page.

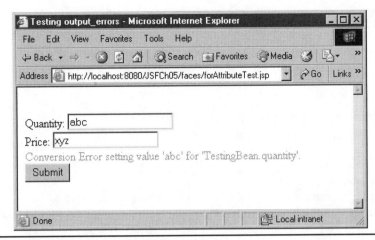

Figure 5-11   *Using the for attribute in the output_errors tag*

The selectboolean_checkbox Tag

Use the `selectboolean_checkbox` tag to obtain a Boolean value from the user. It is rendered as an `<input type=checkbox>` element in the browser and can be bound to a `boolean` type. The `selectBooleanCheckBoxTest.jsp` page in Listing 5-14 demonstrates using this tag.

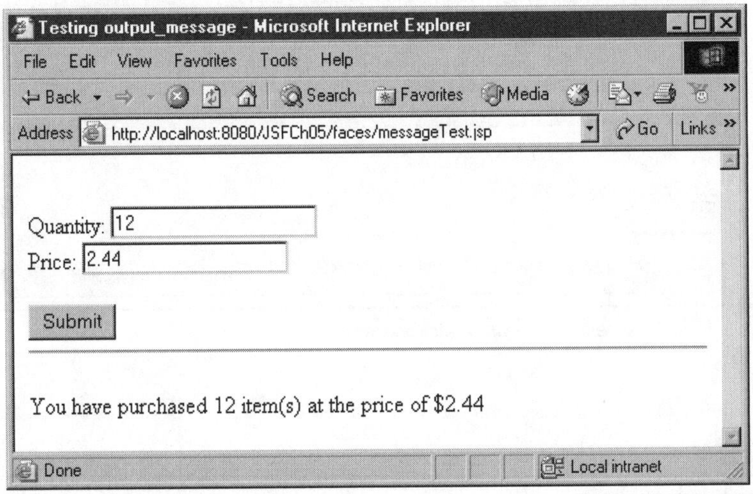

Figure 5-12   *Using the output_message tag*

Listing 5-14   *The selectBooleanCheckBoxTest.jsp Page*

```
<%@ taglib uri="http://java.sun.com/jsf/html" prefix="h" %>
<%@ taglib uri="http://java.sun.com/jsf/core" prefix="f" %>
<html>
<head>
<title>Using selectboolean_checkbox</title>
</head>
<body>
<f:use_faces>
<h:form formName="myForm">
  <br>Apply Discounted Price: <h:selectboolean_checkbox
    valueRef="myBean.discounted"/>
  <br><h:command_button label="Submit" commandName="submit"/>
</h:form>
</f:use_faces>
</body>
</html>
```

To invoke the `selectBooleanCheckBoxTest.jsp` page, use the following URL:
`http://localhost:8080/JSFCh05/faces/selectBooleanCheckBoxTest.jsp`

Figure 5-13 shows the result of invoking the `selectBooleanCheckBoxTest.jsp` page.

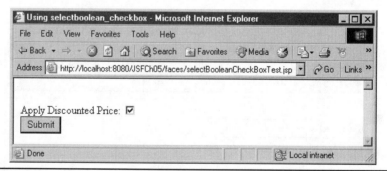

Figure 5-13   *Using the selectboolean_checkbox tag*

Summary

You use the UI components in JSP pages by employing the custom tags defined in the HTML custom tag library. This chapter presented the custom tags that represent the following UI components: `UIForm`, `UIGraphic`, `UICommand`, `UIInput`, `UIOutput`, and `UISelectBoolean`. The next chapter will discuss the custom tags that represent more advanced UI components.

CHAPTER 6

JSF Advanced Components

IN THIS CHAPTER:

Using UIPanel Components

Using Select Components

Summary

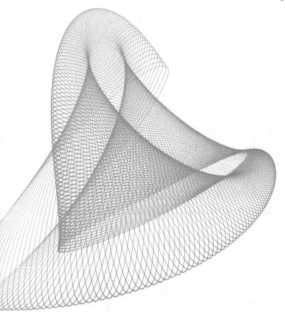

I n Chapter 5, you learned how to use simple tags in your JSP pages, as well as how to map the components to JavaBeans. This chapter will describe the custom tags that allow you to use the more complex UI components, including the `UIPanel`, `UISelectItem`, `UISelectItems`, `UISelectMany`, and `UISelectOne` components.

The `UIPanel` component is represented by four panel tags, rendered as HTML tables. The other components are represented by select tags, rendered as select elements.

Using UIPanel Components

A `UIPanel` component serves as a container for child components, presenting them in a table format. To use the `UIPanel` component from a JSP page, you write one of the panel tags to present information in an HTML table. There are four panel tags you can use: `panel_grid`, `panel_list`, `panel_group`, and `panel_data`. Both `panel_grid` and `panel_list` represent the entire table; `panel_group` and `panel_data` represent rows in the tables. Additionally, you can add a header and a footer to your table using the `facet` tag of the Core custom tag library. For more formatting options, you can use a style sheet to specify styles for your `UIPanel` components.

For the `UIPanel` examples presented in this section, as well as the select component examples later in the chapter, you will use several JavaBeans as model objects. These JavaBeans are registered in the application configuration file, as shown in Listing 6-1. The classes for the JavaBeans are discussed in the sections that include the examples.

Listing 6-1 *JavaBean Registration in the Application Configuration File*

```xml
<?xml version="1.0"?>
<!DOCTYPE faces-config PUBLIC
    "-//Sun Microsystems, Inc.//DTD JavaServer Faces Config 1.0//EN"
    "http://java.sun.com/dtd/web-facesconfig_1_0.dtd">

<faces-config>
  <managed-bean>
    <managed-bean-name>userBean</managed-bean-name>
    <managed-bean-class>ch06.UserBean</managed-bean-class>
    <managed-bean-scope>session</managed-bean-scope>
  </managed-bean>
  <managed-bean>
    <managed-bean-name>shoppingCartBean</managed-bean-name>
    <managed-bean-class>ch06.ShoppingCartBean</managed-bean-class>
    <managed-bean-scope>session</managed-bean-scope>
  </managed-bean>
  <managed-bean>
    <managed-bean-name>selectedCountryBean</managed-bean-name>
    <managed-bean-class>ch06.SelectedCountryBean</managed-bean-class>
```

```
      <managed-bean-scope>session</managed-bean-scope>
  </managed-bean>
  <managed-bean>
    <managed-bean-name>countryListBean</managed-bean-name>
    <managed-bean-class>ch06.CountryListBean</managed-bean-class>
    <managed-bean-scope>application</managed-bean-scope>
  </managed-bean>
  <managed-bean>
    <managed-bean-name>selectedCountriesBean</managed-bean-name>
    <managed-bean-class>
      ch06.SelectedCountriesBean
    </managed-bean-class>
    <managed-bean-scope>session</managed-bean-scope>
  </managed-bean>
</faces-config>
```

Rendering an HTML Table with the panel_grid Tag

You can use the `panel_grid` tag to format a bunch of components into a table. Basically, you nest all input and output tags inside a pair of `panel_grid` tags, and the `panel_grid` tag will format the input and output tags as a table. The most important attribute of the `panel_grid` tag is `columns`, which specifies how many columns the table has.

For example, you can use a `panel_grid` tag for a standard login form that requests a username and password, and store those values in a JavaBean instance. Listing 6-2 shows the UserBean class we will use for this example.

Listing 6-2   *The UserBean*

```
package ch06;
public class UserBean {
  private String userName;
  private String password;

  public String getUserName() {
    return userName;
  }
  public void setUserName(String userName) {
    this.userName = userName;
  }
  public String getPassword() {
    return password;
  }
  public void setPassword(String password) {
```

```
        this.password = password;
    }
}
```

The page with the logon form, `panelGridTest.jsp`, is shown in Listing 6-3. The `panel_grid` columns attribute formats the panel with two columns. Following the `panel_grid` tag are six other tags that will be formatted by the `panel_grid` tag: three `output_text` tags, an `input_text` tag, an `input_secret` tag, and a `command_button` tag.

Listing 6-3   *The panelGridTest.jsp Page*

```
<%@ taglib uri="http://java.sun.com/jsf/html" prefix="h" %>
<%@ taglib uri="http://java.sun.com/jsf/core" prefix="f" %>
<html>
<head>
<title>Using panel_grid</title>
</head>
<body>
<center>
<h2>Please enter your user name and password.</h2>
<br>
<f:use_faces>
<h:form  formName="myForm">
<h:panel_grid columns="2">
   <h:output_text value="User Name:"/>
   <h:input_text valueRef="userBean.userName"/>
   <h:output_text value="Password:"/>
   <h:input_secret valueRef="userBean.password"/>
   <h:output_text value=""/>
   <h:command_button commandName="login" label="login"/>
</h:panel_grid>
</h:form>
</f:use_faces>
</center>
</body>
</html>
```

To invoke the `panelGridTest.jsp` page, use the following URL:

`http://localhost:8080/JSFCh06/faces/panelGridTest.jsp`

Figure 6-1 shows the `panelGridTest.jsp` page in a browser.

Figure 6-1   *Formatting using the panel_grid tag*

When you view the HTML source, you will see something like the following (some spaces have been removed for better viewing):

```
<html>
<head>
<title>Using panel_grid</title>
</head>
<body>
<center>
<h2>Please enter your user name and password.</h2>
<br>
<form method="post"
action="/JSFCh06/faces/panelGridTest.jsp;
jsessionid=88F60D35113A072E2AFFD0F587389120">
<table>
<tr>
<td>User Name:</td>
<td><input type="text" name="id0" value=""></td>
</tr>
<tr>
<td>Password:</td>
<td><input type="password" name="id1" value=""></td>
</tr>
<tr>
<td></td>
<td><input type="submit" name="id2" value="login"></td>
</tr>
</table>
```

```
</form>
</center>
</body>
</html>
```

See how the `panel_grid` tag is rendered as an HTML table? Try changing the value of the `columns` attribute to 3. Then change it to 1 to see the results.

TIP

There are other attributes that you can use for better table formatting: columnClasses, rowClasses, footerClass, and headerClass. You will learn about these attributes in the "Using Style Sheets to Format UIPanel Components" section later in this chapter.

Adding Table Entries with the panel_list and panel_data Tags

The `panel_list` tag is also rendered as a `<table>` element in the browser, just like the `panel_grid` tag. However, the `panel_list` tag is more powerful because it can nest a `panel_data` tag to retrieve data from a source.

To display data in a table rendered by a `panel_list` tag, you need two types of JavaBeans. The first JavaBean is a collection object that contains zero or more instances of the second bean. We will call the first JavaBean the *container bean* and the second JavaBean the *element bean*. The container bean must have at least one property, which is an array, a `java.util.Collection`, a `java.util.Map`, or a `java.util.Iterator`. Each element bean represents a table row. Each cell in the row can be static data or mapped to a property in the element bean. The container bean contains the element beans, thus it holds all of the table data.

The `panel_data` tag is mapped to the container bean using the `valueRef` attribute. The `panel_data` tag must also have the `var` attribute, which refers to the current instance of the element bean. Each input and output tag inside the `panel_data` tag is mapped to a property in the element bean.

For example, you could use `panel_list` and `panel_data` tags to display the contents of a shopping cart in an online store application. This requires an element bean to represent each shopping item. We will use a JavaBean named `shoppingItemBean`, which has the properties `productId`, `productName`, and `quantity`, as shown in Listing 6-4.

Listing 6-4 *The ShoppingItemBean*

```
package ch06;
public class ShoppingItemBean {
  private String productId;
  private String productName;
  private int quantity;

  public ShoppingItemBean(String productId,
    String productName, int quantity) {
```

```
      this.productId = productId;
      this.productName = productName;
      this.quantity = quantity;
  }
  public String getProductId() {
    return productId;
  }
  public void setProductId(String productId) {
    this.productId = productId;
  }
  public String getProductName() {
    return productName;
  }
  public void setProductName(String productName) {
    this.productName = productName;
  }
  public int getQuantity() {
    return quantity;
  }
  public void setQuantity(int quantity) {
    this.quantity = quantity;
  }
}
```

The shopping cart itself is represented by the ShoppingCartBean (the container bean) and has one property, shoppingItems, as shown in Listing 6-5. The getShoppingItems method of the ShoppingCartBean returns a collection containing the instances of ShoppingItemBean.

| **Listing 6-5**   *The ShoppingCartBean* |

```
package ch06;
import java.util.ArrayList;
import java.util.Collection;

public class ShoppingCartBean {
  ArrayList shoppingItems = new ArrayList();
  public ShoppingCartBean() {
    shoppingItems.add(
      new ShoppingItemBean("t1", "Choco Chocolate Wafer", 10));
    shoppingItems.add(
      new ShoppingItemBean("t2", "Marbelee Biscuit", 5));
  }
```

```
public Collection getShoppingItems() {
  return shoppingItems;
}
public void setShoppingItems(Collection shoppingItems) {
  this.shoppingItems = new ArrayList(shoppingItems);
}
}
```

NOTE

The ShoppingCartBean *class has an internal variable of type* ArrayList: shoppingItems *(*java.util.ArrayList *indirectly implements the* java.util.Collection *interface through its parent's superclass* java.util.AbstractCollection*). The constructor contains code to add two instances of* ShoppingItemBean *to the* ArrayList*. In a real-world example, you might use another method to add shopping items to the cart.*

To display the contents of the ShoppingCartBean, you use the panel_list and panel_data tags. The panelListTest.jsp page, shown in Listing 6-6, demonstrates this.

Listing 6-6   *The panelListTest.jsp Page*

```
<%@ taglib uri="http://java.sun.com/jsf/html" prefix="h" %>
<%@ taglib uri="http://java.sun.com/jsf/core" prefix="f" %>
<html>
<head>
<title>Using panel_list</title>
</head>
<body>
<f:use_faces>
<h:form   formName="myForm">
<h:panel_list border="1">
  <h:panel_data var="item" valueRef="shoppingCartBean.shoppingItems">
    <h:output_text valueRef="item.productId"/>
    <h:output_text valueRef="item.productName"/>
    <h:output_number valueRef="item.quantity"/>
  </h:panel_data>
</h:panel_list>
</h:form>
</f:use_faces>
</body>
</html>
```

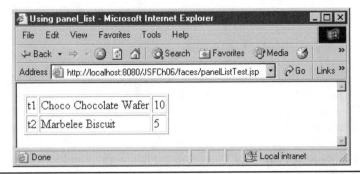

Figure 6-2   *Using the panel_list tag*

Notice that the `var` attribute in the `panel_data` tag contains a name by which each element bean is referred to in each output tag nested inside the `panel_data` tag.

To run the `panelListTest.jsp` page, use the following URL:

```
http://localhost:8080/JSFCh06/faces/panelListTest.jsp
```

Figure 6-2 displays the result in a browser.

Writing Headers and Footers with panel_group

The `panel_group` tag can encapsulate a nested tree of components so that the parent thinks of those components as a single component. A common use of the `panel_group` tag is in a table header or footer, in conjunction with the `facet` tag of the Core custom tag library.

As explained in Chapter 4, a component can become a subordinate of another component by becoming a facet of the owning component. There is no parent-child relationship between the containing component and the nested facet component. In this way, a header or a footer is a nested component in a table, but it is not a child component of a table. Headers and footers are rendered as `<th>` elements in the browser.

Here, we will look at two examples of creating headers and footers: a simple one using a `panel_group` tag inside a `panel_grid` tag and a bit more complex one that uses the `panel_group` tag inside a `panel_list` tag.

The panel_group Tag Within the panel_grid Tag

Listing 6-7 shows the `panelGroupTest.jsp` page, which uses a `panel_grid` tag to format three pairs of country/capital names in a two-column table. One `panel_group` tag is used in the header, and another is used in the footer.

Listing 6-7   *The panelGroupTest.jsp Page*

```
<%@ taglib uri="http://java.sun.com/jsf/html" prefix="h" %>
<%@ taglib uri="http://java.sun.com/jsf/core" prefix="f" %>
```

```
<html>
<head>
<title>Using panel_grid</title>
</head>
<body>
<f:use_faces>
<h:form   formName="myForm">
<h:panel_grid columns="2">

  <f:facet name="header">
  <h:panel_group>
    <h:output_text value="Country"/>
    <h:output_text value="  "/>
    <h:output_text value="Capital"/>
  </h:panel_group>
  </f:facet>

  <h:output_text value="Australia"/>
  <h:output_text value="Canberra"/>
  <h:output_text value="China"/>
  <h:output_text value="Beijing"/>
  <h:output_text value="France"/>
  <h:output_text value="Paris"/>

  <f:facet name="footer">
  <h:panel_group>
    <h:output_text value="source: n/a"/>
  </h:panel_group>
  </f:facet>

</h:panel_grid>
</h:form>
</f:use_faces>
</body>
</html>
```

You can call the panelGroupTest.jsp page by using the following URL:

http://localhost:8080/JSFCh06/faces/panelGroupTest.jsp

The result is shown in Figure 6-3.

The panel_group Tag Within the panel_list Tag

The next example refines the example of using the panel_list tag to display the contents of a shopping cart (Listing 6-6). It uses the ShoppingItemBean (Listing 6-4) and

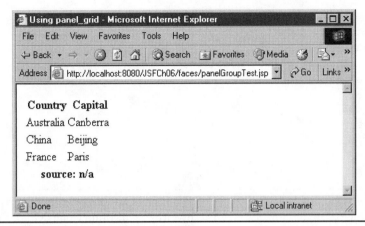

Figure 6-3   *Using panel_group inside panel_grid*

ShoppingCartBean (Listing 6-5). The `panelGroupTest2.jsp` page used for this example, shown in Listing 6-8, is similar to the page shown in Listing 6-6, but it uses two `panel_group` tags to display a header and a footer.

Listing 6-8   *The panelGroupTest2.jsp Page*

```
<%@ taglib uri="http://java.sun.com/jsf/html" prefix="h" %>
<%@ taglib uri="http://java.sun.com/jsf/core" prefix="f" %>
<html>
<head>
<title>Using panel_list</title>
</head>
<body>
<f:use_faces>
<h:form   formName="myForm">
<h:panel_list border="1">
  <f:facet name="header">
  <h:panel_group>
    <h:output_text value="Product Id"/>
    <h:output_text value="Product Name"/>
    <h:output_text value="Quantity"/>
  </h:panel_group>
  </f:facet>
<h:panel_data var="item" valueRef="shoppingCartBean.shoppingItems">
    <h:output_text valueRef="item.productId"/>
    <h:output_text valueRef="item.productName"/>
    <h:output_number valueRef="item.quantity"/>
```

```
    </h:panel_data>
    <f:facet name="footer">
    <h:panel_group>
      <h:output_text value="Code:P1"/>
    </h:panel_group>
    </f:facet>
</h:panel_list>
</h:form>
</f:use_faces>
</body>
</html>
```

You can run `panelGroupTest2.jsp` by invoking the following URL:

`http://localhost:8080/JSFCh06/faces/panelGroupTest2.jsp`

The result is shown in Figure 6-4.

Using Style Sheets to Format UIPanel Components

The `panel_grid` and `panel_list` tags have attributes that allow you to format parts of the table using Cascading Style Sheet (CSS) classes. You can format columns, rows, headers, and footers by using the `columnClasses`, `rowClasses`, `headerClass`, and `footerClass` attributes, respectively.

The example presented here uses the style sheet file named `Styles.css`, shown in Listing 6-9, which is located in the application directory.

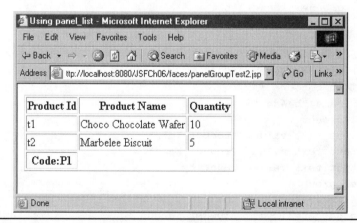

Figure 6-4   *Using the panel_group tag to draw a table header and footer*

Listing 6-9   *The Styles.css File*

```css
body {
  font-family: Arial, Helvetica, sans-serif;
  font-size: 12px;
}
td {
  font-family: Arial, Helvetica, sans-serif;
  font-size: 12px;
}
th {
  font-family: Arial, Helvetica, sans-serif;
  font-size: 12px;
}
.bodystyle {
  font-family: Arial, Helvetica, sans-serif;
  font-size: 12px;
}
.small {
  font-family: Arial, Helvetica, sans-serif;
  font-size: 11px;
}
.medium {
  font-family: Arial, Helvetica, sans-serif;
  font-size: 12px;
}
.header {
  font-family: "Times New Roman", Times, serif;
  font-size: 14px;
  color: #999999;
}
.footer {
  font-family: "Times New Roman", Times, serif;
  font-size: 10px;
  color: #999999;
}
```

The JSP page in Listing 6-10, `cssTest.jsp`, shows how you can format tables rendered by the `panel_grid` and `panel_list` tags.

Listing 6-10   *The cssTest.jsp Page*

```jsp
<%@ taglib uri="http://java.sun.com/jsf/html" prefix="h" %>
<%@ taglib uri="http://java.sun.com/jsf/core" prefix="f" %>
```

```
<html>
<head>
<title>Using panel_list</title>
<link rel="stylesheet" type="text/css"
  href='<%= request.getContextPath() + "/styles.css" %>'>
</head>
<body>
<f:use_faces>
<h:form   formName="myForm">
<h:panel_list border="1" footerClass="footer" headerClass="header"
panelClass="medium"
  columnClasses="small">
  <f:facet name="header">
  <h:panel_group>
    <h:output_text value="Product Id"/>
    <h:output_text value="Product Name"/>
    <h:output_text value="Quantity"/>
  </h:panel_group>
  </f:facet>

  <h:panel_data var="item" valueRef="shoppingCartBean.shoppingItems">
    <h:output_text valueRef="item.productId"/>
    <h:output_text valueRef="item.productName"/>
    <h:output_number valueRef="item.quantity"/>
  </h:panel_data>
  <f:facet name="footer">
  <h:panel_group>
    <h:output_text value="Code:P1"/>
  </h:panel_group>
  </f:facet>
</h:panel_list>
</h:form>
</f:use_faces>
</body>
</html>
```

In the `cssTest.jsp` page, notice that the `link` element's `href` attribute is given the value `request.getContextPath()` plus the style sheet filename:

```
<link rel="stylesheet" type="text/css"
  href='<%= request.getContextPath() + "/styles.css" %>'>
```

This is because the URL to the JSP page contains the `faces` pattern needed to invoke the Faces servlet. To remove the Java code entirely, you can use the Expression Language in JSP 2.0, discussed in Chapter 17.

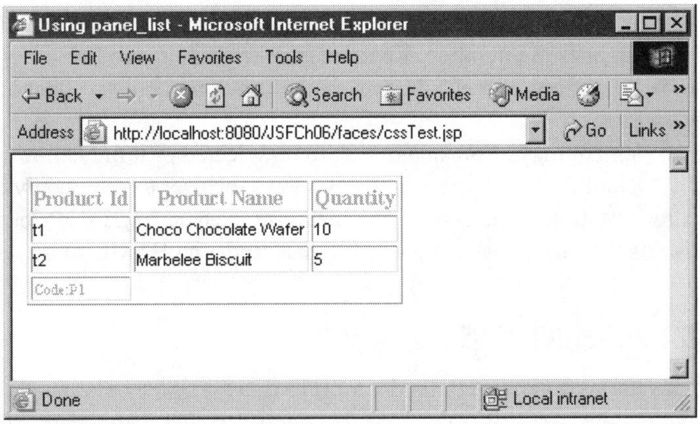

Figure 6-5 *Formatting panels using a style sheet*

Use the following URL to invoke the `cssTest.jsp` page:

```
http://localhost:8080/JSFCh06/faces/cssTest.jsp
```

The result is shown in Figure 6-5.

Using Select Components

You use the `UISelectItem`, `UISelectItems`, `UISelectMany`, and `UISelectOne` components to render various types of selection items, such as check boxes and radio buttons, in JSP pages. To add these components, you use the select tags to render an HTML `<select>` element. Let's have a quick refresher on how the `<select>` element works before going into the details of using the JSP tags.

Reviewing the <select> Element

Recall that a `<select>` element has zero or more `<option>` elements. The format of a `<select>` element with *n* options is as follows:

```
<select>
  <option value="value-1">text-1</option>
  <option value="value-2">text-2</option>
  . . .
  <option value="value-n">text-n</option>
</select>
```

An `<option>` element can have an optional `value` attribute, which represents the value of that option. If no `value` attribute is present in an `<option>` element, the text will be considered the value of the `<option>` element.

Also, a <select> element can have a size attribute, which has the default value of 1. The size attribute defines the number of options displayed in a <select> element at a time. If the number of options exceeds the value of size, a vertical scrollbar allows the user to see all of the options.

A <select> element may allow one option to be selected or it may allow many options to be selected. By default, a <select> element allows the user to select only one option. If you want it to allow multiple options to be selected, use the multiple attribute.

Now, let's discuss the various select tags in JSF that render an HTML <select> element.

Introducing the Select Tags

There are two tags that you can use to render an HTML <select> element that allows the user to select one option: selectone_listbox and selectone_menu. A related tag that performs a similar job is selectone_radio, in which options are displayed as radio buttons.

There are also two tags that render an HTML <select> element that allows multiple selections: selectmany_listbox and selectmany_menu. In addition, the selectmany_checkboxlist tag behaves similarly, but options are rendered as check boxes.

NOTE

The selectone_listbox and selectmany_listbox tags display all of the options. The selectone_menu and selectmany_menu tags allow you to use the size attribute to choose the number of options displayed at one time.

Select Tag Binding

A selectone tag can look complicated. However, remember that the user is allowed to select only one option. Therefore, a selectone tag's data is simply a String. For example, the SelectedCountryBean in Listing 6-11 has the selectedCountry property, which can be bound to a selectone tag, as you will see in some of the examples in the following sections.

Listing 6-11 *The SelectedCountryBean*

```
package ch06;
public class SelectedCountryBean {
  private Object selectedCountry;
  public Object getSelectedCountry() {
    return selectedCountry;
  }
  public void setSelectedCountry(Object selectedCountry) {
    this.selectedCountry = selectedCountry;
  }
}
```

A `selectmany` tag must be bound to a property that is an array of `Object` types, because a `selectmany` tag allows the user to select many options. Listing 6-12 shows the `SelectedCountriesBean`, which can be bound to a `selectmany` tag, as you will see in the upcoming multiple-selection examples.

Listing 6-12   *The SelectedCountriesBean*

```
package ch06;
public class SelectedCountriesBean {
  private Object[] selectedCountries;
  public void setSelectedCountries(Object[] selectedCountries) {
    this.selectedCountries = selectedCountries;
  }
  public Object[] getSelectedCountries() {
    return selectedCountries;
  }
}
```

Option Representation

For each select tag, you can use either the `selectitem` tag or the `selectitems` tag to represent an option or options. The `selectitem` tag is easier to use, and no programming is required. With `selectitem`, the page author defines the items in the list on the JSP page.

Here is an example of using a select tag with `selectitem`:

```
<h:selectone_listbox valueRef="selectedCountryBean.selectedCountry">
  <h:selectitem itemValue="Australia" itemLabel="Australia"/>
  <h:selectitem itemValue="Brazil" itemLabel="Brazil"/>
  <h:selectitem itemValue="China" itemLabel="China"/>
  <h:selectitem itemValue="Denmark" itemLabel="Denmark"/>
  <h:selectitem itemValue="Egypt" itemLabel="Egypt"/>
</h:selectone_listbox>
```

This example displays a list of countries. Each `selectitem` tag represents an option, in this case a country. Each option has an `itemValue` attribute and an `itemLabel` attribute. In the browser, the `itemValue` attribute will be rendered as the value of the `value` attribute of the `<option>` element. The `itemLabel` attribute becomes the text of that option.

As you can see, the `selectitem` tag is easy to use. However, a problem arises when a JSF application uses multiple select tags containing the same options. If you need to make changes to an option, they must be modified in every occurrence of the select tags—a maintenance nightmare.

The alternative to `selectitem` is `selectitems`. The `selectitems` tag solves the maintenance problem, but it is harder to use. The values of a `selectitems` tag come from a JavaBean instance. You map the `selectitems` tag with a JavaBeans property that is an array, a `java.util.Collection`, a `java.util.Map`, or a `java.util.Iterator`. As usual, you use the `valueRef` attribute to do the mapping.

Now, you need to do some programming to represent options with the `selectitems` tag. As explained in Chapter 4, the `javax.faces.component.SelectItem` class represents a select item, which is rendered as an `<option>` element in the browser. The `SelectItem` class has the following constructor:

```
public SelectItem(Object value, String label, String description);
```

The `value` becomes the `value` attribute of the HTML `<option>` element, and the `label` is rendered as the option's text. The `description` describes the select item but is not rendered to the browser.

Basically, the `selectitems` tag is bound to a JavaBean property that is an array, collection, map, or iterator whose elements are instances of the `SelectItem` class. Listing 6-13 shows the `CountryListBean`, which can be bound to a `selectitems` tag. Initial elements of the `ArrayList countryList` are added in the constructor and come from the `countries String` array. In a real application, these values could be from a database. We will use this bean in some examples later in the chapter.

Listing 6-13   *The CountryListBean*

```
package ch06;
import java.util.ArrayList;
import java.util.Collection;
import javax.faces.component.SelectItem;

public class CountryListBean {
  private String countries[] =
    { "Australia", "Brazil", "China", "Denmark", "Egypt" };
  private ArrayList countryList = new ArrayList();

  public CountryListBean() {
    for (int i=0; i<countries.length; i++) {
      countryList.add(
        new SelectItem(countries[i], countries[i], null));
    }
  }
  public void setCountryList(Collection countries) {
    countryList = new ArrayList(countries);
  }
  public Collection getCountryList() {
    return countryList;
  }
}
```

Now that you have an idea of what is required to render <select> items, let's take a close look at each select tag.

The selectone_listbox Tag

The selectone_listbox tag renders a <select> element that lets the user select one of a set of options. All of the options are displayed. The JSP page in Listing 6-14, selectOneListBoxTest.jsp, illustrates the use of this tag to display a list of countries from five selectitem tags.

Listing 6-14 *The selectOneListBoxTest.jsp Page*

```
<%@ taglib uri="http://java.sun.com/jsf/html" prefix="h" %>
<%@ taglib uri="http://java.sun.com/jsf/core" prefix="f" %>
<html>
<head>
<title>Using selectone_listbox with selectitem</title>
</head>
<body>
<f:use_faces>
<h:form formName="myForm">
<h:selectone_listbox valueRef="selectedCountryBean.selectedCountry">
  <h:selectitem itemValue="Australia" itemLabel="Australia"/>
  <h:selectitem itemValue="Brazil" itemLabel="Brazil"/>
  <h:selectitem itemValue="China" itemLabel="China"/>
  <h:selectitem itemValue="Denmark" itemLabel="Denmark"/>
  <h:selectitem itemValue="Egypt" itemLabel="Egypt"/>
</h:selectone_listbox>
<h:command_button commandName="submit" label="submit"/>
<hr>
You selected:
  <h:output_text valueRef="selectedCountryBean.selectedCountry"/>
</h:form>
</f:use_faces>
</body>
</html>
```

The selectone_listbox tag is bound to the selectedCountry property of the SelectedCountryBean (Listing 6-11). You can invoke this JSP page by using the following URL:

```
http://localhost:8080/JSFCh06/faces/selectOneListBoxTest.jsp
```

The result of selecting a country and clicking the submit button is shown in Figure 6-6.

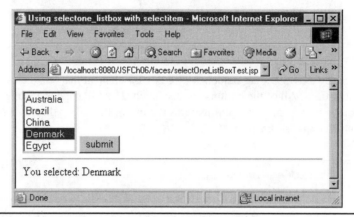

Figure 6-6 *Using the selectone_listbox tag with selectitem tags*

The HTML source code is as follows:

```
<html>
<head>
<title>Using selectone_listbox with selectitem</title>
</head>
<body>
<form method="post" action="/JSFCh06/faces/selectOneListBoxTest.jsp">
<select name="id0" size="5" >
  <option value="Australia">Australia</option>
  <option value="Brazil">Brazil</option>
  <option value="China">China</option>
  <option value="Denmark" selected>Denmark</option>
  <option value="Egypt">Egypt</option>
</select>
<input type="submit" name="id1" value="submit">
<hr>
You selected: Denmark
</form>
</body>
</html>
```

Notice how the `selectone_listbox` tag is rendered as an HTML `<select>` element.

The next example renders the same HTML as the first example. However, instead of using `selectitem` tags, the `selectOneListBoxTest2.jsp` page, shown in Listing 6-15, uses a `selectitems` tag to retrieve values from the `CountryListBean` (Listing 6-13).

Listing 6-15   *The selectOneListBoxTest2.jsp Page*

```
<%@ taglib uri="http://java.sun.com/jsf/html" prefix="h" %>
<%@ taglib uri="http://java.sun.com/jsf/core" prefix="f" %>
<html>
<head>
<title>Using selectone_listbox with selectitems</title>
</head>
<body>
<f:use_faces>
<h:form   formName="myForm">
<h:selectone_listbox valueRef="selectedCountryBean.selectedCountry">
  <h:selectitems valueRef="countryListBean.countryList"/>
</h:selectone_listbox>
<h:command_button commandName="submit" label="submit"/>
<hr>
You selected:
  <h:output_text valueRef="selectedCountryBean.selectedCountry"/>
</h:form>
</f:use_faces>
</body>
</html>
```

You can invoke this JSP page using the following URL:

```
http://localhost:8080/JSFCh06/faces/selectOneListBoxTest2.jsp
```

The resulting page looks similar to the one produced using `selectitem` tags (see Figure 6-6).

The selectone_menu Tag

The `selectone_menu` tag is similar to the `selectone_listbox` tag. However, the `selectone_menu` tag allows you to decide how many select items are displayed at a time, by using the `size` attribute. Listing 6-16 presents the `selectOneMenuTest.jsp` page, which uses a `selectone_menu` tag with five `selectitem` tags.

Listing 6-16   *The selectOneMenuTest.jsp Page*

```
<%@ taglib uri="http://java.sun.com/jsf/html" prefix="h" %>
<%@ taglib uri="http://java.sun.com/jsf/core" prefix="f" %>
<html>
<head>
<title>Using selectone_menu with selectitem</title>
</head>
```

```
<body>
<f:use_faces>
<h:form   formName="myForm">
<h:selectone_menu size="3"
  valueRef="selectedCountryBean.selectedCountry">
  <h:selectitem itemValue="Australia" itemLabel="Australia"/>
  <h:selectitem itemValue="Brazil" itemLabel="Brazil"/>
  <h:selectitem itemValue="China" itemLabel="China"/>
  <h:selectitem itemValue="Denmark" itemLabel="Denmark"/>
  <h:selectitem itemValue="Egypt" itemLabel="Egypt"/>
</h:selectone_menu>
<h:command_button commandName="submit" label="submit"/>
<hr>
You selected:
<h:output_text valueRef="selectedCountryBean.selectedCountry"/>
</h:form>
</f:use_faces>
</body>
</html>
```

You can invoke the `selectOneMenuTest.jsp` page using the following URL:

`http://localhost:8080/JSFCh06/faces/selectOneMenuTest.jsp`

The result of selecting a country and then clicking the submit button is shown in Figure 6-7.

The next example, using the `selectOneMenuTest2.jsp` shown in Listing 6-17, produces the same result as Listing 6-16. However, instead of using `selectitem` tags, it uses a `selectitems` tag bound to the `CountryListBean` (Listing 6-13).

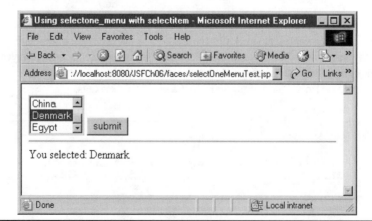

Figure 6-7   *Using selectone_menu with selectitem tags*

Listing 6-17   *The selectOneMenuTest2.jsp Page*

```
<%@ taglib uri="http://java.sun.com/jsf/html" prefix="h" %>
<%@ taglib uri="http://java.sun.com/jsf/core" prefix="f" %>
<html>
<head>
<title>Using selectone_menu with selectitems</title>
</head>
<body>
<f:use_faces>
<h:form  formName="myForm">
<h:selectone_menu size="3"
  valueRef="selectedCountryBean.selectedCountry">
  <h:selectitems valueRef="countryListBean.countryList"/>
</h:selectone_menu>
<h:command_button commandName="submit" label="submit"/>
<hr>
You selected:
<h:output_text valueRef="selectedCountryBean.selectedCountry"/>
</h:form>
</f:use_faces>
</body>
</html>
```

To invoke this page, use the following URL:

```
http://localhost:8080/JSFCh06/faces/selectOneMenuTest2.jsp
```

The result will be the same as shown in Figure 6-7.

The selectone_radio Tag

The `selectone_radio` tag is similar to the `selectone_listbox` and `selectone_menu` tags. However, instead of getting a select element in the browser, you show a set of radio buttons. The options for a `selectone_radio` tag can be a set of `selectitem` tags or a `selectitems` tag.

As an example, consider the `selectOneRadioTest.jsp` page in Listing 6-18. The `selectone_radio` tag is bound to the `selectedCountry` property of the `SelectedCountryBean` (Listing 6-11).

Listing 6-18   *The selectOneRadioTest.jsp Page*

```
<%@ taglib uri="http://java.sun.com/jsf/html" prefix="h" %>
<%@ taglib uri="http://java.sun.com/jsf/core" prefix="f" %>
<html>
```

```
<head>
<title>Using selectone_radio with selectitem</title>
</head>
<body>
<f:use_faces>
<h:form   formName="myForm">
<h:selectone_radio valueRef="selectedCountryBean.selectedCountry">
  <h:selectitem itemValue="Australia" itemLabel="Australia"/>
  <h:selectitem itemValue="Brazil" itemLabel="Brazil"/>
  <h:selectitem itemValue="China" itemLabel="China"/>
  <h:selectitem itemValue="Denmark" itemLabel="Denmark"/>
  <h:selectitem itemValue="Egypt" itemLabel="Egypt"/>
</h:selectone_radio>
<h:command_button commandName="submit" label="submit"/>
<hr>
You selected:
<h:output_text valueRef="selectedCountryBean.selectedCountry"/>
</h:form>
</f:use_faces>
</body>
</html>
```

Test the `selectOneRadioTest.jsp` page by invoking this URL:

`http://localhost:8080/JSFCh06/faces/selectOneRadioTest.jsp`

If you select a country and click the submit button, you will see a page similar to Figure 6-8.

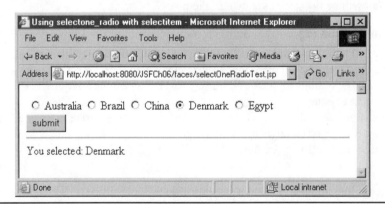

Figure 6-8   *Using selectone_radio with selectitem tags*

If you view the HTML source for this example, here is what you will see:

```
<html>
<head>
<title>Using selectone_radio with selectitem</title>
</head>
<body>
<form method="post" action="/JSFCh06/faces/selectOneRadioTest.jsp">
<table border="0">
<tr>
<td><input type="radio" name="id0" value="Australia"> Australia</td>
<td><input type="radio" name="id0" value="Brazil"> Brazil</td>
<td><input type="radio" name="id0" value="China"> China</td>
<td><input type="radio" checked name="id0" value="Denmark">
 Denmark</td>
<td><input type="radio" name="id0" value="Egypt"> Egypt</td>
</tr>
</table>
<input type="submit" name="id1" value="submit">
<hr>
You selected: Denmark
</form>
</body>
</html>
```

Another example of using the selectone_radio tag is shown in Listing 6-19. The selectOneRadioTest2.jsp is similar to selectOneRadioTest.jsp, except that it uses a selectitems tag.

Listing 6-19   *The selectOneRadioTest2.jsp Page*

```
<%@ taglib uri="http://java.sun.com/jsf/html" prefix="h" %>
<%@ taglib uri="http://java.sun.com/jsf/core" prefix="f" %>
<html>
<head>
<title>Using selectone_radio with selectitems</title>
</head>
<body>
<f:use_faces>
<h:form  formName="myForm">
<h:selectone_radio valueRef="selectedCountryBean.selectedCountry">
  <h:selectitems valueRef="countryListBean.countryList"/>
</h:selectone_radio>
<h:command_button commandName="submit" label="submit"/>
<hr>
```

```
You selected:
  <h:output_text valueRef="selectedCountryBean.selectedCountry"/>
</h:form>
</f:use_faces>
</body>
</html>
```

You can invoke the JSP page using the following URL:

`http://localhost:8080/JSFCh06/faces/selectOneRadioTest2.jsp`

The selectmany_listbox Tag

The `selectmany_listbox` tag renders an HTML `<select>` element that allows the user to make multiple selections. The data of the component represented by this tag can be bound to an array of `Object` types.

As an example, the JSP page shown in Listing 6-20, `selectManyListBoxTest.jsp`, uses a `selectmany_listbox` tag to bind to the `selectedCountries` property of the `SelectedCountriesBean` (Listing 6-12). The `selectmany_listbox` tag uses five `selectitem` tags to get its options.

Listing 6-20   *The selectManyListBoxTest.jsp Page*

```
<%@ taglib uri="http://java.sun.com/jsf/html" prefix="h" %>
<%@ taglib uri="http://java.sun.com/jsf/core" prefix="f" %>
<html>
<head>
<title>Using selectmany_listbox with selectitem</title>
</head>
<body>
<f:use_faces>
<h:form   formName="myForm">
<h:selectmany_listbox
  valueRef="selectedCountriesBean.selectedCountries">
  <h:selectitem itemValue="Australia" itemLabel="Australia"/>
  <h:selectitem itemValue="Brazil" itemLabel="Brazil"/>
  <h:selectitem itemValue="China" itemLabel="China"/>
  <h:selectitem itemValue="Denmark" itemLabel="Denmark"/>
  <h:selectitem itemValue="Egypt" itemLabel="Egypt"/>
</h:selectmany_listbox>
<h:command_button commandName="submit" label="submit"/>
</h:form>
</f:use_faces>
</body>
</html>
```

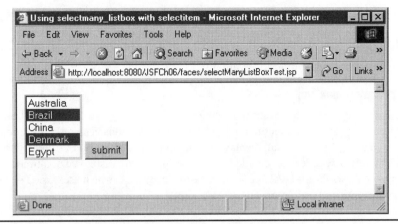

Figure 6-9   *Using the selectmany_listbox tag with selectitem tags*

Use the following URL to invoke the JSP page:

```
http://localhost:8080/JSFCh06/faces/selectManyListBoxTest.jsp
```

You can now select multiple values and get a result similar to Figure 6-9.

In the next example, shown in Listing 6-21, the selectManyListBoxTest2.jsp page uses a selectitems tag with the selectmany_listbox tag.

Listing 6-21   *The selectManyListBoxTest2.jsp Page*

```
<%@ taglib uri="http://java.sun.com/jsf/html" prefix="h" %>
<%@ taglib uri="http://java.sun.com/jsf/core" prefix="f" %>
<html>
<head>
<title>Using selectmany_listbox with selectitems</title>
</head>
<body>
<f:use_faces>
<h:form   formName="myForm">
<h:selectmany_listbox
  valueRef="selectedCountriesBean.selectedCountries">
  <h:selectitems valueRef="countryListBean.countryList"/>
</h:selectmany_listbox>
<h:command_button commandName="submit" label="submit"/>
</h:form>
</f:use_faces>
</body>
</html>
```

To invoke the `selectManyListBoxTest2.jsp` page, use the following URL:

`http://localhost:8080/JSFCh06/faces/selectManyListBoxTest2.jsp`

This produces a result similar to Figure 6-9.

The selectmany_menu Tag

The `selectmany_menu` tag is similar to the `selectmany_listbox` tag—both are rendered as a `<select>` element that allows multiple selections. The only difference is that the `selectmany_listbox` tag displays all the options, and the `selectmany_menu` tag has the `size` attribute to let you decide how many options are displayed at a time.

Listing 6-22 shows the `selectManyMenuTest.jsp` page, which uses a `selectmany_menu` tag with five `selectitem` tags.

Listing 6-22   *The selectManyMenuTest.jsp Page*

```
<%@ taglib uri="http://java.sun.com/jsf/html" prefix="h" %>
<%@ taglib uri="http://java.sun.com/jsf/core" prefix="f" %>
<html>
<head>
<title>Using selectmany_menu with selectitem</title>
</head>
<body>
<f:use_faces>
<h:form  formName="myForm">
<h:selectmany_menu size="3"
  valueRef="selectedCountriesBean.selectedCountries">
  <h:selectitem itemValue="Australia" itemLabel="Australia"/>
  <h:selectitem itemValue="Brazil" itemLabel="Brazil"/>
  <h:selectitem itemValue="China" itemLabel="China"/>
  <h:selectitem itemValue="Denmark" itemLabel="Denmark"/>
  <h:selectitem itemValue="Egypt" itemLabel="Egypt"/>
</h:selectmany_menu>
<h:command_button commandName="submit" label="submit"/>
</h:form>
</f:use_faces>
</body>
</html>
```

You can run the JSP page using the following URL:

`http://localhost:8080/JSFCh06/faces/selectManyMenuTest.jsp`

The result will be similar to Figure 6-10.

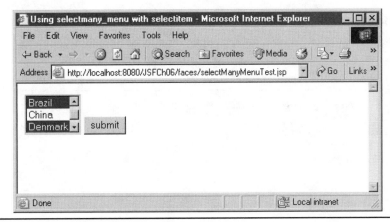

Figure 6-10   *Using selectmany_menu with selectitems tags*

The JSP page in Listing 6-23 produces the same result as the JSP page in Listing 6-22, but it uses a `selectitems` tag instead of five `selectitem` tags.

Listing 6-23   *The selectManyMenuTest2.jsp Page*

```
<%@ taglib uri="http://java.sun.com/jsf/html" prefix="h" %>
<%@ taglib uri="http://java.sun.com/jsf/core" prefix="f" %>
<html>
<head>
<title>Using selectmany_menu with selectitems</title>
</head>
<body>
<f:use_faces>
<h:form   formName="myForm">
<h:selectmany_menu size="3"
  valueRef="selectedCountriesBean.selectedCountries">
  <h:selectitems valueRef="countryListBean.countryList"/>
</h:selectmany_menu>
<h:command_button commandName="submit" label="submit"/>
</h:form>
</f:use_faces>
</body>
</html>
```

To invoke the `selectManyMenuTest2.jsp` page, use the following URL:

`http://localhost:8080/JSFCh06/faces/selectManyMenuTest2.jsp`

The selectmany_checkboxlist Tag

The `selectmany_checkboxlist` tag renders as a set of check boxes. Listing 6-24 shows
a JSP page that uses a `selectmany_checkboxlist` tag with five `selectitem` tags.

Listing 6-24   *The selectManyCheckBoxListTest.jsp Page*

```
<%@ taglib uri="http://java.sun.com/jsf/html" prefix="h" %>
<%@ taglib uri="http://java.sun.com/jsf/core" prefix="f" %>
<html>
<head>
<title>Using selectmany_checkboxlist with selectitem</title>
</head>
<body>
<f:use_faces>
<h:form   formName="myForm">
<h:selectmany_checkboxlist
  valueRef="selectedCountriesBean.selectedCountries">
  <h:selectitem itemValue="Australia" itemLabel="Australia"/>
  <h:selectitem itemValue="Brazil" itemLabel="Brazil"/>
  <h:selectitem itemValue="China" itemLabel="China"/>
  <h:selectitem itemValue="Denmark" itemLabel="Denmark"/>
  <h:selectitem itemValue="Egypt" itemLabel="Egypt"/>
</h:selectmany_checkboxlist>
<h:command_button commandName="submit" label="submit"/>
</h:form>
</f:use_faces>
</body>
</html>
```

To invoke this JSP page, use the following URL:

```
http://localhost:8080/JSFCh06/faces/selectManyCheckBoxListTest.jsp
```

You will see something similar to Figure 6-11.

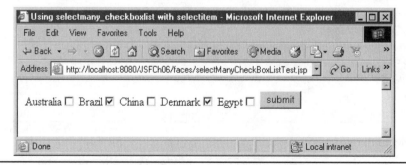

Figure 6-11   *Using selectmany_checkboxlist with selectitem tags*

The HTML sent to the browser is something like the following:

```
<html>
<head>
<title>Using selectmany_checkboxlist with selectitem</title>
</head>
<body>
<form method="post"
action="/JSFCh06/faces/selectManyCheckBoxListTest.jsp">
<label for="id0.id0">Australia
<input name="id0" id="id0.id0" value="Australia"
type="checkbox"></label>
<label for="id0.id1">Brazil
<input name="id0" id="id0.id1" value="Brazil"
type="checkbox"></label>
<label for="id0.id2">China
<input name="id0" id="id0.id2" value="China"
type="checkbox"></label>
<label for="id0.id3">Denmark
<input name="id0" id="id0.id3" value="Denmark"
type="checkbox"></label>
<label for="id0.id4">Egypt<input name="id0" id="id0.id4"
value="Egypt"
type="checkbox"></label>
<input type="submit" name="id1" value="submit">
</form>
</body>
</html>
```

For another example, consider the `selectManyCheckBoxListTest2.jsp` page in Listing 6-25. It uses a `selectmany_checkboxlist` tag with a `selectitems` tag and allows the user to check zero or more options.

Listing 6-25   *The selectManyCheckBoxListTest2.jsp Page*

```
<%@ taglib uri="http://java.sun.com/jsf/html" prefix="h" %>
<%@ taglib uri="http://java.sun.com/jsf/core" prefix="f" %>
<html>
<head>
<title>Using selectmany_checkboxlist with selectitems</title>
</head>
<body>
<f:use_faces>
<h:form   formName="myForm">
<h:selectmany_checkboxlist
```

```
  valueRef="selectedCountriesBean.selectedCountries">
  <h:selectitems valueRef="countryListBean.countryList"/>
</h:selectmany_checkboxlist>
<h:command_button commandName="submit" label="submit"/>
</h:form>
</f:use_faces>
</body>
</html>
```

To invoke the JSP page, use the following URL:

`http://localhost:8080/JSFCh06/faces/selectManyCheckBoxListTest2.jsp`

The result is similar to Figure 6-11.

Summary

In this chapter, you learned how to use the JSF components UIPanel, UISelectItem, UISelectItems, UISelectMany, and UISelectOne in JSP pages using the various panel and select tags. You also learned how to bind those components to object models.

The next chapter will discuss the event handling in JSF and how to write event listeners for your JSF applications.

JSF Event Handling

As you already know, JSF applications are event-driven. Following the Java 2 event model, any object in a JSF application can be designed to generate or receive events. For example, a `UICommand` component can generate an event when the user clicks it.

There are two types of events in JSF: `ActionEvent` and `ValueChangedEvent`. `UICommand` components can fire an `ActionEvent`, and `UIInput` components can fire a `ValueChangedEvent`. For writing implementations of the event listeners, JSF provides the `javax.faces.event` package.

This chapter begins with a discussion of the Java 2 event model, and then focuses on handling events in JSF. You will learn how events are processed and then work through two examples that demonstrate how to write event listeners to handle the two types of events.

Introducing the Java 2 Event Model

JSF event handling follows the Java 2 event model. In this model, any object can notify other objects about a change in its state. The information about the change of the state itself is encapsulated in an event object. In this model, there are three participants involved:

- ▶   The event source, which is the object whose state changes
- ▶   The event object, which encapsulates the state changes in the event source
- ▶   The event listener, which is the object that wants to be notified of the state changes of the event source

In summary, when an event occurs, the event source generates an event object and sends it to the event listener.

Event Sources

Any object can be an event source. However, the class for an event source must provide methods for event listeners to register and deregister their interest in receiving state change notifications from the event source. Also, an event source must maintain a list of interested event listeners. For example, the `javax.faces.component.UICommand` class has two methods for this purpose: `addActionListener` and `removeActionListener`. In addition, an event source must also provide logic to create and deliver event objects to all interested event listeners.

As an example, Listing 7-1 presents the `MyEventSource` class, which belongs to the `ch07.eventmodel` package. `MyEventSource` is the class for objects that will generate events.

Listing 7-1   *The MyEventSource Class*

```
package ch07.eventmodel;
import java.util.ArrayList;
```

```
import java.util.Iterator;

public class MyEventSource {
  private String oldPassword;
  private String password;
  private ArrayList listeners = new ArrayList();

  public void setPassword(String newPassword) {
    if (newPassword==null)
      return;
      oldPassword = this.password;
      this.password = newPassword;
      if (!newPassword.equals(oldPassword)) {
        broadcast();
      }
  }
  public void addEventListener(MyEventListener listener) {
      listeners.add(listener);
  }
  public void removeEventListener(MyEventListener listener) {
      listeners.remove(listener);
  }
  public void broadcast() {
      Iterator iterator = listeners.iterator();
      MyEventObject event =
        new MyEventObject(this, oldPassword, password);
      while (iterator.hasNext()) {
        MyEventListener listener = (MyEventListener) iterator.next();
        listener.handleEvent(event);
    }
  }
}
```

An instance of the MyEventSource class can emit an event when its password property is changed. Notice that the setPassword method calls the broadcast method when the new password passed is different from the current value of the password property.

The listeners ArrayList stores all of the objects interested in the change of the password property. Two methods are provided for registering and deregistering interest in the change of the password property: addEventListener and removeEventListener.

Finally, the broadcast method iterates all registered listeners in the listeners ArrayList and calls their handleEvent method, passing the MyEventObject instance (described in the next section), which encapsulates the value change of the password property in the MyEventSource object.

Event Objects

An event object encapsulates information about a particular type of event, such as the old and new values of the state that changed. The class for an event object must extend the `java.util.EventObject` class. The `EventObject` class has the `getSource` method, which returns the event source. The signature of the `getSource` method is as follows:

```
public Object getSource()
```

In your event object class, you can then implement methods related to the event, such as `getOldValue` and `getNewValue`.

Listing 7-2 shows an example of an event object class called `MyEventObject` class, which also belongs to the `ch07.eventmodel` package. `MyEventObject` encapsulates the information on the state change in the instance of `MyEventSource`.

Listing 7-2   *The MyEventObject Class*

```
package ch07.eventmodel;
import java.util.EventObject;

public class MyEventObject extends EventObject {
  private String oldPassword;
  private String newPassword;
  public MyEventObject(
    Object source, String oldPassword, String newPassword) {
      super(source);
      this.oldPassword = oldPassword;
      this.newPassword = newPassword;
  }
  public String getOldPassword() {
    return oldPassword;
  }
  public String getNewPassword() {
    return newPassword;
  }
}
```

The `MyEventObject` class represents an event object that can be triggered by the `MyEventSource` class (Listing 7-1). Its constructor accepts the event source, as well as the old and new passwords. A listener can call its `getOldPassword` and `getNewPassword` methods to obtain the old and new values of the `password` property of the `EventSource` object.

Event Listeners

An event listener can receive a particular type of event by implementing the appropriate listener interface. All listener interfaces are subinterfaces of the java.util.EventListener interface. This interface does not have any methods and acts as a marker interface. Your event listener interface must then define a method for receiving the appropriate event object.

Listing 7-3 shows the MyEventListener listener (also in the ch07.eventmodel package).

Listing 7-3   *The MyEventListener Interface*

```
package ch07.eventmodel;
import java.util.EventListener;

public interface MyEventListener extends EventListener {
  public void handleEvent(MyEventObject event);
}
```

MyEventSource is the class for objects that will generate events. MyEventListener is an interface that must be implemented by any object interested in getting a notification from instances of MyEventSource. Specifically, it must be implemented by the objects that want to know about the value change of the password property in a MyEventSource instance.

Objects Interested in Event Notification

To demonstrate the example, you need a class to represent any object that may be interested in the event notification from a MyEventSource instance. InterestedParty, shown in Listing 7-4, implements the MyEventListener interface. The implementation of the handleEvent method simply writes to the console the old and new passwords of the event source.

Listing 7-4   *The InterestedParty Class*

```
package ch07.eventmodel;

public class InterestedParty implements MyEventListener {
  public void handleEvent(MyEventObject event) {
    System.out.println("Hi, I'm an InterestedParty");
    System.out.println("Got MyEventObject");
```

```
      System.out.println(
        "Its old password is " + event.getOldPassword());
      System.out.println(
        "Its new password is " + event.getNewPassword());
      System.out.println("-------------------------");
  }
}
```

Event Demonstration

Finally, to demonstrate the example, you need one more class: EventDemo. The
EventDemo class is the main class in this example. In its demo method, the EventDemo
object instantiates the MyEventSource class and registers an InterestedParty with
it. It then invokes the setPassword method on the MyEventSource object, effectively
causing MyEventSource to emit an event. The EventDemo class is shown in Listing 7-5.

Listing 7-5   *The EventDemo Class*

```
package ch07.eventmodel;

public class EventDemo {
  public void demo() {
    MyEventSource source = new MyEventSource();
    InterestedParty interestedParty = new InterestedParty();
    // register interestedParty's interest in
    // the event that MyEventSource can emit
    source.addEventListener(interestedParty);
    // now trigger the event by setting a new value for MyEventSource
    source.setPassword("Hello");
    // trigger another one
    source.setPassword("WOW");
  }
  public static void main(String[] args) {
    EventDemo eventDemo = new EventDemo();
    eventDemo.demo();
  }
}
```

If you run the EventDemo class, you will see the following on your console:

```
Hi, I'm an InterestedParty
Got MyEventObject
Its old password is null
Its new password is Hello
-------------------------
Hi, I'm an InterestedParty
Got MyEventObject
Its old password is Hello
Its new password is WOW
-------------------------
```

Handling Events in JSF

Handling events in JSF is surprisingly easy. Here are the steps:

▶ Write an event listener.

▶ Deploy the event listener under the WEB-INF/classes or WEB-INF/lib directory under the application directory.

▶ In the tag representing the component whose event is to be captured, use an action_listener or a valuechanged_listener tag defined in the Core custom tag library.

JSF provides a set of interfaces and classes for working with events and listeners in the javax.faces.event package, shown in Figure 7-1.

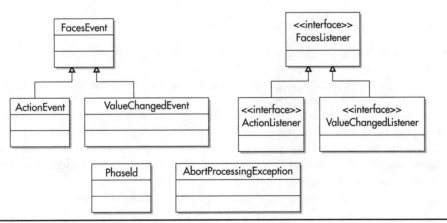

Figure 7-1   *The classes in the javax.faces.event package*

NOTE

The *FacesEvent* class subclasses the `java.util.EventObject,` and the
FacesListener interface extends the `java.util.EventListener` interface.

Just like the Java 2 event model, the JSF event model includes three participants: the event source, the event object, and the event listener. The `UIInput` and `UICommand` components are possible event sources in a JSF application.

Event Objects in JSF

All event objects in JSF must extend the `javax.faces.event.FacesEvent` class for those events to be supported by the request processing lifecycle. The `FacesEvent` class is a subclass of the `java.util.EventObject` class and adds the `getComponent` method, which returns the `UIComponent` component that fired the event.

The `FacesEvent` class has two subclasses: `ActionEvent` and `ValueChangedEvent`. The `ActionEvent` class represents the activation of the UI component, such as a `UICommand` component. The `ActionEvent` class adds one method: `getActionCommand`. This method returns a `String` containing the command that was activated. In the `command_button` and `command_hyperlink` tags, the command corresponds to the `commandName` attribute.

The `ValueChangedEvent` class represents a notification that the local value of a `UIInput` component has been changed. However, if the new value was not validated successfully, the `ValueChangedEvent` will not be fired. There are two methods added to this class: `getOldValue` and `getNewValue`. The `getOldValue` method returns the old value of the component that fired the event. The `getNewValue` method returns the new value. The return type of both `getOldValue` and `getNewValue` is `java.lang.Object`.

Event Listeners in JSF

To capture a JSF event, you need to write a listener. All listeners in JSF application must implement the `javax.faces.event.FacesListener` interface. This interface extends the `java.util.EventListener` interface, which is the interface that must be implemented by all Java event listeners.

The `FacesListener` interface has the `getPhaseId` method, which allows you to specify after which processing phase your listener should be called. The `getPhaseId` method returns an instance of the `javax.faces.event.PhaseId` class representing the phase after which the listener should be called. The `PhaseId` class contains constants that return phases in JSF request processing:

- ▶ RECONSTITUTE_REQUEST
- ▶ APPLY_REQUEST_VALUES
- ▶ PROCESS_VALIDATIONS
- ▶ UPDATE_MODEL_VALUES
- ▶ INVOKE_APPLICATIONS
- ▶ ANY_PHASE

Note: The phases during which events can be handled are Apply Request Values, Process Validations, and Update Model Values. A value of PhaseId.ANY_PHASE returned by the getPhaseId method will make the listener process events during the Apply Request Values phase, if possible.

The FacesListener interface has two subinterfaces: ActionListener and ValueChangedListener. The ActionListener interface is the interface that must be implemented to capture an ActionEvent. This interface adds a new method that will be invoked by the request processing lifecycle: processAction. This method is invoked when the ActionEvent the ActionListener is registered for occurs. The processAction method has the following signature.

```
public void processAction(ActionEvent event)
    throws AbortProcessingException
```

The processAction method is equivalent to the handleEvent method in the MyEventListener interface shown earlier in Listing 7-3.

The ValueChangedListener interface is the interface you implement to capture a ValueChangedEvent. This interface adds one method: processValueChanged. This method is invoked when the ValueChangedEvent observed by this listener occurs. Here is the signature of the processValueChanged method:

```
public void processValueChanged(ValueChangedEvent event)
    throws AbortProcessingException
```

Writing an ActionListener for UICommand Components

A UICommand component raises an ActionEvent when clicked by the user. The example in this section shows how to write an ActionListener and register it with two command buttons. The steps you need to take include writing an ActionListener by implementing the javax.faces.event.ActionListener interface and registering it using the action_listener tag of the Core custom tag library.

NOTE

Until the Early Access 3 version of JSF 1.0, you needed to write your own `ActionListener` *to manage user navigation from one page to another, which was a tedious task. Fortunately, later versions provide a better way of page navigation: they include a default* `ActionListener` *in the* `javax.faces` `.application.Application` *for each Web application. Now, thanks to the default* `ActionListener`, *you just need to edit the application configuration file to manage page navigation. In fact, you should not write an* `ActionListener` *for page navigation, so you do not interfere with the work of the default* `ActionListener`.

The example presents a simple calculator that can add two numbers or subtract one number from another. To add, you click the command button with the label +; to subtract, you click the button with the – label. The first command_button tag has its commandName attribute set to "add", and the second command_button tag's commandName attribute is assigned the value "subtract".

When the user clicks the add button, an ActionEvent is queued. The getCommandName method of this ActionEvent instance returns add. When the user clicks the subtract button, an ActionEvent instance's getCommandName method returns subtract. Because you have only one ActionListener for both buttons, the first thing to do is to inquire which button was clicked by calling the getCommandName method of the ActionEvent object passed to the listener.

The NumberBean in Listing 7-6 is used to store the two numbers and the result of the calculation. The type of the result property is String.

Listing 7-6   *The NumberBean*

```java
package ch07;
public class NumberBean {
  private String firstNumber;
  private String secondNumber;
  private String result;
  public String getFirstNumber() {
    return firstNumber;
  }
  public void setFirstNumber(String number) {
    firstNumber = number;
  }
  public String getSecondNumber() {
    return secondNumber;
  }
  public void setSecondNumber(String number) {
    secondNumber = number;
```

```
  }
  public String getResult() {
    System.out.println("getResult:" + result);
    return result;
  }
  public void setResult(String result) {
    System.out.println("setResult:" + result);
    this.result = result;
  }
}
```

The NumberBean is registered in the application configuration file using the managed-bean tag, as shown in Listing 7-7.

Listing 7-7   *NumberBean Registration in the Application Configuration File*

```
<managed-bean>
  <managed-bean-name>numberBean</managed-bean-name>
  <managed-bean-class>ch07.NumberBean</managed-bean-class>
  <managed-bean-scope>session</managed-bean-scope>
</managed-bean>
```

Implementing the ActionListener Interface

The ch07.MyActionListener class, shown in Listing 7-8, implements the javax.faces .event.ActionListener interface. It provides the implementations of the getPhaseId and processAction methods.

Listing 7-8   *The MyActionListener Class*

```
package ch07;

import javax.faces.FactoryFinder;
import javax.faces.application.Application;
import javax.faces.application.ApplicationFactory;
import javax.faces.context.FacesContext;
import javax.faces.el.ValueBinding;
import javax.faces.event.ActionEvent;
import javax.faces.event.ActionListener;
```

```java
import javax.faces.event.PhaseId;

public class MyActionListener implements ActionListener {

  public PhaseId getPhaseId() {
    return PhaseId.INVOKE_APPLICATION;
  }
  public void processAction(ActionEvent event) {
    System.out.println("processAction");

    FacesContext facesContext = FacesContext.getCurrentInstance();
    Object firstNumber =
getValueBinding("numberBean.firstNumber").getValue(facesContext);
    Object secondNumber =
getValueBinding("numberBean.secondNumber").getValue(facesContext);
    String command = event.getActionCommand();
    if (command.equals("add")) {
      try {
        int firstNo = Integer.parseInt(firstNumber.toString());
        int secondNo = Integer.parseInt(secondNumber.toString());
        String result = Integer.toString(firstNo + secondNo);
        System.out.println("processAction. result:" + result);
        getValueBinding("numberBean.result").
          setValue(facesContext, result);
      }
      catch (Exception e) {
      }
    }
    else if (command.equals("subtract")) {
      try {
        int firstNo = Integer.parseInt(firstNumber.toString());
        int secondNo = Integer.parseInt(secondNumber.toString());
        String result = Integer.toString(firstNo - secondNo);
        System.out.println("processAction. result:" + result);
        getValueBinding("numberBean.result").
          setValue(facesContext, result);
      }
      catch (Exception e) {
      }
    }
  }
```

```
private static ValueBinding getValueBinding(String valueRef) {
   ApplicationFactory factory = (ApplicationFactory)
     FactoryFinder.getFactory(FactoryFinder.APPLICATION_FACTORY);
   Application application = factory.getApplication();
   return application.getValueBinding(valueRef);
}
}
```

The `getPhaseId` method returns `PhaseId.INVOKE_APPLICATION` to indicate that the listener should be invoked after the Invoke Application phase of the request processing lifecycle. The `processAction` method processes the event fired.

The `processAction` method first obtains the `FacesContext` instance for this request and uses the `getValueBinding` method to acquire the values of the `firstNumber` and `secondNumber` properties in the `NumberBean`.

```
FacesContext facesContext = FacesContext.getCurrentInstance();
Object firstNumber =
getValueBinding("numberBean.firstNumber").getValue(facesContext);
   Object secondNumber =
getValueBinding("numberBean.secondNumber").getValue(facesContext);
```

NOTE

The `getValueBinding` *method returns a* `ValueBinding` *object for the specified value reference. This method was discussed in Chapter 3.*

The `processAction` method then checks the command name from the `getActionCommand` method of the `ActionEvent` object. If the command name equals "`add`", the following code will be executed:

```
String command = event.getActionCommand();
if (command.equals("add")) {
   try {
     int firstNo = Integer.parseInt(firstNumber.toString());
     int secondNo = Integer.parseInt(secondNumber.toString());
     String result = Integer.toString(firstNo + secondNo);
     System.out.println("processAction. result:" + result);
     getValueBinding("numberBean.result")
        .setValue(facesContext, result);
   }
   catch (Exception e) {
   }
}
```

This results in the `result` property of the `NumberBean` being assigned the value of
(`firstNumber` + `secondNumber`).

If the command name equals "`subtract`", the following code is run:

```
else if (command.equals("subtract")) {
    try {
      int firstNo = Integer.parseInt(firstNumber.toString());
      int secondNo = Integer.parseInt(secondNumber.toString());
      String result = Integer.toString(firstNo - secondNo);
      System.out.println("processAction. result:" + result);
      getValueBinding("numberBean.result").setValue(facesContext,
result);
    }
    catch (Exception e) {
    }
  }
```

In this case, the `result` property of the `NumberBean` is assigned the value of
(`firstNumber` − `secondNumber`).

Setting Up the UICommand Components for Capturing Events

The `calculator.jsp` page, shown in Listing 7-9, is the JSP page that contains the
required UI components: two `UIInput` components, two `UICommand` components, and
two `UIOutput` components for displaying the result and the error message.

Listing 7-9   *The calculator.jsp Page*

```
<%@ taglib uri="http://java.sun.com/jsf/html" prefix="h" %>
<%@ taglib uri="http://java.sun.com/jsf/core" prefix="f" %>
<html>
<head>
<title>Perform simple calculation</title>
</head>
<body>
<f:use_faces>
<h:form  formName="myForm">
First Number: <h:input_text valueRef="numberBean.firstNumber"/>
<br>Second Number: <h:input_text valueRef="numberBean.secondNumber"/>
<br>Result: <h:output_text valueRef="numberBean.result"/>
```

```
<br>
<h:command_button commandName="add" label=" + ">
  <f:action_listener type="ch07.MyActionListener"/>
</h:command_button>
<h:command_button commandName="subtract" label=" - ">
  <f:action_listener type="ch07.MyActionListener"/>
</h:command_button>
<br><h:output_errors/>
</h:form>
</f:use_faces>
</body>
</html>
```

You can invoke the `calculator.jsp` page using the following URL:

```
http://localhost:8080/JSFCh07/faces/calculator.jsp
```

When the page appears, type numbers in the input boxes and click either the add or the subtract button. Figure 7-2 shows an example of performing an addition.

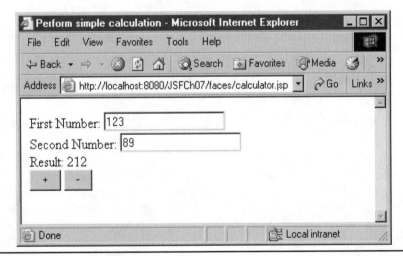

Figure 7-2   *Using an ActionListener*

What About Using JavaBeans for Business Logic?

You've seen that the `ActionListener` encapsulates business logic for your application. You might be wondering if it is possible to use a JavaBean to encapsulate business logic. For very simple applications, the answer is yes.

For example, an application that simply adds two numbers can use a JavaBean that stores data as well as performs the calculation. Consider the following JavaBean named `SimpleNumberBean`:

```java
package ch07;
public class SimpleNumberBean {
  private int firstNumber;
  private int secondNumber;
  public int getFirstNumber() {
    return firstNumber;
  }
  public void setFirstNumber(int number) {
    firstNumber = number;
  }
  public int getSecondNumber() {
    return secondNumber;
  }
  public void setSecondNumber(int number) {
    secondNumber = number;
  }
  public int getResult() {
    return firstNumber + secondNumber;
  }
}
```

See the `getResult` method that returns the result of `firstNumber` + `secondNumber`? The `firstNumber`, `secondNumber`, and `result` properties can be easily bound to `UIInput` and `UIOutput` components, such as in the following JSP page (which you can run from `http://localhost:8080/JSFCh07/faces/usingBean.jsp`):

```jsp
<%@ taglib uri="http://java.sun.com/jsf/html" prefix="h" %>
<%@ taglib uri="http://java.sun.com/jsf/core" prefix="f" %>
<html>
<head>
<title>Using JavaBean for Business Logic</title>
</head>
<body>
<f:use_faces>
```

```
<h:form  formName="myForm">
  First Number:
  <h:input_number valueRef="simpleNumberBean.firstNumber"/>
  <br>Second Number:
  <h:input_number valueRef="simpleNumberBean.secondNumber"/>
  <br>Result:
  <h:output_number valueRef="simpleNumberBean.result"/>
  <br>
  <h:command_button commandName="add" label=" + "/>
</h:form>
</f:use_faces>
</body>
</html>
```

However, as the business logic becomes more complicated—say, needing to perform both addition and subtraction—an event listener provides a more powerful solution. So, JavaBeans can provide business logic in very simple JSF applications, but they can never replace event listeners entirely.

Writing a ValueChangedListener for a UIInput Component

Now, we will use the other type of JSF event, by writing a `ValueChangedListener` to capture a `ValueChangedEvent` fired by a `UIInput` component. This example is a "vowel-counter" application. It will present a `UIInput` component in which the user can enter a word, and then click a button to get the number of vowels in that word.

To store the word and the number of vowels, you use the `TestingBean`, shown in Listing 7-10.

Listing 7-10   *The TestingBean*

```
package ch07;
public class TestingBean {
  private String word;
  private String vowelCount;
  public String getWord() {
    return word;
  }
  public void setWord(String word) {
    this.word = word;
  }
  public String getVowelCount() {
```

```
    return vowelCount;
  }
  public void setVowelCount (String vowelCount) {
    this.vowelCount = vowelCount;
  }
}
```

The TestingBean is registered in the application configuration file using the managed-bean element shown in Listing 7-11.

Listing 7-11   *TestingBean Registration in the Application Configuration File*

```
<managed-bean>
  <managed-bean-name>testingBean</managed-bean-name>
  <managed-bean-class>ch07.TestingBean</managed-bean-class>
  <managed-bean-scope>session</managed-bean-scope>
</managed-bean>
```

Implementing the ValueChangedListener Interface

Listing 7-12 shows the MyValueChangedListener class, which acts as the listener for the ValueChangedEvent raised by the UIInput component.

Listing 7-12   *The MyValueChangedListener Class*

```
package ch07;

import javax.faces.FactoryFinder;
import javax.faces.application.Application;
import javax.faces.application.ApplicationFactory;
import javax.faces.context.FacesContext;
import javax.faces.el.ValueBinding;
import javax.faces.event.AbortProcessingException;
import javax.faces.event.PhaseId;
import javax.faces.event.ValueChangedEvent;
import javax.faces.event.ValueChangedListener;

public class MyValueChangedListener implements ValueChangedListener {

  public PhaseId getPhaseId() {
    System.out.println("getPhaseId");
    return PhaseId.PROCESS_VALIDATIONS;
  }
```

```
  public void processValueChanged(ValueChangedEvent event) throws
AbortProcessingException {
    System.out.println("processValueChanged");
    String word = event.getNewValue().toString().toUpperCase();
    int wordLength = word.length();
    int vowelCount = 0;
    for (int i=0; i<wordLength; i++) {
      char c = word.charAt(i);
      if (c=='A' || c=='E' || c=='I' || c=='O' || c=='U')
        vowelCount++;
    }
    FacesContext facesContext = FacesContext.getCurrentInstance();
    try {
      getValueBinding("testingBean.vowelCount")
        .setValue(facesContext, Integer.toString(vowelCount));
    }
    catch (Exception e) {
      System.out.println(e.toString());
    }
  }
  private static ValueBinding getValueBinding(String valueRef) {
    ApplicationFactory factory = (ApplicationFactory)
      FactoryFinder.getFactory(FactoryFinder.APPLICATION_FACTORY);
    Application application = factory.getApplication();
    return application.getValueBinding(valueRef);
  }
}
```

The MyValueChangedListener class has the usual getValueBinding method. The processValueChanged method starts by assigning to the word variable the new value of the UIInput component emitting the ValueChangedEvent. It does so by calling the getNewValue method of the ValueChangedEvent class.

```
String word = event.getNewValue().toString().toUpperCase();
```

It then iterates each character in word and increments vowelCount for each occurrence of a vowel in the word.

```
    int wordLength = word.length();
    int vowelCount = 0;
    for (int i=0; i<wordLength; i++) {
      char c = word.charAt(i);
      if (c=='A' || c=='E' || c=='I' || c=='O' || c=='U')
        vowelCount++;
    }
```

Next, the `processValueChanged` method retrieves the `FacesContext` instance of the current request and sets the value of the `vowelCount` property of the `TestingBean`.

```
FacesContext facesContext = FacesContext.getCurrentInstance();
try {
  getValueBinding("testingBean.vowelCount")
    .setValue(facesContext, Integer.toString(vowelCount));
}
catch (Exception e) {
  System.out.println(e.toString());
}
```

Setting Up the UIInput Component for Capturing Events

To test the `ValueChangedListener`, use the `vowelCounter.jsp` page shown in Listing 7-13.

Listing 7-13   *The vowelCounter.jsp Page*

```
<%@ taglib uri="http://java.sun.com/jsf/html" prefix="h" %>
<%@ taglib uri="http://java.sun.com/jsf/core" prefix="f" %>
<html>
<head>
<title>Count the number of vowels in a word</title>
</head>
<body>
<f:use_faces>
<h:form  formName="myForm">
Type in a word and we will count the number of vowels in it:
<h:input_text  valueRef="testingBean.word">
  <f:valuechanged_listener type="ch07.MyValueChangedListener"/>
</h:input_text>
<br>The number of vowels:
  <h:output_number valueRef="testingBean.vowelCount"/>
<br><h:command_button commandName="login"
  label="Count the Number of Vowels"/>
<br>
<h:output_errors/>
</h:form>
</f:use_faces>
</body>
</html>
```

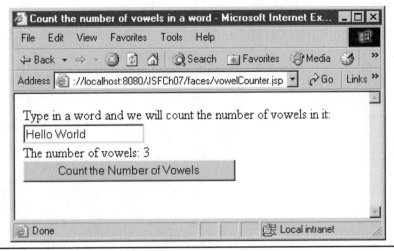

Figure 7-3   *Using a ValueChangedListener*

You can invoke the `vowelCounter.jsp` page by using the following URL:

`http://localhost:8080/JSFCh07/faces/vowelCounter.jsp`

Once you type in a word and click the button, you can see the number of vowels in the word you entered, as shown in Figure 7-3.

Summary

In this chapter, you learned how to handle events in JSF applications by writing listeners that implement one of the interfaces in the `javax.faces.event` package. The examples demonstrated using an `ActionListener` that captures the `ActionEvent` and a `ValueChangedListener` for capturing the `ValueChangedEvent`.

As noted in this chapter, in earlier versions of JSF, the programmer needed to write an `ActionListener` to manage user navigation from one page to another. Now, that task is handled by a default `ActionListener` for the application. Page navigation is an important topic, which is discussed in the next chapter.

Page Navigation

IN THIS CHAPTER:

Defining Navigation Rules

Defining Conditional Page Navigation

Summary

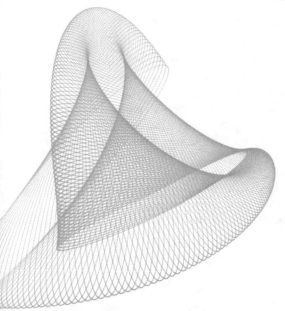

Page navigation is a crucial aspect of JSF application programming. All JSF applications, except those consisting of only one page, will require users to navigate from one page to another.

Users navigate to another page by clicking a `UICommand` component on the page, which is represented by either the `command_button` tag or the `command_hyperlink` tag (described in Chapter 5). Since JSF provides a default `ActionListener` for page navigation management, you do not need to write your own `ActionListener` to manage this function.

This chapter describes how to control page navigation by writing page navigation rules in the application configuration file. Because the application configuration file is an XML document, you can use any text editor to update it. This means that your page navigation rules are easy to modify.

Defining Navigation Rules

In Chapter 2, we worked through a simple example that included page navigation between two pages. You controlled the navigation by using navigation rules in the application configuration file. You learned that you need to specify a navigation rule for each page from which the user can navigate to another page. Here, we will examine how navigation rules are defined in the application configuration file.

Specifying Navigation Rule's Elements

Each navigation rule specifies a page of origin and one or more possible targets. A navigation rule is defined by the `navigation-rule` element in the application configuration file. The element is described as follows:

```
<!ELEMENT navigation-rule (description*, display-name*, icon*,
  from-tree-id?, navigation-case*)>
```

The `description`, `display-name`, `icon`, and `navigation-case` subelements can be omitted entirely or appear many times (denoted by the asterisk). The `from-tree-id` subelement can be omitted or used once (denoted by the question mark).

The two most important subelements of the `navigation-rule` element are `from-tree-id`, which identifies the origin page, and `navigation-case`, which identifies a target page. Each possible target is represented by a `navigation-case` subelement.

The from-tree-id Subelement

A page in a navigation rule is represented by its tree identifier. The value for a `from-tree-id` subelement is the tree identifier of the page of origin. For example, to describe the navigation rule for a JSP page called `login.jsp`, use the following:

```
<from-tree-id>/login.jsp</from-tree-id>
```

The navigation-case Subelement

The `navigation-case` subelement represents a possible target. Each `navigation-case` element specifies the target page for a particular outcome of the `from-tree-id` processing. An outcome can be obtained from the `action` or `actionRef` attributes of the `UICommand` component in the page referenced by `from-tree-id` element.

The `navigation-case` element is described as follows:

```
<!ELEMENT navigation-case (description*, display-name*, icon*,
  from-action-ref?, from-outcome?, to-tree-id)>
```

You use the `description` element to describe the navigation case. The `display-name` and `icon` elements are useful only for an XML tool you use to edit the application configuration file. Neither of these is used very often.

The `to-tree-id` element specifies the target page for this navigation case. The `from-outcome` element is the outcome of processing the `from-tree-id` subelement of `navigation-rule`. It is obtained from the value of the `action` property of the `UICommand` component that triggered the `ActionEvent` in the `from-tree-id` (origin) page. (`UICommand` component properties are described in Chapter 4.)

The `from-action-ref` element also represents the outcome of processing the `from-tree-id` page. However, its value comes from the `actionRef` property of the `UICommand` component that raised the `ActionEvent`.

You will see examples of using the `from-outcome` and `from-action-ref` subelements later in this chapter, in the "Defining Conditional Page Navigation" section. In this chapter's first example, we will use simple `navigation-rule` elements, without those subelements.

Implementing Simple Navigation

The example in this section illustrates the simplest navigation rule. This application consists of two pages: `page1.jsp` and `page2.jsp`. From `page1.jsp`, you can click the button to go to `page2.jsp`, and from `page2.jsp`, you can click the button to go to `page1.jsp`. The navigation rules in Listing 8-1 specify the navigation from both `page1.jsp` and `page2.jsp`.

Listing 8-1   *Simple Navigation Rules in the Application Configuration File*

```
<navigation-rule>
  <from-tree-id>/page1.jsp</from-tree-id>
  <navigation-case>
    <to-tree-id>/page2.jsp</to-tree-id>
  </navigation-case>
</navigation-rule>
<navigation-rule>
  <from-tree-id>/page2.jsp</from-tree-id>
  <navigation-case>
    <to-tree-id>/page1.jsp</to-tree-id>
  </navigation-case>
</navigation-rule>
```

The first `navigation-rule` element specifies the target for `page1.jsp`. It contains the `navigation-case` element with a `to-tree-id` subelement, without a `from-outcome` or `from-action-ref` subelement. This means that, regardless of the outcome, the target page (`page2.jsp`) will be displayed.

The second `navigation-rule` element specifies the target for `page2.jsp`. From `page2.jsp`, the user will go to `page1.jsp`. However, as you will see in the `page1.jsp` page definition, the original page will be redisplayed if there is a processing error.

Both `page1.jsp` and `page2.jsp` use the `TestingBean` shown in Listing 8-2.

Listing 8-2 *The TestingBean Class*

```
package ch08;
public class TestingBean {
  private String value;
  public String getValue() {
    return value;
  }
  public void setValue(String value) {
    this.value = value;
  }
}
```

The bean is registered in the application configuration file, as shown in Listing 8-3.

Listing 8-3 *TestingBean Registration in the Application Configuration File*

```
<managed-bean>
  <managed-bean-name>testingBean</managed-bean-name>
  <managed-bean-class>ch08.TestingBean</managed-bean-class>
  <managed-bean-scope>session</managed-bean-scope>
</managed-bean>
```

The `page1.jsp` page, shown in Listing 8-4, contains a `UIInput` component and a validator that enforces the user to type in four or more characters into the `UIInput` component. (Validators are the topic of Chapter 9.)

Listing 8-4 *The page1.jsp Page*

```
<%@ taglib uri="http://java.sun.com/jsf/html" prefix="h" %>
<%@ taglib uri="http://java.sun.com/jsf/core" prefix="f" %>
<html>
<head>
<title>Page 1</title>
</head>
<body>
```

```
<f:use_faces>
<h:form  formName="myForm">
Enter your user name (minimum 4 characters) :
  <h:input_text valueRef="TestingBean.value">
    <f:validate_length minimum="4"/>
  </h:input_text>
<br>
<h:command_button commandName="submit" label="submit"/>
<br>
<h:output_errors/>
</h:form>
</f:use_faces>
</body>
</html>
```

The page2.jsp page, shown in Listing 8-5, contains a UIOutput component that displays the value entered in the UIInput component in the page1.jsp page. The page2.jsp page also has a command button for the user to go back to page1.jsp.

Listing 8-5   *The page2.jsp Page*

```
<%@ taglib uri="http://java.sun.com/jsf/html" prefix="h" %>
<%@ taglib uri="http://java.sun.com/jsf/core" prefix="f" %>
<html>
<head>
<title>Page 2</title>
</head>
<body>
<f:use_faces>
<h:form  formName="myForm">
Your user name is <h:output_text valueRef="TestingBean.value"/>
<br>
<h:command_button commandName="back" label="Back"/>
</h:form>
</f:use_faces>
</body>
</html>
```

You can invoke the page1.jsp page using the following URL:

```
http://localhost:8080/JSFCh08/faces/page1.jsp
```

When the page appears in your browser, type in a string of four or more characters, as in the example in Figure 8-1, and click submit.

You will see a page similar to the one shown in Figure 8-2. If you click the Back button, you will see the first page again.

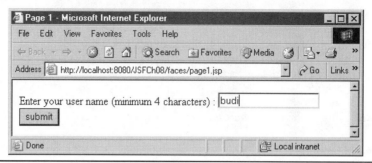

Figure 8-1   *The first page of the simple navigation example*

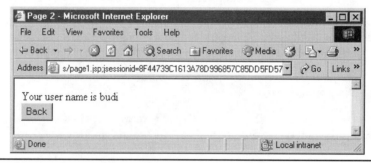

Figure 8-2   *The second page of the simple navigation example*

Back at the first page, if you enter fewer than four characters into the UIInput component, the validator in page1.jsp will add a Message object to the FacesContext instance, causing the navigation to be canceled. As a result, you will see the first page with an error message, as shown in Figure 8-3.

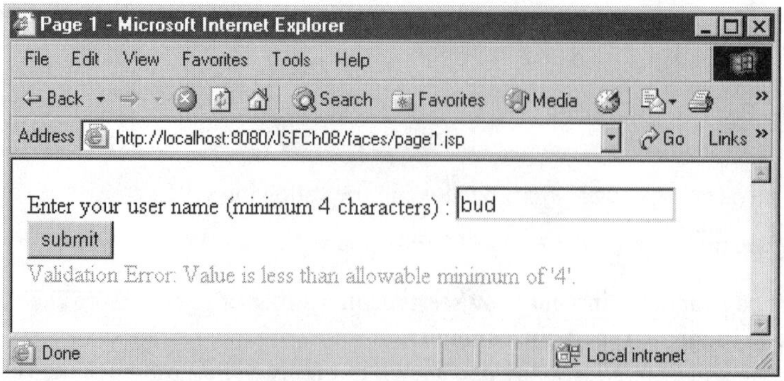

Figure 8-3   *Failed navigation in the simple navigation example*

Defining Conditional Page Navigation

For conditional page navigation, you define navigation rules with multiple navigation cases, which depend on the outcome of processing the target page. Recall that this is the function of the `from-outcome` and `from-actionRef` subelements of the `navigation-rule` element in your application configuration file.

This type of page navigation requires you to invoke an `Action` object, which is an object that performs a task. In JSF, an `Action` object is represented by the abstract `javax.faces` `.application.Action` class. The Action class has the `invoke` method, which is an abstract method that returns a `String`. You write the code to perform the task for the `Action` object in this method. The signature of the `invoke` method is as follows:

```
public abstract String invoke()
```

The `invoke` method will be called by the JSF implementation. An `Action` object can be invoked by a `UICommand` via the `actionRef` attribute of its `command_button` or `command_hyperlink` tag. You will see how this works in the next two examples.

Using Multiple Navigation Cases

To understand how multiple navigation cases work, consider a page that contains a login form. When the user clicks the submit button to log in, JSF can redirect control to either a welcome page (if the login was successful) or back to the login page (if the login failed). In this case, the origin page (the login form) will have two navigation cases: one for a successful login and one for a failed login.

The example contains two JSP pages: `login.jsp` and `welcome.jsp`. The `login.jsp` page contains a login form with two `UIInput` components for the user name and password. To log in, the user clicks the command button. After a successful login, the user will be directed to the `welcome.jsp` page. If the login failed, however, the user will see the `login.jsp` page again, this time with an error message.

The Navigation Rule for Conditional Navigation

The navigation rule for this example is shown in Listing 8-6.

Listing 8-6   *The Conditional Navigation Rule in the Application Configuration File*

```
<navigation-rule>
  <from-tree-id>/login.jsp</from-tree-id>
  <navigation-case>
    <from-outcome>success</from-outcome>
    <to-tree-id>/welcome.jsp</to-tree-id>
  </navigation-case>
  <navigation-case>
```

```
        <from-outcome>failed</from-outcome>
        <to-tree-id>/login.jsp</to-tree-id>
    </navigation-case>
</navigation-rule>
```

The `navigation-rule` element specifies the possible targets for the `login.jsp` page. For the `from-outcome` element value of `success` (a successful login), the `welcome.jsp` page will be displayed. If the `from-outcome` element value is `failed`, the `login.jsp` page is redisplayed. (There is no navigation rule for the `welcome.jsp` page, but you can add one yourself.)

The Command Button Outcome Definition

For the conditional navigation to work, you use the `actionRef` attribute of the `command_button` in the `login.jsp` page to define the source of the command button's outcome. The `login.jsp` and `welcome.jsp` pages are shown in Listings 8-7 and 8-8.

Listing 8-7   *The login.jsp Page*

```
<%@ taglib uri="http://java.sun.com/jsf/html" prefix="h" %>
<%@ taglib uri="http://java.sun.com/jsf/core" prefix="f" %>
<html>
<head>
<title>Login</title>
</head>
<body>
<f:use_faces>
<h:form  formName="loginForm">
<h2>Please enter your user name and password</h2>
<br>User Name: <h:input_text valueRef="loginBean.userName"/>
<br>Password: <h:input_secret valueRef="loginBean.password"/>
<br><h:command_button commandName="login" label="login"
actionRef="loginBean.login"/>
<br/>
<h:output_errors/>
</h:form>
</f:use_faces>
</body>
</html>
```

Listing 8-8   *The welcome.jsp Page*

```
<%@ taglib uri="http://java.sun.com/jsf/html" prefix="h" %>
<%@ taglib uri="http://java.sun.com/jsf/core" prefix="f" %>
```

```
<html>
<head>
<title>Welcome</title>
</head>
<body>
You logged in successfully.
</body>
</html>
```

The command_button tag in the login.jsp page has the actionRef attribute with the value of LoginBean.login:

```
<h:command_button commandName="login" label="login"
  actionRef="loginBean.login"/>
```

This means that the outcome of the command button will come from the login property of the LoginBean.

The LoginBean is listed in Listing 8-9. Pay special attention to the LoginAction class, which will be explained after the code listing.

Listing 8-9   *The LoginBean*

```
package ch08;
import javax.faces.application.Action;
import javax.faces.application.Message;
import javax.faces.application.MessageImpl;
import javax.faces.context.FacesContext;

public class LoginBean {
  private String userName;
  private String password;
  private Action login;
  public String getUserName() {
    return userName;
  }
  public void setUserName(String userName) {
    this.userName = userName;
  }
  public String getPassword() {
    return password;
  }
}
```

```
   public void setPassword(String password) {
     this.password = password;
   }
   public Action getLogin() {
     if (login==null)
       login = new LoginAction();
     return login;
   }

   class LoginAction extends Action {
     public String invoke() {
       if ("ken".equals(userName) && "blackcomb".equals(password))
         return "success";
       else {
         Message loginErrorMessage =
           new MessageImpl(1, "<hr>Login failed", null);
         FacesContext.getCurrentInstance().addMessage(null,
           loginErrorMessage);
         return "failed";
       }
     }
   }
}
```

For a bean's property to represent an action's outcome, the property must be of type
`javax.faces.application.Action`. The `login` property has this type:

```
private Action login;
```

The `getLogin` method returns the `login Action`.

```
public Action getLogin() {
   if (login==null)
     login = new LoginAction();
   return login;
}
```

The implementation of the `Action` class must provide the implementation of the
`invoke` method. According to the navigation rule in Listing 8-6, the value must be either
`success` or `failed`. These are the possible return values of the `invoke` method in the
`LoginAction` class. In this example, the correct user name and password are `ken` and
`blackcomb`.

The example uses the `LoginBean`, which is registered in the application configuration file using the `managed-bean` element, as shown in Listing 8-10.

Listing 8-10   *The LoginBean Registration in the Application Configuration File*

```
<managed-bean>
  <managed-bean-name>loginBean</managed-bean-name>
  <managed-bean-class>ch08.LoginBean</managed-bean-class>
  <managed-bean-scope>session</managed-bean-scope>
</managed-bean>
```

You can invoke the `login.jsp` page using the following URL:

```
http://localhost:8080/JSFCh08/faces/login.jsp
```

You will see the login page in your browser. Type **ken** in the User Name box and **blackcomb** in the Password box, as shown in Figure 8-4. Then click the login button.

The `welcome.jsp` page appears, as shown in Figure 8-5.

Now, invoke the `login.jsp` page again, and enter a different user name and/or password. This time, the `login.jsp` page will be redisplayed with an error message, as shown in Figure 8-6.

A Navigation Rule with the from-action-ref Subelement

In the preceding example, the possible `action` values from the bean are all unique, so you did not need to use the `from-action-ref` subelement in the `navigation-case` element of the navigation rule. However, you could use the `from-action-ref` element if desired, as shown in Listing 8-11.

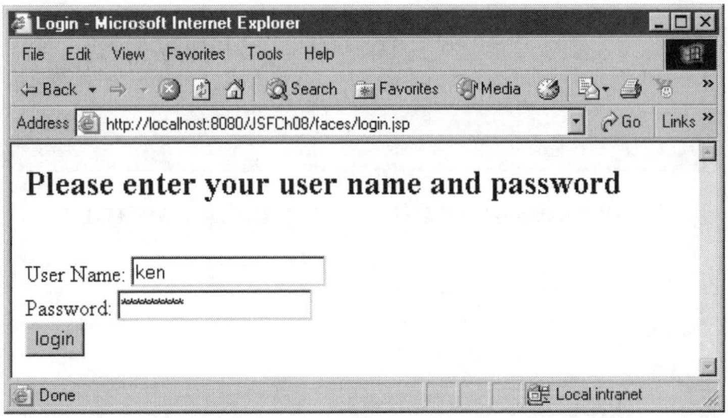

Figure 8-4   *Enter the correct user name and password in the login page.*

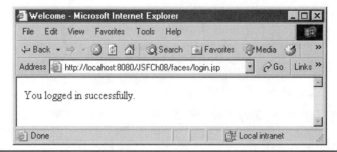

Figure 8-5   *The welcome.jsp page appears after a successful login.*

Listing 8-11   *The Navigation Rule with from-action-ref Elements*

```
<navigation-rule>
  <from-tree-id>/login.jsp</from-tree-id>
  <navigation-case>
    <from-action-ref>loginBean.login</from-action-ref>
    <from-outcome>success</from-outcome>
    <to-tree-id>/welcome.jsp</to-tree-id>
  </navigation-case>
  <navigation-case>
    <from-action-ref>loginBean.login</from-action-ref>
    <from-outcome>failed</from-outcome>
    <to-tree-id>/login.jsp</to-tree-id>
  </navigation-case>
</navigation-rule>
```

Figure 8-6   *Incorrect entries result in a failed login.*

Using from-action-ref Element

Our next example demonstrates how you can get the outcome of the `from-tree-id` processing from either an `action-ref` attribute or an `action` attribute. This example uses a `login2.jsp` page, which is similar to the `login.jsp` page (Listing 8-7), but it contains a hyperlink that goes to the `help.jsp` page when clicked.

Listing 8-12 shows the `navigation-rule` element in the application configuration file for this example.

Listing 8-12   *The Navigation Rule for Navigating to a Help Page*

```
<navigation-rule>
  <from-tree-id>/login2.jsp</from-tree-id>
  <navigation-case>
    <from-outcome>success</from-outcome>
    <to-tree-id>/welcome.jsp</to-tree-id>
  </navigation-case>
  <navigation-case>
    <from-outcome>failed</from-outcome>
    <to-tree-id>/login2.jsp</to-tree-id>
  </navigation-case>
  <navigation-case>
    <from-outcome>help</from-outcome>
    <to-tree-id>/help.jsp</to-tree-id>
  </navigation-case>
</navigation-rule>
```

The `login2.jsp` page, shown in Listing 8-13, uses the `command_button` tag with `actionRef` referencing `loginBean.login`, as in the previous example. It uses the same `LoginBean` (Listing 8-9) and `LoginBean` registration (Listing 8-10) as the previous example. However, this version also contains a `command_hyperlink` tag, for navigating to the `help.jsp` page, shown in Listing 8-14.

Listing 8-13   *The login2.jsp Page*

```
<%@ taglib uri="http://java.sun.com/jsf/html" prefix="h" %>
<%@ taglib uri="http://java.sun.com/jsf/core" prefix="f" %>
<html>
<head>
<title>Login 2</title>
</head>
<body>
<f:use_faces>
```

```
<h:form  formName="loginForm">
<h2>Please enter your user name and password</h2>
<br/>User Name: <h:input_text valueRef="loginBean.userName"/>
<br/>Password: <h:input_secret valueRef="loginBean.password"/>
<br/><h:command_button commandName="login" label="login"
actionRef="loginBean.login"/>
<br/><h:command_hyperlink commandName="forgottenPassword"
  action="help"  label="Forgotten your password?"/>
<h:output_errors/>
</h:form>
</f:use_faces>
</body>
</html>
```

Listing 8-14   *The help.jsp Page*

```
<html>
<head>
<title>Help</title>
</head>
<body>
If you have forgotten your password, please contact the admin
(admin@brainysoftware.com).
</body>
</html>
```

To run this example, you will need to restart your browser to force JSF to create a new instance of the LoginBean. Then you can invoke the login2.jsp page using this URL:

```
http://localhost:8080/JSFCh08/faces/login2.jsp
```

You can enter a user name and password, as shown in Figure 8-7.

If you enter the correct user name and password, you will see the welcome.jsp page. Typing in the wrong user name and password returns you to the login2.jsp page. If you click the hyperlink, you will see the help.jsp page, shown in Figure 8-8.

However, suppose you use success as the value of the action attribute in the command_hyperlink tag in the login2.jsp page in Listing 8-13:

```
<h:command_hyperlink commandName="forgottenPassword"
  action="success" label="Forgotten your password?"/>
```

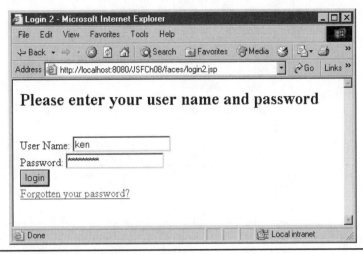

Figure 8-7   *The login2.jsp page includes a help link.*

In this case, you would need to write the `navigation-rule` element as follows, this time including the `from-action-ref` element:

```
<navigation-rule>
  <from-tree-id>/login2.jsp</from-tree-id>
  <navigation-case>
    <from-action-ref>LoginBean.login</from-action-ref>
    <from-outcome>success</from-outcome>
    <to-tree-id>/welcome.jsp</to-tree-id>
  </navigation-case>
  <navigation-case>
    <from-action-ref>LoginBean.login</from-action-ref>
    <from-outcome>failed</from-outcome>
    <to-tree-id>/login2.jsp</to-tree-id>
  </navigation-case>
  <navigation-case>
    <from-outcome>success</from-outcome>
    <to-tree-id>/help.jsp</to-tree-id>
  </navigation-case>
</navigation-rule>
```

Figure 8-8 *The help.jsp page*

Summary

In this chapter, you have learned about page navigation, a very important aspect of JSF application programming. First, you learned how to define navigation rules in the application configuration file and saw how these rules work in a simple navigation example. Then you worked through examples of using conditional page navigation, which provides more flexibility in your applications.

The next chapter covers another topic important to JSF programmers: input validation.

Validators

IN THIS CHAPTER:

Using Standard Validators

Writing Custom Validators

Summary

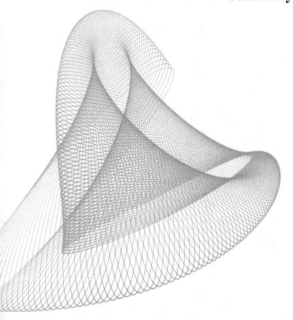

J SF provides a set of classes for validating input values entered into input components. These classes are called *validators*. By using validators to validate user input, programmers can save hours of effort, as the examples in this chapter will demonstrate.

JSF offers some standard validators that you can use in your applications. Alternatively, you can write your own validator if none of the standard validators suits your needs.

In this chapter, you will learn how to use the JSF validators. First, you will be introduced to each of the standard validators. Then you will learn how to write your own custom validators.

Using Standard Validators

Basically, a validator is an implementation class that checks an input value and sends an error message if the input is invalid. You use a validator by nesting it inside an input component whose input needs to be validated. If the validator decides that the user's input is invalid, the JSF Faces servlet redisplays the JSP page from which the form is submitted, without copying the local value to the JavaBean instance bound to the input component.

The JSF implementation provides five standard validators for common validation tasks, including checking that required fields have entries and that input meets length and range requirements. Table 9-1 lists the standard validators.

Validator Class	Tag	Description
RequiredValidator	validate_required	Verifies that the value entered into a component is not null. Additionally, if the local value of the component is of type String, this validator checks that it is not a zero-length String.
LengthValidator	validate_length	Makes sure that the length of a component's local value falls into a certain range. The value must be a String.
LongRangeValidator	validate_longrange	Ensures that a component's local value is within a certain range. The value must be convertible to a long.
DoubleRangeValidator	validate_doublerange	Ensures that a component's local value is within a certain range. The value must be convertible to a floating-point number.
StringRangeValidator	validate_stringrange	Verifies that a component's local value is within a certain range. The value must be a String.

Table 9-1 *JSF Standard Validators*

Creating the TestingBean for Validator Tests

Many of the examples in this chapter use the TestingBean JavaBean, shown in Listing 9-1.

Listing 9-1   *The TestingBean Class*

```
package ch09;
import java.util.Date;

public class TestingBean {
  private boolean discounted;
  private int quantity;
  private float price;
  private Date today;
  private String value;
  public boolean getDiscounted() {
    return discounted;
  }
  public void setDiscounted(boolean discounted) {
    this.discounted = discounted;
  }
  public int getQuantity() {
    return quantity;
  }
  public void setQuantity(int quantity) {
    this.quantity = quantity;
  }
  public float getPrice() {
    return price;
  }
  public void setPrice(float price) {
    this.price = price;
  }
  public Date getToday() {
    return today;
  }
  public void setToday (Date today) {
    this.today = today;
  }
  public String getValue() {
    return value;
  }
```

```
    public void setValue(String value) {
      this.value = value;
    }
  }
}
```

The `TestingBean` is registered in the application configuration file using the `managed-bean` tag, as shown in Listing 9-2.

Listing 9-2   *TestingBean Registration in the Application Configuration File*

```
<managed-bean>
  <managed-bean-name>testingBean</managed-bean-name>
  <managed-bean-class>ch09.TestingBean</managed-bean-class>
  <managed-bean-scope>request</managed-bean-scope>
</managed-bean>
```

Introducing the Validator Tags

Now that we have the `TestingBean` ready for some of the examples, we can see how the standard tags for validators work. Here, we will cover the tags that represent the `RequiredValidator`, `LengthValidator`, `LongRangeValidator`, `DoubleRangeValidator`, and `StringRangeValidator` classes.

The validate_required Tag

The `validate_required` tag checks if a component's local data is not `null` and, in the case where the local value is a `String`, it is not blank. The `validateRequiredTest.jsp` page shown in Listing 9-3 uses a form with an `input_text` tag.

Listing 9-3   *The validateRequiredTest.jsp Page*

```
<%@ taglib uri="http://java.sun.com/jsf/html" prefix="h" %>
<%@ taglib uri="http://java.sun.com/jsf/core" prefix="f" %>
<html>
<head>
<title>Using validate_required</title>
</head>
<body>
<f:use_faces>
<h:form  formName="myForm">
Type in something here:
  <h:input_text valueRef="testingBean.value">
<f:validate_required/>
</h:input_text>
```

```
<br/>
<h:command_button commandName="submit" label="submit"/>
<br/><hr/>
<h:output_errors/>
<br/>
</h:form>
</f:use_faces>
</body>
</html>
```

You can invoke the `validateRequiredTest.jsp` page by using this URL:

`http://localhost:8080/JSFCh09/faces/validateRequiredTest.jsp`

Now, if you click the button without entering a value to the input fields, you will see something similar to Figure 9-1. Notice the validation error message?

The validate_length Tag

The `validate_length` tag checks if a component's local value has the specified length. This tag has the `minimum` and `maximum` attributes, which specify the minimum number and maximum number of characters to be entered, respectively. If no `minimum` attribute is present, zero is assumed. If you do not include the `maximum` attribute, no maximum restriction applies.

You can use the `validate_length` tag with any of the input tags, such as `input_number` and `input_datetime`. If you are using an `input_text` tag, you can also set its `maxLength` attribute to restrict the number of characters the user can enter into the input field.

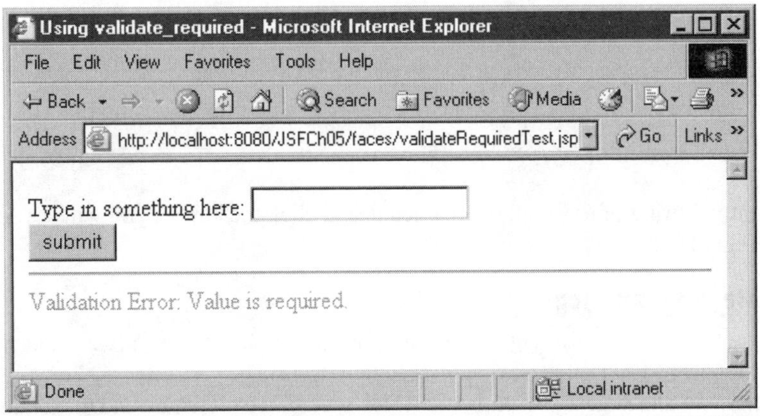

Figure 9-1   *Using the validate_required tag*

The `validateLengthTest.jsp` page, shown in Listing 9-4, illustrates the use of the `validate_length` tag with an `input_text` tag. The value of the `minimum` attribute of the `validate_length` tag is 6, meaning that you must enter a string having six or more characters.

Listing 9-4   *The validateLengthTest.jsp Page*

```
<%@ taglib uri="http://java.sun.com/jsf/html" prefix="h" %>
<%@ taglib uri="http://java.sun.com/jsf/core" prefix="f" %>
<html>
<head>
<title>Using validate_length</title>
</head>
<body>
<f:use_faces>
<h:form   formName="myForm">
Enter a minimum of 6 characters here:
  <h:input_text size="8" valueRef="testingBean.value">
    <f:validate_length minimum="6"/>
  </h:input_text>
<br/>
<h:command_button commandName="submit" label="submit"/>
<br/><hr/>
<h:output_errors/>
<br/>
</h:form>
</f:use_faces>
</body>
</html>
```

You can invoke the `validateRequiredTest.jsp` page by using this URL:

`http://localhost:8080/JSFCh09/faces/validateLengthTest.jsp`

If you enter a string of less than six characters and click the button, you will see something similar to Figure 9-2.

The validate_longrange Tag

The `validate_longrange` tag can validate the value of an `input_number` tag and ensure that the component's local value is within a specified range. The `validate_longrange` tag has the `minimum` and `maximum` attributes, which specify the minimum and maximum values that can be entered. For example, if you want the user to enter a number between 10 and 100, you assign `10` to the `minimum` attribute and `100` to the `maximum` attribute. The number specified with these attributes must be a `long`. You cannot, for example, assign `1.10` to the `minimum` or `maximum` attribute.

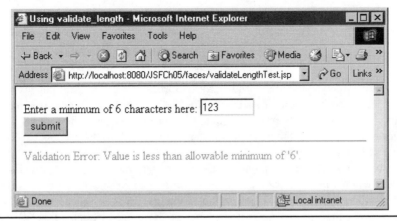

Figure 9-2   *Using the validate_length tag*

Listing 9-5 shows the `validateLongRangeTest.jsp` page, which uses an `input_number` tag with a `validate_longrange` tag. The user must enter a number between 10 and 100.

Listing 9-5   *The validateLongRangeTest.jsp Page*

```
<%@ taglib uri="http://java.sun.com/jsf/html" prefix="h" %>
<%@ taglib uri="http://java.sun.com/jsf/core" prefix="f" %>
<html>
<head>
<title>Using validate_longrange</title>
</head>
<body>
<f:use_faces>
<h:form formName="myForm">
Enter a number between 10 and 100 (inclusive)
  <h:input_number size="3" valueRef="testingBean.quantity">
    <f:validate_longrange minimum="10" maximum="100"/>
  </h:input_number>
<br/>
<h:command_button commandName="submit" label="submit"/>
<br/><hr/>
<h:output_errors/>
</h:form>
```

```
</f:use_faces>
</body>
</html>
```

The `input_number` tag in the `validateLongRangeTest.jsp` page is bound to the `quantity` property of the `TestingBean`. The accessor and mutator (the `get` and `set` methods) of this property print a string to the console whenever they are invoked. If the user enters an invalid value, the `set` method is never invoked, so the process never reaches the Update Model Values phase.

If the user enters a floating-point number, such as 12.3, into the `input_number` tag, the validator will not raise an error. However, since the `quantity` property is of type `int`, the number will be automatically converted to an integer.

You can invoke the `validateRequiredTest.jsp` page by using this URL:

```
http://localhost:8080/JSFCh09/faces/validateLongRangeTest.jsp
```

Now, if you enter a number less than 10 or greater than 100 and click the button, you will see an error message similar to the one in Figure 9-3.

The validate_doublerange Tag

You can use the `validate_doublerange` tag to validate the value of an `input_number` tag and ensure that the component's local value is within a specified range. This tag is similar to `validate_longrange`; however, you can assign a `float` as well as a `long` to the `minimum` and `maximum` attributes.

The `validateDoubleRangeTest.jsp` page, shown in Listing 9-6, uses an `input_number` tag with a `validate_doublerange` tag. The user is allowed to enter only a number between –9.99 and 9.99.

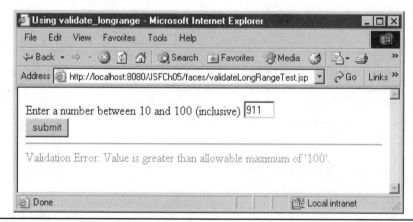

Figure 9-3   *Using the validate_longrange tag*

Listing 9-6   *The validateDoubleRangeTest.jsp Page*

```
<%@ taglib uri="http://java.sun.com/jsf/html" prefix="h" %>
<%@ taglib uri="http://java.sun.com/jsf/core" prefix="f" %>
<html>
<head>
<title>Using validate_doublerange</title>
</head>
<body>
<f:use_faces>
<h:form formName="myForm">
Enter a number between -9.99 and 9.99
  <h:input_number size="3" valueRef="testingBean.price">
    <f:validate_doublerange minimum="-9.99" maximum="9.99"/>
  </h:input_number>
<br/>
<h:command_button commandName="submit" label="submit"/>
<br/><hr/>
<h:output_errors/>
</h:form>
</f:use_faces>
</body>
</html>
```

You can invoke the `validateDoubleRangeTest.jsp` page by using this URL:

`http://localhost:8080/JSFCh09/faces/validateDoubleRangeTest.jsp`

Now, if you enter a number greater than 9.99 or less than –9.99 and click the button, you will see an error message like the one in Figure 9-4.

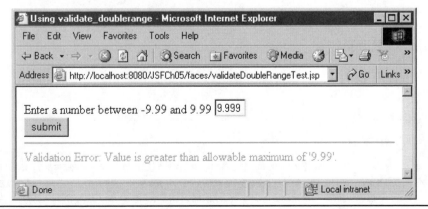

Figure 9-4   *Using the validate_doublerange tag*

The validate_stringrange Tag

For text input validation, you can use the `validate_stringrange` tag. This validator checks if a `String` is within the specified range of text. This tag also has the `minimum` and `maximum` attributes for setting limits. For example, if you assign "A" to the `minimum` attribute, the `validate_stringrange` tag will raise an error if you type in 9, because the ASCII representation of 9 is less than that of *A*. However, *A9* is greater than *A* but less than *AA*.

The `validateStringRangeTest.jsp` page, shown in Listing 9-7, uses a `validate_stringrange` tag with an `input_text` tag and specifies "A" and "z" as the `minimum` and `maximum` values. It also uses a `validate_length` tag to ensure that a valid value is only one character long and is an alphabetic character.

Listing 9-7   *The validateStringRangeTest.jsp Page*

```
<%@ taglib uri="http://java.sun.com/jsf/html" prefix="h" %>
<%@ taglib uri="http://java.sun.com/jsf/core" prefix="f" %>
<html>
<head>
<title>Using validate_stringrange</title>
</head>
<body>
<f:use_faces>
<h:form formName="myForm">
Enter your initial
  <h:input_text size="3" valueRef="testingBean.value">
    <f:validate_stringrange minimum="A" maximum="z"/>
    <f:validate_length maximum="1"/>
  </h:input_text>
<br/>
<h:command_button commandName="submit" label="submit"/>
<br/><hr/>
<h:output_errors/>
</h:form>
</f:use_faces>
</body>
</html>
```

CAUTION

The JSP page in Listing 9-7 shows that you can use many validators to "watch" a component. Sometimes, this is necessary so that you can achieve the validation that you want. However, you should be careful of using many validators at the same time, because the overall restriction may make it impossible for the user to enter a valid value.

You can invoke the `validateStringRangeTest.jsp` page by using this URL:

`http://localhost:8080/JSFCh09/faces/validateStringRangeTest.jsp`

Now, if you type in a number or a string longer than one character and click the button, you will see an error message like the one in Figure 9-5.

Writing Custom Validators

When standard validators do not meet your application requirements, you can resort to writing your own, or, in the foreseeable future, purchase third-party products. There are two ways of writing a custom validator. You can implement the `Validator` interface and use the validator tag from the Core custom tag library, or you can implement the `Validator` interface and use it as a custom tag library. Using the custom tag library is a more involved process, because you need to write a tag handler and a tag library descriptor (TLD), but it allows you to write a more sophisticated validator that can accept attributes.Both methods require you to register your validator class in the application configuration file (`faces-config.xml`).

Introducing the Validator and Message Interfaces

Every validator must implement the `javax.faces.validator.Validator` interface. This interface has the `validate` method, which will be called by the JSF implementation during the request processing lifecycle. The signature of the `validate` method is as follows:

`public void validate(FacesContext context, UIComponent component)`

`context` is the instance of `FacesContext`, and `component` is the component whose local value needs to be validated.

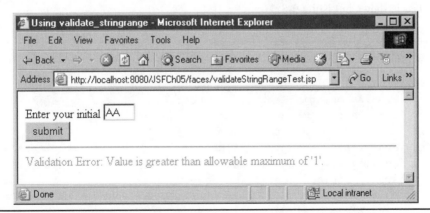

Figure 9-5   *Using the validate_stringrange tag*

From within the `validate` method, you need to obtain the value of the component using its `getValue` method, and then evaluate the value. If the value is valid, you pass `true` to the component's `setValid` method. Otherwise, you pass `false` to the component's `setValid` method and add a `Message` object to the context. This message contains the corresponding error message that will be displayed in an `output_errors` tag, if one exists.

CAUTION

The JSF specification advises that you use the `javax.faces.validator.ValidatorBase` class instead of implementing the `Validator` interface directly, to reduce the impacts of any future changes in the `Validator` interface.

The `javax.faces.application.Message` interface represents a message. With a validator, a `Message` object can contain an error message that can be added to the `FacesContext`. For an invalid component value, your validator needs to create an instance of the `Message` interface. JSF provides the `javax.faces.application.MessageImpl` class, which implements the `Message` interface. You can instantiate the `MessageImpl` class and pass the severity level (an integer), an error message, and the detail of the error.

Creating a Simple Custom Validator

The most common method of writing custom validators is to write an implementation class of the `Validator` interface. To use it, you register the custom validator with the application configuration file and use the validator tag in your JSP page.

Writing the Validator Class

The example in this section is a simple custom validator that is easy to write and to use. It's a `ZipCodeValidator` class that can check if a piece of text qualifies as a zip code. The implementation class is part of the `ch09` package and is named `ZipCodeValidator`. This class is shown in Listing 9-8.

Listing 9-8   *The ZipCodeValidator*

```
package ch09;
import javax.faces.component.UIComponent;
import javax.faces.component.UIOutput;
import javax.faces.context.FacesContext;
import javax.faces.validator.Validator;
import javax.faces.application.Message;
import javax.faces.application.MessageImpl;

public class ZipCodeValidator implements Validator {

  private static final int LENGTH = 5;
```

```
public void validate(FacesContext context, UIComponent component) {
  boolean valid = false;
  if (context==null || component==null)
    throw new NullPointerException();
  if (!(component instanceof UIOutput))
    return;
  String value = ((UIOutput) component).getValue().toString();
  if (value.length()!=LENGTH) {
    Message message =
      new MessageImpl(1, "Length is not equal to 5",
      "A US zip code must be 5-digit");
    context.addMessage(component, message);
  }
  else {
    // temporarily, set valid to true
    valid = true;
    // check if all chars are numbers
    for (int i=0; i<LENGTH; i++) {
      char c = value.charAt(i);
      if (c<'0' || c>'9') {
        valid = false;
        Message message = new
          MessageImpl(1, "A zip code must be all numbers",
          "An invalid character has been entered");
        context.addMessage(component, message);
        break;
      }
    }
  }
  component.setValid(valid);
}
}
```

Registering the Custom Validator

To register this custom validator with the application configuration file, you need to use the
<validator> element. The validator element is defined as follows:

```
<!ELEMENT validator (description*, display-name*, icon*,
  validator-id, validator-class, attribute*, property*)>
```

The mandatory subelements are validator-id and validator-class. The
validator-id element represents the identifier for the validator, and it must be unique
throughout the Web application. The validator-class element represents the fully
qualified name of the validator implementation class. The attribute element identifies a generic

attribute that may be configured on the corresponding UIComponent in order to affect the operation of the Validator. The property element identifies a JavaBeans property of the Validator implementation class that may be configured to affect the operation of the Validator.

Listing 9-9 shows the <validator> tag to register the ZipCodeValidator. You must deploy your ZipCodeValidator class under the WEB-INF/classes/ch09 directory.

Listing 9-9   *ZipCodeValidator Registration in the faces-config.xml File*

```
<validator>
  <description>A validator for validating zip codes</description>
  <validator-id>zipCodeValidator</validator-id>
  <validator-class>ch09.ZipCodeValidator</validator-class>
</validator>
```

Using the Custom Validator

Listing 9-10 shows the validateZipCodeTest.jsp page, which uses the ZipCodeValidator validator.

Listing 9-10   *The validateZipCodeTest.jsp Page*

```
<%@ taglib uri="http://java.sun.com/jsf/html" prefix="h" %>
<%@ taglib uri="http://java.sun.com/jsf/core" prefix="f" %>
<html>
<head>
<title>Using ZipCodeValidator</title>
</head>
<body>
<f:use_faces>
<h:form   formName="myForm">
Your zip code:
  <h:input_text valueRef="testingBean.value">
    <f:validator id="zipCodeValidator" />
  </h:input_text>
<br>
<h:command_button commandName="submit" label="submit"/>
<br/><hr/>
<h:output_errors/>
</h:form>
</f:use_faces>
</body>
</html>
```

Figure 9-6 *Using the ZipCodeValidator*

You can invoke the `validateZipCodeTest.jsp` page by using this URL:

`http://localhost:8080/JSFCh09/faces/validateZipCodeTest.jsp`

Now, if you enter an invalid zip code, you will get an error message. For example, Figure 9-6 depicts what happens if you type in a string longer than five characters.

Creating a Custom Validator with Attributes

The previous example is simple to implement, but it does not give you the luxury of passing values to the properties in your validator class in the form of attributes. This is because the `validator` tag does not support any attributes.

To create a custom validator that can use attributes, you must first write a validator class that directly or indirectly implements the `javax.faces.validator.Validator` interface, just as you do for a simple custom validator. However, to use validator attributes, you include properties in your validator class. For each property, you need an accessor and a mutator. Values will be passed to these properties through the tag's attributes. After you create the validator class, you need to write a tag handler and a TLD, because your custom validator is usable through a custom tag library.

Writing the Validator Class with a Property

As an example, you will refine the `ZipCodeValidator` (Listing 9-8). That validator can be used only with zip codes that are five digits. However, not all zip codes are five digits long. In Australia, for instance, zip codes are called post codes and are four digits long. The `VariableLengthZipCodeValidator`, shown in Listing 9-11, provides flexibility by incorporating the `length` property in the validator class. This way, your validator will be more useful.

Listing 9-11   *The VariableLengthZipCodeValidator Class*

```java
package ch09;
import javax.faces.component.UIComponent;
import javax.faces.component.UIOutput;
import javax.faces.context.FacesContext;
import javax.faces.validator.Validator;
import javax.faces.application.Message;
import javax.faces.application.MessageImpl;

public class VariableLengthZipCodeValidator implements Validator {

  private int length;
  public int getLength() {
    return length;
  }
  public void setLength(int length) {
    this.length = length;
  }

  public void validate(FacesContext context, UIComponent component) {
    boolean valid = false;
    if (context==null || component==null)
      throw new NullPointerException();
    if (!(component instanceof UIOutput))
      return;
    String value = ((UIOutput) component).getValue().toString();
    if (value.length()!=length) {
      Message message = new
        MessageImpl(1, "Length is not equal to " + length,
        "A US zip code must be 5-digit");
      context.addMessage(component, message);
    }
    else {
      // temporarily, set valid to true
      valid = true;
      // check if all chars are numbers
      for (int i=0; i<length; i++) {
        char c = value.charAt(i);
        if (c<'0' || c>'9') {
          valid = false;
          Message message = new
            MessageImpl(1, "A zip code must be all numbers",
            "An invalid character has been entered");
          context.addMessage(component, message);
          break;
```

```
        }
      }
    }
    component.setValid(valid);
  }
}
```

Notice that the static final LENGTH used in the original ZipCodeValidator (Listing 9-8) has been changed to an instance variable named length. There are also getLength and setLength methods to access the property.

Writing a Tag Handler and TLD for the Custom Validator

Because you will use the validator as a tag in a custom tag library, you need to write a tag handler. A tag handler for a custom validator must extend the javax.faces.webapp .ValidatorTag class and override its createValidator method. The tag handler for this example is shown in Listing 9-12.

Listing 9-12   *The VariableLengthZipCodeValidatorTag Class*

```
package ch09;
import javax.faces.webapp.ValidatorTag;
import javax.faces.validator.Validator;
import javax.servlet.jsp.JspException;

public class VariableLengthZipCodeValidatorTag extends ValidatorTag {
  protected int length;
  public VariableLengthZipCodeValidatorTag() {
    super();
    super.setId("VariableLengthZipCodeValidator");
  }

  public int getLength() {
    return length;
  }
  public void setLength(int length){
   this.length = length;
  }

  protected Validator createValidator() throws JspException {
    VariableLengthZipCodeValidator validator =
      (VariableLengthZipCodeValidator) super.createValidator();
    validator.setLength(length);
    return validator;
  }
}
```

Listing 9-13 defines the TLD for the tag handler in Listing 9-12.

Listing 9-13   *The variableLengthZipCodeValidator.tld File*

```
<?xml version="1.0" encoding="ISO-8859-1" ?>
<!DOCTYPE taglib
  PUBLIC "-//Sun Microsystems, Inc.//DTD JSP Tag Library 1.2//EN"
  "http://java.sun.com/dtd/web-jsptaglibrary_1_2.dtd">

<taglib>
  <tlib-version>0.03</tlib-version>
  <jsp-version>1.2</jsp-version>
  <short-name>JSF Tag Library</short-name>

  <tag>
    <name>variable_length_zip_code_validator</name>
    <tag-class>ch09.VariableLengthZipCodeValidatorTag</tag-class>
    <attribute>
      <name>length</name>
      <required>true</required>
      <rtexprvalue>false</rtexprvalue>
    </attribute>
  </tag>
</taglib>
```

Notice that the tag name for using the tag handler is `variable_length_zip_code_validator` and its tag handler is `ch09.VariableLengthZipCodeValidatorTag`. The tag has one mandatory attribute: `length`.

The tag handler must be deployed to the `WEB-INF/classes` directory, and the TLD needs to go in the `WEB-INF` directory.

Registering the Custom Validator with Attributes

As with the simple custom validator in the previous example, you need to register the `VariableLengthZipCodeValidator` in the application configuration file (`faces-config.xml` file), using the `<validator>` element. In this case, you also need to include the `<attribute>` subelement. Listing 9-14 shows the registration.

Listing 9-14   *VariableLengthZipCodeValidator Registration in the faces-config.xml File*

```
<validator>
  <description>
    A validator for validating variable-length zip codes
  </description>
```

```
    <validator-id>VariableLengthZipCodeValidator</validator-id>
    <validator-class>
      ch09.VariableLengthZipCodeValidator
    </validator-class>
    <attribute>
      <description>Length of a valid zip code</description>
      <attribute-name>length</attribute-name>
      <attribute-class>java.lang.Integer</attribute-class>
    </attribute>
  </validator>
```

Using the Custom Validator with Attributes

To use the validator from a JSP page, include the custom tag nested inside the component whose value needs to be validated. The `validateVariableLengthZipCodeTest`
`.jsp` page, shown in Listing 9-15, can be used to test the custom validator.

Listing 9-15   *The validateVariableLengthZipCodeTest.jsp Page*

```
<%@ taglib uri="http://java.sun.com/jsf/html" prefix="h" %>
<%@ taglib uri="http://java.sun.com/jsf/core" prefix="f" %>
<%@ taglib uri="/WEB-INF/variableLengthZipCodeValidator.tld"
  prefix="cd" %>
<html>
<head>
<title>Using VariableLengthZipCodeValidator</title>
</head>
<body>
<f:use_faces>
<h:form  formName="myForm">
Your zip code:
  <h:input_text valueRef="testingBean.value">
    <cd:variable_length_zip_code_validator length="4"/>
  </h:input_text>
<br/>
<h:command_button commandName="submit" label="submit"/>
<br/><hr/>
<h:output_errors/>
</h:form>
</f:use_faces>
</body>
</html>
```

Notice that you need to tell the Web container the location of the TLD and the prefix for your custom validator tag, using the following `taglib` directive:

```
<%@ taglib uri="/WEB-INF/variableLengthZipCodeValidator.tld"
   prefix="cd" %>
```

You can invoke the `validateZipCodeTest.jsp` page by using this URL:

```
http://localhost:8080/JSFCh09/faces/validateVariableLengthZipCodeTest.jsp
```

Using Message Resources in Your Custom Validators

In both of the previous examples, the error messages are hard-coded into the validator class. This is fine if you are sure that you will never want to change the messages. However, what if you might need to modify your error messages? In that case, you should move the error messages to the application configuration file. That way, if you need to change the error messages, you only need to edit the application configuration file, which is much easier to do than rewriting and recompiling the validator class.

Another advantage of moving error messages to the application configuration file is that it allows you to localize those error messages. This means that you can create a JSF application that can produce error messages in different languages, depending on the locale of the server running the application. For this purpose, JSF introduces `MessageResources`, which is a collection of message templates. These templates have message identifiers that are unique throughout the application. `MessageResources` are discussed in Chapter 11, which also presents a modified version of the `ZipCodeValidator` that retrieves error messages from the application configuration file.

Summary

In this chapter, you learned that a validator is an implementation class that checks a user's input and sends an error message if that input is invalid. You were introduced to the five standard validators provided by JSF and saw examples of their use. Then you learned how to write your own custom validators, using both a simple method and a more sophisticated method that allows the use of validator attributes. Finally, you learned that validator error messages can be moved to the application configuration file, which makes them easier to change and also allows for message localization.

The next chapter covers JSF converters, which handle data conversion.

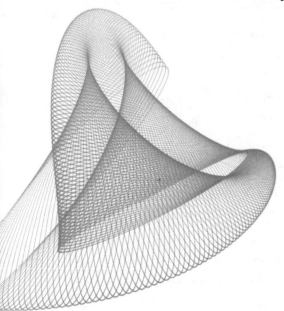

IN THIS CHAPTER:

Using Standard Converters

Writing Custom Converters

Summary

A s you know, a JSF application stores user input and other data in JavaBeans. However, when presenting this data to the browser, the application must render the data in a format understood by the browser. For example, a date is stored as a `java.util.Date` or `java.util.Calendar` object, but in the browser, the date will be displayed as a string. Therefore, a JSF application must handle data conversion between the model view (in JavaBeans) and the presentation view (in the browser) and vice versa.

A `UIInput` component does the data conversion automatically by employing a different renderer for a different data type. You choose a renderer by using an appropriate tag for a `UIInput` component. For example, the `input_date` tag uses a renderer that can handle conversions between strings and dates, and the `input_number` tag can convert numbers to strings and strings to numbers. (Chapter 12 discusses renderers in detail.) If you cannot find a renderer for the data type you are using, you can use one of the standard converters in JSF, or you can write your own converter. This chapter describes how to use the standard converters and how to write and use custom converters.

Using Standard Converters

JSF provides a number of standard converters that you can use with a `UIInput` or a `UIOutput` component. However, not all tags that represent the `UIInput` and `UIOutput` components can be used with a converter. Only four tags have the `converter` attribute and can use a converter: `output_text`, `input_text`, `input_secret`, and `input_hidden`.

The standard converters available in JSF are described in Table 10-1.

Converter Identifier	Configuration Attribute	Pattern Formatter	Valid Values for Attribute
`Boolean`			
`Date`	`dateStyle`	`java.text.DateFormat`	short (default), medium, long, or full
	`timezone`	`java.util.TimeZone`	A time zone
`DateFormat`	`formatPattern`	`java.text.DateFormat`	A valid format pattern
	`timezone`	`java.util.TimeZone`	A time zone
`DateTime`	`dateStyle`	`java.text.DateFormat`	short (default), medium, long, or full
	`timeStyle`	`java.text.DateFormat`	short (default), medium, long, or full
	`timezone`	`java.util.TimeZone`	A time zone
`Number`	`numberStyle`	`java.text.NumberFormat`	Currency, integer (default), number, or percent
`NumberFormat`	`formatPattern`	`java.text.NumberFormat`	Any valid format pattern
`Time`	`timeStyle`	`java.text.DateFormat`	short (default), medium, long, or full
	`timezone`	`java.util.TimeZone`	A time zone

Table 10-1   *JSF Standard Converters*

NOTE

You can use the UIInput component with an appropriate renderer that does the job of a standard converter.

Creating the TestingBean for Converter Tests

The examples in this chapter use the ch10.TestingBean, shown in Listing 10-1.

Listing 10-1   *The TestingBean*

```
package ch10;
import java.util.Date;

public class TestingBean {
  private boolean discounted;
  private int quantity;
  private float price;
  private Date today;
  private String value;

  public boolean getDiscounted() {
    return discounted;
  }
  public void setDiscounted(boolean discounted) {
    this.discounted = discounted;
  }
  public int getQuantity() {
    return quantity;
  }
  public void setQuantity(int quantity) {
    this.quantity = quantity;
  }
  public float getPrice() {
    return price;
  }
  public void setPrice(float price) {
    this.price = price;
  }
  public Date getToday() {
    return today; //new Date(System.currentTimeMillis());
  }
  public void setToday (Date today) {
```

```
  this.today = today;
}
public String getValue() {
  return value;
}
public void setValue(String value) {
  this.value = value;
}
}
```

The `TestingBean` is registered in the application configuration file using the `managed-bean` tag, as shown in Listing 10-2.

Listing 10-2 *TestingBean Registration in the Application Configuration File*

```
<managed-bean>
  <managed-bean-name>testingBean</managed-bean-name>
  <managed-bean-class>ch10.TestingBean</managed-bean-class>
  <managed-bean-scope>session</managed-bean-scope>
</managed-bean>
```

Introducing the Standard Converters

Here, we will cover the seven standard converters: `Boolean`, `Date`, `DateFormat`, `DateTime`, `Number`, `NumberFormat`, and `Time`. As explained earlier in the chapter, you can use the standard converters only with `output_text`, `input_text`, `input_secret`, and `input_hidden` tags. To demonstrate using the converters, the following examples use those tags. However, in practice, you can achieve the same results by using the appropriate tag, rather than one that allows the use of converters:

▶ Instead of using an `input_text` or `output_text` date with the `Date` converter, you can use an `input_date` or `output_date` tag to handle the conversion.

▶ Instead of using an `input_text` or `output_text` tag with the `DateTime` converter, you can use the `input_datetime` or `output_datetime` tag.

▶ Instead of using an `input_text` and `output_text` tag with the `NumberFormat` converter, you can use the `input_number` or `output_number` tag with the `formatPattern` attribute.

▶ Instead of using an `input_text` or `output_text` tag with the `Time` converter, you can use the `input_time` or `output_time` tag.

The Boolean Converter

Using the Boolean converter, your UIInput component can accept true or false. The value entered is case-insensitive; *true*, *TRUE*, or *True* will be converted to boolean true. Anything other than a form of *true* will be converted to boolean false.

Listing 10-3 shows the booleanConverterTest.jsp page, which uses a Boolean converter.

Listing 10-3   *The booleanConverterTest.jsp Page*

```
<%@ taglib uri="http://java.sun.com/jsf/html" prefix="h" %>
<%@ taglib uri="http://java.sun.com/jsf/core" prefix="f" %>
<html>
<head>
<title>Boolean Converter</title>
</head>
<body>
<f:use_faces>
<h:form formName="myForm">
Type in true or false
<h:input_text valueRef="testingBean.discounted" converter="Boolean"/>
<br/>
<h:output_text valueRef="testingBean.discounted"
  converter="Boolean"/>
<br/>
<h:command_button commandName="submit" label="submit"/>
<br/><h:output_errors/>
</h:form>
</f:use_faces>
</body>
</html>
```

The Date Converter

The Date converter converts a string to a date format. You can set two attributes: dateStyle and timezone. The dateConverterTest.jsp, shown in Listing 10-4, contains an input field used with a Date converter.

Listing 10-4   *The dateConverterTest.jsp Page*

```
<%@ taglib uri="http://java.sun.com/jsf/html" prefix="h" %>
<%@ taglib uri="http://java.sun.com/jsf/core" prefix="f" %>
<html>
<head>
<title>Date Converter</title>
```

```
</head>
<body>
<f:use_faces>
<h:form formName="myForm">
<h:input_text valueRef="testingBean.today" converter="Date">
  <f:attribute name="dateStyle" value="long"/>
</h:input_text>
<br/>
Today's date:
<h:output_text valueRef="testingBean.today" converter="Date">
  <f:attribute name="dateStyle" value="long"/>
</h:output_text>
<br/>
<h:command_button commandName="submit" label="submit"/>
<br/><h:output_errors/>
</h:form>
</f:use_faces>
</body>
</html>
```

The DateFormat Converter

The DateFormat converter converts a string to a date and allows you to specify a pattern.
The example in Listing 10-5, dateFormatConverter.jsp, uses DateFormat
converters in an input box and an output box.

Listing 10-5   *The dateFormatConverter.jsp Page*

```
<%@ taglib uri="http://java.sun.com/jsf/html" prefix="h" %>
<%@ taglib uri="http://java.sun.com/jsf/core" prefix="f" %>
<html>
<head>
<title>DateFormat Converter</title>
</head>
<body>
<f:use_faces>
<h:form formName="myForm">
<h:input_text valueRef="testingBean.today" converter="DateFormat">
  <f:attribute name="formatPattern" value="MM/dd/yyyy hh:mm"/>
</h:input_text>
<br/>
Today's date:
<h:output_text valueRef="testingBean.today" converter="DateFormat">
  <f:attribute name="formatPattern" value="MM/dd/yyyy hh:mm"/>
</h:output_text>
<br/>
```

```
<h:command_button commandName="submit" label="submit"/>
<br/><h:output_errors/>
</h:form>
</f:use_faces>
</body>
</html>
```

NOTE

As explained in Chapter 5, you can use the `input_datetime` *and* `output_datetime` *tags, as well as the* `input_number` *and* `output_number` *tags, with the* `formatPattern` *attribute.*

The DateTime Converter

The `DateTime` converter converts a string to a date and vice versa. It allows you to specify the values for its `dateStyle`, `timeStyle`, and `timezone` attributes. Listing 10-6 shows the `dateTimeConverterTest.jsp` page, which uses the `DateTime` converter.

Listing 10-6 *The dateTimeConverterTest.jsp Page*

```
<%@ taglib uri="http://java.sun.com/jsf/html" prefix="h" %>
<%@ taglib uri="http://java.sun.com/jsf/core" prefix="f" %>
<html>
<head>
<title>DateTime Converter</title>
</head>
<body>
<f:use_faces>
<h:form formName="myForm">
<h:input_text valueRef="testingBean.today" converter="DateTime">
  <f:attribute name="dateStyle" value="short"/>
</h:input_text>
<br/>
Today's date:
<h:output_text valueRef="testingBean.today" converter="DateTime">
  <f:attribute name="dateStyle" value="short"/>
</h:output_text>
<br/>
<h:command_button commandName="submit" label="submit"/>
<br/><h:output_errors/>
</h:form>
</f:use_faces>
</body>
</html>
```

The Number Converter

The Number converter converts a string to a number and vice versa. It has the numberStyle attribute, which can be set to currency, integer (default), number, or percent. If you use the Number converter with an input_text tag and assign "currency" to the numberStyle attribute, a currency sign (such as a dollar sign or pound sign) will be added to the input_text tag. Using "percent" as the value of the numberStyle attribute will add a percent sign to the input text.

The numberConverterTest.jsp page, shown in Listing 10-7, includes examples of using the Number converter with each of the numberStyle attributes.

Listing 10-7   *The numberConverterTest.jsp Page*

```
<%@ taglib uri="http://java.sun.com/jsf/html" prefix="h" %>
<%@ taglib uri="http://java.sun.com/jsf/core" prefix="f" %>
<html>
<head>
<title>Number Converter</title>
</head>
<body>
<f:use_faces>
<h:form formName="myForm">
<h:input_text valueRef="testingBean.price" converter="Number">
  <f:attribute name="numberStyle" value="number"/>
</h:input_text>
<br/>
currency numberStyle:
<h:output_text valueRef="testingBean.price" converter="Number">
  <f:attribute name="numberStyle" value="currency"/>
</h:output_text>
<br/>
integer numberStyle:
<h:output_text valueRef="testingBean.price" converter="Number">
  <f:attribute name="numberStyle" value="integer"/>
</h:output_text>
<br/>
number numberStyle:
<h:output_text valueRef="testingBean.price" converter="Number">
  <f:attribute name="numberStyle" value="number"/>
</h:output_text>
<br/>
percent numberStyle:
```

```
<h:output_text valueRef="testingBean.price" converter="Number">
  <f:attribute name="numberStyle" value="percent"/>
</h:output_text>
<br/>
<h:command_button commandName="submit" label="submit"/>
<br/><h:output_errors/>
</h:form>
</f:use_faces>
</body>
</html>
```

The NumberFormat Converter

The `NumberFormat` converter converts a string to a number and vice versa. It has the attribute `formatPattern`, which allows you to specify a format pattern of the string accepted as the input text or displayed as the output text.

The Time Converter

The `Time` converter converts a string to a time and vice versa. Listing 10-8 shows an example of using a `Time` converter with `input_text` and `output_text` tags.

Listing 10-8   *The timeConverterTest.jsp Page*

```
<%@ taglib uri="http://java.sun.com/jsf/html" prefix="h" %>
<%@ taglib uri="http://java.sun.com/jsf/core" prefix="f" %>
<html>
<head>
<title>Time Converter</title>
</head>
<body>
<f:use_faces>
<h:form formName="myForm">
<h:input_text valueRef="testingBean.today" converter="Time">
  <f:attribute name="dateStyle" value="short"/>
</h:input_text>
<br/>
<h:command_button commandName="submit" label="submit"/>
<br/><h:output_errors/>
</h:form>
</f:use_faces>
</body>
</html>
```

Writing Custom Converters

If you need special data type conversion for your application, such as dates in dd.mm.yyyy format to mm/dd/yyyy, you can write a custom converter. You do this by writing a class that implements the `javax.faces.convert.Converter` interface, and then register the converter in the application configuration file. You can then use your custom converter from your JSP page.

Introducing the Converter Interface

The `Converter` interface has two methods that will be called by the JSF implementation: `getAsObject` and `getAsString`.

The `getAsObject` method converts data from the presentation view to the model view. It has the following definition:

```
public Object getAsObject(FacesContext context,
  UIComponent component, String newValue) throws ConverterException;
```

The `UIComponent` passed to this method represents the component that employs the converter, and the `String newValue` is the component's local value.

The `getAsString` method also converts data from the model view to the presentation view. It is defined as follows:

```
public String getAsString(FacesContext context,
  UIComponent component, Object value) throws ConverterException
```

The `UIComponent` passed in to this method represents the component using this converter, and the `Object value` is the object that needs to be converted into a `String`.

Creating a Custom Converter

The example in this section is a custom date converter with a lenient format. It can accept a date in the *MM/dd/yyyy*, *MM-dd-yyyy*, or *MM.dd.yyyy* format. You cannot use an `input_date` tag for this purpose, because it was not designed to accept a date in either the *MM-dd-yyyy* or *MM.dd.yyyy* format.

Writing the Converter Class

The first step in creating a custom converter is to write a class that implements the `javax.faces.convert.Converter` interface. The class for the sample custom date converter, named `MyConverter`, is shown in Listing 10-9.

Listing 10-9   *The MyConverter Class*

```
package ch10;
import java.text.DateFormat;
import java.text.ParseException;
```

```java
import java.util.Date;
import javax.faces.component.UIComponent;
import javax.faces.context.FacesContext;
import javax.faces.convert.Converter;
import javax.faces.convert.ConverterException;

public class MyConverter implements Converter {
  // lenient date format
  // expects MM/dd/yyyy, but also accepts MM-dd-yyyy or MM.dd.yyyy
  public Object getAsObject(FacesContext context,
  UIComponent component, String value)  throws ConverterException {
    if (value==null)
      return null;
    Date result;
    int length = value.length();
    StringBuffer validDate = new StringBuffer(length);
    for (int i=0; i<length; i++) {
      char c = value.charAt(i);
      if (c=='.' || c=='-')
        validDate.append('/');
      else
        validDate.append(c);
    }
    try {
      DateFormat df = DateFormat.getDateInstance(DateFormat.SHORT);
      result = df.parse(validDate.toString());
    }
    catch (ParseException e) {
      throw new ConverterException("Invalid Date Format");
    }
    return result;
  }

  public String getAsString(FacesContext context,
    UIComponent component, Object value)
    throws ConverterException {
    DateFormat df = DateFormat.getDateInstance(DateFormat.SHORT);
    return df.format((Date) value);
  }
}
```

The getAsObject method in the MyConverter class converts the String value into a Date. It starts by obtaining the length of the value and creating a StringBuffer that will contain a valid date.

```
Date result;
int length = value.length();
StringBuffer validDate = new StringBuffer(length);
```

It then iterates all characters in `value` and replaces any occurrence of . and - with a /.

```
for (int i=0; i<length; i++) {
  char c = value.charAt(i);
  if (c=='.' || c=='-')
    validDate.append('/');
  else
    validDate.append(c);
}
```

For example, an entry such as 12-13-2003 or 12.13.2003 will be converted to 12/13/2003.

The `getAsObject` method then uses a `java.text.DateFormat` object to parse the `String` and returns a `Date` object as the return value of the method.

```
try {
  DateFormat df = DateFormat.getDateInstance(DateFormat.SHORT);
  result = df.parse(validDate.toString());
}
catch (ParseException e) {
  throw new ConverterException("Invalid Date Format");
}
return result;
```

The `getAsString` method in the `MyConverter` class uses a `java.text.DateFormat` object to format the `Date` object into a `String`. The method starts by obtaining a `DateFormat` instance from the static `getDateInstance` method, passing `DateFormat.SHORT` to indicate the date style.

```
DateFormat df = DateFormat.getDateInstance(DateFormat.SHORT);
```

It then calls the `format` method to format the date value and returns the result.

```
return df.format((Date) value);
```

Registering the Converter

After you compile and deploy the converter class in your application directory, you need to register it in the application configuration file before you can use it in the application. You do this by using the `converter` element, which must have two subelements: `converter-id` and `converter-class`. The `converter-id` element specifies a unique identifier that is used to refer to this converter in the JSP page. The `converter-class` element defines the fully qualified Java class implementing the `Converter` interface.

Listing 10-10 shows how to register the converter class in your application configuration file.

Listing 10-10   *Custom Converter Registration in the Application Configuration File*

```
<converter>
  <converter-id>myConverter</converter-id>
  <converter-class>ch10.MyConverter</converter-class>
</converter>
```

Using the Converter

Now, that you have created and registered the custom converter class, you can use the converter from a JSP page. As with a standard converter, you can use the `converter` attribute in an `input_text`, `input_hidden`, `input_secret`, or `output_text` tag. Listing 10-11 presents a JSP page called `customConverterTest.jsp`, which uses the custom converter.

Listing 10-11   *The customConverterTest.jsp Page*

```
<%@ taglib uri="http://java.sun.com/jsf/html" prefix="h" %>
<%@ taglib uri="http://java.sun.com/jsf/core" prefix="f" %>
<html>
<head>
<title>Using Custom Converter</title>
</head>
<body>
<f:use_faces>
<h:form formName="myForm">
<h:input_text valueRef="testingBean.today" converter="myConverter"/>
<br/>
The date you entered: <h:output_date valueRef="testingBean.today"
  dateStyle="short"/>
<br/>
<h:command_button commandName="submit" label="submit"/>
<br><h:output_errors/>
</h:form>
</f:use_faces>
</body>
</html>
```

You can invoke this page by using the following URL:

```
http://localhost:8080/JSFCh10/faces/customConverterTest.jsp
```

The result in your browser will resemble the window shown in Figure 10-1.

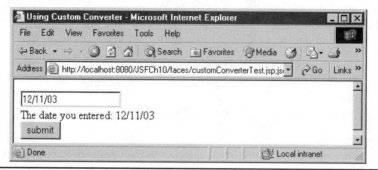

Figure 10-1   *Using the custom converter*

Summary

In this chapter, you have learned about converters. JSF provides several standard converters that you can use with the `output_text`, `input_text`, `input_hidden`, and `input_secret` tags, by using the `converter` attribute. Most of the standard converters are redundant, considering that you can choose a renderer that converts data automatically.

JSF also supports custom converters through the use of the `javax.faces.convert.Converter` interface. In this chapter, you worked through an example of creating a custom converter that accepts dates in several formats.

In the next chapter, you will learn how to design JSF applications for internationalization and localization.

Internationalization and Localization

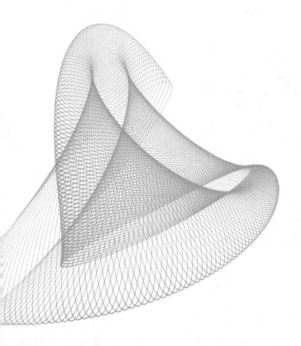

Today Web applications often cater to an audience from different parts of the world. As such, it is sometimes necessary to make your Web sites multi-lingual. To do this, you need to understand internationalization and localization.

Internationalization is designing software applications to support various languages and regions without needing to change their programming logic. *Localization* is designing software applications for a specific locale.

This chapter describes how to support internationalization and localization in your JSF applications. You will learn how to create properties files for locales and use the `ResourceBundle` class to read them, as well as how to localize static and dynamic data. Finally, you will learn how to localize messages in your JSF applications.

Designing an Application for Internationalization

An application designed with internationalization in mind has its textual elements (such as error messages and GUI component labels) displayed in the local language of the computer on which the application runs. This means that the textual contents are not hard-coded; rather, they are retrieved dynamically, normally from a text file. In addition, culture-dependent data, such as dates and currencies, appears in the format that conforms to the user's language and region. Also, adding a new language does not require the recompilation of the application.

Internationalization is abbreviated i18n, because the word *internationalization* starts with an *i* and ends with an *n*, and there are 18 letters between the first *i* and the last *n*.

Localizing an Application

A *locale* is a specific geographical, political, or cultural region. An operation that requires a locale to perform its task is called *locale-sensitive*. For instance, displaying a date is a locale-sensitive operation because the date must be in the format acceptable to the user's country or region. The eleventh day of September 2003 can be written as 9/11/2003 in North America, but that data is written as 11/9/2003 in Australia.

Localization is abbreviated l10n, because the word *localization* starts with an *l* and ends with an *n*, and there are two letters between the beginning and ending letters.

Localizing an application is accomplished by translating text and adding locale-specific components (such as culture-sensitive images and sounds).

Defining a Locale

A locale is represented by the `java.util.Locale` class. There are three main components of a locale: language, country, and variant. The language is obviously the most important part; however, sometimes the language itself is not sufficient to differentiate a locale. For example, the German language is spoken in countries such as Germany and Switzerland. However, the German language spoken in Switzerland is not the same as the one used in Germany. Therefore, it is necessary to specify the country of the language. As another example, the English language used in the United States is not exactly the same as the one used in England. It's *color* in the United States, but *colour* in England, as one example.

The variant argument is a vendor- or browser-specific code. For example, you use WIN for Windows, MAC for Macintosh, and POSIX for POSIX. Where there are two variants, separate them with an underscore, and put the most important one first. For example, a Traditional Spanish collation might construct a locale with parameters for language, country, and variant as es, ES, Traditional_WIN.

In JDK 1.4, the java.util.Locale class has three constructors:

```
public Locale(String language)
public Locale(String language, String country)
public Locale(String language, String country, String variant)
```

The language argument is a valid ISO language code, which is a two-letter, lowercase code specified in ISO 639 (http://ftp.ics.uci.edu/pub/ietf/http/related/iso639.txt). Table 11-1 shows the ISO language code.

Code	Language
aa	Afar
ab	Abkhazian
af	Afrikaans
am	Amharic
ar	Arabic
as	Assamese
ay	Aymara
az	Azerbaijani
ba	Bashkir
be	Byelorussian
bg	Bulgarian
bh	Bihari
bi	Bislama
bn	Bengali; Bangla
bo	Tibetan
br	Breton
ca	Catalan
co	Corsican

Table 11-1   *The ISO Language Code*

Code	Language
cs	Czech
cy	Welsh
da	Danish
de	German
dz	Bhutani
el	Greek
en	English
eo	Esperanto
es	Spanish
et	Estonian
eu	Basque
fa	Persian
fi	Finnish
fj	Fiji
fo	Faroese
fr	French
fy	Frisian
ga	Irish
gd	Scots Gaelic
gl	Galician
gn	Guarani
gu	Gujarati
ha	Hausa
he	Hebrew (formerly iw)
hi	Hindi
hr	Croatian
hu	Hungarian
hy	Armenian
ia	Interlingua
id	Indonesian (formerly in)
ie	Interlingue
ik	Inupiak
is	Icelandic
it	Italian
iu	Inuktitut

Table 11-1 *The ISO Language Code* (continued)

Code	Language
ja	Japanese
jw	Javanese
ka	Georgian
kk	Kazakh
kl	Greenlandic
km	Cambodian
kn	Kannada
ko	Korean
ks	Kashmiri
ku	Kurdish
ky	Kirghiz
la	Latin
ln	Lingala
lo	Laothian
lt	Lithuanian
lv	Latvian, Lettish
mg	Malagasy
mi	Maori
mk	Macedonian
ml	Malayalam
mn	Mongolian
mo	Moldavian
mr	Marathi
ms	Malay
mt	Maltese
my	Burmese
na	Nauru
ne	Nepali
nl	Dutch
no	Norwegian
oc	Occitan
om	(Afan) Oromo
or	Oriya
pa	Punjabi
pl	Polish

Table 11-1   *The ISO Language Code* (continued)

Code	Language
ps	Pashto, Pushto
pt	Portuguese
qu	Quechua
rm	Rhaeto-Romance
rn	Kirundi
ro	Romanian
ru	Russian
rw	Kinyarwanda
sa	Sanskrit
sd	Sindhi
sg	Sangho
sh	Serbo-Croatian
si	Sinhalese
sk	Slovak
sl	Slovenian
sm	Samoan
sn	Shona
so	Somali
sq	Albanian
sr	Serbian
ss	Siswati
st	Sesotho
su	Sundanese
sv	Swedish
sw	Swahili
ta	Tamil
te	Telugu
tg	Tajik
th	Thai
ti	Tigrinya
tk	Turkmen
tl	Tagalog
tn	Setswana
to	Tonga
tr	Turkish

Table 11-1   *The ISO Language Code* (continued)

Code	Language
ts	Tsonga
tt	Tatar
tw	Twi
ug	Uighur
uk	Ukrainian
ur	Urdu
uz	Uzbek
vi	Vietnamese
vo	Volapuk
wo	Wolof
xh	Xhosa
yi	Yiddish (formerly ji)
yo	Yoruba
za	Zhuang
zh	Chinese
zu	Zulu

Table 11-1   *The ISO Language Code* (continued)

The `country` argument is a valid ISO country code, which is a two-letter, uppercase code specified in ISO 3166 (`http://userpage.chemie.fu-berlin.de/diverse/doc/ISO_3166.html`). Table 11-2 lists all the country codes in ISO 3166.

Country	Code
Afghanistan	AF
Albania	AL
Algeria	DZ
American Samoa	AS
Andorra	AD
Angola	AO
Anguilla	AI
Antarctica	AQ
Antigua and Barbuda	AG
Argentina	AR
Armenia	AM

Table 11-2   *ISO 3166 Country Codes*

Country	Code
Aruba	AW
Australia	AU
Austria	AT
Azerbaijan	AZ
Bahamas	BS
Bahrain	BH
Bangladesh	BD
Barbados	BB
Belarus	BY
Belgium	BE
Belize	BZ
Benin	BJ
Bermuda	BM
Bhutan	BT
Bolivia	BO
Bosnia and Herzegowina	BA
Botswana	BW
Bouvet Island	BV
Brazil	BR
British Indian Ocean Territory	IO
Brunei Darussalam	BN
Bulgaria	BG
Burkina Faso	BF
Burundi	BI
Cambodia	KH
Cameroon	CM
Canada	CA
Cape Verde	CV
Cayman Islands	KY
Central African Republic	CF
Chad	TD
Chile	CL
China	CN
Christmas Island	CX
Cocos (Keeling) Islands	CC
Colombia	CO

Table 11-2   *ISO 3166 Country Codes* (continued)

Country	Code
Comoros	KM
Congo, Democratic Republic of (was Zaire)	CD
Congo, People's Republic of	CG
Cook Islands	CK
Costa Rica	CR
Cote D'ivoire	CI
Croatia (local name Hrvatska)	HR
Cuba	CU
Cyprus	CY
Czech Republic	CZ
Denmark	DK
Djibouti	DJ
Dominica	DM
Dominican Republic	DO
East Timor	TL
Ecuador	EC
Egypt	EG
El Salvador	SV
Equatorial Guinea	GQ
Eritrea	ER
Estonia	EE
Ethiopia	ET
Falkland Islands (Malvinas)	FK
Faroe Islands	FO
Fiji	FJ
Finland	FI
France	FR
France, Metropolitan	FX
French Guiana	GF
French Polynesia	PF
French Southern Territories	TF
Gabon	GA
Gambia	GM
Georgia	GE
Germany	DE
Ghana	GH

Table 11-2   *ISO 3166 Country Codes* (continued)

Country	Code
Gibraltar	GI
Greece	GR
Greenland	GL
Grenada	GD
Guadeloupe	GP
Guam	GU
Guatemala	GT
Guinea	GN
Guinea-Bissau	GW
Guyana	GY
Haiti	HT
Heard and McDonald Islands	HM
Honduras	HN
Hong Kong	HK
Hungary	HU
Iceland	IS
India	IN
Indonesia	ID
Iran (Islamic Republic of)	IR
Iraq	IQ
Ireland	IE
Israel	IL
Italy	IT
Jamaica	JM
Japan	JP
Jordan	JO
Kazakhstan	KZ
Kenya	KE
Kiribati	KI
Korea, Democratic People's Republic of	KP
Korea, Republic of	KR
Kuwait	KW
Kyrgyzstan	KG
Lao People's Democratic Republic	LA
Latvia	LV
Lebanon	LB

Table 11-2   *ISO 3166 Country Codes* (continued)

Country	Code
Lesotho	LS
Liberia	LR
Libyan Arab Jamahiriya	LY
Liechtenstein	LI
Lithuania	LT
Luxembourg	LU
Macau	MO
Macedonia, The Former Yugoslav Republic of	MK
Madagascar	MG
Malawi	MW
Malaysia	MY
Maldives	MV
Mali	ML
Malta	MT
Marshall Islands	MH
Martinique	MQ
Mauritania	MR
Mauritius	MU
Mayotte	YT
Mexico	MX
Micronesia, Federated States of	FM
Moldova, Republic of	MD
Monaco	MC
Mongolia	MN
Montserrat	MS
Morocco	MA
Mozambique	MZ
Myanmar	MM
Namibia	NA
Nauru	NR
Nepal	NP
Netherlands	NL
Netherlands Antilles	AN
New Caledonia	NC
New Zealand	NZ
Nicaragua	NI

Table 11-2   *ISO 3166 Country Codes* (continued)

Country	Code
Niger	NE
Nigeria	NG
Niue	NU
Norfolk Island	NF
Northern Mariana Islands	MP
Norway	NO
Oman	OM
Pakistan	PK
Palau	PW
Palestinian Territory, Occupied	PS
Panama	PA
Papua New Guinea	PG
Paraguay	PY
Peru	PE
Philippines	PH
Pitcairn	PN
Poland	PL
Portugal	PT
Puerto Rico	PR
Qatar	QA
Reunion	RE
Romania	RO
Russian Federation	RU
Rwanda	RW
Saint Kitts and Nevis	KN
Saint Lucia	LC
Saint Vincent and The Grenadines	VC
Samoa	WS
San Marino	SM
Sao Tome and Principe	ST
Saudi Arabia	SA
Senegal	SN
Seychelles	SC
Sierra Leone	SL
Singapore	SG
Slovakia (Slovak Republic)	SK

Table 11-2   *ISO 3166 Country Codes* (continued)

Country	Code
Slovenia	SI
Solomon Islands	SB
Somalia	SO
South Africa	ZA
South Georgia and The South Sandwich Islands	GS
Spain	ES
Sri Lanka	LK
St. Helena	SH
St. Pierre and Miquelon	PM
Sudan	SD
Suriname	SR
Svalbard and Jan Mayen Islands	SJ
Swaziland	SZ
Sweden	SE
Switzerland	CH
Syrian Arab Republic	SY
Taiwan	TW
Tajikistan	TJ
Tanzania, United Republic of	TZ
Thailand	TH
Togo	TG
Tokelau	TK
Tonga	TO
Trinidad and Tobago	TT
Tunisia	TN
Turkey	TR
Turkmenistan	TM
Turks and Caicos Islands	TC
Tuvalu	TV
Uganda	UG
Ukraine	UA
United Arab Emirates	AE
United Kingdom	GB
United States	US
United States, Minor Outlying Islands	UM

Table 11-2 *ISO 3166 Country Codes* (continued)

Country	Code
Uruguay	UY
Uzbekistan	UZ
Vanuatu	VU
Vatican City State (Holy See)	VA
Venezuela	VE
Viet Nam	VN
Virgin Islands (British)	VG
Virgin Islands (U.S.)	VI
Wallis and Futuna Islands	WF
Western Sahara	EH
Yemen	YE
Yugoslavia	YU
Zambia	ZM
Zimbabwe	ZW

Table 11-2   *ISO 3166 Country Codes* (continued)

Creating Locale Properties Files

For textual contents, an application that supports internationalization has a separate properties file for each locale. Each file contains key/value pairs, and each key uniquely identifies a locale-specific object. Keys are always `Strings`, and values can be `Strings` or any other type of object. For example, to support American English, French, and German, you will have three properties files, all of which have the same keys.

Here is the English version of the properties file. Note that it has two keys: `greetings` and `farewell`.

```
greetings = Hello
farewell = Goodbye
```

The French version would be as follows:

```
greetings = Bonjour
farewell = Au revoir
```

And the properties file for the German language is as follows:

```
greetings = Hallo
farewell = Tschüß
```

Now, you need a way to easily choose and read the properties file specific to the user's locale and look up the values. The answer in Java is the `java.util.ResourceBundle` class.

The `ResourceBundle` abstract class is used to read a properties file and store locale-specific values. A ResourceBundle class has a base name, which can be any name. In order for a ResourceBundle class to pick up a properties file, the file must be named with the ResourceBundle base name, followed by an underscore, followed by the language code, and optionally followed by another underscore and the country code. The format for a properties filename is as follows:

> *basename_languageCode[_countryCode]*

For example, suppose the base name is `MyResources` and you define three locales as follows:

```
US-en
FR-fr
DE-de
```

Then you would have three properties files:

- `MyResources_en_US.properties`

- `MyResources_fr_FR.properties`

- `MyResources_de_DE.properties`

Reading Properties Files

To begin, you obtain a `ResourceBundle` object by calling the `getBundle` static method, passing the base name and the locale to be used (where `locale` represents a `Locale` object):

```
ResourceBundle messages =
  ResourceBundle.getBundle("MyResources", locale);
```

This will load the `ResourceBundle` object with the values in the corresponding properties file.

If a suitable properties file is not found, the `ResourceBundle` object will use the default properties file, which will be the one whose name equals the base name and has the extension .properties. In this case, the default file would be `MyResources.properties`. If this file is not found, a `java.util.MissingResourceException` will be thrown.

Then, to read a value, you use the `ResourceBundle` class's `getString` method, passing the key.

```
public String getString(String key)
```

If the entry with the specified key is not found, a `java.util.MissingResourceException` will be thrown.

The following example illustrates the effort to support internationalization with three languages: English, French, and German. This example uses four properties files:

- `MyResources_en_US.properties`, shown in Listing 11-1

- ▶ MyResources_fr_FR.properties, shown in Listing 11-2
- ▶ MyResources_de_DE.properties, shown in Listing 11-3
- ▶ MyResources.properties (the default), shown in Listing 11-4

These files are placed in the directory specified in the class path.

Listing 11-1   *The MyResources_en_US.properties File*

```
greetings=Hello
farewell=Goodbye
```

Listing 11-2   *The MyResources_fr_FR.properties File*

```
greetings=Bonjour
farewell=Au revoir
```

Listing 11-3   *The MyResources_de_DE.properties File*

```
greetings=Hallo
farewell=Tschüß
```

Listing 11-4   *The MyResources.properties File*

```
greetings=Hello
farewell=Goodbye
```

The TestingI18N class, shown in Listing 11-5, obtains the ResourceBundle object according to the locale of your computer and prints the localized message for the greetings and farewell keys.

Listing 11-5   *An I18N Example*

```
package ch11;
import java.util.Locale;
import java.util.ResourceBundle;

public class TestingI18N {
  public static void main(String[] args) {
```

```
    Locale locale = Locale.getDefault();
    ResourceBundle messages =
      ResourceBundle.getBundle("MyResources", locale);
    System.out.println(messages.getString("greetings"));
    System.out.println(messages.getString("farewell"));
  }
}
```

The `getDefault` method of the `Locale` class returns the default locale in your computer. If it is German (Germany), the program will return:

```
Hallo
Tschüß
```

If it is French (France), the result is:

```
Bonjour
Au revoir
```

If it is English (United States), the result is:

```
Hello
Goodbye
```

If the locale is none of the above, the result will be from the `MyResources.properties` file:

```
Hello
Goodbye
```

Supporting Internationalization and Localization in JSF Applications

You can easily create multi-lingual applications with JSF. To make use of support for internationalization, your JSF application needs a way to determine the user's locale in order to present the correct localized version. You can get this information from the browser's locale or allow the user to select a language.

Getting the Browser's Locale

The `javax.servlet.ServletRequest` interface has a method called `getLocale` that returns a `java.util.Locale` object containing the browser's locale-specific information. However, browsers do not normally include the information about the country, just the language. Listing 11-6 provides a JSP page called `localeTest.jsp`, which you can use to display the language and country of browser's locale. (But, since the browser may not have the information, do not be surprised if it returns a blank string for the country.)

Listing 11-6 *The localeTest.jsp Page*

```
<%@ page import="java.util.Locale"%>
<html>
<head>
<title>Testing Locale</title>
</head>
<body>
<h2>Locale information</h2>
<%
  Locale locale = request.getLocale();
  out.println("Locale country: " + locale.getCountry());
  out.println("<br>Locale language: " + locale.getLanguage());
%>
</body>
</html>
```

To invoke the `localeTest.jsp` page, use the following URL (this is just a normal JSP page, it does not include processing by a JSF implementation):

```
http://localhost:8080/JSFCh11/localeTest.jsp
```

Localizing Static Data

To support internationalization in a JSF application, you use the JSP Standard Tag Library (JSTL) Internationalization `setBundle` tag. This tag is included in the `standard.jar` file, so all you need to do is make sure that this file is copied into your `WEB-INF/lib` directory. To use the tag in your page, you need to declare the following `taglib` directive on your page:

```
<%@ taglib uri="http://java.sun.com/jstl/fmt" prefix="fmt" %>
```

Then use the `setBundle` tag. This tag has the following attributes:

▶ `basename` is the base name for the `ResourceBundle` object.

▶ `scope` is the scope of the `ResourceBundle` object.

▶ `var` is an identifier to refer to this `ResourceBundle` object from the page.

After you have used the `setBundle` tag, you can use localized text in your `UIOutput` and `UICommand` components by using the `key` and `bundle` attributes in the tags that represent the components. The `bundle` attribute is assigned the value in the `var` attribute of the `setBundle` tag. The `key` attribute specifies the key of the value you want to retrieve from one of the properties files.

Let's look at an example of a login page that uses localized messages. The example uses the `LoginBean` shown in Listing 11-7.

Listing 11-7   *The LoginBean*

```
package ch11;
public class LoginBean {
  private String userName;
  private String password;

  public String getUserName() {
    return userName;
  }
  public void setUserName(String userName) {
    this.userName = userName;
  }
  public String getPassword() {
    return password;
  }
  public void setPassword(String password) {
    this.password = password;
  }
}
```

The `LoginBean` is registered in the application configuration file using the `managed-bean` tag, as shown in Listing 11-8.

Listing 11-8   *The LoginBean Registration in the Application Configuration File*

```
<managed-bean>
  <managed-bean-name>loginBean</managed-bean-name>
  <managed-bean-class>ch11.LoginBean</managed-bean-class>
  <managed-bean-scope>session</managed-bean-scope>
</managed-bean>
```

The example also uses the `staticDataTest.jsp` page, shown in Listing 11-9. This page contains a `UIOutput` component and a `UICommand` component. Notice that the `output_text` and `command_button` tags use the `bundle` and `key` attributes.

Listing 11-9   *The staticDataTest.jsp page*

```
<%@ taglib uri="http://java.sun.com/jsf/html" prefix="h" %>
<%@ taglib uri="http://java.sun.com/jsf/core" prefix="f" %>
<%@ taglib uri="http://java.sun.com/jstl/fmt" prefix="fmt" %>
<html>
<head>
```

```
<title>I18N</title>
</head>
<body>
<fmt:setBundle basename="Login" scope="session" var="loginBundle"/>
<f:use_faces>
<h:form formName="myForm">
<h:output_text bundle="loginBundle" key="userName"/>
<h:input_text valueRef="LoginBean.userName"/>
<br/>
<h:output_text bundle="loginBundle" key="password"/>
<h:input_text valueRef="LoginBean.password"/>
<br/>
<h:command_button commandName="submit"
  bundle="loginBundle" key="loginCommand"/>
<br/><h:output_errors/>
</h:form>
</f:use_faces>
</body>
</html>
```

The application supports two languages: English and German. The properties files are called `Login_en.properties`, shown in Listing 11-10, and `Login_de.properties`, shown in Listing 11-11.

Listing 11-10   *The Login_en.properties File*

```
userName=User Name
password=Password
loginCommand=Login
```

Listing 11-11   *The Login_de.properties File*

```
userName=Benutzername
password=Paßwort
loginCommand=Anmelden
```

You can invoke the `staticDataTest.jsp` page by using the following URL:

`http://localhost:8080/JSFCh11/faces/staticDataTest.jsp`

If the computer you use to request the `staticDataTest.jsp` page has been set to use the English language, you will see a screen similar to the one shown in Figure 11-1. If it has been set to use the German language, you will see a screen similar to the one shown in Figure 11-2. If the language setting is not English or German, the values from the `Login.properties` file are used. The contents of this file are the same as the entries in the `Login_en.properties` file.

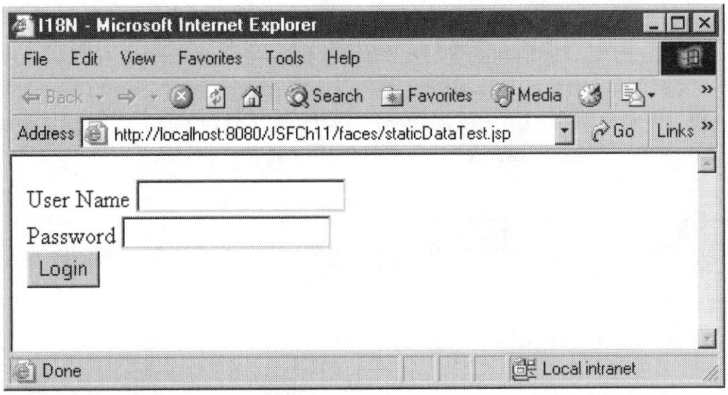

Figure 11-1   *Using the en language*

You can put the properties files under any subdirectory of `WEB-INF/classes`. However, this must be reflected in the `basename` attribute of the `setBundle` tag. For instance, if you put the properties files under the `WEB-INF/classes/ch11` directory, your `setBundle` tag should look like this:

```
<fmt:setBundle basename="ch11.Login"
  scope="session" var="loginBundle"/>
```

Notice that you use a period (.) to separate the directory from the base name.

Localizing Dynamic Data

In the previous example, the application gets the base name for the `ResourceBundle` object from the browser's locale found in the request. However, in some cases where you need locale-specific data, you must load the values dynamically. For example, a JavaBean that is used in a multilingual application does not know the user's locale until the user's first request arrives. Therefore, the JavaBean must load the values dynamically.

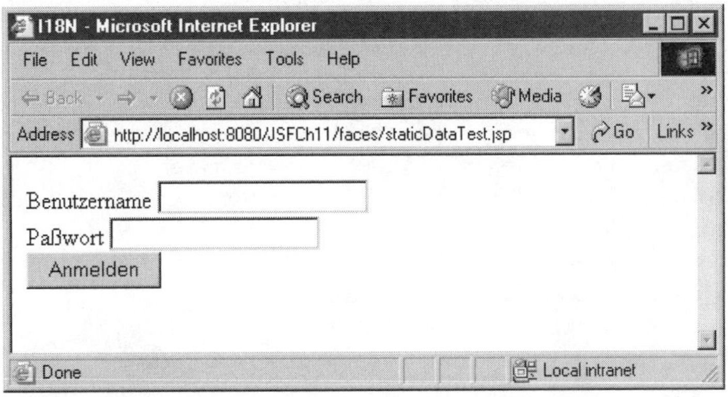

Figure 11-2   *Using the de language*

In the following example, you will allow the user to select one of the two languages supported, English and German, in the first page. Then the second page employs a `UISelect` component whose option values come from a JavaBean called `CountryListBean`. The JavaBean is populated on the fly. The `CountryListBean` is registered in the application configuration file using the `managed-bean` element, as shown in Listing 11-12.

Listing 11-12   *The CountryListBean Registration in the Application Configuration File*

```
<managed-bean>
  <managed-bean-name>CountryListBean</managed-bean-name>
  <managed-bean-class>ch11.CountryListBean</managed-bean-class>
  <managed-bean-scope>session</managed-bean-scope>
</managed-bean>
```

The first page is the `selectLanguage.jsp` page. It hosts a form with a `selectone_menu` tag. The `selectone_menu` tag has two select items, one for English and one for German. Also note that the `selectone_menu` tag uses a `valueChangedListener` of type `ch11.LanguageChangedListener`. The `selectLanguage.jsp` page is shown in Listing 11-13.

Listing 11-13   *The selectLanguage.jsp Page*

```
<%@ taglib uri="http://java.sun.com/jsf/html" prefix="h" %>
<%@ taglib uri="http://java.sun.com/jsf/core" prefix="f" %>
<html>
<head>
<title>Select Language</title>
</head>
<body>
<h2>Please select your language</h2>
<f:use_faces>
<h:form formName="myForm">
<br>Language:
<h:selectone_menu valueRef="countryListBean.language">
  <f:valuechanged_listener type="ch11.LanguageChangedListener"/>
  <h:selectitem itemValue="en" itemLabel="English"/>
  <h:selectitem itemValue="de" itemLabel="German"/>
</h:selectone_menu>
<br>
<h:command_button commandName="submit"
  label="Submit" action="success"/>
<br><h:output_errors/>
</h:form>
</f:use_faces>
```

```
</body>
</html>
```

There are only two pages in this example, so the page navigation is simple. It is defined in the application configuration file using the `navigation-rule` element, as shown in Listing 11-14.

Listing 11-14   *Page Navigation Defined in the Application Configuration File*

```
<navigation-rule>
  <from-tree-id>/selectLanguage.jsp</from-tree-id>
  <navigation-case>
    <to-tree-id>/selectCountry.jsp</to-tree-id>
  </navigation-case>
</navigation-rule>
```

The `selectCountry.jsp` page uses the JSTL Internationalization `setBundle` tag. It loads a value from a `ResourceBundle` object whose base name is `SelectCountry`. Listing 11-15 presents the `selectCountry.jsp` page.

Listing 11-15   *The selectCountry.jsp Page*

```
<%@ taglib uri="http://java.sun.com/jsf/html" prefix="h" %>
<%@ taglib uri="http://java.sun.com/jsf/core" prefix="f" %>
<%@ taglib uri="http://java.sun.com/jstl/fmt" prefix="fmt" %>
<html>
<head>
<title>Select Country</title>
</head>
<body>
<fmt:setBundle basename="ch11.SelectCountry" scope="session"
var="selectCountryBundle"/>
<f:use_faces>
<h:form formName="myForm">
<h:selectone_listbox>
  <h:selectitems valueRef="countryListBean.countryList"/>
</h:selectone_listbox>
<br/>
<h:command_button commandName="submit" bundle="selectCountryBundle"
key="selectCommand"/>
<br/><h:output_errors/>
</h:form>
</f:use_faces>
</body>
</html>
```

There are two languages supported in the `SelectCountry_en.properties` and `SelectCountry_de.properties` files. There is one key in each properties file: `selectCommand`, which is used for the label of the `UICommand` component. These properties files are shown in Listings 11-16 and 11-17.

Listing 11-16   *The SelectCountry_en.properties File*

```
selectCommand=Select
```

Listing 11-17   *The SelectCountry_de.properties File*

```
selectCommand=Wählen
```

Now, consider the `selectone_listbox` tag in the `selectCountry.jsp` page.

```
<h:selectone_listbox>
  <h:selectitems valueRef="countryListBean.countryList"/>
</h:selectone_listbox>
```

The options come from a `selectitems` tag whose `valueRef` is bound to the `countryList` property of the `CountryListBean`. The `CountryListBean` gets the country list from either the `CountryList_en.properties` file, shown in Listing 11-18, or the `CountryList_de.properties` file, shown in Listing 11-19.

Listing 11-18   *The CountryList_en.properties File*

```
country_1=Australia
country_2=Brazil
country_3=China
country_4=Denmark
country_5=Egypt
```

Listing 11-19   *The CountryList_de.properties File*

```
country_1=Australien
country_2=Brazilien
country_3=China
country_4=Dänemark
country_5=Ägypten
```

Before we discuss the `CountryListBean`, let's look at the `LanguageChangedListener` in Listing 11-20. This listener observes the value change in the `select` element in the `selectLanguage.jsp` page.

Listing 11-20   *The LanguageChangedListener*

```
package ch11;

import javax.faces.FactoryFinder;
import javax.faces.application.Application;
import javax.faces.application.ApplicationFactory;
import javax.faces.el.ValueBinding;
import javax.faces.context.FacesContext;
import javax.faces.event.AbortProcessingException;
import javax.faces.event.PhaseId;
import javax.faces.event.ValueChangedEvent;
import javax.faces.event.ValueChangedListener;

public class LanguageChangedListener
  implements ValueChangedListener {

  public PhaseId getPhaseId() {
    System.out.println("getPhaseId");
    return PhaseId.APPLY_REQUEST_VALUES;
  }

  public void processValueChanged(ValueChangedEvent event) throws
    AbortProcessingException {
    String language = event.getNewValue().toString();
    FacesContext facesContext = FacesContext.getCurrentInstance();
    try {
      getValueBinding("countryListBean.language")
        .setValue(facesContext, language);
    }
    catch (Exception e) {
      System.out.println(e.toString());
    }
  }
  private static ValueBinding getValueBinding(String valueRef) {
    ApplicationFactory factory = (ApplicationFactory)
      FactoryFinder.getFactory(FactoryFinder.APPLICATION_FACTORY);
    Application application = factory.getApplication();
    ValueBinding binding = application.getValueBinding(valueRef);
    return binding;
  }
}
```

The `processValueChanged` method is important. It gets the language from the `getNewValue` method of the `ValueChangedEvent` passed in and obtains the reference to the current `FacesContext` object.

```
String language = event.getNewValue().toString();
FacesContext facesContext = FacesContext.getCurrentInstance();
```

Next, it will set the value of the `language` property in the `CountryListBean`. This will make the `CountryListBean` load the appropriate country list. The `CountryListBean` is shown in Listing 11-21.

Listing 11-21   *The CountryListBean*

```java
package ch11;
import java.util.ArrayList;
import java.util.Collection;
import java.util.Locale;
import java.util.ResourceBundle;
import javax.faces.component.SelectItem;
import javax.faces.context.FacesContext;

public class CountryListBean {

  private ArrayList countryList = new ArrayList();
  private String language;

  public void setCountryList(Collection countries) {
    countryList = new ArrayList(countries);
  }
  public Collection getCountryList() {
    return countryList;
  }

  public void setLanguage(String language) {
    if (language==null)
      return;
    String oldLanguage = this.language;
    this.language = language;
    // only load values if the new language is different
    if (!language.equals(oldLanguage)) {
      Locale locale = new Locale(language);
      FacesContext facesContext = FacesContext.getCurrentInstance();
      facesContext.setLocale(locale);
      loadValues();
    }
  }
}
```

```
private void loadValues() {
  countryList.clear();
  Locale currentLocale =
    FacesContext.getCurrentInstance().getLocale();
  ResourceBundle rb =
    ResourceBundle.getBundle("ch11/CountryList", currentLocale);
  for (int i=1; i<6; i++) {
    String key = "country_" + i;
    String value = rb.getString(key);
    SelectItem item = new SelectItem(value, value, null);
    countryList.add(item);
  }
 }
}
```

Whenever the `setLanguage` method of the `CountryListBean` is called, it will compare the new value with the old language. If they are different, it calls the `loadValues` method. The `loadValues` method gets the user's locale from the `FacesContext` object and constructs a `ResourceBundle` object, passing the locale. It then adds the five countries from the `CountryList_en.properties` file or the `CountryList_de.properties` file.

You can invoke the `selectLanguage.jsp` page by using the following URL:

`http://localhost:8080/JSFCh11/faces/selectLanguage.jsp`

You will see the `selectLanguage.jsp` page shown in Figure 11-3.

Select either English or German and click Submit. When you select English, you will see the country list shown in Figure 11-4. Selecting German shows the country list in Figure 11-5.

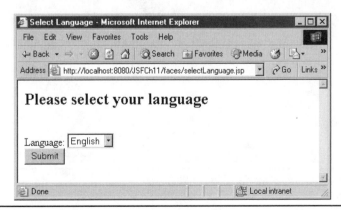

Figure 11-3   *Selecting a language*

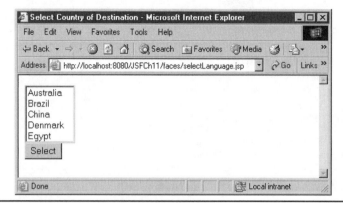

Figure 11-4   *The country list for the English language*

Localizing Error Messages in Validators

JSF also allows you to write locale-specific messages in the application configuration file, so you do not need to use properties files. You will most likely use this technique to localize error messages for your custom validators. You use the `MessageResources` object for this purpose. A `MessageResources` object is analogous to a `ResourceBundle` object.

In the application configuration file, a `MessageResources` object is represented by the `message-resources` element. A `message-resources` element represents a set of message elements for localized messages. A `message-resources` element has an identifier that is unique throughout the entire application. This identifier is equivalent to the base name of a `ResourceBundle` object.

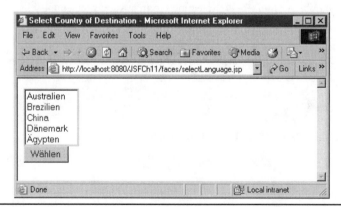

Figure 11-5   *The country list for the German language*

The `message-resource` element is defined as follows.

```
<!ELEMENT message-resources (description*, display-name*,
  icon*, message-resources-id, message-resources-class?, message*)>
```

As you can see, a `message-resources` element must have a `message-resources-id` subelement, and it may have an optional `message-resources-class` subelement and zero or more messages. The `message-resources-class` element, when present, represents the `MessageResources` implementation class.

A `message` element represents an individual localizable message and is analogous to a key/value pair in a properties file. The `message` element is defined as follows:

```
<!ELEMENT message (message-id, message-class?, summary*,
  detail*, severity?)>
```

The `message-id` is a unique key. The `summary` represents a value for a particular language. Therefore, if your application supports two languages, each message will have two `summary` elements.

For example, using a `ResourceBundle` object with `ZipCodeFormat` as the base name for supporting two languages, English and German, you would have two properties files: `ZipCodeFormat_en.properties` and `ZipCodeFormat_de.properties`. These properties files are shown in Listings 11-22 and 11-23.

Listing 11-22   *The ZipCodeFormat_en.properties File*

```
invalidLength=Length is not equal to 5
invalidFormat=A zip code must be all numbers
```

Listing 11-23   *The ZipCodeFormat_de.properties File*

```
invalidLength=Die Länge ist nicht gleich 5
invalidFormat= Eine Postleitzahl muß alle Zahlen sein
```

To use `MessageResources` instead of these properties files, include the `message-resources` element given in Listing 11-24 in your application configuration file:

Listing 11-24   *The message-resources Element in the Application Configuration File*

```
<message-resources>
  <message-resources-id>zipCodeFormat</message-resources-id>
  <message>
    <message-id>invalidLength</message-id>
    <summary xml:lang="en">Length is not equal to 5</summary>
    <summary xml:lang="de">Die Länge ist nicht gleich 5</summary>
```

```
    </message>
    <message>
      <message-id>invalidFormat</message-id>
      <summary xml:lang="en">
        A zip code must be all numbers
      </summary>
      <summary xml:lang="de">
        Eine Postleitzahl muß alle Zahlen sein
      </summary>
    </message>
</message-resources>
```

To retrieve a value from your class, you need to retrieve the `javax.faces.context` `.MessageResources` abstract class for the application. You obtain the `MessageResources` instance by using the following code:

```
ApplicationFactory appFactory = (ApplicationFactory)
  FactoryFinder.getFactory(FactoryFinder.APPLICATION_FACTORY);
Application application = appFactory.getApplication();
MessageResources mr =
  application.getMessageResources("ZipCodeFormat");
```

Once you have the `MessageResources` instance, you call its `getMessage` method to get the value for the specified message identifier (`key`). The user's locale will determine which language should be used. The `getMessage` method returns an instance of `javax` `.faces.application.Message` and has six overloads. The simplest overload has the following signature:

```
public abstract Message getMessage(FacesContext context,
  String messageId)
```

As an example, let's rewrite the custom validator in Chapter 9, but this time with localized messages. You will use the `message-resources` element in Listing 11-24 in your application configuration file.

In addition, you need to register your validator using the `validator` element in your application configuration file, as shown in Listing 11-25.

Listing 11-25   *The Validator Registration in the Application Configuration File*

```
<validator>
  <description>
    A validator for validating zip codes, with localized messages
  </description>
  <validator-id>ZipCodeValidator</validator-id>
  <validator-class>ch09.ZipCodeValidator</validator-class>
</validator>
```

This example uses the `TestingBean` class, shown in Listing 11-26, to store the value of the zip code.

Listing 11-26 *The TestingBean Class*

```
package ch11;
public class TestingBean {
  private String value;
  public String getValue() {
    return value;
  }
  public void setValue(String value) {
    this.value = value;
  }
}
```

The `TestingBean` is registered in the application configuration file using the `managed-bean` tag, as shown in Listing 11-27.

Listing 11-27 *The TestingBean Registration in the Application Configuration File*

```
<managed-bean>
  <managed-bean-name>testingBean</managed-bean-name>
  <managed-bean-class>ch11.TestingBean</managed-bean-class>
  <managed-bean-scope>session</managed-bean-scope>
</managed-bean>
```

Listing 11-28 presents the `validateZipCodeTest.jsp` page to test your validator.

Listing 11-28 *The validateZipCodeTest.jsp Page*

```
<%@ taglib uri="http://java.sun.com/jsf/html" prefix="h" %>
<%@ taglib uri="http://java.sun.com/jsf/core" prefix="f" %>
<html>
<head>
<title>Using ZipCodeValidator</title>
</head>
<body>
<f:use_faces>
<h:form  formName="myForm">
Your zip code:
  <h:input_text valueRef="TestingBean.value">
    <f:validator id="ZipCodeValidator" />
```

```
    </h:input_text>
<br>
<h:command_button commandName="submit" label="submit"/>
<br><hr>
<h:output_errors/>
<br>
</h:form>
</f:use_faces>
</body>
</html>
```

You can invoke the `validateZipCodeTest.jsp` page using the following URL:

`http://localhost:8080/JSFCh11/faces/validateZipCodeTest.jsp`

Figure 11-6 shows an error message displayed in English. The German version will look similar.

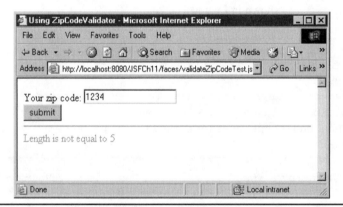

Figure 11-6   *An error message in English*

Summary

In this chapter, you learned what internationalization and localization are and how to support both in your JSF applications. You also learned about `ResourceBundle` and how to localize static and dynamic data. Finally, this chapter showed you how to localize messages in your JSF applications.

CHAPTER
12

Renderers

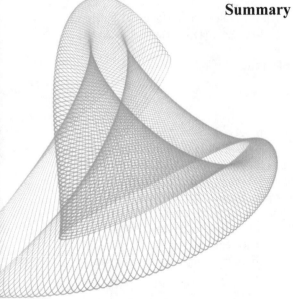

A very important step in the JSF request processing lifecycle is rendering the user interface (UI) component. This chapter will discuss component rendering in detail. This information is particularly important to JSF developers who want to write custom components (the subject of the next chapter).

First, we will cover how renderers work. Then you will be introduced to the renderers used for rendering JSF standard UI components. Finally, you will learn how to write a custom renderer and use it to render a standard component.

How Does Rendering Work?

In the JSF request processing lifecycle, there are two operations involved in the process of rendering a UI component: decoding and encoding. Decoding occurs during the Apply Request Values phase, when component values are decoded from the incoming request. Encoding occurs during the Render Response phase, and it involves generating output, such as HTML elements, for the client.

Direct Implementation versus Delegated Implementation

A UI component can choose to perform rendering itself or delegate rendering to an external renderer. A UI component that renders itself is said to apply the *direct implementation* programming model. A UI component that employs an external renderer uses the *delegated implementation* programming model.

A UI component tells the JSF implementation whether it wants to render itself or delegate rendering to an external renderer by using its `rendererType` property. If this property value is `null`, the UI component will render itself. Otherwise, it must assign a renderer name to its `rendererType` property to use delegated rendering. The renderer names are found in the JSF implementation's `RenderKit`, which is a collection of standard renderers. A renderer is represented by the `javax.faces.render.Renderer` class. All standard components delegate their rendering to external renderers.

Now, let's see what happens during the decoding and encoding operations.

Decoding and Encoding Operations

During the Apply Request Values phase of the request processing lifecycle, the JSF implementation calls the `decode` method of the root component in the component tree associated with the current request. Because the `decode` method in a UI component always calls the `decode` methods of its child components, if any, the `decode` methods in all components in the tree will be called during the Apply Request Values phase. If a UI component implements the delegated implementation programming model, in its `decode` method, it obtains the associated renderer and calls the renderer's `decode` method.

During the Render Response phase, the JSF implementation calls the `encodeBegin`, `encodeChildren`, and `encodeEnd` methods of the root of the component tree. Each of these methods of the root component calls the corresponding method in the child components; in effect, the encodeBegin, encodeChildren, and encodeEnd methods of each component in the component tree will be called. Again, in the delegated implementation programming model, these methods call the corresponding methods of the associated renderer.

Therefore, a component that performs its own rendering must provide implementations of its decode, encodeBegin, encodeChildren, and encodeEnd methods. On the other hand, if the rendering of a component is to be delegated to an external renderer, the component does not need to provide the implementation of those methods.

Using Standard Renderers

The JSF implementation provides renderers for rendering standard UI components. Each standard UI component has an external renderer, which is hard-coded in the component's class implementation. For the curious, this section presents an example that prints the component tree and the renderer type used by each component in the tree. Then we will cover the RenderKit class and its collection of renderers.

Getting Component Renderer Types

The example presented here is a modification of the first application presented in Chapter 2, the event listener and component tree example. It uses an ActionListener that displays the component tree of the requested page, but modifies it a bit to also display each UI component's renderer type. The ActionListener is shown in Listing 12-1.

Listing 12-1   *The ActionListener to Display Component Renderer Types*

```
package ch12;

import java.util.Iterator;
import javax.faces.component.UIComponent;
import javax.faces.context.FacesContext;
import javax.faces.event.ActionEvent;
import javax.faces.event.ActionListener;
import javax.faces.event.PhaseId;
import javax.faces.tree.Tree;

public class MyActionListener implements ActionListener {

  public PhaseId getPhaseId() {
    return PhaseId.APPLY_REQUEST_VALUES;
  }
```

```
public void processAction(ActionEvent event) {
  FacesContext facesContext = FacesContext.getCurrentInstance();
  Tree tree = facesContext.getTree();
  UIComponent root = tree.getRoot();
  System.out.println("----------- Component Tree -------------");
  navigateComponentTree(root, 0);
  System.out.println("----------------------------------------");
}

private void navigateComponentTree(UIComponent component,
    int level) {
  // indent
  for (int i=0; i<level; i++)
    System.out.print("  ");
  // print component id
  System.out.print(component.getComponentId() + ". ");
  // print renderer type
  System.out.println("(Renderer: " +
    component.getRendererType() + ")");
  // navigate children
  Iterator children = component.getChildren();
  while (children.hasNext()) {
    UIComponent child = (UIComponent) children.next();
    navigateComponentTree(child, level + 1);
  }
 }
}
```

The `ActionListener` in Listing 12-1 is to be registered with a `UICommand` component. When the `UICommand` component is clicked, the `processAction` method of the `ActionListener` will be called. The `processAction` method acquires the root of the component tree of the current request from the `FacesContext` instance and passes it to the `navigateComponentTree` method. The `navigateComponentTree` is called recursively, as discussed in Chapter 2. For each component, the `navigateComponentTree` method prints the component's identifier and renderer type:

```
System.out.print(component.getComponentId() + ". ");
// print renderer type
System.out.println("(Renderer: " + component.getRendererType() + ")");
```

Now, you need a JSP page containing various UI components plus a button to submit the form. Listing 12-2 shows the `displayRenderer.jsp` page that you can use to find out the renderer types of various components.

Listing 12-2 *The displayRenderer.jsp Page*

```jsp
<%@ taglib uri="http://java.sun.com/jsf/html" prefix="h" %>
<%@ taglib uri="http://java.sun.com/jsf/core" prefix="f" %>
<html>
<head>
<title>Display Renderer on Console</title>
</head>
<body>
<f:use_faces>
<h:form id="myForm" formName="addForm" >
  <h:input_number id="input_number" value="10"/>
  <br/>
  <h:input_text id="input_text"/>
  <br/>
  <h:output_number id="output_number"/>
  <br/>
  <h:output_text id="output_text"/>
  <br/>
  <h:selectmany_menu id="selectmany_menu" size="3">
    <h:selectitem itemValue="Australia" itemLabel="Australia"/>
  </h:selectmany_menu>
  <br/>
  <h:selectone_listbox id="selectone_listbox">
    <h:selectitem itemValue="Australia" itemLabel="Australia"/>
  </h:selectone_listbox>
  <br/>
  <h:panel_grid id="panel_grid" columns="2"/>
  <br/>
  <h:command_button id="submitButton"
    label="Display Tree and Renderer" commandName="display" >
    <f:action_listener type="ch12.MyActionListener" />
  </h:command_button>
</h:form>
</f:use_faces>
</body>
</html>
```

The `displayRenderer.jsp` page uses various components with names identical to the tag representing the component. This is to make it easier to recognize the component type later.

Note also that your application must have the usual deployment descriptor and the library files. To run the application, direct your browser to the following URL:

```
http://localhost:8080/JSFCh12/faces/displayRenderer.jsp
```

Figure 12-1 shows what you will see in your browser.

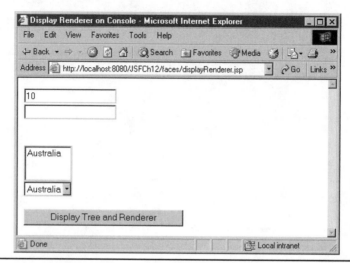

Figure 12-1   *Printing renderer types*

Now, simply click the Display Tree and Renderer button. On your console that runs the Web container, you will see the following result.

```
----------- Component Tree -------------
null. (Renderer: null)
  myForm. (Renderer: Form)
    input_number. (Renderer: Number)
    input_text. (Renderer: Text)
    output_number. (Renderer: Number)
    output_text. (Renderer: Text)
    selectmany_menu. (Renderer: Menu)
      null. (Renderer: null)
    selectone_listbox. (Renderer: Listbox)
      null. (Renderer: null)
    panel_grid. (Renderer: Grid)
    submitButton. (Renderer: Button)
---------------------------------------
```

Now, you know the type of the renderer associated with each standard UI component. Note that the renderer type is the name that identifies the renderer in the `RenderKit` class in the JSF implementation.

Exploring RenderKit

As mentioned previously, each standard UI component is associated with an external renderer. The JSF implementation has a `RenderKit` that contains the collection of renderers responsible for rendering standard UI components.

You can obtain a `RenderKit` instance by first acquiring the `javax.faces.render` `.RenderKitFactory` object, using the following code:

```
RenderKitFactory factory = (RenderKitFactory)
  FactoryFinder.getFactory(FactoryFinder.RENDER_KIT_FACTORY);
```

Then you call the `getRenderKit` method of the `RenderKitFactory` object:

```
RenderKit renderKit = factory.getRenderKit(renderKitId);
```

where *renderKitId* is the identifier of `RenderKit`. For the default `RenderKit` that a JSF implementation must provide, *renderKitId* is a `String` constant denoted by `RenderKitFactory.DEFAULT_RENDER_KIT`.

You can get a renderer by calling the `getRenderer` method of the `RenderKit` object, passing the renderer type. For example, to obtain the renderer of type `Number`, you use the following code:

```
Renderer renderer = renderKit.getRenderer("Number");
```

As you can see from the output of the example in the previous section, the renderer type for a `Form` component is `Form`. Tables 12-1 through 12-6 list the other renderers provided in the standard `RenderKit`, organized by the UI component they render. For each renderer, the data type, render-dependent attributes, decode behavior, and encode behavior are given. (The UI components are discussed in Chapters 5 and 6.)

NOTE:

The `UICommand` component can be rendered either by the `Button` or `Hyperlink` renderers. With `Button`, the `UICommand` is rendered as either an HTML `<input type="submit">` or `<input type="reset">`. With `Hyperlink`, the `UICommand` is rendered as the `<a>` element.

Render Type	Data Type	Render-Dependent Attribute	Decode Behavior	Encode Behavior
Button	String	label, type	Submit FormEvent to application.	Render `<input>` with the specified type (submit, reset). The button text is specified by the `label` attribute.
Button	String	key, bundle, type	Submit FormEvent to application.	Render `<input>` with the specified type (submit, reset). The button text is localized, based on the `key` and `bundle` attributes.
Hyperlink	String	None	Submit CommandEvent to application.	Render `<a>` that generates a hyperlink back to the tree identifier of the tree, so that a command event can be queued.
Hyperlink	String	href		Render `<a>` that links to the specified URL. Nested `UIParameter` components can be used to configure request parameters that will be added to the specified URL. URL rewriting will be performed to maintain session state when cookies are not being used.

Table 12-1   *The Renderer Types for the UICommand Component*

Render Type	Data Type	Render-Dependent Attribute	Encode Behavior
Image	String		Render <img> with a src attribute obtained from the current value of the underlying component.
Image		key, bundle	Render <img>with a src attribute localized from ResourceBundle. If no cookie is being used to maintain session state, URL rewriting will be performed.

Table 12-2 *Renderer Types for UIGraphic*

Note that UIGraphic does not have a decode behavior.

Render Type	Data Type	Render-Dependent Attribute	Decode Behavior	Encode Behavior
Date	Date, long	dateStyle, timezone	Get DateFormat instance, parse text input, convert as necessary, and store.	Get current value, convert to Date, create localized DateFormat instance for the specified dateStyle, set time zone, and render formatted result as <input type="text">.
DateTime	Date, long	formatPattern, timezone	Get DateFormat instance, parse text input, convert as necessary, and store.	Get current value, convert to Date, create localized SimpleDateFormat based on formatPattern, set time zone if it is specified, and render formatted result as <input>.
DateTime	Date, long	dateStyle, timeStyle, timezone	Get DateFormat instance, parse text input, convert as necessary, and store.	Get current value, convert to Date, create localized DateFormat date/time instance, set time zone if it's specified, and render formatted result as <input>.
Hidden	Any	converter	Convert as necessary and store.	Get current value, convert to String, and render as <input type=hidden>.
Number	Numeric	formatPattern	Get NumberFormat instance, parse text input, convert as necessary, and store.	Get current value, convert to appropriate numeric value, create localized NumberFormat instance based on numberStyle, and render formatted result as <input type=text>.
Number	Numeric	numberStyle	Get NumberFormat instance, parse text input, convert as necessary, and store.	Get current value, convert to appropriate numeric value, create localized NumberFormat instance based on numberStyle, and render formatted result as <input type=text>.
Secret	Any	converter, redisplay	Convert as necessary and store.	Get current value, convert to String, and render as <input type=password>. If the redisplay attribute is true, redisplay the current value.

Table 12-3 *Renderer Types for UIInput*

Render Type	Data Type	Render-Dependent Attribute	Decode Behavior	Encode Behavior
Text	Any	converter	Convert as necessary and store.	Get current value, convert to String, and render as `<input type=text>`.
Textarea	Any	converter	Convert as necessary and store.	Get current value, convert to String, and render as `<textarea>`.

Table 12-3 *Renderer Types for UIInput* (continued)

Note that UIOutput does not have a decode behavior.

Render Type	Data Type	Render-Dependent Attribute	Encode Behavior
Date	Date, long	dateStyle, timezone	Get current value, convert to Date, create localized DateFormat instance for the specified dateStyle, set time zone if it is specified, and render formatted result.
DateTime	Date, long	formatPattern, timezone	Get current value, convert to Date, create localized SimpleDateFormat instance for the specified formatPattern, set time zone if it is specified, and render formatted result.
DateTime	Date, long	dateStyle, timeStyle	Get current value, convert to Date, create localized DateFormat instance for the specified dateStyle, set time zone if it is specified, and render formatted result.
Errors	None	For	Render the collection of error messages associated with the specified client identifier, or the global errors not associated with any component (if for is an empty string), or all errors (if for is not specified).
Label	None	For	Render the nested components surrounded by an HTML `<label>` element with the specified for attribute.
Message	Any	Converter	Get current value, convert to String, treat as a MessageFormat pattern (nested UIParameter components may be used to provide values for parameter substitution), and render formatted result.
Message	Any	converter, key, bundle	Get localized resource from ResourceBundle, treat as a MessageFormat pattern (nested UIParameter components may be used to provide values for parameter substitution), and render formatted result.
Number	Numeric	formatPattern	Get current value, convert to appropriate numeric value, create localized NumberFormat instance based on numberStyle, and render formatted result.
Number	Numeric	numberStyle	Get current value, convert to appropriate numeric value, create localized NumberFormat instance based on numberStyle, and render formatted result.

Table 12-4 *Renderer Types for UIOutput*

Render Type	Data Type	Render-Dependent Attribute	Encode Behavior
Text	Any	Converter	Get current value, convert to `String`, and render literally.
Time	`Date`, `long`	`timeStyle`, `timezone`	Get current value, convert to `Date`, create localized `DateFormat` instance for the specified `timeStyle`, set time zone if it is specified, and render formatted result.

Table 12-4   *Renderer Types for UIOutput* (continued)

Note that UIPanel does not have decode behavior.

Render Type	Data Type	Render-Dependent Attribute	Encode Behavior
Data	`array`, `Collection`, `Map`	`Var`	Nested child components represent the template for a row to be generated for each element of a collection represented by the current value of this component. Each element of the collection will be exposed as a request attribute named by var, so that model reference expressions in the template components can access the values for the current element. There should be one child component per column to be created.
Grid	None	`columnClasses`, `columns`, `footerClass`, `headerClass`, `rowClasses`	Render `<table>` from the child components, based on the following: A. If headerClass is present, the first child is rendered as a header row, formatted according to this CSS style class; B. Each intervening child is rendered in a separate table data element, with a new row started each columns children; C. If footerClass is present, the last child is rendered as a footer row across all the columns, formatting according to this CSS style class.
Group	None		Render the child components as specified by their own renderer type settings. This renderer exists to allow the creation of arbitrary groups where a parent component expects to see a single child.
List	None	`columnClasses`, `footerClass`, `headerClass`, `rowClasses`	Render a `<table>` from the child components, based on the following: A. If headerClass is present, the first child should be a UIPanel with a renderer type of Group, representing the column headers for the table to be rendered; B. Next children should be zero or more UIPanel components with a renderer type of Data that represent the data collection(s) to be iterated over, and whose children represent a template for each row to be rendered; C. If footerClass is present, the last child should be a UIPanel with a renderer type of Group, representing the column footers for the table to be rendered.

Table 12-5   *Renderer Types for UIPanel*

Render Type	Data Type	Render-Dependent Attribute	Decode Behavior	Encode Behavior
UISelectBoolean Component				
`Checkbox`	`boolean`		Convert as necessary and store.	Get current value, convert to `boolean`, and render as `<input type=checkbox>`.
UISelectMany Component				
`Checkbox`	`String`	`layout`	Convert as necessary and store.	Get current value, convert to `String`, get available items from nested `UISelectItem` and `UISelectItems` components, and render as a series of `<input type=checkbox>` elements, laid out according to the `layout` attribute (`PAGE_DIRECTION` or `LINE_DIRECTION`).
`Listbox`	`String[]`		Convert as necessary and store.	Get current value(s), convert to `String[]`, get available items from nested `UISelectItem` and `UISelectItems` components, and render as `<select>` that displays all possible values.
`Menu`	`String[]`	`size`	Convert as necessary and store.	Get current value(s), convert to `String[]`, get available items from nested `UISelectItem` and `UISelectItems` components, and render as `<select>` element that displays the number of elements specified by the `size` attribute.
UISelectOne Component				
`Listbox`	`String`		Convert as necessary and store.	Get current value, convert to `String`, get available items from nested `UISelectItem` and `UISelectItems` components, and render as `<select>` that displays all possible values.
`Menu`	`String`	`size`	Convert as necessary and store.	Get current value, convert to `String`, get available items from nested `UISelectItem` and `UISelectItems` components, and render as `<select>` that displays the number of elements specified by the `size` attribute.
`Radio`	`String`	`layout`	Convert as necessary and store.	Get current value, convert to `String`, get available items from nested `UISelectItem` and `UISelectItems` components, and render as a series of radio buttons, laid out according to the `layout` attribute (`PAGE_DIRECTION` or `LINE_DIRECTION`).

Table 12-6   *Renderer Types for UISelectBoolean, UISelectMany, and UISelectOne Components*

Writing a Custom Renderer

To create a custom renderer, you must extend the `javax.faces.render.Renderer` abstract class. Here, we will first take a look at the `Renderer` class, and then create a sample custom renderer for a standard UI component. (Chapter 13 covers the process of writing a custom renderer for a custom UI component.)

Examining the Renderer Class

The `Renderer` class has the `decode`, `encodeBegin`, `encodeChildren`, `encodeEnd`, and `getClientId` methods. In your custom renderer, you must provide implementations for any of these methods that are required by the component. Each of these methods is discussed in the following sections.

The decode Method

The `decode` method will be called during the Apply Request Values phase of the request processing lifecycle. In this method, a renderer decodes the component's local value from the incoming request. The signature of this method is as follows:

```
public abstract void decode(FacesContext context,
  UIComponent component)    throws java.io.IOException
```

The JSF implementation passes the `FacesContext` instance associated with the current request and the `UIComponent` that needs to be rendered. The implementation of the `decode` method in a renderer accesses the `FacesContext` instance to obtain the new local value for the component, performing the necessary conversion. If the conversion is successful, the `decode` method saves the new local value of this component by passing it to the `UIComponent`'s `setValue` method and sets its `valid` property to `true`.If the conversion fails, the `decode` method does the following:

▶ Saves the state information inside the component so that the encoding process can reproduce the previous input to be redisplayed

▶ Adds an error message by instantiating a `Message` object and adding it to the `FacesContext` instance by calling the `FacesContext`'s `addMessage` method

▶ Sets the valid property of the component to `false`

The `decode` method may also queue events for later processing by any registered event listener. Queuing events is accomplished by calling the `addFacesEvent` method on the `FacesContext` instance.

The encodeBegin Method

The `encodeBegin` method is called during the Render Response phase of the request processing lifecycle. The method signature is as follows:

```
public abstract void encodeBegin(FacesContext context,
  UIComponent component)    throws java.io.IOException
```

The JSF implementation passes the `FacesContext` instance associated with the current request and the `UIComponent` that needs to be rendered.

The implementation of this method renders the beginning of the current state of the specified `UIComponent` to the output stream or writer associated with the response being created. If the conversion performed in the `decode` method failed, the `encodeBegin` method should retrieve the previous input stored in the `UIComponent` instance and redisplay it to the user. If the conversion was successful, the value to be displayed is retrieved from the `UIComponent` by calling the `currentValue` method on the component.

The encodeChildren Method

The `encodeChildren` method is called during the Render Response phase of the request processing lifecycle. The method signature is as follows:

```
public abstract void encodeChildren(FacesContext context,
  UIComponent component)    throws java.io.IOException
```

The JSF implementation passes the `FacesContext` instance associated with the current request and the `UIComponent` that needs to be rendered.

The implementation of the `encodeChildren` method renders the child components of the specified `UIComponent`, following the rules described for the `encodeBegin` method. The method will be called only if the `rendersChildren` property of the component is `true`.

The encodeEnd Method

The `encodeEnd` method is called during the Render Response phase of the request processing lifecycle. The method signature is as follows:

```
public abstract void encodeEnd(FacesContext context,
  UIComponent component)    throws java.io.IOException
```

The JSF implementation passes the `FacesContext` instance associated with the current request and the `UIComponent` that needs to be rendered.

The `encodeEnd` method renders the ending of the current state of the specified `UIComponent`, following the rules described for the `encodeBegin` method.

The getClientId Method

The `getClientId` method generates and returns a new client identifier for the component being rendered. The signature of this method is as follows:

```
public abstract String getClientId(FacesContext context,
  UIComponent component)
```

The JSF implementation passes the `FacesContext` instance associated with the current request and the `UIComponent` that needs to be rendered.

Creating a Custom Renderer

As noted earlier, a custom renderer must extend the `javax.faces.render.Renderer` class. Once you have a custom renderer class, you need to enable the use of `UIOutput` with your renderer in a JSP page, via a custom tag. Having a custom tag means you need a tag handler and a tag library descriptor (TLD) file, too. Finally, to use the renderer, you need to register the renderer in your application configuration file.

To summarize, here are the steps for writing a custom renderer to be used with a standard UI component:

1. Write a renderer class, extending `javax.faces.render.Renderer`.
2. Write a tag handler for handling the custom tag to represent the `UIOutput` with your custom renderer.
3. Write a TLD.

To demonstrate creating a custom renderer, we will go through the steps in writing a custom renderer for the `UIOutput` component. The renderer in this example is called `BoldOutputRenderer`, and it displays the value of the `UIOutput` in bold. The HTML tags rendered are as follows:

```
<b>[value]</b>
```

where `[value]` represents the value of the `UIOutput` component.

Writing the Renderer Class

The first step to writing a custom renderer is to extend the `javax.faces.render.Renderer` class. The class for our custom renderer is shown in Listing 12-3. It's called `BoldOutputRenderer`.

Listing 12-3   *The BoldOutputRenderer Class*

```
package ch12;

import java.io.IOException;
import javax.faces.component.UIComponent;
import javax.faces.component.UIOutput;
import javax.faces.context.FacesContext;
import javax.faces.context.ResponseWriter;
import javax.faces.render.Renderer;

public class BoldOutputRenderer extends Renderer {

  public void decode(FacesContext context, UIComponent component)
    throws IOException {
  }
```

```
public void encodeBegin(FacesContext context,
    UIComponent component)      throws IOException {
  if (context == null)
    throw new NullPointerException("FacesContext null");
  if (!component.isRendered())
    return;
  ResponseWriter writer = context.getResponseWriter();
  Object currentValue =
    ((UIOutput) component).currentValue(context);
  writer.write("<b>");
  if(currentValue != null)
    writer.write(currentValue.toString());
  writer.write("</b>");
}

public void encodeEnd(FacesContext context, UIComponent component)
  throws IOException {
}
public void encodeChildren(FacesContext context,
    UIComponent component)      throws IOException {
}
public String getClientId(FacesContext context,
    UIComponent component) {
  return null;
}
}
```

For this example, we are using a very simple `BoldOutputRenderer` class. The only implementation it has is for the `encodeBegin` method. The `UIOutput` component does not need the `decode` method, because it does not accept user input. It does not need the `encodeChildren` method either, because a `UIOutput` component never has children. The `encodeEnd` method is not implemented because the `encodeBegin` handles all of the encoding. After making sure that the `FacesContext` is not `null` and the component's `isRendered` method returns `true`, the `encodeBegin` method obtains the `ResponseWriter` object from the `FacesContext` instance. You need the `ResponseWriter` object to write the output to the client.

```
ResponseWriter writer = context.getResponseWriter();
```

Then you need to get the value of the `UIOutput`. You do this by calling the `currentValue` method of the `UIOutput` class.

```
Object currentValue = ((UIOutput) component).currentValue(context);
```

Next, you can start writing to the `ResponseWriter` object by calling its `write` method.

```
writer.write("<b>");
if(currentValue != null)
  writer.write(currentValue.toString());
writer.write("</b>");
```

Writing the Tag Handler

To render the `UIOutput` component using your custom renderer, you need to create a special custom tag for this purpose. The custom tag will need a tag handler. The tag handler for a custom renderer must extend the `javax.faces.webapp.UIComponentTag` class. The tag handler for this example, the `BoldOutputTag` class, is shown in Listing 12-4.

Listing 12-4   *The BoldOutputTag Class*

```
package ch12;

import javax.faces.webapp.UIComponentTag;
import javax.faces.component.UIComponent;
import javax.faces.component.UIOutput;

public class BoldOutputTag extends UIComponentTag {

  private String value;
  private String valueRef;

  public String getRendererType() {
    return "BoldOutputRenderer";
  }
  public String getComponentType() {
    return "BoldOutput";
  }
  public String getValue() {
    return value;
  }
  public void setValue(String value) {
    this.value = value;
  }

  public String getValueRef() {
    return valueRef;
  }
  public void setValueRef(String valueRef) {
```

```
    this.valueRef = valueRef;
  }

  protected void overrideProperties(UIComponent component) {
    super.overrideProperties(component);
    UIOutput outputComponent = (UIOutput) component;
    if(valueRef != null)
      outputComponent.setValueRef(valueRef);
    if (outputComponent.getValue()==null)
      outputComponent.setValue(getValue());
  }
}
```

The most important point to note is that your tag handler must provide the implementations for the getRendererType and getComponentType methods.

```
public String getRendererType() {
  return "BoldOutputRenderer";
}
public String getComponentType() {
  return "BoldOutput";
}
```

The getRendererType method returns the renderer type to be used with the component represented by the custom tag in JSP pages. This method must return a name used to refer to the custom renderer. To use this renderer, you must have the render-kit element in your application configuration file. The getComponentType method returns a value that identifies the UIOutput component. Using this component requires a component element in your application configuration file to identify the component type and class. Listing 12-6 later in this chapter shows the application configuration file entries that are necessary for using our custom renderer in an application.

The tag handler also has two properties: value and valueRef. The value property allows you to initialize the value for the UIOutput component. The valueRef property is for binding the component to a model object. For these properties, you need the overrideProperties method, which passes the attributes in the custom tag to the component class. This method, and other details of the javax.faces.webapp.UIComponentTag class, will be discussed in Chapter 13.

Writing the Tag Library Descriptor (TLD)

The TLD for the custom renderer is named customRenderer.tld. It defines the bold_output tag mapped to the ch12.BoldOutputTag tag handler. It also defines the set of attributes that can be used with the bold_output tag. The customRenderer.tld file is shown in Listing 12-5.

Listing 12-5 *The customRenderer.tld File*

```xml
<?xml version="1.0" encoding="ISO-8859-1" ?>
<!DOCTYPE taglib
  PUBLIC "-//Sun Microsystems, Inc.//DTD JSP Tag Library 1.2//EN"
  "http://java.sun.com/dtd/web-jsptaglibrary_1_2.dtd">

<taglib>
  <tlib-version>0.03</tlib-version>
  <jsp-version>1.2</jsp-version>
  <short-name>Using Custom Renderer</short-name>
  <tag>
    <name>bold_output</name>
    <tag-class>ch12.BoldOutputTag</tag-class>
    <attribute>
      <name>id</name>
      <required>false</required>
      <rtexprvalue>false</rtexprvalue>
    </attribute>
    <attribute>
      <name>value</name>
      <required>false</required>
      <rtexprvalue>false</rtexprvalue>
    </attribute>
    <attribute>
      <name>valueRef</name>
      <required>false</required>
      <rtexprvalue>false</rtexprvalue>
    </attribute>
  </tag>
</taglib>
```

Now that you have created a custom renderer, let's see how to use it in an application.

Using the Custom Renderer

To use a custom renderer in application, you need to register the component and `render-kit` in your application configuration file. Then you can create the JSP page that uses the component with the custom renderer.

Registering a Custom Renderer in the Application Configuration File

Listing 12-6 shows the application configuration file entries for registering our sample custom renderer.

Listing 12-6   *Registering the Renderer in the Application Configuration File*

```xml
<?xml version="1.0"?>
<!DOCTYPE faces-config PUBLIC
   "-//Sun Microsystems, Inc.//DTD JavaServer Faces Config 1.0//EN"
   "http://java.sun.com/dtd/web-facesconfig_1_0.dtd">

<faces-config>
   <!-- registering the custom component BoldOutput -->
   <component>
     <component-type>BoldOutput</component-type>
     <component-class>javax.faces.component.UIOutput</component-class>
   </component>

   <!-- registering the renderer PositiveIntegerRenderer -->
   <render-kit>
     <renderer>
       <renderer-type>BoldOutputRenderer</renderer-type>
       <renderer-class>ch12.BoldOutputRenderer</renderer-class>
     </renderer>
   </render-kit>
</faces-config>
```

In your application configuration file, you register a new component type,
`BoldOutput`, which identifies the `javax.faces.component.UIOutput` class.
You also define a new renderer called `BoldOutputRenderer`, which identifies the
`ch12.BoldOutputRenderer` class. Notice that the `renderer-class` element
contains the fully qualified name of the renderer implementation class.

Creating the JSP Page

In an application, the custom tag `bold_output` represents the `UIOutput`
component used with our sample custom renderer. The application has a JSP page
called `boldOutputTest.jsp`, which uses this tag, as shown in Listing 12-7.

Listing 12-7   *The boldOutputTest.jsp Page*

```jsp
<%@ taglib uri="http://java.sun.com/jsf/html" prefix="h" %>
<%@ taglib uri="http://java.sun.com/jsf/core" prefix="f" %>
<%@ taglib uri="/WEB-INF/customRenderer.tld" prefix="d" %>
<html>
<head>
<title>Use Custom Renderer</title>
</head>
<body>
```

```
<f:use_faces>
<h:form id="myForm" formName="addForm" >
  <h:output_text value="normal text"/>
  <br/>
<d:bold_output value="bold text"/>
  <br/>
  <h:command_button label="Submit" commandName="submit"/>
</h:form>
</f:use_faces>
</body>
</html>
```

First, notice that you need to include the `customRenderer.tld` file in the JSP page to use the `bold_output` tag.

```
<%@ taglib uri="/WEB-INF/customRenderer.tld" prefix="d" %>
```

Then you use the `bold_output` tag as follows in the JSP page.

```
<d:bold_output value="bold text"/>
```

The `bold_output` tag will be handled by the `ch12.BoldOutputTag` tag handler, as defined in the TLD in Listing 12-5.

```
<tag>
  <name>bold_output</name>
  <tag-class>ch12.BoldOutputTag</tag-class>
  ...
```

The `getComponentType` method of the `BoldOutputTag` class (shown in Listing 12-4) returns `BoldOutput`, the name you registered to identify `javax.faces.component.UIOutput` in the application configuration file. Therefore, the `bold_output` custom tag in a JSP page is associated with the component identified by `BoldOutput`, which is `javax.faces.component.UIOutput`.

The renderer type for the `UIOutput` component represented by the `bold_output` element is obtained from the `getRendererType` method of the `BoldOutputTag` class, which returns `BoldOutputRenderer`. From the following element in the application configuration, the JSF implementation knows that the renderer to render the `UIOutput` component represented by a `bold_output` element is an instance of the `ch12.BoldOutputRenderer` class:

```
<render-kit>
  <renderer>
    <renderer-type>BoldOutputRenderer</renderer-type>
    <renderer-class>ch12.BoldOutputRenderer</renderer-class>
  </renderer>
</render-kit>
```

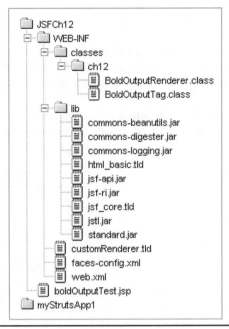

Figure 12-2 *The directory structure for the application with a custom renderer*

Running the Application with the Custom Renderer

Before running the application, make sure that you have all the necessary parts for the JSF application. Figure 12-2 shows the directory structure for this application.

To run the application, direct your browser to the following URL:

```
http://localhost:8080/JSFCh12/faces/boldOutputTest.jsp
```

The result in your browser will look similar to Figure 12-3. You can see that the output from the `bold_output` tag is printed in bold.

Figure 12-3 *Using the custom renderer*

Summary

This chapter explained how renderers work and the two processes involved in rendering: decoding and encoding. It also listed all of the renderers used with standard UI components. The last section of this chapter provided step-by-step instructions for writing and using custom renderers.

The next chapter covers custom components. You will learn how to write a custom component that performs its own rendering, as well as custom components that use external renderers.

Custom User Interface Components

IN THIS CHAPTER:

T
he JSF implementation includes a number of UI components that are sufficient for most applications. However, some applications may require nonstandard UI components. If necessary, you can write your own custom components for your JSF applications. In the future, it's probable that many third-party vendors will provide custom components, and it's easy to see how making JSF custom components could grow into a separate industry. In many cases, it's easier and cheaper to purchase custom components from third-party vendors than it is to write one yourself. However, if the component you need is not available in the market, you should be ready to write it yourself as a viable option.

This chapter explains the techniques for writing your own custom components and presents four sample custom components:

▶ `UIPositiveNumber` is an input component that can accept a positive number.

▶ `UIPositiveInteger` is a modification of `UIPositiveNumber` with a custom renderer.

▶ `UICalendar` is a date selector with a custom renderer.

▶ `FlexibleHyperlink` is a hyperlink that can have a dynamic value for its label.

But first, you need to decide whether you really need a custom component. As explained in the first section of this chapter, a custom renderer may be a better choice.

Custom Component or Custom Renderer?

Before you write a custom component, you should first consider whether you need a new component or just a custom renderer that you can plug into an existing component. (Custom renderers are discussed in Chapter 12.) Keep in mind that writing a custom component could be a lengthy process, involving extensive coding and testing.

Basically, the justification for writing a new component is that if the new component will provide functionality not available in existing components, then it's worth the effort. Here are some requirements that might prompt you to write a new component:

▶ You need a composite component that aggregates many existing components, such as a calendar that consists of three select boxes for choosing the date, month, and year.

▶ You want to use a specific event. For example, you may need a number-input box that triggers a `ValueChangedEvent` *only* if the current value is greater than the previous value.

▶ You need a component that supports the rendering to nonbrowser clients, such as a phone.

You do not need a custom component if you just want to render the component differently. For example, if you have a calendar component that takes input in the date-month-year order, and you want it to be in the month-date-year order, all you need is a custom renderer.

Similarly, you do not need a custom component if you just want to validate or convert a component's data to a type not supported by its renderer. In those cases, you need a custom validator (covered in Chapter 9) or a custom converter (covered in Chapter 10).

Writing a Custom Component

When writing a custom component, you need to consider the following:

▶ The behavior of your custom component. This affects the choice of the parent class your component needs to extend.

▶ Whether your custom component will need a separate renderer or if it should do the rendering itself.

▶ The type of events that can be triggered by the component. Any event triggered by your custom component must be queued to the `FacesContext`.

Understanding the steps to writing a custom component will be easier if you keep in mind how you use the standard components, so let's have a brief review of standard components first.

A UI component extends the `javax.faces.component.UIComponentBase` class. This class provides the basic functionality of a UI component and implements the required `javax.faces.component.UIComponent` interface.

NOTE

A custom component must implement the `javax.faces.component.UIComponent` interface. However, rather than implementing this interface directly, it is recommended that you extend the `javax.faces.component.UIComponentBase` class, so that any future changes to the `UIComponent` interface will have minimum impact on your custom components. `UIComponentBase` implements `UIComponent` and provides default implementations for its methods.

The JSF implementation calls several methods of the `UIComponent` interface during the component's lifetime. For example, during the Apply Request Values phase of the request processing lifecycle, the JSF implementation calls the `processDecodes` method of the root component in the component tree. The `processDecodes` method in a component will call the `processDecodes` method in all of its child components, as well as the `decode` method in the component itself.

Deciding Which Class to Extend

You should extend the class that provides the closest functionality to the new class. If your custom component is used for receiving input from the user, it is appropriate to inherit the `javax.faces.component.UIInput` class, because `UIInput` provides the basic functionality for an input component. For example, if you want an input box that can take a positive number, extending `javax.faces.component.UIInput` is the best choice.

If your component will be used only for displaying a value and not for obtaining user input, extending the `javax.faces.component.UIOutput` class is a better choice, because `UIOutput` is simpler, and `UIOutput` is the parent class of `UIInput`. For example, if you want a component that can display different icons for different file types, you would need to inherit `javax.faces.component.UIOutput`.

If you want a list box that submits its containing form every time its value changes, your best option would be to subclass `javax.faces.component.UISelectOne` or `javax.faces.component.UISelectMany`.

If your custom component will be an entirely different component, you should extend the `javax.faces.component.UIComponentBase` class, the convenience base class for all UI components.

Deciding How to Handle Rendering

Next, you need to decide if your custom component will perform the rendering itself. In Chapter 12, we discussed the rendering process of a component, which includes the decoding of user input into the component's state and the encoding of the component into a format that the JSF client understands. When using JSF in a Web application, encoding translates the component's internal state into HTML tags.

If your component will do its own rendering, you will need to provide implementations for the `decode`, `encodeBegin`, and `encodeEnd` methods of the `UIComponent` interface. If it will not perform the rendering, you need to write an external renderer for your component.

Using a Custom Component in a JSP Page

The next step is to figure out how your custom component can be used in a JSP page and how you can pass attribute values to the component. As you have learned, you use custom tags and tag handlers for this purpose. For example, here is the calendar tag with a "d" prefix that represents a custom component called `UICalendar`:

```
<%@ taglib uri="/WEB-INF/customComponents.tld" prefix="d" %>
...
<d:calendar/>
```

The first line is the `taglib` directive that shows the `prefix` and the `uri` of the tag library descriptor (TLD).

In the TLD, you describe the tag for your custom component, any attributes that can be passed in to the component, and the tag handler that handles the tag in the JSP page and passes values to the UI component. The tag handler for this purpose must extend the `javax.faces.webapp.UIComponentTag` abstract class. You must implement the following methods of the `UIComponentTag` class for your custom component to function:

▶ `getRendererType` This method should return `null` if your component is to perform its own rendering. Alternatively, if your component will use an external renderer, it should return the type of the external renderer.

▶ `getComponentType`   This method should return the type of the custom component.

▶ `overrideProperties`   This method overrides properties of the specified component if the corresponding properties of this tag handler were explicitly set and the corresponding attribute of the component is not set.

You'll see the use of the `UIComponentTag` class in the custom components built in this chapter.

Creating the TestingBean for Testing Custom Components

For the examples in this chapter, we will use the `TestingBean` shown in Listing 13-1. You need to bind the custom UI components to this bean to be able to see them work.

Listing 13-1   *The TestingBean Class*

```
package ch13;
import java.util.Date;

public class TestingBean {
  private int quantity;
  private float price;
  private Date today;
  private String value = "Click here";

  public int getQuantity() {
    return quantity;
  }
  public void setQuantity(int quantity) {
    this.quantity = quantity;
  }
  public float getPrice() {
    return price;
  }
  public void setPrice(float price) {
    this.price = price;
  }
  public Date getToday() {
    return today; //new Date(System.currentTimeMillis());
  }
  public void setToday (Date today) {
    this.today = today;
  }
  public String getValue() {
```

```
      return value;
    }
    public void setValue(String value) {
      this.value = value;
    }
}
```

The `TestingBean` is registered in the application configuration file using the `managed-bean` tag, as shown in Listing 13-2.

Listing 13-2   *The TestingBean Registration in the Application Configuration File*

```
<managed-bean>
  <managed-bean-name>testingBean</managed-bean-name>
  <managed-bean-class>ch13.TestingBean</managed-bean-class>
  <managed-bean-scope>session</managed-bean-scope>
</managed-bean>
```

Creating an Input Component for Positive Numbers

Our first example of a custom component, `UIPositiveNumber`, is an input component that can accept a positive number. In the browser, the `UIPositiveNumber` component is rendered as `<input type=text>`. It does the rendering itself, so you must provide the implementations of the `decode`, `encodeBegin`, and `encodeEnd` methods.

There are two classes that you must write: the class representing the component and the component tag handler that enables the component to be used from a JSP page as a custom tag action. Both of these classes are members of the `ch13.positivenumber` package.

Writing the UIPositiveNumber Class

The `UIPositiveNumber` class, shown in Listing 13-3, extends the `javax.faces.component.UIInput` class. The `UIInput` component needs to maintain the previous value entered by the user, so that it can emit a `ValueChangedEvent` if the new value is different from the previous value. You are responsible for making sure that the `UIInput` component maintains its previous value. You can do this by using the `setPrevious` method of the `UIInput` class.

Listing 13-3   *The UIPositiveNumber Class*

```
package ch13.positivenumber;
import java.io.IOException;
import java.util.Map;
```

```java
import javax.faces.application.Message;
import javax.faces.application.MessageImpl;
import javax.faces.component.UIInput;
import javax.faces.context.FacesContext;
import javax.faces.context.ResponseWriter;

public class UIPositiveNumber extends UIInput {

  public void decode(FacesContext context) throws IOException {
    if(context == null)
      throw new NullPointerException("FacesContext null.");
    setPrevious(currentValue(context));
    String clientId = getClientId(context);
    Map requestMap =
      context.getExternalContext().getRequestParameterMap();
    String newValue = (String) requestMap.get(clientId);
    try {
      // check if newValue is valid
      int intValue = Integer.parseInt(newValue.trim());
      if (intValue < 0)
        throw new Exception();
      setValue(new Integer(intValue));
      setValid(true);
    }
    catch(Exception e) {
      // add error message
      Message message = new MessageImpl(1,
        "Error. Input must be a positive integer.", null);
      context.addMessage(this, message);
      setValid(false);
      setValue(newValue);
    }
  }

  public void encodeBegin(FacesContext context) throws IOException {
    if (context == null)
      throw new NullPointerException("FacesContext null");
    if (!isRendered())
      return;
    ResponseWriter writer = context.getResponseWriter();
    Object currentValue = currentValue(context);
    String clientId = getClientId(context);
    writer.write("<input type=\"text\"");
    writer.write(" name=\"");
    writer.write(clientId);
```

```
      writer.write("\"");
      writer.write(" id=\"");
      writer.write(clientId);
      writer.write("\"");
      if(currentValue != null)
        writer.write(" value=\"" + currentValue + "\"");
      writer.write(">");
   }


   public void encodeEnd(FacesContext context) throws IOException {
   }


}
```

The `UIPositiveNumber` class implements the `decode` and `encodeBegin` methods and leaves the `encodeEnd` method blank. In its `decode` method, the `UIPositiveNumber` class calls its `setPrevious` method, retrieves the value entered by the user, and validates that the value is a positive integer.

It starts by calling the `currentValue` method, which returns the current value of the component. The current value is "current" before the invocation of the current page and passing it to the `setPrevious` method.

```
setPrevious(currentValue(context));
```

This will make the current value the previous value. The current value will then be replaced by the new value entered by the user.

Next, the `decode` method tries to obtain the new value entered by the user.

```
      String clientId = getClientId(context);
      Map requestMap =
        context.getExternalContext().getRequestParameterMap();
      String newValue = (String) requestMap.get(clientId);
```

Then the `decode` method validates that the new value is a positive integer. If it is, the next step is to call the `setValue` method, passing the new `Integer`, and call the `setValid` method, passing `true` to indicate that the component has a valid value.

```
      try {
        // check if newValue is valid
        int intValue = Integer.parseInt(newValue.trim());
        if (intValue < 0)
          throw new Exception();
        setValue(new Integer(intValue));
        setValid(true);
      }
```

If the new value is not an integer, the `parseInt` method of the `Integer` class in the `try` block will throw an exception. Also, if it is an integer but its value is negative, this throws an exception. In effect, the code in the `catch` block will be executed. The code creates a `Message` object and adds it to the current instance of `FacesContext`. It then also indicates that the current value is not valid by passing `false` to the `setValid` method. Last, it passes the `newValue` to the `setValue` method, so that the value can be redisplayed.

```
catch(Exception e) {
  // add error message
  Message message = new MessageImpl(1,
    "Error. Input must be a positive integer.", null);
  context.addMessage(this, message);
  setValid(false);
  setValue(newValue);
}
```

The `encodeBegin` method is called during the Render Response phase of the request processing lifecycle. In this method, you must first obtain the `ResponseWriter` object from the current instance of `FacesContext` so that you write to the `Response` object.

```
ResponseWriter writer = context.getResponseWriter();
```

Then you render the component as an `<input type="text">` element by calling the `write` method of the `ResponseWriter` object.

```
  Object currentValue = currentValue(context);
  String clientId = getClientId(context);
  writer.write("<input type=\"text\"");
  writer.write(" name=\"");
  writer.write(clientId);
  writer.write("\"");
  writer.write(" id=\"");
  writer.write(clientId);
  writer.write("\"");
  if(currentValue != null)
    writer.write(" value=\"" + currentValue + "\"");
  writer.write(">");
}
```

Now that you have understood how the `UIPositiveNumber` class works, let's look at the `PositiveNumberTag` class.

Writing the PositiveNumberTag Tag Handler

The `PositiveNumberTag` class, shown in Listing 13-4, is the tag handler for the `UIPositiveNumber` component.

Listing 13-4 *The PositiveNumberTag Class*

```java
package ch13.positivenumber;
import javax.faces.component.UIComponent;
import javax.faces.webapp.UIComponentTag;

public class PositiveNumberTag extends UIComponentTag {

  private String value;
  private String valueRef;

  public String getValue() {
    System.out.println("PositiveNumberTag. getValue:" + value);
    return value;
  }
  public void setValue(String value) {
    System.out.println("PositiveNumberTag. setValue:" + value);
    this.value = value;
  }
  public String getValueRef() {
    System.out.println("PositiveNumberTag. getValueRef:" + valueRef);
    return valueRef;
  }
  public void setValueRef(String valueRef) {
    System.out.println("PositiveNumberTag. setValueRef:" + valueRef);
    this.valueRef = valueRef;
  }
  public String getRendererType() {
    return null;
  }
  public String getComponentType() {
    return "PositiveNumber";
  }
  protected void overrideProperties(UIComponent component) {
    super.overrideProperties(component);
    UIPositiveNumber positiveNumberComponent =
      (UIPositiveNumber) component;
    if(valueRef != null)
      positiveNumberComponent.setValueRef(valueRef);
    if (positiveNumberComponent.getValue()==null)
      positiveNumberComponent.setValue(getValue());
  }
}
```

The `PositiveNumberTag` class's `getRendererType` returns `null` to indicate to the JSF implementation that the `UIPositiveNumber` component will handle its own rendering. The `getComponentType` method returns "`PositiveNumber`". There are also two properties: `value` and `valueRef`. The `overrideProperties` method allows these properties to be set by specifying the corresponding attributes in the tag representing the `UIPositiveNumber` class.

Adding the UIPositiveNumber Tag Definition

Now that you have the component class and the tag handler, you need to register the `UIPositiveNumber` component in the `customComponents.tld` file. Listing 13-5 shows the tag definition for the `UIPositiveNumber` component.

NOTE

All of the custom UI components in this chapter share the same TLD file (`customComponents.tld`). This file must be copied to the `WEB-INF` directory of any application using any of the custom components

---

Listing 13-5   *UIPositiveNumber Tag Definition in the TLD File*

```
<tag>
  <name>input_positivenumber</name>
  <tag-class>ch13.positivenumber.PositiveNumberTag</tag-class>
  <attribute>
    <name>id</name>
    <required>false</required>
    <rtexprvalue>false</rtexprvalue>
  </attribute>
  <attribute>
    <name>value</name>
    <required>false</required>
    <rtexprvalue>false</rtexprvalue>
  </attribute>
  <attribute>
    <name>valueRef</name>
    <required>false</required>
    <rtexprvalue>false</rtexprvalue>
  </attribute>
</tag>
```

Using the UIPositiveNumber Component

To use the `UIPositiveNumber` component from an application, you must register the component in the application configuration file, as shown in Listing 13-6.

Listing 13-6 *UIPositiveNumber Registration in the Application Configuration File*

```
<!-- registering the custom component PositiveNumber -->
<component>
  <component-type>PositiveNumber</component-type>
  <component-class>
    ch13.positivenumber.UIPositiveNumber
  </component-class>
</component>
```

You can use the `positiveNumberTest.jsp` page, shown in Listing 13-7, to test the `UIPositiveNumber` component.

Listing 13-7 *The positiveNumberTest.jsp Page*

```
<%@ taglib uri="http://java.sun.com/jsf/html" prefix="h" %>
<%@ taglib uri="http://java.sun.com/jsf/core" prefix="f" %>
<%@ taglib uri="/WEB-INF/customComponents.tld" prefix="d" %>
<html>
<head>
<title>Using UIPositiveNumber</title>
</head>
<body>
<f:use_faces>
<h:form formName="myForm">
  Enter a positive number:
  <d:input_positivenumber valueRef="testingBean.quantity"/>
  <br/>
  <h:command_button label="submit" commandName="submit"/>
  <hr/>
  <br/>
  <h:output_errors/>
</h:form>
</f:use_faces>
</body>
</html>
```

To invoke the `positiveNumberTest.jsp` page, use the following URL:

```
http://localhost:8080/JSFCh13/faces/positiveNumberTest.jsp
```

Figure 13-1 shows an example of what happens when you enter a negative number in the `UIPositiveNumber` component.

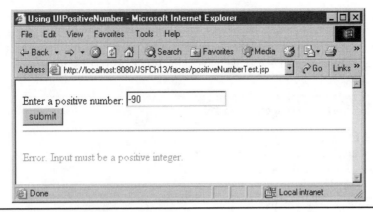

Figure 13-1   *Using UIPositiveNumber*

Using a Custom Renderer with a Custom Input Component

Our next example, the UIPositiveInteger component, is similar to UIPositiveNumber. It is an input component that accepts a positive integer. However, unlike UIPositiveNumber, UIPositiveInteger has a custom renderer.

There are three classes for the UIPositiveInteger component:

▶ UIPositiveInteger, representing the component class

▶ PositiveIntegerTag, representing the component tag handler

▶ PositiveIntegerRenderer, representing the external renderer for UIPositiveInteger

Writing the UIPositiveInteger Class and Tag Handler

The UIPositiveInteger class is shown in Listing 13-8. You will notice that there is not much to this class. Since rendering is performed by an external renderer, the UIPositiveInteger class does not need to do anything.

Listing 13-8   *The UIPositiveInteger Class*

```
package ch13.positiveinteger;
import javax.faces.component.UIInput;
public class UIPositiveInteger extends UIInput {
}
```

The `PositiveIntegerTag` class, shown in Listing 13-9, is similar to the `PositiveNumberTag` class in the previous example. It has two properties, `value` and `valueRef`, which can be set using attributes in the tag representing the component. However, notice that its `getRendererType` method returns `PositiveIntegerRenderer`.

Listing 13-9   *The PositiveIntegerTag Class*

```
package ch13.positiveinteger;
import javax.faces.component.UIComponent;
import javax.faces.webapp.UIComponentTag;

public class PositiveIntegerTag extends UIComponentTag {
  private String value;
  private String valueRef;
  public String getValue() {
    return value;
  }
  public void setValue(String value) {
    this.value = value;
  }
  public String getValueRef() {
    return valueRef;
  }
  public void setValueRef(String valueRef) {
    this.valueRef = valueRef;
  }
  public String getRendererType() {
    return "PositiveIntegerRenderer";
  }
  public String getComponentType() {
    return "PositiveInteger";
  }
  protected void overrideProperties(UIComponent component) {
    super.overrideProperties(component);
    UIPositiveInteger positiveIntegerComponent =
      (UIPositiveInteger) component;
    if(valueRef != null)
      positiveIntegerComponent.setValueRef(valueRef);
    if (positiveIntegerComponent.getValue()==null)
      positiveIntegerComponent.setValue(getValue());
  }
}
```

Writing the Renderer for UIPositiveInteger

The decode method of the PositiveIntegerRenderer class, shown in Listing 13-10, does the job of the decode method of the UIPositiveNumber class in the previous example. Its encodeBegin method does the job of the encodeBegin method of the UIPositiveNumber class. However, the PositiveIntegerRenderer class's getClientId method returns an identifier that is unique in the component's closest naming container.

Listing 13-10	*The PositiveIntegerRenderer Class*

```java
package ch13.positiveinteger;

import java.io.IOException;
import java.util.Map;
import javax.faces.application.Message;
import javax.faces.application.MessageImpl;
import javax.faces.component.NamingContainer;
import javax.faces.component.UIComponent;
import javax.faces.component.UIInput;
import javax.faces.context.FacesContext;
import javax.faces.context.ResponseWriter;
import javax.faces.render.Renderer;

public class PositiveIntegerRenderer extends Renderer {

  public void decode(FacesContext context, UIComponent component)
    throws IOException {
    if(context == null)
      throw new NullPointerException("FacesContext null");
    UIInput input = (UIInput) component;
    input.setPrevious(input.currentValue(context));
    String clientId = input.getClientId(context);
    Map requestMap =
      context.getExternalContext().getRequestParameterMap();
    String newValue = (String) requestMap.get(clientId);
    try {
      // check if newValue is valid
      int intValue = Integer.parseInt(newValue.trim());
      if (intValue < 0)
        throw new Exception();
      input.setValue(new Integer(intValue));
      input.setValid(true);
    }
    catch(Exception ce) {
      // add error message
      Message message =
        new MessageImpl(1, "Error. Input must be a positive integer.", null);
      context.addMessage(component, message);
      input.setValid(false);
```

```java
      input.setValue(newValue);
    }
  }


  public void encodeBegin(FacesContext context, UIComponent component) throws IOException {
    if (context == null)
      throw new NullPointerException("FacesContext null");
    if (!component.isRendered())
      return;
    ResponseWriter writer = context.getResponseWriter();
    Object currentValue = ((UIInput) component).currentValue(context);
    String clientId = getClientId(context, component);
    writer.write("<input type=\"text\"");
    writer.write(" name=\"");
    writer.write(clientId);
    writer.write("\"");
    writer.write(" id=\"");
    writer.write(clientId);
    writer.write("\"");
    if(currentValue != null)
      writer.write(" value=\"" + currentValue + "\"");
    writer.write(">");
  }


  public void encodeEnd(FacesContext context, UIComponent component) throws
IOException {
  }
  public void encodeChildren(FacesContext context, UIComponent component) throws
IOException {
  }


  private NamingContainer getClosestNamingContainer(UIComponent component) {
    // returns the component's closest container that is a naming container
    // if no parent is found or no parent is a naming container, check if
    // the component itself is a naming container. If yes, return the component
    // Otherwise, return null
    UIComponent parent = component.getParent();
    while (parent!=null) {
      if (parent instanceof NamingContainer)
        return (NamingContainer) parent;
      else
        parent = parent.getParent();
    }
    // no parent is a naming container
    if (component instanceof NamingContainer)
      return (NamingContainer) component;
    return null;
  }


  public String getClientId(FacesContext context,
    UIComponent component) {
    String clientId = null;
```

```
    NamingContainer closestContainer =
      getClosestNamingContainer(component);
    if (closestContainer!=null) {
      if (component.getComponentId() == null)
        return closestContainer.generateClientId();
      else
        return component.getComponentId();
    }
    throw new NullPointerException();
  }
}
```

The return value of the getClientId method is the same as the getComponentId method of the component if its closest NamingContainer is not null and the getComponentId method of the component is not null. Otherwise, its return value is the return value of the generateClientId method of the closest NamingContainer.

Adding the UIPositiveInteger Tag Definition to the TLD

For the UIPositiveInteger component to be used from a JSP page, its tag must be defined in the customComponents.tld file. Listing 13-11 shows the tag definition for UIPositiveInteger.

Listing 13-11   *The UIPositiveInteger Tag Definition in the TLD File*

```
  <tag>
    <name>input_positiveinteger</name>
    <tag-class>ch13.positiveinteger.PositiveIntegerTag</tag-class>
    <attribute>
      <name>id</name>
      <required>false</required>
      <rtexprvalue>false</rtexprvalue>
    </attribute>
    <attribute>
      <name>value</name>
      <required>false</required>
      <rtexprvalue>false</rtexprvalue>
    </attribute>
    <attribute>
      <name>valueRef</name>
      <required>false</required>
      <rtexprvalue>false</rtexprvalue>
    </attribute>
  </tag>
```

Using the UIPositiveInteger Component

Any application that wishes to use the UIPositiveInteger component must register the UIPositiveInteger component and its renderer in the application configuration file. Listing 13-12 shows how to register the custom component and renderer.

Listing 13-12   *UIPositiveInteger and Renderer Registration in the Application Configuration File*

```
<!-- registering the custom component PositiveInteger -->
<component>
  <component-type>PositiveInteger</component-type>
  <component-class>
    ch13.positiveinteger.UIPositiveInteger
  </component-class>
</component>

<!-- registering the renderer PositiveIntegerRenderer -->
<render-kit>
  <renderer>
    <renderer-type>PositiveIntegerRenderer</renderer-type>
    <renderer-class>
      ch13.positiveinteger.PositiveIntegerRenderer
    </renderer-class>
  </renderer>
</render-kit>
```

You can use the positiveIntegerTest.jsp page, shown in Listing 13-13 to test the UIPositiveInteger component.

Listing 13-13   *The positiveIntegerTest.jsp Page*

```
<%@ taglib uri="http://java.sun.com/jsf/html" prefix="h" %>
<%@ taglib uri="http://java.sun.com/jsf/core" prefix="f" %>
<%@ taglib uri="/WEB-INF/customComponents.tld" prefix="d" %>
<html>
<head>
<title>Using UIPositiveInteger</title>
</head>
<body>
<f:use_faces>
<h:form formName="myForm">
  Enter a positive integer:
  <d:input_positiveinteger valueRef="testingBean.quantity"/>
  <br/>
```

```
    <h:command_button label="submit" commandName="submit"/>
    <hr/>
    <br/>
    <h:output_errors/>
</h:form>
</f:use_faces>
</body>
</html>
```

You can invoke the `positiveIntegerTest.jsp` page by using the following URL:

`http://localhost:8080/JSFCh13/faces/positiveIntegerTest.jsp`

The `UIPositiveInteger` component behaves similarly to the `UIPositiveNumber` component. Figure 13-2 shows `UIPositiveInteger` in action.

Creating a Calendar Input Component

The sample custom component presented in this section, `UICalendar`, allows the user to select a date. It is a UI component that can accept a date between January 1, 1900, and December 31, 9999. It has a custom renderer and can trigger a `ValueChangedEvent`.

The user interface is two `<select>` elements for the month and the date parts, plus an input box for the year part of the date. The HTML tags rendered are similar to the following:

```
<select name="clientId" id="clientId">
    // options for the months
</select>
<select name="clientId_date" id="clientId_date">
    // options for the dates
</select>
<input type="text" name="clientId_year" size="4" maxLength="4">
```

where `clientId` is the client identifier.

The component has three classes:

▶ `UICalendar`, which represents the UI component

▶ `CalendarTag`, which represents the component tag handler

▶ `CalendarRenderer`, which represents an external renderer for `UICalendar`

Writing the UICalendar Class and Tag Handler

The `UICalendar` class (see Listing 13-14) extends `javax.faces.component.UIInput` and adds three properties: `enteredDate`, `enteredMonth`, and `enteredYear`. The three properties hold the date, month, and year parts of the date, respectively.

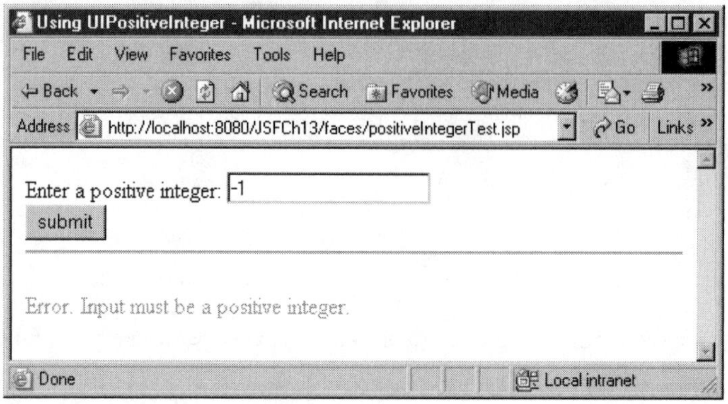

Figure 13-2   *Using UIPositiveInteger*

Listing 13-14   *The UICalendar Class*

```
package ch13.calendar;

import javax.faces.component.UIInput;

public class UICalendar extends UIInput {
  private String enteredDate;
  private String enteredMonth;
  private String enteredYear;

  public String getEnteredDate() {
    return enteredDate;
 }
  public void setEnteredDate(String date) {
    enteredDate = date;
  }
  public String getEnteredMonth() {
    return enteredMonth;
  }
  public void setEnteredMonth(String month) {
    enteredMonth = month;
  }
  public String getEnteredYear() {
    return enteredYear;
  }
  public void setEnteredYear(String year) {
    enteredYear = year;
  }
}
```

The CalendarTag class, shown in Listing 13-15, provides the implementations for the getRendererType and getComponentType methods. It also adds two properties, value and valueRef, which can be set using the attributes of the tag representing the UICalendar component.

Listing 13-15 *The CalendarTag Class*

```
package ch13.calendar;

import javax.faces.webapp.UIComponentTag;
import javax.faces.component.UIComponent;

public class CalendarTag extends UIComponentTag {

  private String value;
  private String valueRef;

  public String getRendererType() {
    return "CalendarRenderer";
  }
  public String getComponentType() {
    return "Calendar";
  }
  public String getValue() {
    return value;
  }
  public void setValue(String value) {
    this.value = value;
  }
  public String getValueRef() {
    return valueRef;
  }
  public void setValueRef(String valueRef) {
    this.valueRef = valueRef;
  }
  protected void overrideProperties(UIComponent component) {
    super.overrideProperties(component);
    UICalendar calendarComponent = (UICalendar) component;
    if(valueRef != null)
      calendarComponent.setValueRef(valueRef);
    if (calendarComponent.getValue()==null)
      calendarComponent.setValue(getValue());
  }
}
```

Writing the Calendar Renderer

The CalendarRenderer class, shown in Listing 13-16, provides the implementations of the decode and encodeBegin methods, which work the same way as the renderer in the previous example (Listing 13-10).

Listing 13-16 *The CalendarRenderer Class*

```java
package ch13.calendar;

import java.io.IOException;
import java.util.Calendar;
import java.util.Date;
import java.util.Map;
import javax.faces.application.Message;
import javax.faces.application.MessageImpl;
import javax.faces.component.NamingContainer;
import javax.faces.component.UIComponent;
import javax.faces.context.FacesContext;
import javax.faces.context.ResponseWriter;
import javax.faces.event.ValueChangedEvent;
import javax.faces.render.Renderer;

public class CalendarRenderer extends Renderer {

  public void decode(FacesContext context, UIComponent component)
    throws IOException {
    if(context == null)
      throw new NullPointerException("FacesContext null");

    UICalendar calendarComponent = (UICalendar) component;
    String clientId = calendarComponent.getClientId(context);
    Map requestMap =
    context.getExternalContext().getRequestParameterMap();
    String newMonthValue = (String) requestMap.get(clientId);
    String newDateValue =
      (String) requestMap.get(clientId + "_date");
    String newYearValue =
      (String) requestMap.get(clientId + "_year");
    calendarComponent.setEnteredDate(newDateValue);
    calendarComponent.setEnteredMonth(newMonthValue);
    calendarComponent.setEnteredYear(newYearValue);
    if (isDateValid(newDateValue, newMonthValue, newYearValue)) {
      int d, m, y;
      // no need to catch NumberFormatException
```

```
        // because isValid has done it
        d = Integer.parseInt(newDateValue);
        m = Integer.parseInt(newMonthValue);
        y = Integer.parseInt(newYearValue);
        Calendar theDate = Calendar.getInstance();
        theDate.set(y, m-1, d, 0, 0, 0);
        Date newDate = theDate.getTime();
        Date oldDate = (Date) calendarComponent.currentValue(context);
        if (newDate!=null) {
          if (oldDate==null)
            context.addFacesEvent(new
              ValueChangedEvent(calendarComponent, oldDate,newDate));
          else {
            // oldDate != null, compare date, month, and year
            Calendar oldDateCal = Calendar.getInstance();
            oldDateCal.setTime(oldDate);
            if (d!=oldDateCal.get(Calendar.DATE) ||
              m!=oldDateCal.get(Calendar.MONTH) + 1 ||
              y!=oldDateCal.get(Calendar.YEAR))
              context.addFacesEvent(new
ValueChangedEvent(calendarComponent,
oldDate, newDate));
          }
        }

        calendarComponent.setValue(newDate);
        calendarComponent.setValid(true);
      }
      else {
        // add error message
        Message message = new
          MessageImpl(1, "Error. Invalid date.", null);
        context.addMessage(component, message);
        calendarComponent.setValid(false);
      }

  }

  public void encodeBegin(FacesContext context,
    UIComponent component) throws IOException {
    if (context == null)
      throw new NullPointerException("FacesContext null");
    if (!component.isRendered())
      return;
    ResponseWriter writer = context.getResponseWriter();
```

```java
      Object currentValue =
        ((UICalendar) component).currentValue(context);
      String clientId = component.getClientId(context);

  writer.write(getRenderedText(context, clientId, component));
    }

  private boolean isDateValid(String date,
      String month, String year) {
      if (date==null || month==null || year==null)
        return false;
      int d, m, y;
      try {
        d = Integer.parseInt(date);
        m = Integer.parseInt(month);
        y = Integer.parseInt(year);
      }
      catch (NumberFormatException e) {
        return false;
      }
      if (d>31 || d<1 || m>12 || m<1 || y<1900 || y>9999)
        return false;
      if (d==31 && (m==2 || m==4 || m==6 || m==9 || m==11))
        return false;
      if (d==30 && m==2)
        return false;
      // leap year: has Feb 29, and:
      // 1. year is evenly divisible by 400 or
      // 2. year is evenly divisible by 4 but not by 100
      // therefore, 1904, 2000, 2004 etc are leap years,
      // but 1900, 2100, etc are not
      if (m==2 && d==29) {
        if (y % 400==0)
          return true;
        if (y%100==0)
          return false;
        if (y%4==0)
          return true;
        else
          return false;
      }
      return true;
    }

  private String getRenderedText(FacesContext context,
```

```
String clientId, UIComponent component) {
UICalendar calendarComponent = (UICalendar) component;
String dateValue, monthValue, yearValue;
Date date = (Date) calendarComponent.currentValue(context);
if (date!=null && component.isValid()) {
  Calendar cal = Calendar.getInstance();
  cal.setTime(date);
  dateValue = Integer.toString(cal.get(Calendar.DATE));
  monthValue = Integer.toString(cal.get(Calendar.MONTH) + 1);
  yearValue = Integer.toString(cal.get(Calendar.YEAR));
}
else {
  dateValue = calendarComponent.getEnteredDate();
  monthValue = calendarComponent.getEnteredMonth();
  yearValue = calendarComponent.getEnteredYear();
}
StringBuffer buffer = new StringBuffer(300);
buffer.append("<select name=\"" + clientId + "\"");
buffer.append(" id=\"" + clientId + "\"");
buffer.append(">\n");
buffer.append("<option ");
if ("1".equals(monthValue))
  buffer.append("selected ");
buffer.append("value=\"1\">January</option>\n");
buffer.append("<option ");
if ("2".equals(monthValue))
  buffer.append("selected ");
buffer.append("value=\"2\">February</option>\n");
buffer.append("<option ");
if ("3".equals(monthValue))
  buffer.append("selected ");
buffer.append("value=\"3\">March</option>\n");
buffer.append("<option ");
if ("4".equals(monthValue))
  buffer.append("selected ");
buffer.append("value=\"4\">April</option>\n");
buffer.append("<option ");
if ("5".equals(monthValue))
  buffer.append("selected ");
buffer.append("value=\"5\">May</option>\n");
buffer.append("<option ");
if ("6".equals(monthValue))
  buffer.append("selected ");
buffer.append("value=\"6\">June</option>\n");
buffer.append("<option ");
```

```
    if ("7".equals(monthValue))
      buffer.append("selected ");
    buffer.append("value=\"7\">July</option>\n");
    buffer.append("<option ");
    if ("8".equals(monthValue))
      buffer.append("selected ");
    buffer.append("value=\"8\">August</option>\n");
    buffer.append("<option ");
    if ("9".equals(monthValue))
      buffer.append("selected ");
    buffer.append("value=\"9\">September</option>\n");
    buffer.append("<option ");
    if ("10".equals(monthValue))
      buffer.append("selected ");
    buffer.append("value=\"10\">October</option>\n");
    buffer.append("<option ");
    if ("11".equals(monthValue))
      buffer.append("selected ");
    buffer.append("value=\"11\">November</option>\n");
    buffer.append("<option ");
    if ("12".equals(monthValue))
      buffer.append("selected ");
    buffer.append("value=\"12\">December</option>\n");
    buffer.append("</select>\n");

    // the date
    buffer.append("<select name=\"" + clientId + "_date\"");
    buffer.append(" id=\"" + clientId + "_date\"");
    buffer.append(">");
    for (int i=1; i<32; i++) {
      buffer.append("<option");
      if (Integer.toString(i).equals(dateValue))
        buffer.append(" selected");
      buffer.append(">");
      buffer.append(i);
      buffer.append("</option>\n");
    }

    buffer.append("</select>\n");
    // the year
    buffer.append("<input name=\"" + clientId + "_year\" size=\"4\"
maxLength=\"4\"");
    if (yearValue!=null)
      buffer.append(" value=\"" + yearValue + "\"");
    buffer.append(">");
```

```java
    return buffer.toString();
  }

  public void encodeEnd(FacesContext context,
    UIComponent component) throws IOException {
  }
  public void encodeChildren(FacesContext context,
    UIComponent component) throws IOException {
  }

  private NamingContainer getClosestNamingContainer(
    UIComponent component) {
    // returns the component's closest container
    // that is a naming container
    // if no parent is found or no parent is a naming container,
    // check if the component itself is a naming container.
    // If yes, return the component
    // Otherwise, return null
    UIComponent parent = component.getParent();
    while (parent!=null) {
      if (parent instanceof NamingContainer)
        return (NamingContainer) parent;
      else
        parent = parent.getParent();
    }
    // no parent is a naming container
    if (component instanceof NamingContainer)
      return (NamingContainer) component;
    return null;
  }

  public String getClientId(FacesContext context,
    UIComponent component) {
    String clientId = null;
    NamingContainer closestContainer =
      getClosestNamingContainer(component);
    if (closestContainer!=null) {
      if (component.getComponentId() == null)
        return closestContainer.generateClientId();
      else
        return component.getComponentId();
    }
    throw new NullPointerException();
  }
}
```

The decode method obtains the three parts of the date: the month, the day, and the year. It uses the following code:

```
Map requestMap = context.getExternalContext().
  getRequestParameterMap();
String newMonthValue = (String) requestMap.get(clientId);
String newDateValue =
  (String) requestMap.get(clientId + "_date");
String newYearValue =
  (String) requestMap.get(clientId + "_year");
```

Then it validates the part by calling the isDateValid method. The encodeBegin method renders the component to the client.

Adding the UICalendar Tag Definition to the TLD

For the UICalendar component to be usable from a JSF application, its tag must be defined in the customComponents.tld file. Listing 13-17 shows the definition of the calendar tag, which represents the UICalendar component.

Listing 13-17   *The UICalendar Tag Definition in the TLD File*

```
<tag>
  <name>calendar</name>
  <tag-class>ch13.calendar.CalendarTag</tag-class>
  <attribute>
    <name>id</name>
    <required>true</required>
    <rtexprvalue>false</rtexprvalue>
  </attribute>
  <attribute>
    <name>value</name>
    <required>false</required>
    <rtexprvalue>false</rtexprvalue>
  </attribute>
  <attribute>
    <name>valueRef</name>
    <required>false</required>
    <rtexprvalue>false</rtexprvalue>
  </attribute>
  <attribute>
    <name>format</name>
    <required>false</required>
```

```
        <rtexprvalue>false</rtexprvalue>
    </attribute>
  </tag>
```

Using the UICalendar Component

To use the `UICalendar` component in an application, you must register it and its renderer in the application configuration file, as shown in Listing 13-18.

Listing 13-18   *UICalendar and Renderer Registration in the Application Configuration File*

```
<!-- registering the custom component Calendar -->
<component>
  <component-type>Calendar</component-type>
  <component-class>ch13.calendar.UICalendar</component-class>
</component>

<!-- registering the renderer CalendarRenderer -->
<render-kit>
  <renderer>
    <renderer-type>CalendarRenderer</renderer-type>
    <renderer-class>ch13.calendar.CalendarRenderer</renderer-class>
  </renderer>
</render-kit>
```

You can test the calendar component using the `calendarTest.jsp` page, shown in Listing 13-19.

Listing 13-19   *The calendarTest.jsp Page*

```
<%@ taglib uri="http://java.sun.com/jsf/html" prefix="h" %>
<%@ taglib uri="http://java.sun.com/jsf/core" prefix="f" %>
<%@ taglib uri="/WEB-INF/customComponents.tld" prefix="d" %>
<html>
<head>
<title>Using Calendar Component</title>
</head>
<body>
<f:use_faces>
<h:form formName="myForm">
Select a date:
<d:calendar id="x" valueRef="testingBean.today">
  <f:valuechanged_listener type="ch13.calendar.DateChangedListener"/>
```

```
</d:calendar>
<br/>
<h:command_button label="submit" commandName="submit"/>
<hr/>
<br/>
<h:output_errors/>
</h:form>
</f:use_faces>
</body>
</html>
```

Notice that a `ValueChangedListener` called `DateChangedListener` is used to listen for any value changes in the `UICalendar` component. The `DateChangedListener` is shown in Listing 13-20.

Listing 13-20 *The DateChangedListener Class*

```
package ch13.calendar;

import java.util.Date;
import javax.faces.event.PhaseId;
import javax.faces.event.ValueChangedEvent;
import javax.faces.event.ValueChangedListener;

public class DateChangedListener implements ValueChangedListener {

  public void processValueChanged(ValueChangedEvent event) {
    Date oldDate = (Date) event.getOldValue();
    Date newDate = (Date) event.getNewValue();
    System.out.println("DateChangedListener. Old date:" + oldDate);
    System.out.println("DateChangedListener. New date:" + newDate);
  }

  public PhaseId getPhaseId() {
    return PhaseId.APPLY_REQUEST_VALUES;
  }
}
```

The `DateChangedListener` simply prints the old and new dates to the console. You can invoke the `calendarTest.jsp` page using the following URL:

```
http://localhost:8080/JSFCh13/faces/calendarTest.jsp
```

Figure 13-3 shows the calendar component.

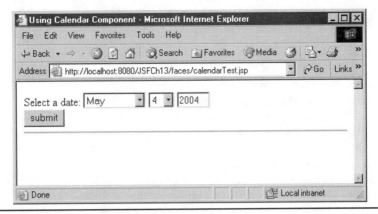

Figure 13-3 *Using the custom calendar component*

Creating a Flexible Hyperlink Component

As a final example, this section presents a component called FlexibleHyperlink, which is a hyperlink that can have a dynamic value for its label.

The command_hyperlink tag is one of the two tags that represent the UICommand component. Using command_hyperlink, a UICommand component is rendered as a hyperlink in the browser. The label attribute of the command_hyperlink tag is used to set the text of the hyperlink. However, the label attribute can take only a static value. It cannot get its value from a value reference expression.

The FlexibleHyperlink component provides a hyperlink with the labelRef attribute. This attribute takes a value reference expression so that the hyperlink can get its text from a model object or another source. The FlexibleHyperlink component consists of only a tag handler. It uses a UICommand component and the Hyperlink renderer. This means that to use the FlexibleHyperlink component in an application, you do not need to register it in the application configuration file. However, you still need to define the tag for the FlexibleHyperlink component in the customComponents.tld file.

Writing the FlexibleHyperlink Tag Handler

Listing 13-21 shows the FlexibleHyperlinkTag class, the component tag handler. Notice that the getRendererType method returns "Hyperlink", indicating to the JSF implementation that it uses the Hyperlink standard renderer. The getComponentType method returns "Command", which means it uses the UICommand standard component.

Listing 13-21 *The FlexibleHyperlinkTag Class*

```
package ch13.flexiblehyperlink;

import javax.faces.FactoryFinder;
import javax.faces.application.Application;
import javax.faces.application.ApplicationFactory;
import javax.faces.el.ValueBinding;
import javax.faces.component.UIComponent;
import javax.faces.component.UICommand;
import javax.faces.webapp.UIComponentTag;

public class FlexibleHyperlinkTag extends UIComponentTag {

  protected String href;
  protected String label;
  protected String labelRef;
  protected String commandName;
  protected String image;
  protected String actionRef;
  protected String action;

  public String getCommandName() {
    return commandName;
  }
  public void setCommandName(String commandName) {
    this.commandName = commandName;
  }
  public String getHref() {
    return href;
  }
  public void setHref(String href) {
    this.href = href;
  }
  public String getLabel() {
    return label;
  }
  public void setLabel(String label) {
    this.label = label;
  }
  public String getLabelRef() {
    return labelRef;
  }
  public void setLabelRef(String labelRef) {
```

```java
    this.labelRef = labelRef;
}
public String getImage() {
  return image;
}
public void setImage(String image) {
  this.image = image;
}
public String getActionRef() {
  return actionRef;
}
public void setActionRef(String actionRef) {
  this.actionRef = actionRef;
}
public String getAction() {
  return action;
}
public void setAction(String action) {
  this.action = action;
}
public String getRendererType() {
  return "Hyperlink";
}
public String getComponentType() {
  return "Command";
}
public UIComponent createComponent(){
  return new UICommand();
}
protected void overrideProperties(UIComponent component) {
  super.overrideProperties(component);
  UICommand hyperlink = (UICommand)component;
  if (hyperlink.getCommandName()==null)
    hyperlink.setCommandName(getCommandName());
  if (hyperlink.getActionRef()==null && actionRef!=null)
    hyperlink.setActionRef(actionRef);
  if (hyperlink.getAction()==null && action!=null)
    hyperlink.setAction(action);
  if (component.getAttribute("labelRef")==null) {
    ApplicationFactory factory = (ApplicationFactory)
      FactoryFinder.getFactory(FactoryFinder.APPLICATION_FACTORY);
    Application application = factory.getApplication();
    ValueBinding binding =
      application.getValueBinding(getLabelRef());
```

```
    component.setAttribute("label", binding.getValue(context));
  }
  if (component.getAttribute("image")==null)
    component.setAttribute("image", getImage());
  if (component.getAttribute("href")==null)
    component.setAttribute("href", getHref());
}


}
```

The most important part of the `FlexibleHyperlinkTag` class is the following fragment in the `overridesProperties` method:

```
if (component.getAttribute("labelRef")==null) {
  ApplicationFactory factory = (ApplicationFactory)
    FactoryFinder.getFactory(FactoryFinder.APPLICATION_FACTORY);
  Application application = factory.getApplication();
  ValueBinding binding =
    application.getValueBinding(getLabelRef());
  component.setAttribute("label", binding.getValue(context));
}
```

This code states that if a `labelRef` is present in the custom tag, use a `ValueBinding` object to obtain the value of the value reference expression represented by `labelRef`. Then call the `setAttribute` method of the component to set the value of the `label` property. This way, the value of the `label` property is determined dynamically.

Adding the FlexibleHyperlink Tag Definition to the TLD

As with the other custom components, to use the `FlexibleHyperlink` component, you must first define its tag in the `customComponents.tld` file, using the tag element shown in Listing 13-22.

Listing 13-22   *FlexibleHyperlink Tag Definition in the TLD File*

```
<tag>
  <name>flexible_hyperlink</name>
  <tag-class>
    ch13.flexiblehyperlink.FlexibleHyperlinkTag
  </tag-class>
  <body-content>JSP</body-content>
    <attribute>
      <name>id</name>
```

```xml
        <required>false</required>
        <rtexprvalue>false</rtexprvalue>
    </attribute>
    <attribute>
        <name>actionRef</name>
        <required>false</required>
        <rtexprvalue>false</rtexprvalue>
    </attribute>
    <attribute>
        <name>action</name>
        <required>false</required>
        <rtexprvalue>false</rtexprvalue>
    </attribute>
    <attribute>
        <name>rendered</name>
        <required>false</required>
        <rtexprvalue>false</rtexprvalue>
    </attribute>
<attribute>
  <name>href</name>
  <required>false</required>
  <rtexprvalue>false</rtexprvalue>
</attribute>
<attribute>
  <name>image</name>
  <required>false</required>
  <rtexprvalue>false</rtexprvalue>
</attribute>
<attribute>
  <name>label</name>
  <required>false</required>
  <rtexprvalue>false</rtexprvalue>
</attribute>
<attribute>
  <name>labelRef</name>
  <required>false</required>
  <rtexprvalue>false</rtexprvalue>
</attribute>
<attribute>
  <name>commandName</name>
  <required>false</required>
  <rtexprvalue>false</rtexprvalue>
</attribute>
<attribute>
```

```
      <name>key</name>
      <required>false</required>
      <rtexprvalue>false</rtexprvalue>
    </attribute>
    <attribute>
      <name>bundle</name>
      <required>false</required>
      <rtexprvalue>false</rtexprvalue>
    </attribute>
    <attribute>
      <name>commandClass</name>
      <required>false</required>
      <rtexprvalue>false</rtexprvalue>
    </attribute>
  </tag>
```

Testing the Hyperlink Component

To test the FlexibleHyperlink component, use the flexibleHyperlinkTest.jsp page, shown in Listing 13-23.

Listing 13-23   *The flexibleHyperlinkTest.jsp Page*

```
<%@ taglib uri="http://java.sun.com/jsf/html" prefix="h" %>
<%@ taglib uri="http://java.sun.com/jsf/core" prefix="f" %>
<%@ taglib uri="/WEB-INF/customComponents.tld" prefix="d" %>
The following is a flexible hyperlink:
<f:use_faces>
<h:form formName="myForm">
  <d:flexible_hyperlink href="browse.jsp"
    labelRef="testingBean.value"/>
</h:form>
</f:use_faces>
```

You can invoke the flexibleHyperlinkTest.jsp page using the following URL:

http://localhost:8080/JSFCh13/faces/flexibleHyperlinkTest.jsp

Figure 13-4 shows the FlexibleHyperlink component in a browser.

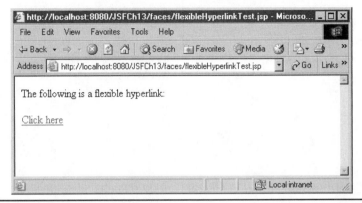

Figure 13-4   *Using the FlexibleHyperlink component*

Summary

JSF provides a number of standard UI components which we discussed in Chapters 5 and 6. While in most cases these standard components are sufficient, there are circumstances where you need to roll up your sleeve and write your own custom UI components. These special circumstances were discussed at the beginning of this chapter.

A custom component can do the rendering itself or delegate rendering to a custom renderer and fire events. In this chapter, you learned how to write four custom components: `UIPositiveNumber`, `UIPositiveInteger`, `UICalendar`, and `FlexibleHyperlink`.

Online Store Application

In the previous chapters, you have learned the basics of JSF and how to build each component of a JSF application. To illustrate the use of JSF in the real world, this chapter presents an online store application named BuyDirect, an Internet store that sells electronic goods.

This chapter begins with an overview of the application, and then discusses the application development process. We will cover page design, database design and access, model objects, the application configuration file entries for bean registration and navigation rules, the deployment descriptor, and the JSP pages.

Introducing the BuyDirect Application

The BuyDirect application allows users to do the following:

- ▶ Search for certain products based on product names or descriptions.

- ▶ Browse the list of products by category.

- ▶ View a product's details.

- ▶ Add a product to the shopping cart.

- ▶ View the shopping cart.

- ▶ Check out and place an order.

The main objective of this application is to show how to use JSF in a real-world application. Admittedly, the application is not a complete solution yet. For example, you cannot edit the shopping cart, and it lacks an administration section for changing the product information and handling the orders. However, it provides basic functionality, and finalizing it should not be difficult.

The BuyDirect application has ten JSP pages, one `ActionListener` (`AppActionListener`), one context listener (`AppContextListener`), and eight JavaBeans. In addition, there are also the deployment descriptor and the JSF application configuration file, as well as a number of image files in the `images` directory. Figure 14-1 shows the directory structure of this application.

Designing the Application Pages

For consistency, each page in the BuyDirect application uses the same design. There is a header at the top of the page and a menu on the left side. The page template is shown in Figure 14-2.

Here are the HTML tags that make up the page:

```
<html>
<head>
<title><!-- The title --></title>
</head>
<body>
<table>
<tr>
  <td colspan="2">
```

```
      <!-- The header -->
  </td>
</tr>
<tr>
  <td valign="top">
    <!-- The menu -->
  </td>
  <td valign="top">
    <!-- Content -->
</td>
</tr>
<tr>
  <td colspan="2">
    <!-- The footer -->
</td>
</tr>
</table>
</body>
</html>
```

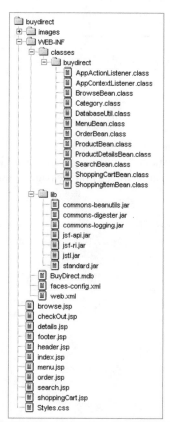

Figure 14-1   *The BuyDirect application directory structure*

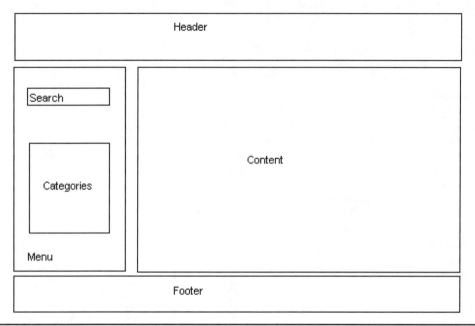

Figure 14-2 *The BuyDirect application page design*

Using a Style Sheet

Each page in the application links to a Cascading Style Sheet (CSS) file called `Styles.css`, residing in the application directory. Using a style sheet provides a more flexible way of formatting than embedding formatting directly on the page. The `Styles.css` file is shown in Listing 14-1.

Listing 14-1 *The Styles.css File*

```
body {
  background:#ffffff;
  font-family: verdana;
  font-size: 8pt;
  font-weight: bold;
  color: #000000;
} A:link {
  font-family: verdana;
  font-size: 8pt;
  color: #000000;
  text-decoration:underline
```

```
} A:visited {
  font-family: verdana;
  font-size: 8pt;
  color: #000000;
  text-decoration:underline
}

A:hover {
  font-family: verdana;
  font-size: 8pt;
  color: #CCCCCC;
  text-decoration:none
}

.Header {
  background: #CCCCCC;
  color: #FFFFFF;
}

.HeaderText1 {
  font-family: verdana;
  font-size: 13pt;
  font-weight: bold;
}

.HeaderText2 {
  font-family: verdana;
  font-size: 11pt;
  font-weight: bold;
}

.MenuHeader {
  font-family: verdana;
  font-size: 12pt;
  font-weight: bold;
  background: #CCCCCC;
  color: #FFFFFF;
}

.MenuItem:link {
  font-family: verdana;
  font-size: 8pt;
  font-weight: bold;
  color: #000000;
  text-decoration:none
```

```
    }

    .MenuItem:visited {
      font-family: verdana;
      font-size: 8pt;
      font-weight: bold;
      color: #000000;
      text-decoration:none
    }

    .MenuItem:hover {
      font-family: verdana;
      font-size: 8pt;
      font-weight: bold;
      color: #bbccdd;
      text-decoration:none
    }

    .OuterTable {
      background:#CCCCCC;
    }

    .InnerTable {
      background:#EDEDED;
    }

    .PageHeader {
      font-family: verdana;
      font-size: 16pt;
      font-weight: bold;
      color: #CCCCCC;
    }

    .SecondPageHeader {
      font-family: verdana;
      font-size: 14pt;
      font-weight: bold;
      color: #CCCCCC;
    }

    .TableHeader {
      font-family: verdana;
      font-size: 12pt;
      font-weight: bold;
      color: #FFFFFF;
```

```
}

.TableItem {
  font-family: verdana;
  font-size: 9pt;
  color: #000000;
}

.AlternatingTableItem {
  font-family: verdana;
  font-size: 9pt;
  color: #000000;
}

.Footer {
  font-family: verdana;
  font-size: 8pt;
  color: #000000;
}

.NormalLarge {
  font-family: verdana;
  font-size: 11pt;
  font-weight: bold;
  color: #000000;
}

.NormalSmall {
  font-family: verdana;
  font-size: 10pt;
  color: #000000;
}

.ErrorMessage {
  font-family: verdana;
  font-size: 10pt;
  color: #FF0000;
}
```

Understanding the Page Control Flow

The control flow of the BuyDirect application is straightforward, similar to shopping in an online store such as Amazon.com. Here, we will take a look at the design of each page in the application.

The Main Page

The main page of this application serves as a welcome page, as shown in Figure 14-3. Users can use the menu box on the left side of the page to search for a product or browse the products by category. In fact, the menu box is available from every page, enabling users to search and browse without needing to go back to the main page.

The Search Page

Users can search for a product by entering a keyword in the Search box and clicking the Go button. All of the products found are summarized on the search page, shown in Figure 14-4. Each product is listed with its name and price, as well as a Details link. The user clicks the Details link to view the product details and to purchase the product.

The Browse Page

The application allows users to browse products by category by clicking one of the links in the menu box. Currently, there are five categories for BuyDirect: Digital Camera, DVD Player, Camcorder, TV, and Analog. Like the search page, the browse page lists each product's name and price with a Details link, as shown in Figure 14-5. However, this page lists products from the same category, rather than those matching a certain search key.

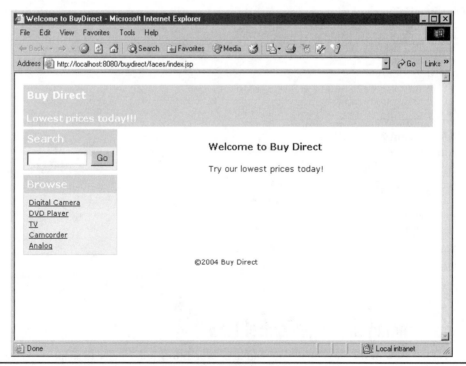

Figure 14-3   *The main page of the BuyDirect application*

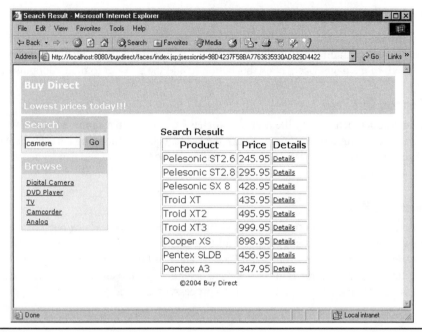

Figure 14-4   *The search page of the BuyDirect application*

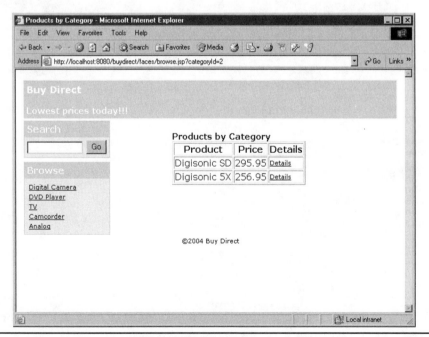

Figure 14-5   *The browse page of the BuyDirect application*

The Product Details Page

Clicking the Details link in either the search or browse page displays the details of the selected product, including a description, as shown in Figure 14-6. Notice the Buy button at the bottom of the page. Users click this button to add the product to their shopping cart.

The Shopping Cart Page

All of the products selected by the user for purchase are stored in a shopping cart. Every time the user adds a product to the shopping cart, the contents of the shopping cart are displayed, as in Figure 14-7. Users click the Check Out button at the bottom of the page when they are finished shopping.

The Check Out Page

When users are satisfied with their selections, they can proceed to the check out page to have their purchases processed. As shown in Figure 14-8, this page contains five input fields: Contact Name, Delivery Address, Name on Credit Card, Credit Card Number, and Expiry Date. All of the input fields are mandatory. If the user fails to enter a value into any of the input fields, an error message appears. Clicking the Pay button processes the order.

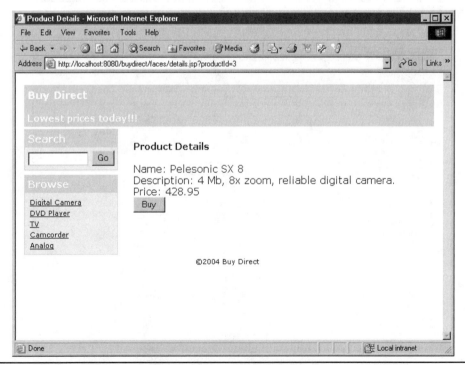

Figure 14-6   *The product details page of the BuyDirect application*

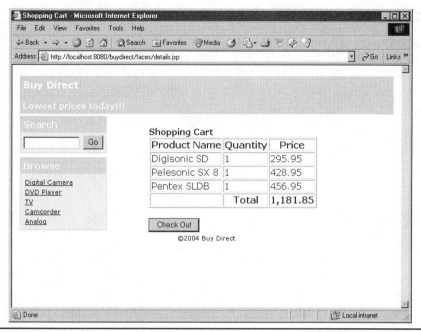

Figure 14-7   *The shopping cart page of the BuyDirect application*

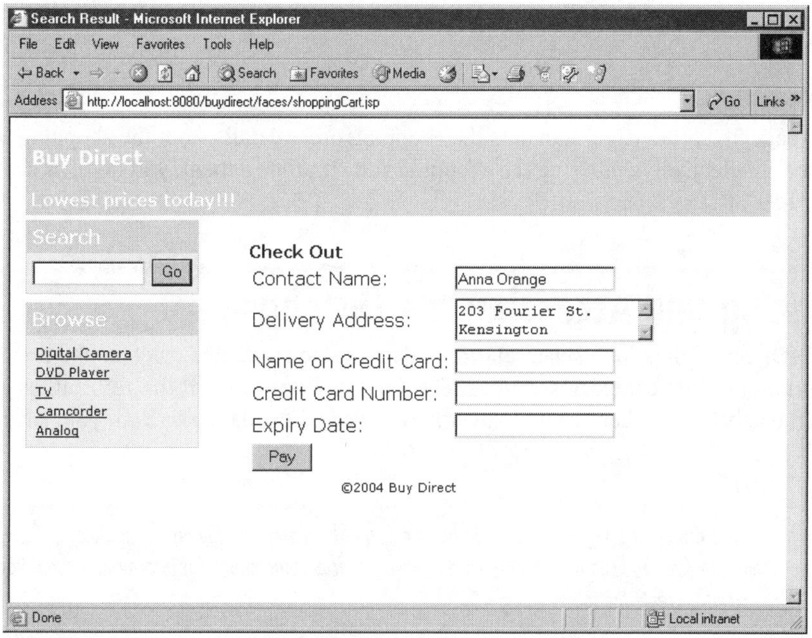

Figure 14-8   *The check out page of the BuyDirect application*

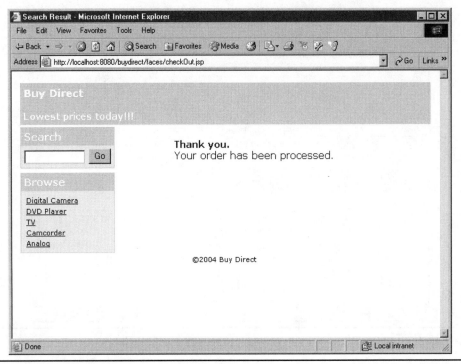

Figure 14-9   *The order page of the BuyDirect application*

The Order Page

The last page, the order page, transfers the shopping order details from the shopping cart to the database, effectively emptying the shopping cart. It prints a thank you note, as shown in Figure 14-9.

Designing and Accessing the Database

This BuyDirect application uses a relational database to store data, such as the product information, product categories, and orders. First, we will look at the four tables in the relational database, and then we will cover how to access the database from your Java code.

NOTE

The code listing for `buydirect` *includes a script file to generate the database tables and populate them with data. You should consult your database server documentation for information about how to run the script to create the tables.*

Structuring the Database Tables

The BuyDirect application uses four tables: Categories, Products, Orders, and OrderDetails. The Categories table stores product categories, as shown in Table 14-1.

The Products table stores the details of each product sold in the online store. Table 14-2 lists the column names and data types in this table.

The Orders table, shown in Table 14-3, holds order information, including delivery addresses, credit card details, and contact names. There is a unique identifier for each order to link all shopping items in that order. These shopping items are stored in the OrderDetails table, shown in Table 14-4.

Column Name	Data Type
Id	AutoNumber
Description	Text

Table 14-1   *The Categories Table in the Database*

Column Name	Data Type
ProductId	AutoNumber
CategoryId	Number
Name	Text
Description	Text
Price	Number

Table 14-2   *The Products Table in the Database*

Column Name	Data Type
OrderId	Number
ContactName	Text
DeliveryAddress	Text
CCName	Text
CCNumber	Text
CCExpiryDate	Text

Table 14-3   *The Orders Table in the Database*

Column Name	Data Type
Id	AutoNumber
OrderId	Number
ProductId	Number
Quantity	Number
Price	Number

Table 14-4   *The OrderDetails Table in the Database*

Connecting to the Database

Java Database Connectivity (JDBC) is the technology for accessing a database and manipulating its data in a Java application. JDBC has two parts: the JDBC Core Application Programming Interface (API) and the JDBC Optional Package API. The most recent version of JDBC is 3.0 and it is included in Java 2, Standard Edition (J2SE) version 1.4.1 and later. (At the time of the writing of this book, JDBC version 4.0 was being developed.)

Basically, to access a database, you simply connect to the database server. Then you can send a SQL query to retrieve data from a table, update records, insert new records, delete data, and so on.

You need to perform four steps to access a database with JDBC:

▶ Load the JDBC database driver.

▶ Create a connection.

▶ Create a statement.

▶ Create a result set, if you expect the database server to send back some data.

NOTE

JDBC drivers normally come in a .jar file. To use the driver from a Web application, you need to copy this jar file to the `WEB-INF/lib` *directory under your application directory. If you are using the JDBC-ODBC bridge, however, you do not need to install the driver, because it's already included in your Java Development Kit (JDK).*

Setting Up an ODBC Data Source Name

You need to set up an Open Database Connectivity (ODBC) Data Source Name (DSN) on your computer if you want to use the Microsoft Access database provided on the CD-ROM that accompanies this book. To set up an ODBC DSN, follow these steps:

1. Open the ODBC Data Source Administration dialog box from the Control Panel.

2. Click the System DSN tab.

3. Click the Add button.

4. Select a driver name from the list of ODBC drivers.

5. Enter the information requested in the Setup dialog box that appears. For accessing the `buydirect.mdb` Microsoft Access database, the name for the DSN must be **buydirect**.

6. Click OK to close the dialog box.

The `DatabaseUtil` class, explained in the next section, provides methods for the rest of the application. For production, you may also want to use connection pooling to make your application more scalable.

Using the DatabaseUtil Class

As part of our BuyDirect application, various business objects need to access the database. A utility class called `DatabaseUtil` class is provided for this purpose. This class provides the methods used by other classes to access and manipulate the data in the database.

DatabaseUtil Class Methods

The `DatabaseUtil` class methods work with the `Category`, `ProductBean`, `OrderBean`, `ShoppingCartBean`, and `ShoppingItemBean` classes, which are described in the "Defining Classes for the Application" section later in this chapter. The `DatabaseUtil` class provides the following methods:

▶ `getCategories`   This method accepts no argument and returns an `ArrayList` containing all of the categories from the Categories table. Each category is represented by the `Category` class. The signature of the `getCategories` method is as follows:

```
public ArrayList getCategories()
```

▶ `searchProducts`   This method returns an `ArrayList` containing all of the products found for a given search key. A product is represented by the `ProductBean` class. Here is the signature of the `searchProducts` method:

```
public ArrayList searchProducts(String searchKey)
```

▶ `getProductsByCategory`   This method returns an `ArrayList` containing all of the products belonging to the specified category identifier passed in as the argument to this method. A product is represented by the `ProductBean` class. The signature of the `getProductsByCategory` method is as follows:

```
public ArrayList getProductsByCategory(String categoryId)
```

▶ `getProductDetails`   This method accepts a product identifier and returns the details of the product encapsulated in an instance of `ProductBean`. The signature of the `getProductDetails` method is as follows:

```
public ProductDetailsBean getProductDetails(String productId)
```

▶ `insertOrder`   You use this method to insert a purchase order. This method accepts two arguments: an order and a shopping cart. An order, represented by the `OrderBean` class, contains the delivery and payment information (the contact name, delivery address, and credit card details). The shopping cart, represented by the `ShoppingCartBean` class, contains all the shopping items. A shopping item is represented by the `ShoppingItemBean` class. Here is the signature of the `insertOrder` method:

```
public synchronized void insertOrder(OrderBean order,
  ShoppingCartBean shoppingCart) {
```

In addition, the `DatabaseUtil` class has two methods for initializing values required for accessing the database: `setJdbcDriver` and `setDbUrl`.

The DatabaseUtil Instance

The application needs only one instance of this class. To avoid creating multiple instances of this class, the application instantiates the class at startup and stores it in `ServletContext`, in the attribute named `DATABASE_UTIL`. The instance can then be retrieved by using the following code:

```
FacesContext facesContext = FacesContext.getCurrentInstance();
ServletContext servletContext = (ServletContext)
  facesContext.getExternalContext().getContext();
DatabaseUtil dbUtil = (DatabaseUtil)
  servletContext.getAttribute("DATABASE_UTIL");
```

To store the `DatabaseUtil` instance at application startup, you use the servlet context listener called `AppContextListener`, shown in Listing 14-2.

Listing 14-2   *The AppContextListener Class*

```
package buydirect;

import javax.servlet.ServletContext;
import javax.servlet.ServletContextEvent;
import javax.servlet.ServletContextListener;

public class AppContextListener implements ServletContextListener {

  public void contextInitialized(ServletContextEvent event) {
    DatabaseUtil dbUtil = new DatabaseUtil();
    ServletContext servletContext = event.getServletContext();
    String jdbcDriver =
      servletContext.getInitParameter("jdbcDriver");
    String dbUrl = servletContext.getInitParameter("dbUrl");
    dbUtil.setJdbcDriver(jdbcDriver);
    dbUtil.setDbUrl(dbUrl);
    servletContext.setAttribute("DATABASE_UTIL", dbUtil);
  }
  public void contextDestroyed(ServletContextEvent event) {
    ServletContext servletContext = event.getServletContext();
    servletContext.removeAttribute("DATABASE_UTIL");
  }
}
```

The `DatabaseUtil` instance needs the `dbUrl` and `jdbcDriver` information provided as context initial parameters in the deployment descriptor (`web.xml` file), as follows:

```
<context-param>
  <param-name>dbUrl</param-name>
  <param-value>jdbc:odbc:buydirect</param-value>
</context-param>
<context-param>
  <param-name>jdbcDriver</param-name>
  <param-value>sun.jdbc.odbc.JdbcOdbcDriver</param-value>
</context-param>
```

NOTE

You need to change the values of the `dbUrl` and `jdbcDriver` parameters to the values of your database server's database URL and JDBC driver.

This means that you can use any database server from any vendor, as long as you provide the correct JDBC driver and URL to the database. Note that you must also copy the JDBC driver to the `WEB-INF/lib` directory.

The DatabaseUtil Class

The `DatabaseUtil` class is shown in Listing 14-3.

Listing 14-3   *The DatabaseUtil Class*

```
package buydirect;

import java.sql.*;
import java.util.ArrayList;
import java.util.Collection;
import java.util.Iterator;

public class DatabaseUtil {


  String dbUrl = "jdbc:odbc:buydirect";
  String jdbcDriver = "sun.jdbc.odbc.JdbcOdbcDriver";

  public void setDbUrl(String dbUrl) {
    this.dbUrl = dbUrl;
  }
  public void setJdbcDriver(String jdbcDriver) {
    this.jdbcDriver = jdbcDriver;
```

```java
      }

   public ArrayList getCategories() {
     ArrayList categories = new ArrayList();
     String sql = "SELECT Id, Description FROM Categories";
     try {
       Class.forName(jdbcDriver);
       Connection connection = DriverManager.getConnection(dbUrl);
       Statement statement = connection.createStatement();
       ResultSet resultSet = statement.executeQuery(sql);
       while (resultSet.next()) {
         String id = resultSet.getString(1);
         String description = resultSet.getString(2);
         Category category = new Category(id, description);
         categories.add(category);
       }
       resultSet.close();
       statement.close();
       connection.close();
     }
     catch (ClassNotFoundException e) {
     }
     catch (SQLException e) {
     }
     catch (Exception e) {
     }
     return categories;
   }

   public ProductBean getProductDetails(String productId) {
     String sql =
       "SELECT ProductId, Name, Description, Price FROM Products" +
       " WHERE ProductId=" + productId;
     ProductBean result = null;
     try {
       Class.forName(jdbcDriver);
       Connection connection = DriverManager.getConnection(dbUrl);
       Statement statement = connection.createStatement();
       ResultSet resultSet = statement.executeQuery(sql);
       if (resultSet.next()) {
         String id = resultSet.getString(1);
         String name = resultSet.getString(2);
         String description = resultSet.getString(3);
         float price = resultSet.getFloat(4);
         result = new ProductBean(id, name, description, price);
```

```java
      }
      resultSet.close();
      statement.close();
      connection.close();
    }
    catch (ClassNotFoundException e) {
    }
    catch (SQLException e) {
    }
    catch (Exception e) {
    }
    return result;
  }
  public ArrayList searchProducts(String searchKey) {
    ArrayList products = new ArrayList();
    String sql = "SELECT ProductId, Name, Price FROM Products" +
      " WHERE Name LIKE '%" + searchKey + "%'" +
      " OR Description LIKE '%" + searchKey + "%'";
    try {
      Class.forName(jdbcDriver);
      Connection connection = DriverManager.getConnection(dbUrl);
      Statement statement = connection.createStatement();
      ResultSet resultSet = statement.executeQuery(sql);
      while (resultSet.next()) {
        String id = resultSet.getString(1);
        String name = resultSet.getString(2);
        float price = resultSet.getFloat(3);
        ProductBean product = new ProductBean(id, name, price);
        products.add(product);
      }
      resultSet.close();
      statement.close();
      connection.close();
    }
    catch (ClassNotFoundException e) {
    }
    catch (SQLException e) {
      System.out.println(e.toString());
    }
    catch (Exception e) {
    }
    return products;
  }

  public ArrayList getProductsByCategory(String categoryId) {
```

```
ArrayList products = new ArrayList();
String sql = "SELECT ProductId, Name, Price FROM Products" +
  " WHERE CategoryId=" + categoryId;
  System.out.println("getProductsBYCategory. categoryId = " +
    categoryId);
try {
  Class.forName(jdbcDriver);
  Connection connection = DriverManager.getConnection(dbUrl);
  Statement statement = connection.createStatement();
  ResultSet resultSet = statement.executeQuery(sql);
  while (resultSet.next()) {
    String id = resultSet.getString(1);
    String name = resultSet.getString(2);
    float price = resultSet.getFloat(3);
    ProductBean product = new ProductBean(id, name, price);
    products.add(product);
  }
  resultSet.close();
  statement.close();
  connection.close();
}
catch (ClassNotFoundException e) {
}
catch (SQLException e) {
  System.out.println(e.toString());
}
catch (Exception e) {
}
return products;
}
public synchronized void insertOrder(OrderBean order,
  ShoppingCartBean shoppingCart) {
  long orderId = System.currentTimeMillis();

  ArrayList products = new ArrayList();
  String contactName = order.getContactName();
  String deliveryAddress = order.getDeliveryAddress();
  String creditCardName = order.getCreditCardName();
  String creditCardNumber = order.getCreditCardNumber();
  String creditCardExpiryDate = order.getCreditCardExpiryDate();
  String sql = "INSERT INTO Orders" +
    " (OrderId, ContactName, DeliveryAddress, CCName," +
    " CCNumber, CCExpiryDate)" +
```

```java
        " VALUES" +
        " (" + orderId + "," +
        "'" + contactName + "'," +
        "'" + deliveryAddress + "'," +
        "'" + creditCardName + "'," +
        "'" + creditCardNumber + "'," +
        "'" + creditCardExpiryDate + "')";
    try {
      Class.forName(jdbcDriver);
      Connection connection = DriverManager.getConnection(dbUrl);
      Statement statement = connection.createStatement();
      statement.executeUpdate(sql);

      Iterator shoppingItems =
        shoppingCart.getShoppingItems().iterator();
      while (shoppingItems.hasNext()) {
        ShoppingItemBean item =
          (ShoppingItemBean) shoppingItems.next();
        String productId = item.getProductId();
        int quantity = item.getQuantity();
        float price = item.getPrice();
        sql = "INSERT INTO OrderDetails" +
          " (OrderId, ProductId, Quantity, Price)" +
          " VALUES" +
          " (" + orderId + "," +
          productId + "," +
          quantity + "," +
          price + ")";
        statement.executeUpdate(sql);
      }
      statement.close();
      connection.close();
    }
    catch (ClassNotFoundException e) {
    }
    catch (SQLException e) {
      System.out.println(e.toString());
    }
    catch (Exception e) {
    }
  }
}
```

Representing the Model Objects and Registering Beans

A number of classes represent model objects in this application. Also, several of the JavaBeans must be registered in the application configuration file.

Defining Classes for the Application

The following classes are used in this application:

- ► Category
- ► MenuBean
- ► ProductBean
- ► ProductDetailsBean
- ► ShoppingItemBean
- ► ShoppingCartBean
- ► OrderBean
- ► BrowseBean

Each of these classes is discussed in the following sections.

The Category Class

The Category class, shown in Listing 14-4, contains information about a product category. There are two properties in this class: id and description.

Listing 14-4   *The Category Class*

```
package buydirect;
public class Category {
  private String id;
  private String description;
  public Category(String id, String description) {
    this.id = id;
    this.description = description;
  }
  public String getId() {
    return id;
  }
  public void setId(String id) {
    this.id = id;
  }
  public String getDescription() {
```

```
      return description;
  }
  public void setDescription(String description) {
    this.description = description;
  }
}
```

The MenuBean Class

The menu box to the left side of each Web page contains hyperlinks that users can click to browse products by category. The hyperlinks are obtained from the instance of the MenuBean class, shown in Listing 14-5.

Listing 14-5   *The MenuBean Class*

```
package buydirect;

import java.util.ArrayList;
import java.util.Iterator;
import javax.faces.context.FacesContext;
import javax.servlet.ServletContext;

public class MenuBean {

  String menu;
  long lastUpdate;
  String browsePage = "browse.jsp";

  int updateInterval = 1; // in minutes
  public MenuBean() {
    updateMenu();
  }

  public String getBrowsePage() {
    return browsePage;
  }
  public void setBrowsePage(String page) {
    browsePage = page;
  }
  public int getUpdateInterval() {
    return updateInterval;
  }
  public void setUpdateInterval(int interval) {
    updateInterval = interval;
```

```
    }
    public String getMenu() {
      long now = System.currentTimeMillis();
      if (now > lastUpdate + updateInterval * 60 * 1000)
        updateMenu();
      return menu;
    }

    private void updateMenu() {
      // get DatabaseUtil instance
      FacesContext facesContext = FacesContext.getCurrentInstance();
      ServletContext servletContext = (ServletContext)
      facesContext.getExternalContext().getContext();
      DatabaseUtil dbUtil = (DatabaseUtil)
        servletContext.getAttribute("DATABASE_UTIL");
      StringBuffer buffer = new StringBuffer(512);
      buffer.append("<table>\n");
      ArrayList categories = dbUtil.getCategories();
      Iterator iterator = categories.iterator();
      while (iterator.hasNext()) {
        Category category = (Category) iterator.next();
        buffer.append("<tr><td>");
        buffer.append("<a href=\"" + browsePage + "?categoryId=" +
          category.getId() + "\">" + category.getDescription() +
            "</a>");
        buffer.append("</td></tr>\n");
      }
      buffer.append("</table>\n");
      menu = buffer.toString();
      lastUpdate = System.currentTimeMillis();
    }
}
```

The MenuBean class has three properties: menu, browsePage, and lastUpdate. The menu property is read-only, and its value is a collection of hyperlinks in a table row. Each hyperlink has this format:

```
<tr>
<td>
  <a href="[browse page]?categoryId=[category identifier]">
    [description]</a>
</td>
</tr>
```

where `[browse page]` is the JSP page that lists products by category and is indicated by the `browsePage` property. By default, the value of the `browsePage` property is `browse.jsp`. As an example, the first category (with category identifier 1) is Digital Camera. Therefore, the hyperlink for this category is as follows:

```
<tr>
<td>
  <a href="browse.jsp?categoryId=1">Digital Camera</a>
</td>
</tr>
```

The `MenuBean` class provides the value for its `menu` property to all of the application users. The `menu` property gets its value from the Categories table and does not change unless the content of the Categories table is modified. Therefore, to save resources, we employ a caching mechanism. The `menu` property will update its value for every specific interval only. The last update time is stored in the `lastUpdate` variable. When called, the `getMenu` method will compare the present time with the `lastUpdate` value. If the `menu` property value needs to be updated, the `updateMenu` private method is called.

```
public String getMenu() {
  long now = System.currentTimeMillis();
  if (now > lastUpdate + updateInterval * 60 * 1000)
    updateMenu();
  return menu;
}
```

The `updateMenu` method obtains the `DatabaseUtil` instance from the `ServletContext` attribute whose key is `DATABASE_UTIL` and calls the `getCategories` method of the `DatabaseUtil` class:

```
FacesContext facesContext = FacesContext.getCurrentInstance();
ServletContext servletContext = (ServletContext)
  facesContext.getExternalContext().getContext();
DatabaseUtil dbUtil = (DatabaseUtil)
  servletContext.getAttribute("DATABASE_UTIL");
StringBuffer buffer = new StringBuffer(512);
buffer.append("<table>\n");
ArrayList categories = dbUtil.getCategories();
```

After it gets the `ArrayList` containing all of the categories, the `updateMenu` method iterates the `ArrayList` to produce the value for the `menu` property:

```
Iterator iterator = categories.iterator();
while (iterator.hasNext()) {
  Category category = (Category) iterator.next();
  buffer.append("<tr><td>");
  buffer.append("<a href=\"" + browsePage + "?categoryId=" +
```

```
      category.getId() + "\">" + category.getDescription() +
      "</a>");
    buffer.append("</td></tr>\n");
  }
  buffer.append("</table>\n");
  menu = buffer.toString();
```

Lastly, it updates the value of the `lastUpdate` variable:

```
lastUpdate = System.currentTimeMillis();
```

The ProductBean Class

The `ProductBean` class, shown in Listing 14-6, encapsulates the information about a product. It has four properties: `id`, `name`, `description`, and `price`.

Listing 14-6   *The ProductBean Class*

```
package buydirect;

public class ProductBean {
  private String id;
  private String name;
  private String description;
  private float price;

  public ProductBean() {
  }

  public ProductBean(String id, String name, float price) {
    this.id = id;
    this.name = name;
    this.price = price;
  }

  public ProductBean(String id, String name,
    String description, float price) {
    this.id = id;
    this.name = name;
    this.description = description;
    this.price = price;
  }

  public String getId() {
    return id;
```

```
  }
  public void setId(String id) {
    this.id = id;
  }
  public String getName() {
    return name;
  }
  public void setName(String name) {
    this.name = name;
  }
  public String getDescription() {
    return description;
  }
  public void setDescription(String description) {
    this.description = description;
  }
  public float getPrice() {
    return price;
  }
  public void setPrice(float price) {
    this.price = price;
  }
}
```

The ProductDetailsBean Class

The `ProductDetailsBean` class extends the `ProductBean` class and adds two more
properties: imageDir and imageUrl. The `imageDir` property specifies the directory
under the application directory where all of the image files are stored. The `imageUrl`
property specifies the URL to the image file for this product. The `ProductDetailsBean`
class is shown in Listing 14-7.

Listing 14-7   *The ProductDetailsBean Class*

```
package buydirect;

import javax.faces.context.ExternalContext;
import javax.faces.context.FacesContext;
import javax.servlet.ServletContext;

public class ProductDetailsBean extends ProductBean {

  private String imageUrl;
  private String imageDir;
```

```
    public ProductDetailsBean() {
      FacesContext facesContext = FacesContext.getCurrentInstance();
      if (facesContext!=null) {
        String productId = (String) facesContext.getExternalContext().
          getRequestParameterMap().get("productId");
        // get DatabaseUtil instance
        ServletContext servletContext = (ServletContext)
          facesContext.getExternalContext().getContext();
        DatabaseUtil dbUtil = (DatabaseUtil)
          servletContext.getAttribute("DATABASE_UTIL");
        ProductBean product = dbUtil.getProductDetails(productId);
        setId(productId);
        setName(product.getName());
        setDescription(product.getDescription());
        setPrice(product.getPrice());
      }
    }

    public String getImageDir() {
      return imageDir;
    }
    public void setImageDir(String imageDir) {
      this.imageDir = imageDir;
    }

    public String getImageUrl() {
      FacesContext facesContext = FacesContext.getCurrentInstance();
      String contextPath =
        facesContext.getExternalContext().getRequestContextPath();
      return  getImageDir() + getId() + ".gif";
    }
    public void setImageUrl(String url) {
      this.imageUrl = url;
    }
}
```

The `ProductDetailsBean` provides a product's details. The constructor of
this bean is called when the JSF implementation instantiates this class. The constructor
retrieves the information about the product from the Products table by calling the
`getProductDetails` method of the `DatabaseUtil` class, and then populates
all of its properties. The product identifier is obtained from the `Request` object in the
`ExternalContext` object in the `FacesContext` object. Therefore, the page that uses
the `ProductDetailsBean` must be called by passing a parameter called `productId`.
Here is the part of the `ProductDetailsBean` class's constructor that extracts the
product identifier from the `productId` parameter:

```
String productId = (String) facesContext.getExternalContext().
    getRequestParameterMap().get("productId");
```

The ShoppingItemBean Class

The ShoppingItemBean class, shown in Listing 14-8, represents a shopping item. It has four properties: productId, productName, price, and quantity.

Listing 14-8   *The ShoppingItemBean Class*

```
package buydirect;

public class ShoppingItemBean {

  private String productId;
  private String productName;
  private float price;
  private int quantity;

  public ShoppingItemBean(
    String productId, String productName,
    float price, int quantity) {
    this.productId = productId;
    this.productName = productName;
    this.price = price;
    this.quantity = quantity;
  }

  public String getProductId() {
    return productId;
  }
  public void setProductId(String productId) {
    this.productId = productId;
  }
  public String getProductName() {
    return productName;
  }
  public void setProductName(String productName) {
    this.productName = productName;
  }
  public int getQuantity() {
    return quantity;
  }
  public void setQuantity(int quantity) {
    this.quantity = quantity;
```

```
  }
  public float getPrice() {
    return price;
  }
  public void setPrice(float price) {
    this.price = price;
  }
}
```

The ShoppingCartBean Class

The ShoppingCartBean class represents a shopping cart. This class is shown in Listing 14-9.

Listing 14-9 *The ShoppingCartBean Class*

```
package buydirect;

import java.util.ArrayList;
import java.util.Collection;
import java.util.Iterator;

public class ShoppingCartBean {
  ArrayList shoppingItems = new ArrayList();
  public ShoppingCartBean() {
  }
  public Collection getShoppingItems() {
    return shoppingItems;
  }
  public void setShoppingItems(Collection shoppingItems) {
    this.shoppingItems = new ArrayList(shoppingItems);
  }
  public void addShoppingItem(ShoppingItemBean item) {
    shoppingItems.add(item);
  }
  public void removeShoppingItems() {
    shoppingItems.clear();
  }
  public float getTotal() {
    float total = 0;
    Iterator iterator = shoppingItems.iterator();
    while (iterator.hasNext()) {
      ShoppingItemBean item = (ShoppingItemBean) iterator.next();
      total += item.getPrice() * item.getQuantity();
```

```
    }
    return total;
  }
}
```

The `ShoppingCartBean` class provides the `shoppingItems` property, whose value is a collection of `ShoppingItemBean` instances added by the user. Also, it provides three other methods:

▶ `addShoppingItem` adds a `ShoppingItemBean` to the collection.

▶ `removeShoppingItems` clears the `shoppingItems` collection.

▶ `getTotal` calculates the amount of the purchase.

The `getTotal` method iterates all `ShoppingItemBean` instances in the collection and multiplies its `price` and `quantity` properties:

```
float total = 0;
Iterator iterator = shoppingItems.iterator();
while (iterator.hasNext()) {
   ShoppingItemBean item = (ShoppingItemBean) iterator.next();
   total += item.getPrice() * item.getQuantity();
}
return total;
```

The OrderBean Class

The `OrderBean` class, shown in Listing 14-10, encapsulates user information for a purchase order. This class has five properties: `contactName`, `deliveryAddress`, `creditCardName`, `creditCardNumber`, and `creditCardExpiryDate`.

Listing 14-10   *The OrderBean Class*

```
package buydirect;

public class OrderBean {
  private String contactName;
  private String deliveryAddress;
  private String creditCardName;
  private String creditCardNumber;
  private String creditCardExpiryDate;

  public String getContactName() {
    return contactName;
  }
```

```
    public void setContactName(String contactName) {
      this.contactName = contactName;
    }
    public String getDeliveryAddress() {
      return deliveryAddress;
    }
    public void setDeliveryAddress(String deliveryAddress) {
      this.deliveryAddress = deliveryAddress;
    }
    public String getCreditCardName() {
      return creditCardName;
    }
    public void setCreditCardName(String creditCardName) {
      this.creditCardName = creditCardName;
    }
    public String getCreditCardNumber() {
      return creditCardNumber;
    }
    public void setCreditCardNumber(String creditCardNumber) {
      this.creditCardNumber = creditCardNumber;
    }
    public String getCreditCardExpiryDate() {
      return creditCardExpiryDate;
    }
    public void setCreditCardExpiryDate(String creditCardExpiryDate) {
      this.creditCardExpiryDate = creditCardExpiryDate;
    }
}
```

The SearchBean Class

The SearchBean class encapsulates the search key and search result for a product search.
This class is presented in Listing 14-11.

Listing 14-11   *The SearchBean Class*

```
package buydirect;

import java.util.ArrayList;
import java.util.Collection;
import javax.faces.context.FacesContext;
import javax.servlet.ServletContext;

public class SearchBean {
```

```
  private String searchKey;

  public String getSearchKey() {
    return searchKey;
  }
  public void setSearchKey(String searchKey) {
    this.searchKey = searchKey;
  }
  public Collection getSearchResult() {
    // get DatabaseUtil instance
    FacesContext facesContext = FacesContext.getCurrentInstance();
    ServletContext servletContext = (ServletContext)
    facesContext.getExternalContext().getContext();
    DatabaseUtil dbUtil = (DatabaseUtil)
      servletContext.getAttribute("DATABASE_UTIL");
    return dbUtil.searchProducts(searchKey);
  }
}
```

The searchKey property contains the search key. The getSearchResult method returns a collection containing all of the products resulting from a search. The getSearch method obtains its value by calling the searchProducts method of the DatabaseUtil class.

The BrowseBean Class

The BrowseBean class, shown in Listing 14-12, encapsulates all of the products in a category. The bean is referenced by the browse page and retrieves all of the products belonging to a category from the Products table. The browse page must be called by passing a parameter called categoryId, so that the BrowseBean class knows which category to use in its constructor.

Listing 14-12   *The BrowseBean Class*

```
package buydirect;

import java.util.ArrayList;
import java.util.Collection;
import javax.faces.context.FacesContext;
import javax.servlet.ServletContext;

public class BrowseBean {

  private String categoryId;
  public BrowseBean() {
```

```
      FacesContext facesContext = FacesContext.getCurrentInstance();
      if (facesContext!=null)
        categoryId = (String)
          facesContext.getExternalContext().
          getRequestParameterMap().get("categoryId");
    }
    public String getCategoryId() {
      return categoryId;
    }
    public void setCategoryId(String categoryId) {
      this.categoryId = categoryId;
    }
    public Collection getResult() {
      // get DatabaseUtil instance
      FacesContext facesContext = FacesContext.getCurrentInstance();
      ServletContext servletContext = (ServletContext)
      facesContext.getExternalContext().getContext();
      DatabaseUtil dbUtil = (DatabaseUtil)
        servletContext.getAttribute("DATABASE_UTIL");
      return dbUtil.getProductsByCategory(categoryId);
    }
}
```

Notice how the constructor obtains the category identifier from the Request object in the ExternalContext object. It assigns this value to its categoryId property. When the getResult method is called, the categoryId property value is passed to the getProductsByCategory method of the DatabaseUtil instance.

Registering the Beans in the Application Configuration File

You must register the MenuBean, SearchBean, BrowseBean, ProductBean, ProductDetailsBean, and OrderBean in the application configuration file, so that they can be instantiated properly. Listing 14-13 shows the managed-bean tags in the application configuration file.

Listing 14-13   *Managed-Bean Registration in the Application Configuration File*

```
<managed-bean>
  <managed-bean-name>MenuBean</managed-bean-name>
  <managed-bean-class>buydirect.MenuBean</managed-bean-class>
  <managed-bean-scope>application</managed-bean-scope>
</managed-bean>
<managed-bean>
```

```
    <managed-bean-name>SearchBean</managed-bean-name>
    <managed-bean-class>buydirect.SearchBean</managed-bean-class>
    <managed-bean-scope>request</managed-bean-scope>
</managed-bean>
<managed-bean>
    <managed-bean-name>BrowseBean</managed-bean-name>
    <managed-bean-class>buydirect.BrowseBean</managed-bean-class>
    <managed-bean-scope>request</managed-bean-scope>
</managed-bean>
<managed-bean>
    <managed-bean-name>ProductBean</managed-bean-name>
    <managed-bean-class>buydirect.ProductBean</managed-bean-class>
    <managed-bean-scope>request</managed-bean-scope>
</managed-bean>
<managed-bean>
    <managed-bean-name>ProductDetailsBean</managed-bean-name>
    <managed-bean-class>
      buydirect.ProductDetailsBean
    </managed-bean-class>
    <managed-bean-scope>request</managed-bean-scope>
    <managed-property>
      <property-name>imageDir</property-name>
      <value>images/</value>
    </managed-property>
</managed-bean>
<managed-bean>
    <managed-bean-name>ShoppingCartBean</managed-bean-name>
    <managed-bean-class>
      buydirect.ShoppingCartBean
    </managed-bean-class>
    <managed-bean-scope>session</managed-bean-scope>
</managed-bean>
<managed-bean>
    <managed-bean-name>OrderBean</managed-bean-name>
    <managed-bean-class>buydirect.OrderBean</managed-bean-class>
    <managed-bean-scope>session</managed-bean-scope>
</managed-bean>
```

The MenuBean has the application context because the instance is used by
the whole application. The SearchBean, BrowseBean, ProductBean, and
ProductDetailsBean have the request scope because they are specific to a particular
user request. Notice that the ProductDetailsBean has its imageDir property set by
using the managed-property tag. The ShoppingCartBean and OrderBean have
the session scope because they must live throughout a user's session.

Establishing Navigation Rules

You need navigation rules to manage the flow of your program. You use the JSP page names to define the navigation rules in the application file. Table 14-5 presents the JSP page name for each BuyDirect application page that needs navigation rules. (We will discuss these and the other JSP pages in the application in the "Creating the JSP Pages" section later in this chapter.)

Listing 14-14 shows the `navigation-rule` tags in the application configuration file.

Listing 14-14   *Navigation Rules in the Application Configuration File*

```
<navigation-rule>
  <from-tree-id>*</from-tree-id>
  <navigation-case>
    <from-outcome>search</from-outcome>
    <to-tree-id>/search.jsp</to-tree-id>
  </navigation-case>
</navigation-rule>
<navigation-rule>
  <from-tree-id>/search.jsp</from-tree-id>
  <navigation-case>
    <from-outcome>detail</from-outcome>
    <to-tree-id>/details.jsp</to-tree-id>
  </navigation-case>
</navigation-rule>
<navigation-rule>
  <from-tree-id>/browse.jsp</from-tree-id>
  <navigation-case>
    <from-outcome>detail</from-outcome>
    <to-tree-id>/details.jsp</to-tree-id>
  </navigation-case>
</navigation-rule>
<navigation-rule>
  <from-tree-id>/details.jsp</from-tree-id>
  <navigation-case>
    <from-outcome>buy</from-outcome>
    <to-tree-id>/shoppingCart.jsp</to-tree-id>
  </navigation-case>
</navigation-rule>
<navigation-rule>
```

```
    <from-tree-id>/shoppingCart.jsp</from-tree-id>
    <navigation-case>
      <from-outcome>checkOut</from-outcome>
      <to-tree-id>/checkOut.jsp</to-tree-id>
    </navigation-case>
  </navigation-rule>
  <navigation-rule>
    <from-tree-id>/checkOut.jsp</from-tree-id>
    <navigation-case>
      <from-outcome>order</from-outcome>
      <to-tree-id>/order.jsp</to-tree-id>
    </navigation-case>
  </navigation-rule>
```

The following sections discuss how these navigation rules work for each page.

Navigating to the Search Page

Every page allows users to search for a product. Therefore, any page can potentially navigate to the `search.jsp` page, and this is indicated by the following `navigation-rule` tag:

```
<navigation-rule>
  <from-tree-id>*</from-tree-id>
  <navigation-case>
    <from-outcome>search</from-outcome>
    <to-tree-id>/search.jsp</to-tree-id>
  </navigation-case>
</navigation-rule>
```

Page	JSP Filename
Main page	`index.jsp`
Search page	`search.jsp`
Browse page	`browse.jsp`
Product details page	`details.jsp`
Shopping cart page	`shoppingCart.jsp`
Check out page	`checkOut.jsp`
Order page	`order.jsp`

Table 14-5   *The JSP Filenames for BuyDirect Application Pages that Require Navigation Rules*

Navigating to the Product Details Page

From the list of products in both the search page and browse page, users can click the Details hyperlink to view the details of a specific product. Therefore, you need the following two navigation rules:

```
<navigation-rule>
  <from-tree-id>/search.jsp</from-tree-id>
  <navigation-case>
    <from-outcome>detail</from-outcome>
    <to-tree-id>/details.jsp</to-tree-id>
  </navigation-case>
</navigation-rule>
<navigation-rule>
  <from-tree-id>/browse.jsp</from-tree-id>
  <navigation-case>
    <from-outcome>detail</from-outcome>
    <to-tree-id>/details.jsp</to-tree-id>
  </navigation-case>
</navigation-rule>
```

Navigating to the Shopping Cart Page

After viewing the details of a product, users can decide to buy that product. Therefore, the details page must be able to navigate to the shopping cart page. This is made possible by the following `navigation-rule` tag:

```
<navigation-rule>
  <from-tree-id>/details.jsp</from-tree-id>
  <navigation-case>
    <from-outcome>buy</from-outcome>
    <to-tree-id>/shoppingCart.jsp</to-tree-id>
  </navigation-case>
</navigation-rule>
```

Navigating to the Check Out and Order Pages

From the shopping cart page, users can check out. The following `navigation-rule` tag defines the transition from the shopping cart page to the check out page.

```
<navigation-rule>
  <from-tree-id>/shoppingCart.jsp</from-tree-id>
  <navigation-case>
    <from-outcome>checkOut</from-outcome>
    <to-tree-id>/checkOut.jsp</to-tree-id>
  </navigation-case>
</navigation-rule>
```

Finally, after users enter their delivery and payment details, they can pay. This requires navigation from the check out page to the order page, enabled by the following `navigation-rule` tag:

```
<navigation-rule>
  <from-tree-id>/checkOut.jsp</from-tree-id>
  <navigation-case>
    <from-outcome>order</from-outcome>
    <to-tree-id>/order.jsp</to-tree-id>
  </navigation-case>
</navigation-rule>
```

Adding the ActionListener

The application uses an `ActionListener` called `AppActionListener`. In our application, the `ActionListener`'s `processAction` method is invoked when the user clicks the Buy button in the product details page and when the user clicks the Pay button in the check out page. Two private methods, `getValueBinding` and `getDatabaseUtil`, are used from various points in the `AppActionListener` class. The `getValueBinding` method returns a `ValueBinding` object for the specified value reference. The `getDatabaseUtil` method returns the `DatabaseUtil` instance in `ServletContext`.

The `AppActionListener` class is shown in Listing 14-15.

Listing 14-15   *The AppActionListener Class*

```
package buydirect;

import java.util.Iterator;
import javax.faces.FactoryFinder;
import javax.faces.application.Application;
import javax.faces.application.ApplicationFactory;
import javax.faces.context.FacesContext;
import javax.faces.el.ValueBinding;
import javax.faces.event.ActionEvent;
import javax.faces.event.ActionListener;
import javax.faces.event.PhaseId;
import javax.faces.component.UICommand;
import javax.faces.component.UIComponent;
import javax.faces.component.UIInput;
import javax.faces.tree.Tree;
import javax.servlet.ServletContext;

public class AppActionListener implements ActionListener {
```

```java
    public PhaseId getPhaseId() {
      return PhaseId.INVOKE_APPLICATION;
    }


    public void processAction(ActionEvent event) {
      String actionCommand = event.getActionCommand();
      if ("buy".equals(actionCommand)) {
        FacesContext facesContext = FacesContext.getCurrentInstance();
        String productId = (String)
facesContext.getExternalContext().
getRequestParameterMap().get("productId");
        ShoppingCartBean cart =
          (ShoppingCartBean) getValueBinding("ShoppingCartBean").
getValue(facesContext);
        ProductBean product = getDatabaseUtil().
getProductDetails(productId);
        ShoppingItemBean shoppingItem = new
          ShoppingItemBean(product.getId(), product.getName(),
product.getPrice(), 1);
        cart.addShoppingItem(shoppingItem);
      }
      else if ("order".equals(actionCommand)) {
        // insert a record into the database
        FacesContext facesContext = FacesContext.getCurrentInstance();
        OrderBean order = (OrderBean)
getValueBinding("OrderBean").getValue(facesContext);
        ShoppingCartBean cart = (ShoppingCartBean)
getValueBinding("ShoppingCartBean").getValue(facesContext);
        getDatabaseUtil().insertOrder(order, cart);
        // empty shopping cart
        cart.removeShoppingItems();
      }

    }


  private ValueBinding getValueBinding(String valueRef) {
    ApplicationFactory factory =
(ApplicationFactory)FactoryFinder.
getFactory(FactoryFinder.APPLICATION_FACTORY);
    Application application = factory.getApplication();
    return application.getValueBinding(valueRef);
  }

  private DatabaseUtil getDatabaseUtil() {
    FacesContext facesContext = FacesContext.getCurrentInstance();
```

```
    ServletContext servletContext = (ServletContext)
facesContext.getExternalContext().getContext();
    return (DatabaseUtil)
servletContext.getAttribute("DATABASE_UTIL");
  }
}
```

The `processAction` method starts by obtaining the action command by invoking `getActionCommand` on the `ActionEvent` instance.

```
String actionCommand = event.getActionCommand();
```

When the user clicks the Buy button in the product details page, the `ActionListener` executes the code within the following `if` block:

```
    if ("buy".equals(actionCommand)) {
        ...
    }
```

The `processAction` method obtains the product identifier from the `Request` object in the `ExternalContext` instance in `FacesContext` and assigns it to the `productId` `String` variable.

```
    FacesContext facesContext = FacesContext.getCurrentInstance();
    String productId = (String)
facesContext.getExternalContext().
getRequestParameterMap().get("productId");
```

It then retrieves the `ShoppingCartBean` from `FacesContext`.

```
    ShoppingCartBean cart =
(ShoppingCartBean) getValueBinding("ShoppingCartBean").
getValue(facesContext);
```

Next, it obtains the product information by calling the `getProductDetails` method of the `DatabaseUtil` instance and uses it to create an instance of the `ShoppingItemBean` class.

```
    ProductBean product = getDatabaseUtil().
getProductDetails(productId);
    ShoppingItemBean shoppingItem = new
  ShoppingItemBean(product.getId(), product.getName(),
product.getPrice(), 1);
```

The `processAction` method then adds the `ShoppingItemBean` instance to the shopping cart.

```
    cart.addShoppingItem(shoppingItem);
```

When the user clicks the Pay button in the check out page, the `ActionListener` executes the code within the following `if` block:

```
else if ("order".equals(actionCommand)) {
    ...
}
```

The code within the `if` block inserts the order information and clears the shopping cart. It first obtains the `OrderBean` instance and the `ShoppingCartBean` instance:

```
// insert a record into the database
FacesContext facesContext = FacesContext.getCurrentInstance();
OrderBean order = (OrderBean)
getValueBinding("OrderBean").getValue(facesContext);
    ShoppingCartBean cart = (ShoppingCartBean)
getValueBinding("ShoppingCartBean").getValue(facesContext);
```

Then it calls the `insertOrder` method of the `DatabaseUtil` instance, passing the `OrderBean` and `ShoppingCartBean` instances:

```
getDatabaseUtil().insertOrder(order, cart);
```

Lastly, the `ActionListener` calls the `removeShoppingItems` method of the `ShoppingCartBean` to clear the shopping cart.

```
// empty shopping cart
cart.removeShoppingItems();
```

Writing the Deployment Descriptor

Just like any other JSF application, the BuyDirect application needs a deployment descriptor that specifies the `FacesServlet` servlet and the servlet mapping. In addition, you need to declare several `context-param` tags and a listener for the `AppContextListener` class. The deployment descriptor for this application is shown in Listing 14-16.

Listing 14-16 *The Deployment Descriptor for the BuyDirect Application*

```
<?xml version="1.0"?>
<!DOCTYPE web-app PUBLIC
  "-//Sun Microsystems, Inc.//DTD Web Application 2.3//EN"
  "http://java.sun.com/dtd/web-app_2_3.dtd">

<web-app>
  <context-param>
    <param-name>dbUrl</param-name>
    <param-value>jdbc:odbc:buydirect</param-value>
```

```
    </context-param>
    <context-param>
      <param-name>jdbcDriver</param-name>
      <param-value>sun.jdbc.odbc.JdbcOdbcDriver</param-value>
    </context-param>
    <context-param>
      <param-name>pageWidth</param-name>
      <param-value>678</param-value>
    </context-param>
    <context-param>
      <param-name>menuWidth</param-name>
      <param-value>155</param-value>
    </context-param>

    <listener>
      <listener-class>buydirect.AppContextListener</listener-class>
    </listener>

    <!-- Faces Servlet -->
    <servlet>
      <servlet-name>Faces Servlet</servlet-name>
      <servlet-class>javax.faces.webapp.FacesServlet</servlet-class>
      <load-on-startup> 1 </load-on-startup>
    </servlet>

    <!-- Faces Servlet Mapping -->
    <servlet-mapping>
      <servlet-name>Faces Servlet</servlet-name>
      <url-pattern>/faces/*</url-pattern>
    </servlet-mapping>
</web-app>
```

Creating the JSP Pages

The BuyDirect application uses the JSP pages listed earlier in Table 14-5, along with three other pages: `header.jsp`, `footer.jsp`, and `menu.jsp`. These three pages are pages called from other pages. All of the pages, except the include pages, reference the `Styles.css` file, using the following code:

```
<link rel="stylesheet" type="text/css"
  href="<%= request.getContextPath() + "/Styles.css" %>">
```

The `request.getContextPath` method will result in a context path similar to /buydirect/Styles.css. This way, the `Styles.css` file is called without the invocation of `FacesServlet`, because the URL to the `Styles.css` file does not contain the `/faces/` pattern.

On the other hand, simply using the following code would produce the URL pattern `/buydirect/faces/Styles.css`:

```
<link rel="stylesheet" type="text/css"
  href="Styles.css" %>">
```

This would occur because the calling page itself has the `/buydirect/faces/` path. It would invoke the `FacesServlet` servlet, which you do not want to happen, because it would mean extra work in the server.

Each of the JSP pages is explained in the following sections.

The header.jsp and footer.jsp Pages

The `header.jsp` page is the header for all the other JSP pages. It is shown in Listing 14-17.

Listing 14-17   *The header.jsp Page*

```
<table border="0" width="100%" cellpadding="5"
cellspacing="0" class="Header">
<tr>
  <td align="left">
    <div class="HeaderText1">Buy Direct</div>
    <br>
    <div class="HeaderText2">Lowest prices today!!!</div>
  </td>
</tr>
</table>
```

The `footer.jsp` page, shown in Listing 14-18, is the footer for all the other JSP pages.

Listing 14-18   *The footer.jsp Page*

```
<center>
<div class="Footer">&copy;2004 Buy Direct</div>
</center>
```

The menu.jsp Page

The `menu.jsp` page is an include page that provides the contents for the menu box on the left side of each page. Listing 14-19 shows the `menu.jsp` page.

Listing 14-19   *The menu.jsp Page*

```html
<!-- the main table containing two other tables:
Search table and Browse table -->
<table border="0" cellpadding="0" cellspacing="0"
  width="<h:output_text valueRef="initParam.menuWidth"/>">
<tr>
<td>

<!-- the Search table -->
<table cellspacing="0" cellpadding="1" width="100%"
  border="0" class="OuterTable">
<tr>
  <td>
    <table cellspacing="0" cellpadding="5"
      width="100%" border="0" class="InnerTable">
    <tr>
      <td class="MenuHeader">Search</td>
    </tr>
    <tr valign="middle">
      <td rowspan="2">
        <h:input_text size="13" valueRef="SearchBean.searchKey"/>
        <h:command_button commandName="search" label=" Go "
action="search">
          <f:action_listener type="buydirect.AppActionListener"/>
        </h:command_button>
      </td>
    </tr>
    </table>
  </td>
</tr>
</table>

</td>
</tr>

<!-- space between the Search table and Browse table -->
<tr>
<td height="7"></td>
</tr>

<tr>
<td>
```

```
<!-- the Browse table -->
<table cellspacing="0" cellpadding="1"
  width="100%" border="0"
  class="OuterTable">
<tr>
  <td>

    <table cellspacing="0" cellpadding="5" width="100%"
      border="0" class="InnerTable">
    <tr>
      <td class="MenuHeader">Browse</td>
    </tr>
    <tr valign="top">
      <td>
        <h:output_text valueRef="MenuBean.menu"/>
      </td>
    </tr>
    </table>
  </td>
</tr>
</table>


</td>
</tr>
</table>
```

The menu.jsp page contains a main table with three rows. The width of this table is governed by the value obtained from the deployment descriptor:

```
width="<h:output_text valueRef="initParam.menuWidth"/>">
```

The first row of the main table contains a table for the Search box, the second row contains a blank row, and the third row contains a table with hyperlinks to browse products by category. The main table in the menu.jsp page has the following skeleton:

```
<table>
<tr>
  <td>
    <!-- the table containing the Search box -->
  </td>
</tr>
<tr>
  <td>
    <!-- blank row -->
  </td>
```

```
</tr>
<tr>
  <td>
    <!-- the table containing the hyperlinks to
      browse products by category -->
  </td>
</tr>
</table>
```

The first table in the main table, the Search table, uses a `UIInput` component to receive the search key and a `UICommand` component to invoke an `ActionEvent`. The event is captured by the `buydirect.AppActionListener` class.

```
<h:input_text size="13" valueRef="SearchBean.searchKey"/>
    <h:command_button commandName="search" label=" Go "
action="search">
        <f:action_listener type="buydirect.AppActionListener"/>
    </h:command_button>
```

The second table in the main table, the Browse table, uses a `UIOutput` component, which gets its value from the menu property of the `MenuBean`.

```
<h:output_text valueRef="MenuBean.menu"/>
```

The index.jsp Page

The `index.jsp` page is the main page in the application. It contains nothing other than the welcome message, printed in bold, as shown in Listing 14-20.

Listing 14-20   *The index.jsp Page*

```
<%@ taglib uri="http://java.sun.com/jsf/html" prefix="h" %>
<%@ taglib uri="http://java.sun.com/jsf/core" prefix="f" %>
<html>
<head>
<title>Welcome to BuyDirect</title>
<link rel="stylesheet" type="text/css"
  href="<%= request.getContextPath() + "/Styles.css" %>">
</head> .
<body>
<f:use_faces>
<h:form formName="myForm">
<table border="0" cellspacing="4" cellpadding="0"
  width="<h:output_text valueRef="initParam.pageWidth"/>">
```

```
<tr>
  <td colspan="2">
    <%-- The header --%>
    <%@ include file="header.jsp"%>
  </td>
</tr>
<tr>
  <td valign="top">
    <%-- The menu --%>
    <%@ include file="menu.jsp"%>
  </td>
  <td valign="top">


<!-------------- the beginning of the Welcome page ------------->
    <br>
    <div class="NormalLarge">Welcome to Buy Direct</div>
    <br>
    <div class="NormalSmall">Try our lowest prices today!</div>
<!-------------------- the end of the Welcome page ------------->


  </td>
</tr>
<tr>
  <td colspan="2">
    <%-- The footer --%>
    <%@ include file="footer.jsp"%>
  </td>
</tr>
</table>

</h:form>
</f:use_faces>

</body>
</html>
```

The search.jsp Page

The search.jsp page is used to display the search result. The main part of the search.jsp page is printed in bold, as shown in Listing 14-21.

Listing 14-21   *The search.jsp Page*

```jsp
<%@ taglib uri="http://java.sun.com/jsf/html" prefix="h" %>
<%@ taglib uri="http://java.sun.com/jsf/core" prefix="f" %>
<html>
<head>
<title>Search Result</title>
<link rel="stylesheet" type="text/css"
  href="<%= request.getContextPath() + "/Styles.css" %>">
</head>
<body>
<f:use_faces>
<h:form formName="myForm">
<table border="0" cellspacing="4" cellpadding="0"
  width="<h:output_text valueRef="initParam.pageWidth"/>">
<tr>
  <td colspan="2">
    <%-- The header --%>
    <%@ include file="header.jsp"%>
  </td>
</tr>
<tr>
  <td valign="top">
    <%-- The menu --%>
    <%@ include file="menu.jsp"%>
  </td>
  <td valign="top">
    <br>
    <div class="NormalLarge">Search Result</div>


<!-------------- the beginning of the Search page ------------->
<h:panel_list border="1">
  <f:facet name="header">
    <h:panel_group>
      <h:output_text value="Product"/>
      <h:output_text value="Price"/>
      <h:output_text value="Details"/>
    </h:panel_group>
  </f:facet>

  <h:panel_data var="product" valueRef="SearchBean.searchResult">
    <h:output_text valueRef="product.name"/>
```

```
    <h:output_text valueRef="product.price"/>
    <h:command_hyperlink href="details.jsp"
      label="Details" commandName="Details">
      <f:parameter name="productId" valueRef="product.id"/>
    </h:command_hyperlink>

  </h:panel_data>
</h:panel_list>
<!-------------------- the end of the Search page ------------->


  </td>
</tr>
<tr>
  <td colspan="2">
    <%-- The footer --%>
    <%@ include file="footer.jsp"%>
  </td>
</tr>
</table>

</h:form>
</f:use_faces>
</body>
</html>
```

The panel_data tag gets a collection from the searchResult property of the
SearchBean. The collection contains ProductBean instances whose name or description
matches the search key. Two UIOutput components are used to print the product name and
description. The third column is a hyperlink with a parameter called productId. The hyperlink
gets its value from the id property of the PropertyBean. Here is the panel_data tag again:

```
<h:panel_data var="product" valueRef="SearchBean.searchResult">
  <h:output_text valueRef="product.name"/>
  <h:output_text valueRef="product.price"/>
  <h:command_hyperlink href="details.jsp" label="Details" commandName="Details">
    <f:parameter name="productId" valueRef="product.id"/>
  </h:command_hyperlink>
</h:panel_data>
```

The browse.jsp Page

The browse.jsp page displays products in a category. It is shown in Listing 14-22.

Listing 14-22 *The browse.jsp Page*

```jsp
<%@ taglib uri="http://java.sun.com/jsf/html" prefix="h" %>
<%@ taglib uri="http://java.sun.com/jsf/core" prefix="f" %>
<html>
<head>
<title>Products by Category</title>
<link rel="stylesheet" type="text/css"
  href="<%= request.getContextPath() + "/Styles.css" %>">
</head>
<body>
<f:use_faces>
<h:form formName="myForm">
<table border="0" cellspacing="4" cellpadding="0"
  width="<h:output_text valueRef="initParam.pageWidth"/>">
<tr>
  <td colspan="2">
    <%-- The header --%>
    <%@ include file="header.jsp"%>
  </td>
</tr>
<tr>
  <td valign="top">
    <%-- The menu --%>
    <%@ include file="menu.jsp"%>
  </td>
  <td valign="top">
    <br>
    <div class="NormalLarge">Products by Category</div>


<!--------------- the beginning of the Browse page ------------->
<h:panel_list border="1">
  <f:facet name="header">
    <h:panel_group>
      <h:output_text value="Product"/>
      <h:output_text value="Price"/>
      <h:output_text value="Details"/>
    </h:panel_group>
  </f:facet>

  <h:panel_data var="product" valueRef="BrowseBean.result">
    <h:output_text valueRef="product.name"/>
    <h:output_text valueRef="product.price"/>
```

```
    <h:command_hyperlink href="details.jsp" label="Details"
      commandName="Details">
      <f:parameter name="productId" valueRef="product.id"/>
    </h:command_hyperlink>

  </h:panel_data>
</h:panel_list>
<!------------------- the end of the Browse page ------------->


  </td>
</tr>
<tr>
  <td colspan="2">
    <%-- The footer --%>
    <%@ include file="footer.jsp"%>
  </td>
</tr>
</table>

</h:form>
</f:use_faces>
</body>
</html>
```

The `browse.jsp` page is similar to the `search.jsp` page, except that it displays all of the products belonging to a category, rather than the products that match a specific keyword. The following is the part of the `browse.jsp` page that produces the dynamic data:

```
<h:panel_data var="product" valueRef="BrowseBean.result">
  <h:output_text valueRef="product.name"/>
  <h:output_text valueRef="product.price"/>
  <h:command_hyperlink href="details.jsp"
    label="Details" commandName="Details">
    <f:parameter name="productId" valueRef="product.id"/>
  </h:command_hyperlink>
</h:panel_data>
```

The `panel_data` tag gets its contents from the `result` property of the `BrowseBean`. The `result` property is a collection containing `ProductBean` instances that belong to the specified category.

The details.jsp Page

The `details.jsp` page displays the details of a product. Listing 14-23 shows this page.

Listing 14-23   *The details.jsp Page*

```
<%@ taglib uri="http://java.sun.com/jsf/html" prefix="h" %>
<%@ taglib uri="http://java.sun.com/jsf/core" prefix="f" %>
<html>
<head>
<title>Product Details</title>
<link rel="stylesheet" type="text/css"
  href="<%= request.getContextPath() + "/Styles.css" %>">
</head>
<body>
<f:use_faces>
<h:form formName="myForm">
<table border="0" cellspacing="4" cellpadding="0"
  width="<h:output_text valueRef="initParam.pageWidth"/>">
<tr>
  <td colspan="2">
    <%-- The header --%>
    <%@ include file="header.jsp"%>
  </td>
</tr>
<tr>
  <td valign="top">
    <%-- The menu --%>
    <%@ include file="menu.jsp"%>
  </td>
  <td valign="top">
    <br>
    <div class="NormalLarge">Product Details</div>


<!-------------- the beginning of the Details page ------------->

<h:input_hidden id="productId" valueRef="ProductDetailsBean.id"/>

<%-- the valueRef in graphic_image is not good
<h:graphic_image width="150" valueRef="ProductDetailsBean.imageUrl"/>
--%>


<br/>
Name: <h:output_text valueRef="ProductDetailsBean.name"/>
<br/>
Description:
<h:output_text valueRef="ProductDetailsBean.description"/>
```

```
<br/>
Price:
<h:output_number valueRef="ProductDetailsBean.price"/>
<br/>
<h:command_button label="Buy" commandName="buy" action="buy">
  <f:action_listener type="buydirect.AppActionListener"/>
</h:command_button>

<!-------------------- the end of the Details page --------------->


  </td>
</tr>
<tr>
  <td colspan="2">
    <%-- The footer --%>
    <%@ include file="footer.jsp"%>
  </td>
</tr>
</table>

</h:form>
</f:use_faces>
</body>
</html>
```

The details.jsp page is called by passing the productId parameter in the URL.
When the details.jsp page is called, the JSF implementation creates an instance of
ProductDetailsBean. The constructor of the ProductDetailsBean class acquires
the value of the productId parameter and populates the other properties, which then
become the sources for other values.

The shoppingCart.jsp Page

The shoppingCart.jsp page displays the contents of the ShoppingCartBean for a
particular user. It is shown in Listing 14-24.

Listing 14-24   *The shoppingCart.jsp Page*

```
<%@ taglib uri="http://java.sun.com/jsf/html" prefix="h" %>
<%@ taglib uri="http://java.sun.com/jsf/core" prefix="f" %>
<html>
<head>
```

```
<title>Shopping Cart</title>
<link rel="stylesheet" type="text/css"
  href="<%= request.getContextPath() + "/Styles.css" %>">
</head>
<body>
<f:use_faces>
<h:form formName="myForm">
<table border="0" cellspacing="4" cellpadding="0"
  width="<h:output_text valueRef="initParam.pageWidth"/>">
<tr>
  <td colspan="2">
    <%-- The header --%>
    <%@ include file="header.jsp"%>
  </td>
</tr>
<tr>
  <td valign="top">
    <%-- The menu --%>
    <%@ include file="menu.jsp"%>
  </td>
  <td valign="top">
    <br>
    <div class="NormalLarge">Shopping Cart</div>


<!-- the beginning of the Shopping Cart page -->
<h:panel_list border="1">
  <f:facet name="header">
    <h:panel_group>
      <h:output_text value="Product Name"/>
      <h:output_text value="Quantity"/>
      <h:output_text value="Price"/>
    </h:panel_group>
  </f:facet>
  <h:panel_data var="item" valueRef="ShoppingCartBean.shoppingItems">
    <h:output_text valueRef="item.productName"/>
    <h:output_number valueRef="item.quantity"/>
    <h:output_number valueRef="item.price"/>
  </h:panel_data>
  <f:facet name="footer">
    <h:panel_group>
      <h:output_text value=" "/>
      <h:output_text value="Total"/>
      <h:output_number valueRef="ShoppingCartBean.total"/>
    </h:panel_group>
```

```
  </f:facet>
</h:panel_list>

<br>
<h:command_button action="checkOut"
  commandName="checkOut" label="Check Out">
  <f:action_listener type="buydirect.AppActionListener"/>
</h:command_button>

<!-- the end of the Shopping Cart page -->


  </td>
</tr>
<tr>
  <td colspan="2">
    <%-- The footer --%>
    <%@ include file="footer.jsp"%>
  </td>
</tr>
</table>

</h:form>
</f:use_faces>
</body>
</html>
```

The main part of the `shoppingCart.jsp` page (printed in bold) is a `UIPanel` component with a header facet and a footer facet. The dynamic part uses a `panel_data` tag, which gets its data from the `shoppingItems` property of the `ShoppingCartBean`. It has three columns that display the product name, quantity, and price, respectively:

```
<h:panel_data var="item" valueRef="ShoppingCartBean.shoppingItems">
  <h:output_text valueRef="item.productName"/>
  <h:output_number valueRef="item.quantity"/>
  <h:output_number valueRef="item.price"/>
</h:panel_data>
```

The total purchase value is displayed at the footer. The value comes from the `total` property of the `ShoppingCartBean`:

```
<f:facet name="footer">
  <h:panel_group>
    <h:output_text value=" "/>
    <h:output_text value="Total"/>
```

```
                    <h:output_number valueRef="ShoppingCartBean.total"/>
</h:panel_group>
  </f:facet>
```

Below the `UIPanel` component is a `UICommand` component that the user can click to check out:

```
<h:command_button action="checkOut"
  commandName="checkOut" label="Check Out">
    <f:action_listener type="buydirect.AppActionListener"/>
</h:command_button>
```

The checkOut.jsp Page

The `checkOut.jsp` page displays five input fields for delivery details and payment details. The `checkOut.jsp` page is shown in Listing 14-25.

Listing 14-25   *The checkOut.jsp Page*

```
<%@ taglib uri="http://java.sun.com/jsf/html" prefix="h" %>
<%@ taglib uri="http://java.sun.com/jsf/core" prefix="f" %>
<html>
<head>
<title>Search Result</title>
<link rel="stylesheet" type="text/css"
  href="<%= request.getContextPath() + "/Styles.css" %>">
</head>
<body>
<f:use_faces>
<h:form formName="myForm">
<table border="0" cellspacing="4" cellpadding="0"
  width="<h:output_text valueRef="initParam.pageWidth"/>">
<tr>
  <td colspan="2">
    <%-- The header --%>
    <%@ include file="header.jsp"%>
  </td>
</tr>
<tr>
  <td valign="top">
    <%-- The menu --%>
    <%@ include file="menu.jsp"%>
  </td>
  <td valign="top">
    <br>
    <div class="NormalLarge">Check Out</div>
```

```
<!--------------- the beginning of the Check Out page ------------->
<table>
<tr>
  <td>Contact Name:</td>
  <td>
    <h:input_text id="contactName" valueRef="OrderBean.contactName">
      <f:validate_required/>
    </h:input_text>
  </td>
  <td><h:output_errors for="contactName"/></td>
</tr>
<tr>
  <td>Delivery Address:</td>
  <td>
    <h:input_textarea id="deliveryAddress"
      valueRef="OrderBean.deliveryAddress">
      <f:validate_required/>
    </h:input_textarea>
  </td>
  <td><h:output_errors for="deliveryAddress"/></td>
</tr>
<tr>
  <td>Name on Credit Card:</td>
  <td>
    <h:input_text id="ccName" valueRef="OrderBean.creditCardName">
      <f:validate_required/>
    </h:input_text>
  </td>
  <td><h:output_errors for="ccName"/></td>
</tr>
<tr>
  <td>Credit Card Number:</td>
  <td>
    <h:input_text id="ccNumber"
      valueRef="OrderBean.creditCardNumber">
      <f:validate_required/>
    </h:input_text>
  </td>
  <td><h:output_errors for="ccNumber"/></td>
</tr>
<tr>
  <td>Expiry Date:</td>
  <td>
    <h:input_text id="ccExpiryDate"
```

```
      valueRef="OrderBean.creditCardExpiryDate">
        <f:validate_required/>
      </h:input_text>
    </td>
    <td><h:output_errors for="ccExpiryDate"/></td>
</tr>
<tr>
    <td colspan="2">
      <h:command_button action="order" commandName="order" label="Pay">
        <f:action_listener type="buydirect.AppActionListener"/>
      </h:command_button>
    </td>
</table>
<!-------------------- the end of the Check Out page ------------->



    </td>
</tr>
<tr>
    <td colspan="2">
      <%-- The footer --%>
      <%@ include file="footer.jsp"%>
    </td>
</tr>
</table>


</h:form>
</f:use_faces>
</body>
</html>
```

Notice that for each `UIInput` component, a `required_validator` tag is used to make the component a mandatory field. At the end of the page is a `UICommand` button that the user can click to begin processing the order.

```
<h:command_button action="order" commandName="order" label="Pay">
    <f:action_listener type="buydirect.AppActionListener"/>
</h:command_button>
```

The order.jsp Page

The `order.jsp` page displays a thank you note after the purchase order is processed. The `order.jsp` page is shown in Listing 14-26.

Listing 14-26 *The order.jsp Page*

```jsp
<%@ taglib uri="http://java.sun.com/jsf/html" prefix="h" %>
<%@ taglib uri="http://java.sun.com/jsf/core" prefix="f" %>
<html>
<head>
<title>Search Result</title>
<link rel="stylesheet" type="text/css"
  href="<%= request.getContextPath() + "/Styles.css" %>">
</head>
<body>
<f:use_faces>
<h:form formName="myForm">
<table border="0" cellspacing="4" cellpadding="0"
  width="<h:output_text valueRef="initParam.pageWidth"/>">
<tr>
  <td colspan="2">
    <%-- The header --%>
    <%@ include file="header.jsp"%>
  </td>
</tr>
<tr>
  <td valign="top">
    <%-- The menu --%>
    <%@ include file="menu.jsp"%>
  </td>
  <td valign="top">
    <br>
    <div class="NormalLarge">Thank you.</div>


<!--------------- the beginning of the Order page ------------->

Your order has been processed.

<!-------------------- the end of the Order page ------------->


  </td>
</tr>
<tr>
  <td colspan="2">
    <%-- The footer --%>
    <%@ include file="footer.jsp"%>
```

```
    </td>
</tr>
</table>

</h:form>
</f:use_faces>
</body>
</html>
```

Running the Application

To run the application, direct your browser to the following URL:

```
http://localhost:8080/buydirect/faces/index.jsp
```

Summary

This chapter described how to build the BuyDirect online store application. The application uses various components in JSF, such as the UI components and validators, and has a number of managed beans.

   The application is not a complete solution for an online store. However, it provides basic functionality that encompasses many features found in a commercial online store application. You could easily expand it to include capabilities for modifying the shopping cart and managing the store, for example.

The Application Configuration File

IN THIS CHAPTER:

Locating Application Configuration Files

Understanding the Application
Configuration Format

Summary

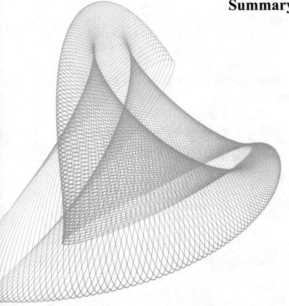

Throughout this book, you've seen examples of application configuration file entries. For each sample application, you named the application configuration file `faces-config.xml` and saved it under the `WEB-INF directory` of the application directory. A JSF application does not have to have an application configuration file. However, for a serious application, chances are you will need one.

You've used the application configuration file to register JavaBeans, validators, page-navigation rules, and other configurations. This chapter explains the application configuration file in detail. You will learn where the application configuration file can reside and each element it can contain.

Locating Application Configuration Files

A JSF application can have one or many application configuration files. The JSF implementation will load and process these configuration files automatically when the application starts, before any request is processed.

Normally, you put the application configuration file under the `WEB-INF` directory when developing the JSF application, so that you can edit it quickly using your favorite text editor. However, when deploying an application or a component, you can choose to bundle the application configuration file in the JAR file together with the application or component, so that the application or component can be deployed by simply copying the JAR file.

The JSF implementation locates application configuration files by first searching through any library files (JAR files) deployed to the `WEB-INF/lib` directory of the application directory. In each JAR file, if a resource named `/META-INF/faces-config.xml` is present, it is loaded as a JSF configuration resource.

If the JSF implementation cannot find a `faces-config.xml` in a JAR file, it checks if the context initialization parameter `javax.faces.application.CONFIG_FILES` exists in the application deployment descriptor. If it finds this parameter, it treats the parameter as a comma-delimited list of context-relative resource paths (starting with a `/`) and loads each of the specified resources. If one of the resources in the list cannot be found, JSF raises a fatal error that will prevent the application startup process from continuing.

If the context initialization parameter does not exist, the JSF implementation will load the `faces-config.xml` file under the `WEB-INF` directory, if such a file exists.

Understanding the Application Configuration Format

Application configuration files are XML documents that conform to the `web-facesconfig_1_0.dtd` from `http://java.sun.com/dtd/`, as specified in the following DOCTYPE declaration of every application configuration file.

```
<!DOCTYPE faces-config PUBLIC
    "-//Sun Microsystems, Inc.//DTD JavaServer Faces Config 1.0//EN"
    "http://java.sun.com/dtd/web-facesconfig_1_0.dtd">
```

TIP

If you are not familiar with XML or document type definition (DTD), download a free online tutorial on XML from http://www.brainysoftware.com.

Structuring an Application Configuration File

The root element of the application configuration file is `faces-config`. Here is the skeleton of an application configuration file:

```
<?xml version="1.0"?>
<!DOCTYPE faces-config PUBLIC
  "-//Sun Microsystems, Inc.//DTD JavaServer Faces Config 1.0//EN"
  "http://java.sun.com/dtd/web-facesconfig_1_0.dtd">

<faces-config>
  <!-- configuration goes here -->
<faces-config>
```

The `faces-config` element can have subelements, as described by the following `ELEMENT` definition:

```
<!ELEMENT faces-config ((application|component|converter|
managed-bean|message-resources|navigation-rule|
referenced-bean|render-kit|validator)*)>
```

An application configuration file can have any number of its subelements, in any order. In other words, elements of the same type do not need to be grouped together. For example, it is valid to have the following configuration, in which there are two `navigation-rule` elements with a `validator` element between them:

```
<?xml version="1.0"?>
<!DOCTYPE faces-config PUBLIC
  "-//Sun Microsystems, Inc.//DTD JavaServer Faces Config 1.0//EN"
  "http://java.sun.com/dtd/web-facesconfig_1_0.dtd">

<faces-config>
  <navigation-rule>
    ...
  </navigation-rule>
  <validator>
    ...
  </validator>
  <navigation-rule>
    ...
  </navigation-rule>

<faces-config>
```

Reviewing the Application Configuration File Elements

You've been introduced to the elements that can be present within the `faces-config` element in the previous chapters, in the context of the examples presented in those chapters. These subelements include `application`, `component`, `converter`, `managed-bean`, `message-resources`, `navigation-rule`, `referenced-bean`, `render-kit`, and `validator`. Here, we will focus on each element, with examples of how they work.

The application Element

The JSF implementation creates an `Application` object for each Web application and provides default implementations of its action listener, navigation handler, property resolver, and variable resolver. If you want to use custom versions of any of these, you configure them in the `application` element of the application configuration file.

NOTE

JSF will use the default implementations for the action listener, navigation handler, property resolver, and/or variable resolver if you do not specify an `application` element in any of the application configuration files in a JSF application.

You use the `application` element to configure the `javax.faces.application` `.Application` instance, which is the per-application-singleton class for a Web application. The `application` element is defined as follows:

```
<!ELEMENT application ((action-listener|navigation-handler|
property-resolver|variable-resolver)*)>
```

If present, any subelement of the `application` element contains the fully qualified class name of the corresponding implementation class. For example, if an `action-listener` subelement exists in the `application` element, it must contain the fully qualified class name of the `ActionListener` implementation class.

As an example, here is an `application` element used to load custom `ActionListener` and `NavigationHandler` classes:

```
<application>
  <action-listener>myPackage.MyActionListener</action-listener>
  <navigation-handler>
    myPackage.MyNavigationHandler
  </navigation-handler>
</application>
```

The component Element

You use the `component` element to register a user interface component. The definition of the `component` element is as follows:

```
<!ELEMENT component (description*, display-name*, icon*,
component-type, component-class, attribute*, property*)>
```

The `component-type` specifies the name used to refer to the component. The `component-class` element specifies the fully qualified name of the implementation class of the component.

As an example, the following `component` element is used to register a custom component called `Calendar` whose implementation class is `myPackage.UICalendar`:

```
<component>
  <component-type>Calendar</component-type>
  <component-class>myPackage.UICalendar</component-class>
</component>
```

Custom components are discussed in Chapter 13.

The converter Element

As explained in Chapter 10, you can use the `converter` element to register a custom converter (for data conversion). It has the following definition:

```
<!ELEMENT converter (description*, display-name*, icon*,
converter-id, converter-class, attribute*, property*)>
```

A `converter` element must have `converter-id` and `converter-class` elements. The `converter-id` element specifies an identifier that must be unique throughout the Web application. The `converter-class` element specifies the fully qualified name of the implementation class for the converter.

As an example, here is a `converter` element that registers a custom converter named `MyConverter` and whose class is `myPackage.MyConverter`:

```
<converter>
  <converter-id>MyConverter</converter-id>
  <converter-class>myPackage.MyConverter</converter-class>
</converter>
```

Standard and custom converters are discussed in Chapter 10.

The managed-bean Element

As you have seen in many examples in previous chapters, you register a JavaBean that will be created at runtime by using the `managed-bean` element in the application configuration file. The `managed-bean` element is defined as follows:

```
<!ELEMENT managed-bean (description*, display-name*, icon*,
managed-bean-name, managed-bean-class, managed-bean-scope,
managed-property*)>
```

A `managed-bean` element must contain the following three subelements:

▶   `managed-bean-name` This element specifies the name that will be used to refer to the JavaBean throughout the application. The `managed-bean-name` element must conform to the variable naming conventions of the Java programming language.

▶ managed-bean-class This element contains the fully qualified class name for the JavaBean.

▶ managed-bean-scope This element defines the scope of the JavaBean. The possible values for this element are application, session, request, or none. If the managed-bean-scope element has a value other than none, the JavaBean created will be stored in the corresponding object. For example, if the value is session, the JavaBean is stored in the Session object of a given user.

Optionally, the managed-bean element may contain any number of description, display-name, icon, and managed-property elements.

As an example, the following managed-bean element loads and instantiates a JavaBean of type myPackage.TestingBean, which will be referred to as testingBean from anywhere in the application. An instance of TestingBean is created and stored in every Session object.

```
<managed-bean>
  <managed-bean-name>testingBean</managed-bean-name>
  <managed-bean-class>myPackage.TestingBean</managed-bean-class>
  <managed-bean-scope>session</managed-bean-scope>
</managed-bean>
```

Using the managed-property element, you can also initialize a settable property of the JavaBean. Here is the definition of the managed-property element:

```
<!ELEMENT managed-property (description*, display-name*, icon*,
property-name, property-class?, (map-entries|null-value|value|
value-ref|values))>
```

The property-name element specifies the property name of the JavaBean and it is followed by an optional property-class element and one of the following elements: map-entries, null-value, value, value-ref, or values.

The property-class element represents the Java type of the value associated with this property name. It must be of type "JavaType". If the property-class element is not specified, it can be inferred from existing classes. However, you should specify this element if the application configuration file will be the source for generating the corresponding classes.

NOTE

A "JavaType" is either the fully qualified name of a Java class that is instantiated to provide the functionality of the enclosing element or the name of a Java primitive type (such as int or char). The class name or primitive type may optionally be followed by [], to indicate that the underlying data must be an array, rather than a scalar variable.

The following sections describe each element that can follow the property-name element and an optional property-class element.

Using map-entries   The `map-entries` element represents a set of key-value pairs that will be added to the computed value of a managed property of type `java.util.Map`. Optionally, you may also declare the Java class types of the key and entry values. The description of the `map-entries` element is as follows:

```
<!ELEMENT map-entries (key-class?, value-class?, map-entry*)>
```

The `map-entry` subelement represents an entry to be added to the `Map` object. It has the following description:

```
<!ELEMENT map-entry (key, (null-value|value|value-ref)*)>
```

As an example, consider the following `managed-bean` element:

```
<managed-bean>
<managed-bean-name>testingBean</managed-bean-name>
<managed-bean-class>ch15.TestingBean</managed-bean-class>
<managed-bean-scope>session</managed-bean-scope>
<managed-property>
  <property-name>countryList</property-name>
  <map-entries>
    <map-entry>
      <key>au</key>
      <value>Australia</value>
    </map-entry>
    <map-entry>
      <key>br</key>
      <value>Brazil</value>
    </map-entry>
    <map-entry>
      <key>cn</key>
      <value>China</value>
    </map-entry>
  </map-entries>
</managed-property>
</managed-bean>
```

Using null-value   The `null-value` element indicates that the managed property in which the `null-value` element is nested will be explicitly set to `null` if the managed bean for the `managed-property` element is automatically created. This is different from omitting the `managed-property` element entirely, which will result in no property setter being called for this property. Here is an example of using the `null-value` subelement:

```
<managed-property>
  <property-name>countryList</property-name>
  <property-class>java.util.Map</property-class>
```

```
    <null-value/>
  </managed-property>
```

Using value   You use the `value` element to initialize a managed bean's property. The following is an example of `managed-bean` element used to register a JavaBean called `TestingBean`. The `managed-bean` element contains a `managed-property` element to initialize the `firstNumber` property to 9.

```
<managed-bean>
  <managed-bean-name>testingBean</managed-bean-name>
  <managed-bean-class>ch15.TestingBean</managed-bean-class>
  <managed-bean-scope>application</managed-bean-scope>
  <managed-property>
    <property-name>firstNumber</property-name>
    <value>9</value>
  </managed-property>
</managed-bean>
```

And, here is the `firstNumber` property in `TestingBean`:

```
int firstNumber;
public int getFirstNumber() {
  return firstNumber;
}
public void setFirstNumber(int number) {
  firstNumber = number;
}
```

Using value-ref   You use the `value-ref` element if you want to initialize the property of a managed bean with a value that is to be retrieved from another source, such as another managed bean.

Using values   The `values` element will initialize a managed bean's property with a set of initialization elements, such as a collection or an array. The `values` element is defined as follows:

```
<!ELEMENT values (value-class?, (null-value|value|value-ref)*)>
```

The following example illustrates the use of the `values` element:

```
<managed-property>
  <property-name>cities</property-name>
  <values>
    <value>Berlin</value>
    <value>San Francisco</value>
    <value>Sydney</value>
  </values>
</managed-property>
```

The message-resources Element

The `message-resources` element of the application configuration file represents a set of message elements for localized messages related to a message resource identifier. The `message-resources` element is defined as follows:

```
<!ELEMENT message-resources (description*, display-name*,
icon*, message-resources-id, message-resources-class?, message*)>
```

The `message-resources-id` element defines an identifier for the message resources, and it must be unique throughout the Web application. The `message-resources-class` element represents the fully qualified class name of a `MessageResources` implementation. If no `message-resources-class` is present, the default implementation will be used.

The `message` element defines an individual localized message. Its definition is as follows:

```
<!ELEMENT message (message-id, message-class?, summary*,
detail*, severity?)>
```

The `message` element must contain a `message-id` element and optionally one `message-class` element, zero or many `summary` elements, zero or many `detail` elements, and an optional `severity` element.

The `message-id` element represents the identifier for the message and must be unique within the scope of the containing `message-resources` instance.

The `message-class` element represents the implementation for a message. If no `message-class` is present, the default implementation will be used.

The `summary` element contains the summary error message and can optionally have an `xml:lang` attribute that indicates a language code:

```
<!ATTLIST summary          xml:lang          %Language;          #IMPLIED>
```

The following is an example of a `message-resources` element:

```
<message-resources>
  <message-resources-id>zipCodeFormat</message-resources-id>
  <message>
    <message-id>invalidLength</message-id>
    <summary xml:lang="en">Length is not equal to 5</summary>
    <summary xml:lang="de">Laenge ist nicht gleich 5</summary>
  </message>
  <message>
    <message-id>invalidFormat</message-id>
    <summary xml:lang="en">A zip code must be all numbers</summary>
    <summary xml:lang="de">
      Eine Postleitzahl muss alle Zahlen sein
    </summary>
  </message>
</message-resources>
```

Chapter 11 discusses how to use message resources to localize applications.

The navigation-rule Element

As you learned in Chapter 8, the `navigation-rule` element allows you to define a rule for page navigation. Its definition is as follows:

```
<!ELEMENT navigation-rule (description*, display-name*,
icon*, from-tree-id?, navigation-case*)>
```

The `from-tree-id` subelement is the tree identifier of the page of origin, such as `login.jsp`.

The `navigation-case` subelement represents a possible target. A `navigation-rule` element can have zero or several `navigation-case` subelements. Each `navigation-case` element specifies the target page for a particular outcome of the `from-tree-id` processing. An outcome can be obtained from the `action` or `actionRef` attribute of the `UICommand` component in the `from-tree-id` element. The `navigation-case` element is described as follows:

```
<!ELEMENT navigation-case (description*, display-name*,
icon*, from-action-ref?, from-outcome?, to-tree-id)>
```

The `to-tree-id` element specifies the target page for this navigation case. The `from-outcome` element is the outcome of processing the `from-tree-id` page. It is obtained from the value of the `action` property of the `UICommand` component that triggered the `ActionEvent` in the `from-tree-id` page.

The `from-action-ref` element also represents the outcome of processing the `from-tree-id` page. However, its value comes from the `actionRef` property of the `UICommand` component that raised the `ActionEvent`.

Here is an example of a `navigation-rule` element:

```
<navigation-rule>
  <from-tree-id>/login.jsp</from-tree-id>
  <navigation-case>
    <from-outcome>success</from-outcome>
    <to-tree-id>/welcome.jsp</to-tree-id>
  </navigation-case>
  <navigation-case>
    <from-outcome>failed</from-outcome>
    <to-tree-id>/login.jsp</to-tree-id>
  </navigation-case>
</navigation-rule>
```

The referenced-bean Element

The `referenced-bean` element represents a design-time promise that a Java object of the specified type will exist at runtime in some scope, under the specified key. This can be used by design-time tools to construct user interface dialog boxes based on the properties of the specified class. The presence or absence of a `referenced-bean` element has no impact on the JSF runtime environment inside a Web application.

The definition for the `referenced-bean` element is as follows:

```
<!ELEMENT referenced-bean (description*, display-name*,
icon*, referenced-bean-name, referenced-bean-class)>
```

The render-kit Element

You use the `render-kit` element if you want your JSF application to use a `RenderKit` that is different from the default `RenderKit` (JSF's collection of standard renderers). The `render-kit` element is defined as follows:

```
<!ELEMENT render-kit (description*, display-name*,
icon*, render-kit-id?, render-kit-class?, renderer*)>
```

The `render-kit-id` element represents an identifier for the `RenderKit` represented by the `render-kit` element. If no `render-kit-id` is specified, the identifier of the default `RenderKit` (`RenderKitFactory.DEFAULT_RENDER_KIT`) is assumed.

The `render-kit-class` element represents the fully qualified class name of a concrete `RenderKit` implementation class.

The `renderer` element represents a `Renderer` implementation. It is defined as follows:

```
<!ELEMENT renderer (description*, display-name*, icon*,
renderer-type, renderer-class, attribute*, component-type*,
component-class*)>
```

Each `renderer` element must have the `renderer-type` element, which represents an identifier for the renderer, and a `renderer-class` element, which represents the fully qualified class name of the `Renderer` implementation. The `attribute`, `component-type`, and `component-class` elements are optional.

As an example, here is a `render-kit` tag that registers a custom renderer:

```
<render-kit>
  <renderer>
    <renderer-type>CustomRenderer</renderer-type>
    <renderer-class>myPackage.MyCustomRenderer</renderer-class>
  </renderer>
</render-kit>
```

Standard and custom renderers are discussed in Chapter 12.

The validator Element

As you learned in Chapter 9, the `validator` element is used to register a custom validator so that it can be used in the JSF application. The `validator` element is defined as follows:

```
<!ELEMENT validator (description*, display-name*, icon*,
validator-id, validator-class, attribute*, property*)>
```

The `validator-id` element represents the identifier for the validator, and it must be unique throughout the Web application. The `validator-class` element represents the fully qualified name of the validator implementation class.

Nested `attribute` elements identify generic attributes that may be configured on the corresponding `UIComponent` component in order to affect the operation of the validator. The `attribute` element is defined as follows:

```
<!ELEMENT attribute (description*, display-name*, icon*,
attribute-name, attribute-class)>
```

Nested `property` elements identify JavaBean properties of the `Validator` implementation class that may be configured to affect the operation of the validator. The `property` element is defined as follows:

```
<!ELEMENT property (description*, display-name*, icon*,
property-name, property-class)>
```

The following is an example of a `validator` tag that is identified as `ZipCodeValidator` and whose class is `myPackage.ZipCodeValidator`. The `validator` element has an `attribute` subelement, whose name is `length` and whose class is `java.lang.Integer`.

```
<validator>
  <description>
    A validator for validating zip codes, with localized messages
  </description>
  <validator-id>ZipCodeValidator</validator-id>
  <validator-class>myPackage.ZipCodeValidator</validator-class>
  <attribute>
    <description>Length of a valid zip code</description>
    <attribute-name>length</attribute-name>
    <attribute-class>java.lang.Integer</attribute-class>
  </attribute>
</validator>
```

Summary

There are many aspects of JSF applications that you can configure by editing the application configuration file of your application. The examples presented in this book give you a good of idea of how you can use customized components, page navigation, validators, renderers, and so on. These require specific application configuration file elements. Registering JavaBeans is another common requirement handled in the application configuration file.

This chapter discussed the possible locations of an application configuration file. Then it explained each element that can exist in an application configuration file.

CHAPTER
16

Summing Up:
How JSF Works

IN THIS CHAPTER:

N ow that you have learned about writing JSF applications and seen plenty of examples, you may be interested in knowing what happens behind the scenes in a JSF implementation. Chapters 2 and 3 provided a general introduction to how JSF works, but this chapter presents an in-depth look at the internal workings of a JSF implementation.

It starts by presenting an overview of JSF processing. Then it discusses the related classes and interfaces required in the request processing lifecycle: `FacesServlet`, `FacesContext`, `Application`, and `Lifecycle`. The final sections describe the six phases in the request processing lifecycle. These phases are easier to understand after you are familiar with what is being processed.

An Overview of JSF Processing

Each request in a JSF application is processed in the request processing lifecycle, which has six phases: Reconstitute Component Tree, Apply Request Values, Process Validations, Update Model Values, Invoke Application, and Render Response. These are discussed in detail in the "The Lifecycle Object" section later in the chapter.

For the processing, obviously the JSF implementation needs the user information and other information, such as the values keyed in to an input field, the user's locale, and so on. This information is submitted as an HTTP request, and the Web container encapsulates this information in the `javax.servlet.ServletRequest` object. In addition, the JSF implementation may need the information on the environment, which can be found in the `javax.servlet.ServletContext` object. To send the response to the user, the JSF implementation needs to write to the `javax.servlet.ServletResponse` object. JSF encapsulates these three objects in a new object of type `javax.faces.context.FacesContext`.

For a request to be processed, it is directed to a `FacesServlet`. For each request, `FacesServlet` acquires a `FacesContext` object and a `Lifecycle` object. The `FacesContext` object is constructed by passing the `javax.servlet.ServletContext`, `javax.servlet.ServletRequest`, and `javax.servlet.ServletResponse` objects from the Web container. Therefore, the `FacesContext` object contains all of the per-request state information for processing a JSF request and rendering the response. The `service` method of the `FacesServlet` then acquires an instance of `javax.faces.lifecycle.Lifecycle`, which is responsible for processing the JSF request. The `Lifecycle` instance executes the six phases of the request processing lifecycle by calling certain methods of the root of the component tree (these methods are described in the "The Lifecycle Object" section later in this chapter).

Also, a JSF application can have a configuration file whose content will be parsed and loaded, to be available from any component, event listener, validator, converter, or renderer in the JSF application. The Web container parses the application configuration when it loads the context, with the aid of a `javax.servlet.ServletContextListener`.

The FacesServlet

Each Web application employs a `FacesServlet`, which is a servlet represented by the `javax.faces.webapp.FacesServlet` class. All requests to JSF are directed to the `FacesServlet`, because their URL patterns contain the `/faces/` pattern, thanks to the following declaration in the application deployment descriptor (`web.xml` file):

```
<!-- Faces Servlet -->
<servlet>
  <servlet-name>Faces Servlet</servlet-name>
  <servlet-class>javax.faces.webapp.FacesServlet</servlet-class>
  <load-on-startup>1</load-on-startup>
</servlet>

<!-- Faces Servlet Mapping -->
<servlet-mapping>
  <servlet-name>Faces Servlet</servlet-name>
  <url-pattern>/faces/*</url-pattern>
</servlet-mapping>
```

The `FacesServlet` class implements the `javax.servlet.Servlet` interface. The `Servlet` interface has the lifecycle methods `init`, `service`, and `destroy`. These methods are described in the following sections.

The init Method

The `init` method of the `Servlet` interface has the following signature:

```
public void init(ServletConfig servletConfig) throws ServletException
```

where `servletConfig` is an instance of `javax.servlet.ServletConfig` passed in by the Web container.

The `ServletConfig` instance contains the information on the servlet configuration. From the `ServletConfig` instance, the servlet can obtain the initial parameters in the deployment descriptor (through the `getInitParameter` and `getInitParameterNames` methods), as well as the reference to the `ServletContext` instance (using the `ServletConfig` interface's `getServletContext` method). Because of the importance of the `ServletConfig` instance, the `FacesContext` stores it in a class-level variable, to be used from the `service` method.

In the `init` method, the `FacesServlet` class performs some initialization, which is acquiring and storing the `javax.faces.lifecycle.LifecycleFactory` and `javax.faces.context.FacesContextFactory` instances. The `LifecycleFactory` returns an instance of `javax.faces.lifecycle.Lifecycle`, which processes each incoming request. The `FacesContextFactory` instance is used to return an instance of `javax.faces.context.FacesContext` associated with each incoming request.

The JSF implementation provides the `javax.faces.FactoryFinder` class, which has the `getFactory` method. This method returns a `Factory` object and has the following signature:

```
public static Object getFactory(String factoryName)
  throws FacesException
```

NOTE

Since the source code of Sun's JSF reference implementation is not available, the code in this chapter has been derived from the JavaServer Faces Specification. The author makes no guarantee of the accuracy of the code.

The `FactoryFinder` class also has five static final `Strings` that you can use as names of various factories: `APPLICATION_FACTORY`, `FACES_CONTEXT_FACTORY`, `LIFECYCLE_FACTORY`, `RENDER_KIT_FACTORY`, and `TREE_FACTORY`. For example, to obtain a `FacesContextFactory` instance, use the following code:

```
FacesContextFactory fcFactory = (FacesContextFactory)
  FactoryFinder.getFactory(FactoryFinder.FACES_CONTEXT_FACTORY);
```

And to acquire an instance of `LifecycleFactory`, use the following code:

```
LifecycleFactory lcFactory = (LifecycleFactory)
  FactoryFinder.getFactory(FactoryFinder.LIFECYCLE_FACTORY);
```

The service Method

For each incoming request, the Web container calls `FacesServlet`'s `service` method. The `service` method performs four steps: obtains a `Lifecycle` instance, obtains a `FacesContext` instance, has the `Lifecycle` object process the request, and then releases the `FacesContext` instance. These steps are described in the following sections.

Obtaining a Lifecycle Instance

The `service` method obtains a `javax.faces.lifecycle.Lifecycle` instance by calling the `createLifecycle` method of the `LifecycleFactory`, passing a lifecycle identifier. The default identifier is defined by the static final `LifecycleFactory` `.DEFAULT_LIFECYCLE`.

```
Lifecycle lifecycle = lifecycleFactory.createLifecycle(
  LifecycleFactory.DEFAULT_LIFECYCLE);
```

Obtaining a FacesContext Instance

The `service` method next obtains a `javax.faces.context.FacesContext` instance by calling the `createFacesContext` method of the `javax.faces.context`

.FacesContextFactory class. The FacesContext instance contains information about the request and servlet context itself (as explained in the upcoming section about FacesContext). Here is the signature of the createFacesContext method:

```
public FacesContext getFacesContext(Object context, Object request,
  Object response, Lifecycle lifecycle) throws FacesException
```

To get an instance of FacesContext, pass the ServletContext (obtained by calling the getServletContext method on ServletConfig), the javax .servlet.Request instance (passed in to the service method by the Web container), the javax.servlet.Response instance (also passed from the Web container to the service method), and the Lifecycle instance (which the service method obtained by calling the createLifecycle method of the LifecycleFactory).

```
FacesContext facesContext = facesContextFactory.
  createFacesContext(servletContext, request, response, lifecycle);
```

As you can see, the FacesContext instance is passed the ServletContext, the Request object, and the Response object. Therefore, the FacesContext has all of the information that is normally required in non-JSF servlet processing. Some of this information can be retrieved from the FacesContext instance, as explained in the section about FacesContext.

You can also obtain a reference to FacesContext from any JSF element (such as a UI component, validator, converter, or renderer) by calling the FacesContext class's getInstance static method.

Processing the Request

The Lifecycle object is responsible for processing the request. After the FacesServlet's service method acquires a Lifecycle instance, it calls the execute method of the Lifecycle class, passing the FacesContext object (obtained by calling the createFacesContext method of the javax.faces .context.FacesContextFactory class). The execute method is responsible for executing the six phases of the JSF request processing lifecycle. The execute method could throw a FacesException, if something happens during the processing. If this occurs, the execute method will rethrow the exception as a javax.servlet.ServletException.

```
try {
  lifecycle.execute(facesContext);
}
catch (FacesException e) {
  // re-throw FacesException as a ServletException
  throw new ServletException();
}
```

Releasing the FacesContext Instance

The `service` method calls the `release` method of the `FacesContext` instance, causing it to be returned to a pool, if the JSF implementation employs one.

```
facesContext.release();
```

The destroy Method

You do not need to be concerned with the `destroy` method, because the garbage collector will do the clean up. However, it is reasonable to assign `null` to class-level variables:

```
lifecycleFactory = null;
facesContextFactory = null;
```

The FacesContext Object

An instance of `FacesContext` is created for each JSF request by passing the three objects passed in by the Web container: `javax.servlet.ServletContext`, `javax.servlet.ServletRequest`, and `javax.servlet.ServletResponse`. The `FacesServlet` servlet holds a reference to the `javax.faces.context.FacesContextFactory` object, which is responsible for returning a `FacesContext` instance.

Recall that to obtain a `FacesServlet` instance, you call the `getFacesContext` method of the `FacesContextFactory` class. The `getFacesContext` method has the following signature:

```
public FacesContext getFacesContext(Object context, Object request,
   Object response, Lifecycle lifecycle) throws FacesException
```

Per-Request State Information in FacesContext

Because the `FacesContext` instance is constructed by passing the `ServletContext`, `ServletRequest`, and `ServletResponse` objects from the Web container, it contains all of the per-request state information used for processing the associated JSF request. However, the `FacesContext` instance wraps the information, and you can obtain it by calling methods in the `FacesContext` class. For example, you can obtain the locale of the request (which the `FacesContext` instance got from the `ServletRequest` object) by invoking the `FacesContext` class's `getLocale` method.

Other information is encapsulated in the `javax.faces.context.ExternalContext` of the `FacesContext`. You can obtain this `ExternalContext` object by calling the `getExternalContext` method of the `FacesContext` class. Each method of `ExternalContext` returns a piece of information originally from either the `ServletRequest` object or the `ServletContext` object passed to construct the `FacesContext` object. (The `ExternalContext` methods are discussed in Chapter 3.)

FacesContext Handling in the Lifecycle Phases

The FacesContext instance is passed to each phase of the request processing lifecycle, and each phase may modify the FacesContext object. For example, the Apply Request Values phase can queue Event objects to be processed in the next phases by calling the addFacesEvent method of the FacesContext class. The Event objects can be later retrieved by calling the getFacesEvents method. The getTree method returns the component tree associated with the request, and the setTree method is used to assign a new component tree to this request.

If there is an error encountered during the request lifecycle processing, the FacesContext class's addMessage method can be called to add a javax.faces.application.Message object. You must also pass the UIComponent associated with the Message to the addMessage method.

Any phase in the request processing lifecycle can also opt to branch to the Render Response phase, bypassing any phases that have not been executed. To do this, it needs to call the renderResponse method of the FacesContext. In addition, a phase can also indicate to the JSF implementation that it should terminate the request processing lifecycle entirely, including the Render Response phase, because the HTTP response for this request has already been generated (such as in the case of a redirect). You do this by calling the responseComplete method of the FacesContext class.

The FacesContext class provides a static method for you to obtain the reference to the FacesContext instance associated with the current request processing: getCurrentInstance. You can call this method from any point in the request processing lifecycle.

The Application Object

A JSF application can optionally have an application configuration file, where you register your navigation rules, JavaBeans, custom validators, event listeners, renderers, and converters. These objects must be made available to the JSF implementation for a successful processing of any page in your JSF application. Therefore, these objects need to be loaded before the first request comes in.

The most appropriate way to load the necessary objects is by employing a ServletContextListener interface's contextInitialized method. This method is invoked when your JSF application is loaded by the Web container. The JSF implementation provides a way to handle this automatically, so you do not need to worry about loading and parsing the application configuration file yourself. This is taken care of by a JSF class that implements the ServletContextListener interface and overrides its contextInitialized method.

After reading the application configuration file and loading the classes needed, the JSF implementation stores the instances of these classes (your custom validators, event listeners, and so on) in an object of type javax.faces.application.Application. The Application object represents a per-Web-application singleton object containing objects whose classes are registered in the application configuration file. The instance of Application must be available from any point in the request processing lifecycle. The JSF implementation gets an instance of Application by calling the getApplication method of the javax .faces.application.ApplicationFactory class.

Most of the methods in the Application class are self-explanatory. For example, you can get a validator by calling the getValidator method, passing the validator identifier. All validator identifiers can be retrieved by calling the getValidatorIds method.

The Default ActionListener

The Application instance returned from the getApplication method of the ApplicationFactory must contain an instance of the javax.faces.event .ActionListener interface, which is called the default ActionListener. The default ActionListener helps in page navigation. In JSF, page navigation is driven by the navigation rules in the application configuration file. An ActionListener must provide implementations for the processAction and the getPhaseId methods.

Now, there must be a mechanism to allow the user to navigate from one page to another. You know that in the browser, the user can move to another page by clicking a button or a hyperlink. A button or a hyperlink in JSF is represented by the javax.faces.component .UICommand, and a UICommand triggers an ActionEvent when clicked. However, an event will not cause any effect unless there is a listener registered for that event. For the sake of page navigation, a default ActionListener is automatically registered to all ActionEvent events triggered by UICommand components. This way, you do not need to add an ActionListener specifically to manage page navigation. The default ActionListener is automatically registered with any UICommand component in the component tree during the Reconstitute Component Tree phase of the request processing lifecycle.

When a button or a hyperlink is clicked, it fires an ActionEvent, and the JSF implementation will call its processAction method. In its processAction method, the default ActionListener must get the javax.faces.application .NavigationHandler instance (obtainable by calling the getNavigationHandler of the Application class) and invoke its handleNavigation method. The NavigationHandler class's handleNavigation method has the following signature:

```
public abstract void handleNavigation(FacesContext facesContext,
    String actionRef, String action)
```

Therefore, the default ActionListener must first prepare the values for the actionRef or the action arguments. The FacesContext instance is readily available by calling the FacesContext.getCurrentInstance method.

Both action and actionRef values are retrieved from the UICommand component by calling the getAction and getActionRef methods of the UICommand class. The UICommand component gets the action and actionRef values from the action and actionRef attributes, respectively. The rules for passing the action and actionRef values are as follows:

▶ If the source `UICommand` instance's `action` property is not `null`, pass this value as the `action` argument of the `handleNavigation` method and pass `null` as the `actionRef` argument.

▶ If the source `UICommand` instance's `action` property is `null`, evaluate the value of its `actionRef` property to retrieve an `Action` object.

  ▶ If no `Action` object is retrieved, or if the `Action` object does not implement the `javax.faces.application.Action` interface, throw an `IllegalArgumentException`.

  ▶ If an `Action` object is successfully retrieved, call its `invoke` method, and the result becomes the outcome. Pass this outcome as the value of the `actionRef` argument of the `handleNavigation` method.

Another requirement for the default `ActionListener` is that its `getPhaseId` method must return `PhaseId.INVOKE_APPLICATION`, so that it is invoked only after the Invoke Application phase in the request processing lifecycle.

NOTE

You can change the default `ActionListener` by calling the `Application` class's `setActionListener` method. However, this should be considered for only a very advanced JSF application or framework.

The Default NavigationHandler

The `Application` instance must also contain an instance of the `javax.faces.application.NavigationHandler` class. This class has one method, `handleNavigation`, which is called by the default `ActionListener`.

The Lifecycle Object

The `FacesServlet` object's `service` method acquires an instance of `javax.faces.lifecycle.Lifecycle`. This `Lifecycle` object is responsible for executing the six phases in the request processing lifecycle. Execution starts when the `FacesServlet` servlet calls the `execute` method of the `Lifecycle` class. From the `execute` method, the `Lifecycle` must first obtain the component tree of the current request and call several methods of the root of the component tree. These methods are discussed in the following sections about the six phases in the request processing lifecycle.

NOTE

Before reading further, make sure you are familiar with the `UIComponent` interface (the topic of Chapter 4) and the `Validator` interface (explained in Chapter 9).

The request processing lifecycle is shown in Figure 16-1. Notice that in addition to the six phases, there are four occasions (after the Apply Request Values, Process Validations, Model Values, and Invoke Applications phases) where the `Lifecycle` instance will try to invoke the listeners interested in any of the `Event` objects queued in the `FacesContext` instance. This will be discussed in the "Event Processing" section later in this chapter.

Note also that in your event listener, you have the chance to force the `Lifecycle` object to jump to the Render Response phase (by calling the `FacesContext` class's `renderResponse` method) or terminate the request processing lifecycle immediately (by calling the `FacesContext` class's `responseComplete` method).

Now, we will look at each of the request processing lifecycle phases in detail.

The Reconstitute Component Tree Phase

The Reconstitute Component Tree phase starts the request processing lifecycle by attempting to obtain state information required to construct the component tree representing the JSF request. Such state information can be found in the incoming request, or it may previously have been saved on the server. A component tree has a tree identifier, which is the path information portion of the request URI. For a request with URI `/faces/index.jsp`, for instance, the tree identifier is `/index.jsp`.

If the Reconstitute Component Tree phase finds the state information for constructing the component tree, the JSF implementation does the following:

▶ Reconstructs the component tree. This includes reconstructing any saved event listeners and validators, and setting the appropriate `RenderKit`.

▶ Saves the component tree in the `FacesContext` by passing the tree to the `setTree` method. Other phases of the request processing lifecycle can obtain the component tree from the `FacesContext` instance by calling its `getTree` method.

▶ Obtains the root of the component tree and call its `processReconstitutes` method. The `processReconstitutes` method implementation in a component calls the `processReconstitutes` method of all facets and child components and invokes the `reconstitute` method in that component itself. Therefore, calling the `processReconstitutes` method of the root component invokes the `processReconstitutes` method of each component in the tree, as well as invokes the root component's and child components' `reconstitute` methods.

▶ Registers the default `ActionListener` from the `Application` object with every `UICommand` component in the tree. (The default `ActionListener` is discussed earlier in the chapter, in the "The Application Object" section.)

If the state information for constructing the component tree is not available, the JSF implementation calls the `getTree` method of the `TreeFactory` instance and stores the tree in the `FacesContext` object by calling its `setTree` method.

As the last step in this phase, the JSF implementation passes the `Locale` object derived from the saved state information or the incoming request to the `setLocale` method of the `FacesContext` object.

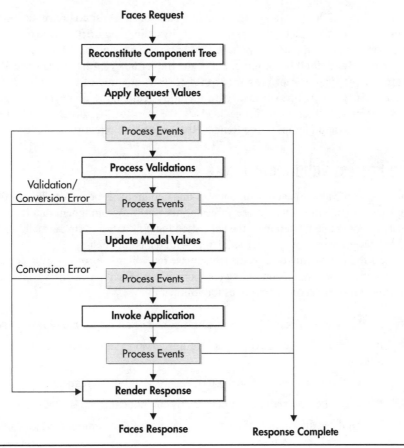

Figure 16-1   *The request processing lifecycle*

The Apply Request Values Phase

In the Apply Request Values phase, the local value of each component in the component tree is updated from the current request. A value can come from a request parameter, a header, a cookie, and so on. The JSF implementation does this by calling the processDecodes method of the root component. The processDecodes method implementation in a component calls the processDecodes method of all facets and child components and invokes the decode method in that component itself. Therefore, calling the processDecodes method of the root component invokes the processDecodes method of each component in the tree, as well as invokes the root component's and child components' decode methods.

During this phase, a component or a renderer may queue events. These events will be processed during the event processing steps in the request processing lifecycle.

In addition, if the decoding of a value in a component causes a conversion error, the JSF implementation will queue `Message` objects by calling the `addMessage` method of `FacesContext`, and the component's `valid` property will be set to `false`.

A `decode` method in a component in the tree or an event listener may call the `responseComplete` or the `renderResponse` method of the `FacesContext` instance. If the `responseComplete` method is called, the lifecycle processing of the current request will terminate immediately. If the `renderResponse` method is called, the JSF implementation jumps to the Render Response phase directly, skipping the other phases.

The Process Validations Phase

After the local value of each component is updated, in the Process Validations phase, the JSF implementation will validate those values, if necessary. A component that requires validation must provide implementation of the validation logic in its `validate` method. Alternatively, the JSF programmer can register validators with the component.

The JSF implementation executes this phase by calling the `processValidators` method of the root component in the component tree. The `processValidators` method implementation in a component does the following:

▶ Invokes the `processValidators` method of all facets and child components.

▶ If the value of the `valid` property of this component is `true`, the method does the following:

   ▶ Calls the `validate` method of each `Validator` registered for this component.

   ▶ Calls the `validate` method of this component.

   ▶ Updates the value of the `valid` property of this component based on the result of the `validate` method.

▶ If the value of the `valid` property of this component is `false`, the method calls the `FacesContext.renderResponse` method, so that the JSF implementation will jump to the Render Response phase after the end of the Process Validations phase.

During this phase, a registered validator or the `validate` method of a component may queue events, call the `FacesContext.renderResponse` method, or call the `FacesContext.responseComplete` method.

The Update Model Values Phase

The Update Model Values phase can be reached only if the local values of all components in the tree are valid. In this phase, the JSF implementation updates the application's model data by calling the `processUpdates` method of the root component in the component tree. The `processUpdates` method implementation in a component does the following:

▶ Calls the `processUpdates` method of all facets and child components.

▶ Calls the `updateModel` of this component.

▶ If the value of the `valid` property of this component is now `false`, the method calls the `FacesContext.renderResponse` method.

During this phase, a component's `updateModel` method may queue events or call the `FacesContext.responseComplete` or `FacesContext.renderResponse` method.

The Invoke Application Phase

During the Invoke Application phase, the JSF implementation handles any application-level events. This may include events such as submitting a form or linking to another page.

The Render Response Phase

In the Render Response phase, the JSF implementation renders the response to the client. It obtains the `javax.faces.lifecycle.ViewHandler` instance and calls its `renderView` method. In this method, the `ViewHandler` instance performs a `RequestDispatcher.forward` call to a Web application resource whose context-relative path is equal to the component tree identifier of the component tree.

Event Processing

The Apply Request Values, Process Validations, Update Model Values, and Invoke Application phases in the request processing lifecycle may queue events in the `FacesContext` instance associated with the current request. Therefore, the JSF implementation must handle these events after these phases.

To process events, the JSF implementation does the following:

▶ Obtains all `javax.faces.event.FacesEvent` objects by calling the `getFacesEvents` method of the `FacesContext` instance associated with the current request. The `getFacesEvents` method returns a `java.util.Iterator` containing all `FacesEvent` objects that have been queued.

▶ For each `FacesEvent` object in the `Iterator`, acquires the component that is the source of the event by calling the `getComponent` method of the `FacesEvent` class. Then it calls the `broadcast` method of the source component, passing the event instance and an identifier for the current phase of the request processing lifecycle.

The Java code for processing events would look something like the following. The `phaseId` variable is a `javax.faces.event.PhaseId` object for each corresponding phase after which the event processing takes place. For example, for event processing after the Apply Request Values phase, the value of `phaseId` will be `PhaseId.APPLY_REQUEST_VALUES`.

```
PhaseId phaseId = ... // assign a PhaseId for this event processing
FacesContext facesContext = FacesContext.getCurrentInstance();
Iterator iterator = facesContext.getFacesEvents();
while (iterator.hasNext()) {
  FacesEvent facesEvent = (FacesEvent) iterator.next();
  UIComponent source = facesEvent.getComponent();
  boolean result = source.broadcast(facesEvent, phaseId);
  if (result==false)
    iterator.remove();
}
```

Note that the `broadcast` method of the `UIComponent` interface returns `false` if the `FacesEvent` object does not have any listeners interested in this event in the future phases of the request processing lifecycle. In that case, the `FacesEvent` object can be removed from the `FacesContext` object.

Summary

This chapter presented a detailed description on how JSF works. It began with an overview, and then continued from the `FacesServlet` servlet through each of the request processing lifecycle phases and event processing.

The next chapter discusses a new JSP 2.0 feature that you can use in your JSF applications: the expression language (EL).

The JSP 2.0 Expression Language

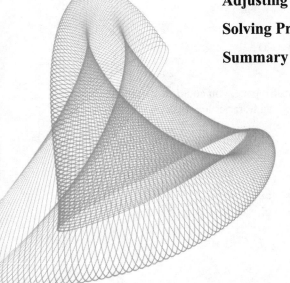

IN THIS CHAPTER:

Introducing the JSP Expression Language

Accessing JavaBeans

Using EL Operators

Adjusting EL-Related Settings

Solving Problems with the EL

Summary

J SP 2.0 adds a new feature that is especially useful for JSP page authors: the expression language (EL). Inspired by both ECMAScript and the XPath expression languages, the JSP 2.0 EL is designed to significantly ease the authoring of JSP pages and reduce (if not eliminate) scripts (JSP declarations, expressions, scriptlets) from a JSP page. EL expressions can appear both in text and in an attribute value of a standard action or a custom action.

The EL in JSP programming is not entirely new. The EL first appeared in the JSP Standard Tag Library (JSTL) 1.0 specification, and JSP 1.2 programmers could use the language by importing the standard libraries into their applications. Now that the EL is part of JSP, JSP programmers can use it without the JSTL. However, JSTL still provides other libraries useful for page authoring. JSTL 1.1, which is called the maintenance release, is discussed in Chapter 18. This chapter explains how the EL can help you to write better JSF applications. You will learn how to write simple EL expressions to use the EL to access object properties, EL implicit objects, and JavaBeans. You will also learn about the EL operators and EL-related application settings.

Introducing the JSP Expression Language

In JSF, the EL can help reduce Java code in a JSP page. For example, recall that the BuyDirect application, presented in Chapter 14, used the following Java code in the JSP pages to reference the CSS file:

```
<link rel="stylesheet" type="text/css"
  href="<%= request.getContextPath() + "/Styles.css" %>">
```

This uses the JSP expression `<%= request.getContextPath() %>`, to call the `getContextPath` method on the `HttpServletRequest` object.

With the EL in JSP 2.0, you can just write the following:

```
<link rel="stylesheet" type="text/css"
  href="${pageContext.request.contextPath}/Styles.css">
```

Now, there is no more script in your JSP page!

You can argue that to eliminate a script from the JSP page, you could wrap it in a custom tag library and use the custom tag. However, custom tag libraries are relatively hard to write, especially compared with using the EL.

To use the EL feature, you must use the Servlet 2.4 deployment descriptor. A Servlet 2.4 deployment descriptor has the following skeleton:

```
<?xml version="1.0" encoding="ISO-8859-1"?>
<web-app xmlns="http://java.sun.com/xml/ns/j2ee"
  xmlns:xsi="http://www.w3.org/2001/XMLSchema-instance"
  xsi:schemaLocation=
"http://java.sun.com/xml/ns/j2ee web-app_2_4.xsd"
  version="2.4">
```

```
...
</web-app>
```

Constructing EL Expressions

An EL expression has the following syntax:

```
${expression}
```

The `${` characters precede an expression, and a closing curly bracket (`}`) ends it.

For example, to write the expression a+b, you use the following construction:

```
${a+b}
```

> **NOTE**
>
> *The `${` sequence of characters denotes the beginning of an EL expression. If you want to send the literal `${` instead, you need to escape the first character: `\${`.*

You can also concatenate two expressions. A sequence of expressions will be evaluated from left to right, coerced to strings, and concatenated. For example, if a+b equals 8 and c+d equals 10, the following two expressions produce 810:

```
${a+b}${c+d}
```

And this expression results in 8some10text:

```
${a+b}some${c+d}text
```

If you use an expression in an attribute value of a custom tag, the expression will be evaluated and the resulting string coerced to the attribute's expected type:

```
<my:tag someAttribute="${expression}"/>
```

An expression is evaluated from left to right. For the general syntax exprA[exprB], the evaluation rule is as follows:

1. Evaluate exprA into valueA.
2. If valueA is null, return null.
3. Evaluate exprB into valueB.
4. If valueB is null, return null.
5. If valueA is a Map, check if valueB is a key in the Map. If yes, return valueA.get(valueB). Otherwise, return null.
6. If valueA is a List or an array:

   Coerce valueB to an int. If coercion fails, throw an exception.

If `valueA.get(valueB)` or `Array.get(valueA, valueB)` throws `ArrayIndexOutOfBoundsException` or `IndexOutOfBoundsException`, return `null`.

Otherwise, return `valueA.get(valueB)` or `Array.get(valueA, valueB)`.

7. At this point, `valueA` must be a JavaBean, therefore coerce `valueB` to `String`. If `valueB` is a readable property of `valueA`, call the getter of the property and return the value from the getter method. If the getter method throws an exception, generate an error.

8. Otherwise, generate an error.

As you would expect, the EL uses reserved words, which you cannot use as identifiers. The reserved words are listed in Table 17-1.

Accessing Object Properties

The return type of an expression can by anything. If an expression results in an object that has a property, you can access that property by using the [ ] or . operator. The [ ] and . operators are treated the same; [ ] is a more generalized form, but . is a nice shortcut.

To access the property of an object, use one of the following forms:

```
${object["propertyName"]}
${object.propertyName}
```

If *propertyName* is not a valid Java variable name, you must use the [ ] syntax.

For example, the implicit object `header` represents a `Map` containing all request headers. To access the `host` header, you can use either of these forms:

```
${header["host"]}
${header.host}
```

and	le
div	lt
empty	mod
eq	ne
false	not
ge	null
gt	or
instanceof	true

Table 17-1   *JSF EL Reserved Words*

However, to access the `accept-language` header, you can use only the [ ] operator, because `accept-language` is not a legal Java variable name.

If an object's property is an object that also has a property, you can use either [ ] or . to access the property. For example, `pageContext` represents the `PageContext` object for the current JSP page. One of the properties of `pageContext` is `request`, which represents the `ServletRequest` object. The `ServletRequest` object has the `requestURI` property. The following expression results in the value of the `requestURI` property:

```
${pageContext.request.requestURI}
```

To access the value of the `requestURI` property, you can also use any of the following forms:

```
${pageContext["request"]["requestURI"]}
${pageContext.request["requestURI"]}
${pageContext["request"].requestURI}
```

Accessing EL Implicit Objects

One of the uses of the EL is to access information that is normally available through Java code, such as context initial parameters, request parameters, request headers, cookies, session objects, and so on. Using the EL, you can access this information through EL implicit objects. Table 17-2 lists all the implicit objects available in the EL.

Object	Description
pageContext	The `javax.servlet.jsp.PageContext` object for the current JSP page.
initParam	A `Map` containing all of the context initialization parameters, with the parameter names as the keys.
Param	A `Map` containing all of the request parameters, with the parameter names as the keys. The value for each key is the first parameter value of the specified name. If there are two request parameters with the same name, only the first is retrieved. To access all parameter values that share the same name, use the `paramValues` object instead.
paramValues	A `Map` containing all of the request parameters, with the parameter names as the keys. The value for each key is an array of `String` values containing all the values for the specified parameter name. If the parameter has only one value, it still returns an array having one element.
Header	A `Map` containing the request headers, with the header names as the keys. The value for each key is the first header of the specified header name. If a header has more than one value, only the first value is returned. To obtain multiple-value headers, use the `headerValues` object instead.

Table 17-2   *The EL Implicit Objects*

Object	Description
headerValues	A Map containing all of the request headers, with the header names as the keys. The value for each key is an array of String values containing all the values for the specified header name. If the header has only one value, it returns a one-element array.
Cookie	A Map containing all Cookie objects in the current request object. The cookie names are the Map keys, and each key is mapped to a Cookie object.
applicationScope	A Map containing all of the attributes in the ServletContext object, with the attribute names as the keys.
sessionScope	A Map containing all of the attributes in the session object, with the attribute names as the keys.
requestScope	A Map containing all of the attributes in the current request object, with the attribute names as the keys.
pageScope	A Map containing all of the attributes with the page scope, with the attribute names as the keys.

Table 17-2   *The EL Implicit Objects* (continued)

The following sections discuss each of the EL implicit objects. The example in the "Using Simple EL Expressions" section, after these descriptions, demonstrates using the implicit objects.

The pageContext Implicit Object

The pageContext implicit object represents the javax.servlet.jsp.PageContext object for the current JSP page. It is the most comprehensive object, because it encapsulates all other JSP implicit objects (such as out, request, response, and so on). Table 17-3 summarizes the JSP implicit objects and how to use EL expressions to access them.

NOTE

The JSP implicit objects should not be confused with the EL implicit objects.

For example, you can obtain the current ServletRequest object using the following expression:

```
${pageContext.request}
```

You can obtain the request URI of the request object using the following expression:

```
${pageContext.request.requestURI}
```

This is equivalent to invoking the getRequestURI method on the request implicit object.

To obtain request parameters, use the param and paramValues implicit objects.

JSP Implicit Object	Type	EL Expression to Access the JSP Object
request	javax.servlet.http .HttpServletRequest	${pageContext.request}
response	javax.servlet.http .HttpServletResponse	${pageContext.response}
out	javax.servlet.jsp.JspWriter	${pageContext.out}
session	javax.servlet.http.HttpSession	${pageContext.session}
application	javax.servlet.ServletContext	${pageContext .servletContext}
config	javax.servlet.ServletConfig	${pageContext .servletConfig}
pageContext	javax.servlet.jsp.PageContext	${pageContext}
page	javax.servlet.jsp.HttpJspPage	${pageContext.page}
exception	java.lang.Throwable	${page.exception}

Table 17-3   *Accessing JSP Implicit Objects*

The initParam Implicit Object

You use the `initParam` implicit object to retrieve the value of a context initial parameter. For example, suppose you have a parameter called `bgColor` that specifies the background color for all your pages, and you declare the following `context-param` element in your deployment descriptor:

```
<context-param>
   <param-name>bgColor</param-name>
   <param-value>green</param-value>
</context-param>
```

You can use the following EL expression to obtain the value of `bgColor`:

```
<body bgcolor="${initParam.bgColor}">
```

The param and paramValues Implicit Objects

The `param` implicit object represents a `Map` containing all of the request parameters. You use this implicit object to retrieve a parameter value. For example, here is how you retrieve the parameter called `name`:

```
{$param.name}
```

The `paramValues` implicit object represents a `Map` containing all of the request parameters, with the parameter names as the keys. The value for each key is an array of `String` values containing all of the values for the specified parameter name. If the parameter has only one value, it still returns an array with one element. For example, to obtain the first and second values of the `favSinger` parameter, use the following expressions:

```
${paramValues.favSinger[0]}
${paramValues.favSinger[1]}
```

The header and headerValues Implicit Objects

The `header` implicit object represents a `Map` containing all of the request headers, with the header names as the keys. For example, to obtain the value of the `host` header, use the following expression:

```
${header.host}
```

If the header name is not a valid Java variable name, such as `accept-language`, you must use the `[ ]` operator:

```
${header["accept-language"]}
```

The `headerValues` implicit object represents a `Map` containing all of the request headers, with the header names as the keys. Unlike `header`, however, the `Map` returned by the `headerValues` object returns an array of `String` values. For example, to obtain the first value of the `accept-language` header, use this expression:

```
${headerValues["accept-language"][0]}
```

The cookie Implicit Object

The `cookie` implicit object represents a `Map` containing all of the cookies in the current `ServletRequest` object. For example, to obtain the value of a cookie called `password`, use the following expression:

```
${cookie.password.value}
```

To obtain the `maxAge` value of the same cookie, use this expression:

```
${cookie.password.maxAge}
```

The Scope Implicit Objects

You use the `applicationScope` implicit object to obtain the value of an application-scoped attribute. For example, if you have an application-scoped attribute called `myAttr`, use this expression to access the attribute:

```
${applicationScope.myAttr}
```

The `sessionScope`, `requestScope`, and `pageScope` implicit objects are similar to `applicationScope`. However, the scopes they address are session, request, and page, respectively.

Using Simple EL Expressions

The `implicitObjectsTest.jsp` page, shown in Listing 17-1, provides examples of using EL expressions to access the EL implicit objects.

Listing 17-1   *The implicitObjectsTest.jsp Page*

```
<%
  if (request.getQueryString()==null) {
    response.sendRedirect(request.getRequestURI() +
"?name=aria&favSinger=Diana+Krall&favSinger=Norah+Jones");
  }
  application.setAttribute("appAttr", "application scope");
  session.setAttribute("sessAttr", "session scope");
  request.setAttribute("reqAttr", "request scope");
  pageContext.setAttribute("pageAttr", "page scope");
%>

<%@ page import="java.util.Enumeration"%>
<html>
<head>
<title>Testing Simple EL Expressions</title>
</head>
<body>
<table>
<tr>
  <th>Expression</th>
  <th>Result</td>
</tr>
<tr>
  <td>\${pageContext.request.requestURI}</td>
  <td>${pageContext.request.requestURI}</td>
</tr>
<tr>
  <td>\${pageContext["request"].contextPath}</td>
  <td>${pageContext["request"].contextPath}</td>
</tr>
<tr>
  <td>\${pageContext["response"]["contentType"]}</td>
  <td>${pageContext["response"]["contentType"]}</td>
</tr>
<tr>
  <td>\${pageContext.response["bufferSize"]}</td>
  <td>${pageContext.response["bufferSize"]}</td>
</tr>
<tr>
  <td>\${pageContext.out.bufferSize}</td>
  <td>${pageContext.out.bufferSize}</td>
</tr>
<tr>
```

```
  <td>\${pageContext.out.remaining}</td>
  <td>${pageContext.out.remaining}</td>
</tr>
<tr>
  <td>\${pageContext.session.id}</td>
  <td>${pageContext.session.id}</td>
</tr>
<tr>
  <td>\${pageContext.servletContext.serverInfo}</td>
  <td>${pageContext.servletContext.serverInfo}</td>
</tr>
<tr>
  <td>\${pageContext.servletConfig.servletName}</td>
  <td>${pageContext.servletConfig.servletName}</td>
</tr>
<tr>
  <td>\${pageContext.page}</td>
  <td>${pageContext.page}</td>
</tr>
<tr>
  <td>\${initParam.bgColor}</td>
  <td>${initParam.bgColor}</td>
</tr>
<tr>
  <td>\${param.name}</td>
  <td>${param.name}</td>
</tr>
<tr>
  <td>\${paramValues.favSinger[0]}</td>
  <td>${paramValues.favSinger[0]}</td>
</tr>
<tr>
  <td>\${paramValues.favSinger[1]}</td>
  <td>${paramValues.favSinger[1]}</td>
</tr>
<tr>
  <td>\${header.host}</td>
  <td>${header.host}</td>
</tr>
<tr>
  <td>\${header["accept-language"]}</td>
  <td>${header["accept-language"]}</td>
</tr>
<tr>
```

```
   <td>\${headerValues["accept-language"][0]}</td>
   <td>${headerValues["accept-language"][0]}</td>
</tr>
<tr>
   <td>\${cookie.JSESSIONID.value}</td>
   <td>${cookie.JSESSIONID.value}</td>
</tr>
<tr>
   <td>\${applicationScope.appAttr}</td>
   <td>${applicationScope.appAttr}</td>
</tr>
<tr>
   <td>\${sessionScope.sessAttr}</td>
   <td>${sessionScope.sessAttr}</td>
</tr>
<tr>
   <td>\${requestScope.reqAttr}</td>
   <td>${requestScope.reqAttr}</td>
</tr>
<tr>
   <td>\${pageScope.pageAttr}</td>
   <td>${pageScope.pageAttr}</td>
</tr>
</table>
</body>
</html>
```

You invoke the `implicitObjectsTest.jsp` by using the following URL:

```
http://localhost:8080/JSFCh17/implicitObjectsTest.jsp
```

It will then redirect itself to pass a few parameters, as follows:

```
if (request.getQueryString()==null) {
  response.sendRedirect(request.getRequestURI() +
    "?name=aria&favSinger=Diana+Krall&favSinger=Norah+Jones");
}
```

This way, you do not need to type the parameters yourself.

Next, it initializes four attributes with different scopes:

```
application.setAttribute("appAttr", "application scope");
session.setAttribute("sessAttr", "session scope");
request.setAttribute("reqAttr", "request scope");
pageContext.setAttribute("pageAttr", "page scope");
```

The rest of the page is a table that provides the results for the EL expressions. Figure 17-1 shows the result of invoking the `implicitObjectsTest.jsp` page.

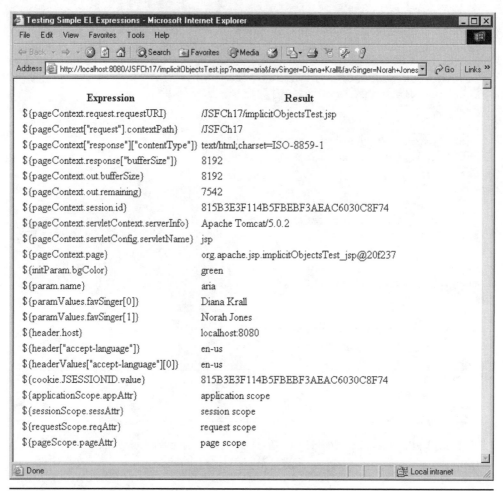

Figure 17-1   Using EL implicit objects

Accessing JavaBeans

In previous chapters, you have seen that you can display the property value of a JavaBean using a UIOutput component. The good news is there is another, shorter, way of displaying a JavaBean's property: using an EL expression.

As usual, your JavaBean must be registered in the application configuration file using a managed-bean element. The value in the managed-bean-name element under \<managed-bean\> is the variable with which you refer to the bean in your EL expression.

You can then use the . or [ ] operator to access the bean property, using the following syntax:

```
${beanName.propertyName}
```

For example, to access the userName property of a bean named TestingBean, use the following expression:

```
${TestingBean.userName}
```

If the property is an object that itself has a property, you can access the property of the second object, too, again using the . or [ ] operator. Or, if the property is a Map, List, or an array, you can use the same rule explained in the previous section on the evaluation rule to access the Map's values or the elements of the List or the array.

As an example, consider the JavaBean named testingBean, shown in Listing 17-2.

Listing 17-2   *The TestingBean*

```java
package ch17;

import java.util.ArrayList;
import java.util.HashMap;
import java.util.List;
import java.util.Map;

public class TestingBean {
  private String userName = "alpha4";
  private String[] ids = { "1001", "1002", "2003" };
  private List cities;
  private Map credentials;

  public TestingBean() {
    cities = new ArrayList();
    cities.add("New Delhi");
    cities.add("Jakarta");
    credentials = new HashMap();
    credentials.put("1001", "chiro");
    credentials.put("1002", "physio");
    credentials.put("2003", "semiconductor");
  }
  public String getUserName() {
    return userName;
  }
  public void setUserName(String userName) {
    System.out.println("setUserName:" + userName);
    this.userName = userName;
  }
  public List getCities() {
```

```
    return cities;
  }
  public Map getCredentials() {
    return credentials;
  }
  public String[] getIds() {
    return ids;
  }
}
```

This JavaBean is registered in the application configuration file using the managed-bean element, as shown in Listing 17-3.

Listing 17-3   *TestingBean Registration in the Application Configuration File*

```
<managed-bean>
  <managed-bean-name>testingBean</managed-bean-name>
  <managed-bean-class>ch17.TestingBean</managed-bean-class>
  <managed-bean-scope>application</managed-bean-scope>
  <managed-property>
    <property-name>userName</property-name>
    <value>touchfone</value>
  </managed-property>
</managed-bean>
```

The javaBeanTest.jsp page, shown in Listing 17-4, demonstrates how to access the properties of the TestingBean using both a UIOutput component and EL expressions.

Listing 17-4   *The javaBeanTest.jsp Page*

```
<%@ taglib uri="http://java.sun.com/jsf/html" prefix="h" %>
<%@ taglib uri="http://java.sun.com/jsf/core" prefix="f" %>
<html>
<head>
<title>Accessing JavaBean Properties Using EL Expressions</title>
</head>
<body>
<f:use_faces>
<h:form formName="myForm" >
  <h:output_number id="output" valueRef="TestingBean.userName"/>
```

```
</h:form>
</f:use_faces>

<hr/>
<br/>User Name: ${TestingBean.userName}
<br/>First city: ${TestingBean.cities[0]}
<br/>Second city: ${TestingBean.cities[1]}
<br/>First id: ${TestingBean.ids[0]}
<br/>Second id: ${TestingBean.ids[1]}
<br/>Third id: ${TestingBean.ids[2]}
<br/>First password: ${TestingBean.credentials[TestingBean.ids[0]]}
<br/>Second password: ${TestingBean.credentials[TestingBean.ids[1]]}
<br/>Third password: ${TestingBean.credentials[TestingBean.ids[2]]}
</body>
</html>
```

You can invoke the `javaBeanTest.jsp` page using the following URL:

`http://localhost:8080/JSFCh17/faces/javaBeanTest.jsp`

The result is shown in Figure 17-2.

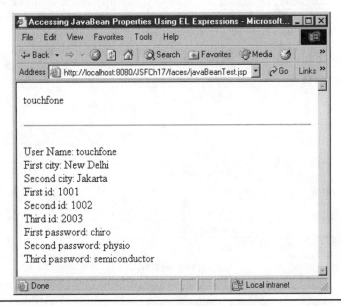

Figure 17-2   *Using EL expressions to access JavaBean properties*

Using EL Operators

Along with the . and [ ] operators for accessing properties, the EL provides a number
of other operators for various operations, as listed in Table 17-4. These operators involve
operands (such as a + b) and allow you to perform some operations; however, you should
use them with caution. Bear in mind that operators are normally used when writing business
logic, and the presentation layer is normally not a place for business logic.

This is not to say that operators cannot be useful in JSP pages. For example, suppose you
want to define a default background color (yellow) for your JSP page. However, if a context
initial parameter named bgColor is specified, you want to use the specified value as the
background color. To accomplish this, you can use the conditional operator, of the form
statement ? *expr1* : *expr2*, to send certain output based on the value of a variable.
You can write the following HTML body element:

```
<body bgColor=
"${initParam.bgColor==null? "yellow" : initParam.bgColor}">
```

If no bgColor context initial parameter exists in the deployment descriptor, you will have
the following body element:

```
<body bgColor="yellow">
```

Otherwise, the value of the bgColor attribute of your body element will be whatever value
is specified for the bgColor context initial parameter in the deployment descriptor.

Operator	Description
Arithmetic Operators	
+	Addition
−	Subtraction
*	Multiplication
/ and div	Division
% and mod	Remainder/modulo
Relational Operators	
== and eq	Equality (for example, ${1==2} returns false)
!= and ne	Nonequality
> and gt	Greater than
>= and ge	Greater than or equal
< and lt	Less than (for example, ${"a"<"b"} returns true)
<= and le	Less than or equal
Logical Operators	
&& and and	AND

Table 17-4   *The EL Operators*

Operator	Description
|| and or	OR
! and not	NOT
Conditional Operator	
${statement? A:B}	If *statement* evaluates to true, then the output of the expression is A. Otherwise, the output is B.
Empty Operator	
${empty A}	Examines if a value is null or empty. If A is null or if A is a zero-length string, the expression returns true. It also returns true if A is an empty Map, an empty array, or an empty Collection. Otherwise, it returns false.

Table 17-4   *The EL Operators* (continued)

NOTE

The division and remainder operators have two forms to be consistent with XPath and ECMAScript.

An EL expression is evaluated from the highest to lowest precedence, and then from left to right. The *, /, div, %, and mod operators have the same level of precedence, and are evaluated first. Then the + and − have the same precedence, and are evaluated after the first group, because they have a lower precedence. Therefore, the expression ${1+2*8} results in 17, not 24.

The operatorTest.jsp page, shown in Listing 17-5, demonstrates how to use the EL operators.

Listing 17-5   *The operatorTest.jsp Page*

```
<%@ taglib uri="http://java.sun.com/jsf/html" prefix="h" %>
<%@ taglib uri="http://java.sun.com/jsf/core" prefix="f" %>
<html>
<head>
<title>Using EL Operators</title>
</head>
<body>
<table border="1">
<tr>
  <th>Expression</th>
  <th>Result</td>
</tr>
<tr>
  <td>\${1+2}</td>
```

```
   <td>${1+2}</td>
 </tr>
 <tr>
   <td>\${1*2+3}</td>
   <td>${1*2+3}</td>
 </tr>
 <tr>
   <td>\${1/2}</td>
   <td>${1/2}</td>
 </tr>
 <tr>
   <td>\${11 mod 2}</td>
   <td>${11 mod 2}</td>
 </tr>
 <tr>
   <td>\${1==2}</td>
   <td>${1==2}</td>
 </tr>
 <tr>
   <td>\${1 le 2}</td>
   <td>${1 le 2}</td>
 </tr>
 <tr>
   <td>\${empty "aString"}</td>
   <td>${empty "aString"}</td>
 </tr>
 </table>
 </body>
 </html>
```

You can invoke this page by using the following URL:

`http://localhost:8080/JSFCh17/faces/operatorTest.jsp`

The result of invoking this page is shown in Figure 17-3.

Adjusting EL-Related Settings

When you use the EL in a JSF application, you may need to adjust some settings to ensure that the application behaves as intended. First, you may not want the EL to be evaluated on one or more JSP pages. Second, you may want to disable scripts on certain JSP pages.

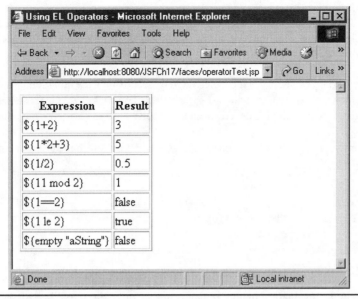

Figure 17-3   *Using EL operators*

Deactivating EL Evaluation

In some cases, you may want to deactivate EL evaluation in a JSP page. For example, if you are using a JSP 2.4 container for hosting a JSP 2.3 application. When you deactivate EL evaluation in a JSP page, every occurrence of the construct $ {expression} will not be evaluated as an EL expression.

There are two ways to deactivate EL evaluation in a JSP page: with a page directive attribute and with a deployment descriptor element.

The page Directive's isELIgnored Attribute

The default value of the page directive's isELIgnored attribute is false. You can deactivate EL evaluation by setting the isELIgnored attribute to true:

```
<%@ page isELIgnored="true" %>
```

Using the isELIgnored attribute is recommended if you want to deactivate EL evaluation in one or a few JSP pages.

The jsp-property-group Element

The other way of deactivating EL evaluation is by using the jsp-property-group element in the deployment descriptor. The jsp-property-group element is a subelement of a jsp-config element. You use jsp-property-group to apply certain settings to a set of JSP pages in the application.

NOTE

If you use a deployment descriptor that is compliant with Servlet 2.3 or earlier, the EL evaluation is already disabled by default.

To use the `jsp-property-group` element to deactivate EL evaluation, you must have two subelements: `url-pattern` and `el-ignored`. The `url-pattern` element specifies the URL pattern to which the EL deactivation will apply. The `el-ignored` element must be set to `true`.

As an example, here is how you deactivate the EL evaluation in the JSP page named `ignored.jsp`:

```
<jsp-config>
  <jsp-property-group>
    <url-pattern>/ignored.jsp</url-pattern>
    <el-ignored>true</el-ignored>
  </jsp-property-group>
</jsp-config>
```

To deactivate EL evaluation in all JSP pages in the application, use `*.jsp` as the value of the `url-pattern` element:

```
<jsp-config>
  <jsp-property-group>
    <url-pattern>*.jsp</url-pattern>
    <el-ignored>true</el-ignored>
  </jsp-property-group>
</jsp-config>
```

EL evaluation in a JSP page will be deactivated if either the `isELIgnored` attribute of its `page` directive is set to `true` or if its URL matches the pattern in the `jsp-property-group` whose subelement `el-ignored` is set to `true`. For example, if the `page` directive's `isELIgnored` attribute of a JSP page is set to `false`, but its URL matches the pattern of JSP pages whose EL evaluation is deactivated in the deployment descriptor, the EL evaluation of that page will be deactivated.

Disabling Scripting Elements

JSP pages should contain only the presentation portion of a Web application. All business rules should be located either in JavaBeans or in custom tag libraries. In other words, JSP pages should be script-less: free of declarations, expressions, and scriptlets. However, this is sometimes hard to enforce.

Starting with JSP 2.0, project managers and software architects can easily disable scripting elements by using the `scripting-invalid` element inside a `jsp-property-group`. When the `scripting-invalid` element is set to `true`, scripting is not allowed, but the EL will still be evaluated. This way, you can allow the EL but not scripts. The other required subelement inside the `jsp-property-group` element is `url-pattern`, which defines the URL pattern to which the scripting disabling applies.

Here is how you disable scripting in all JSP pages in an application:

```
<jsp-config>
  <jsp-property-group>
    <url-pattern>*.jsp</url-pattern>
    <scripting-invalid>true</scripting-invalid>
  </jsp-property-group>
</jsp-config>
```

CAUTION

There can be only one occurrence of the `jsp-config` element in the deployment descriptor. Therefore, if you have specified a `jsp-property-group` for deactivating the EL, you must put your `jsp-property-group` for disabling scripting under the same `jsp-config` element.

Solving Problems with the EL

To give you an idea of how EL expressions can be used in a practical application, let's revisit the simple login application used to demonstrate page navigation in Chapter 8 (Listings 8-7 and 8-8).

First, for the `login.jsp` page, you want to ensure that the current page is not directly invoked by using the URL for the JSP page. Instead, if the user tries to do this, the page will forward the invocation to `/faces/login.jsp`. You can accomplish this by using EL expressions within `<c:if>` tags, as follows:

```
<c:if test="${requestScope['javax.servlet.forward.servlet_path']==null}">
  <jsp:forward page="${initParam.loginPage}"/>
</c:if>
```

Listing 17-6 shows the improved `login.jsp` page.

Listing 17-6   *The login.jsp Page with EL Expressions*

```
<%@ taglib uri="http://java.sun.com/jsf/html" prefix="h" %>
<%@ taglib uri="http://java.sun.com/jsf/core" prefix="f" %>
<%@ taglib uri="http://java.sun.com/jsp/jstl/core" prefix="c" %>
<%--
The following <c:if> makes sure that the current page
is not directly invoked
by using http://localhost:8080/JSFCh17/login.jsp
If the user tries to do so, it will forward to /faces/login.jsp.
--%>
```

```
<c:if test=
"${requestScope['javax.servlet.forward.servlet_path']==null}">
  <jsp:forward page="${initParam.loginPage}"/>
</c:if>
<html>
<head>
<title>Login</title>
</head>
<body>
<f:use_faces>
<h:form   formName="loginForm">
<h2>Please enter your user name and password</h2>
<br>User Name: <h:input_text valueRef="loginBean.userName"/>
<br>Password: <h:input_secret valueRef="loginBean.password"/>
<br><h:command_button commandName="login" label="login"
actionRef="LoginBean.login"/>
<br>
<h:output_errors/>
</h:form>
</f:use_faces>
</body>
</html>
```

Similarly, you can use EL expressions to provide restricted access for the `welcome.jsp` page. You can make sure that a user can access that page only if there is a session attribute named `loggedIn`, and send the user back to the login page if this attribute is not found. Again, include the EL expressions in `<c:if>` tags, as follows:

```
<c:if test="${sessionScope.loggedIn==null}">
  <jsp:forward page="${initParam.loginPage}"/>
</c:if>
```

Listing 17-7 shows this version of the `welcome.jsp` page.

Listing 17-7   *The welcome.jsp Page with EL Expressions*

```
<%@ taglib uri="http://java.sun.com/jsf/html" prefix="h" %>
<%@ taglib uri="http://java.sun.com/jsf/core" prefix="f" %>
<%@ taglib uri="http://java.sun.com/jsp/jstl/core" prefix="c" %>
<%--
  The following <c:if> makes sure that the user can only see
  this page if there is a session attribute named 'loggedIn'.
```

```
    If this attribute is not found, forward to /faces/login.jsp.
--%>
<c:if test="${sessionScope.loggedIn==null}">
  <jsp:forward page="${initParam.loginPage}"/>
</c:if>
<html>
<head>
<title>Welcome</title>
</head>
<body>
You logged in successfully.
</body>
</html>
```

Summary

The JSP 2.0 EL is a powerful feature added to the latest version of JSP. By using the EL properly, you can write shorter JSP pages and can sometimes eliminate the use of UIOutput components.

This chapter demonstrated how to use EL to access implicit objects and JavaBean properties, as well as how to use EL operators. You also learned how to configure two EL-related settings to deactivate the EL and disable scripting.

The JSP Standard
Tag Library

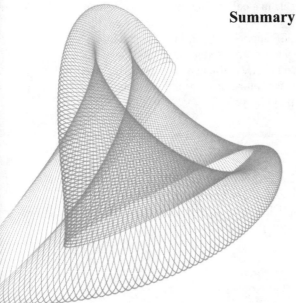

Y ou are familiar with the custom tag technology that can help you write scriptless JSP pages. You have probably written some tags and heard about the JSP Standard Tag Library (JSTL), which provides reusable tags.

This chapter covers how to use JSTL tags with JSF. First, you will learn when JSTL tags may be helpful. Then you will be introduced to the JSTL tags that are commonly used in JSF applications. Finally, you will see how the JSTL can help solve common problems in JSF applications.

Why Use JSTL Tags in a JSF Application?

In a nutshell, the JSTL provides tags with the following functionality:

▶ Common and structural tasks such as iteration, collection, and conditional processing

▶ XML document processing

▶ Internationalization and text formatting

▶ Database access and data manipulation

You'll notice that, in many ways, the functions provided by both JSF and the JSTL overlap. For example, the JSTL provides date/number formatting and internationalization tags. In Chapter 5, you learned how you can use various tags for formatting dates, times, and numbers. Chapter 11 explained how JSF can be used to internationalize your Web site. For these overlapping functions, it is recommended that you use the JSF tags. For those functions not available in JSF, JSTL actions are a welcome addition.

In a JSF application, you may want to use the JSTL to display JavaBeans properties, display implicit objects' properties, iterate over objects in a collection, test a condition, help with data formatting, and so on.

However, some tags are not suitable for use in a JSF application. For instance, the SQL library provides tags to quickly access the database and manipulate the data in it. However, in JSF applications, it's better to write data-access code in a JavaBean or a listener. Accessing a database directly from JSP page would mess up your application control flow. In addition, the JSTL SQL library does not support connection pooling (yet).

Introducing the JSTL

The JSTL specification was developed by the JSR-52 expert group under the Java Community Process (http://www.jcp.org), with the aim of expediting the JSP application development process. The latest specification, version 1.1, was released on June 16, 2003, and is downloadable from http://java.sun.com/products/jsp/jstl/.

The implementation was built by the open-source community under the Apache Software Foundation's Jakarta Taglibs project (`http://jakarta.apache.org/taglibs/`).

> **NOTE**
>
> *This chapter discusses JSTL 1.1. The examples presented here require a Web container that supports Servlet 2.4 and JSP 2.0, such as Tomcat 5.*

Physically, the JSTL comes in two JARs: `jstl.jar` and `standard.jar`. These files are included in the Java Web Services Developer Pack (JWSDP) 1.2, which can be downloaded from `http://jakarta.apache.org/taglibs/doc/standard-doc/intro.html`.

Even though the JSTL is always referred to as a library (singular), it actually exposes its actions via multiple tag libraries. The tags in JSTL 1.1 can be categorized into five areas, which are summarized in Table 18-1.

The following sections describe how to use the JSTL from JSP pages and the more commonly used JSTL tags for JSF applications, grouped by action types.

Using the JSTL from a JSP Page

Pay special attention to the URI and prefix of each library listed in Table 18-1. To use the JSTL from a JSP page, you must use the `taglib` directive on top of your page and employ its `uri` and `prefix` attributes. Here is an example:

```
<%@ taglib uri="http://java.sun.com/jsp/jstl/core" prefix="c" %>
```

Area	Subfunction	URI	Prefix
Core	Variable support Flow control URL management Miscellaneous	http://java.sun.com/jsp/jstl/core	c
XML	Core Flow control Transformation	http://java.sun.com/jsp/jstl/xml	x
I18n	Locale Message formatting Number and date formatting	http://java.sun.com/jsp/jstl/fmt	fmt
Database	SQL	http://java.sun.com/jsp/jstl/sql	sql
Functions	Collection length String manipulation	http://java.sun.com/jsp/jstl/functions	fn

Table 18-1   *The JSTL Tag Libraries*

A JSTL tag handler may need to expose information that can be accessed from the calling JSP page (the JSP page that uses the tag associated with the tag handler). This information is stored in a variable. There are four places where this kind of variable can be stored: the `ServletContext` (application), the `session` object, the `request` object, or the `PageContext` object. Storing this variable in one of these objects is practical, because each can be accessed from a tag handler as well as from a JSP page's scripting language or from EL expressions (discussed in Chapter 17). The variable is stored as an attribute of one of these four objects. Such an attribute is called a *scoped* variable, because it can have one of the four scopes (application, session, request, page), depending on where it is stored.

A JSTL tag normally has the attribute `scope`, which allows you to determine where a scoped variable exposed by the tag handlers is to be stored. The `scope` attribute can have the value `page`, `request`, `session`, or `application`. You can use `session` for the `scope` attribute if the JSP page is participating in session management. If the `scope` attribute is not present, its default value is `page`. Also, JSTL tags, by convention, use the attribute named `var` for scoped variables.

If you use an EL expression to access a scoped variable, the JSP container searches for a scoped variable using the `findAttribute` method of the `JspContext` object in the following order: page, request, session, application.

Performing General-Purpose Actions

General-purpose JSTL tags include `<c:out>`, `<c:set>`, `<c:remove>`, and `<c:catch>`. The first three are used for manipulating scoped variables, and `<c:catch>` is for catching a thrown exception.

The <c:out> Tag

The `<c:out>` tag evaluates an expression and outputs the result to the current `JspWriter` object. The syntax for `<c:out>` has two forms. One form is without body content:

```
<c:out value="value" [escapeXml="{true|false}"] [default="defaultValue"]/>
```

The other form is with body content:

```
<c:out value="value" [escapeXml="{true|false}"]>
  default value
</c:out>
```

NOTE

The [ ] indicates an optional attribute. The underlined value indicates the default value.

The body content is JSP. Table 18-2 lists the `<c:out>` attributes.

Attribute	rtexprvalue	Type	Description
Value	true	Object	The expression to be evaluated
escapeXml	true	Boolean	Indicates whether the characters <, >, &, ', and " in the resulting string will be converted to their corresponding character-entity codes
default	true	Object	The default value

Table 18-2   *The <c:out> Attributes*

NOTE

The body content can be empty, JSP, or tagdependent.

NOTE

The rtexprvalue columns in the tables in this chapter indicate the values of the rtexprvalue *element in the TLD. If the value is* false, *only a static string value can be assigned to the attribute. If the value is* true, *the attribute can be assigned a request-time attribute value, which can be a Java expression, an EL expression, or a value set by a* <jsp:attribute> *tag.*

For example, the following action prints the value of the scoped variable x:

```
<c:out value="${x}"/>
```

By default, <c:out> encodes special characters to their corresponding character-entity codes, as follows:

<	&lt;
>	&gt;
'	&#039;
"	&#034;
&	&amp;

Even if you do not have a scoped variable to display, you can use <c:out> to encode any string that contains one or more of those characters, as in this example:

```
<c:out value="Use <br/> to change lines"/>
```

If you are sure a variable does not contain any of the five special characters, you can safely use the shorter EL expression:${x}.

The `default` attribute in `<c:out>` lets you assign a default value that will be displayed if the EL expression assigned to its `value` attribute results in `null`. For example, in the following `<c:out>` action, if the variable `myVar` is not found in the `session` object, the value of the `myVar` application scoped variable is displayed. If the latter is also not found, an empty string is sent to the output.

```
<c:out value="${sessionScope.myVar}"
  default="${applicationScope.myVar}"/>
```

The `encodeXml` attribute indicates whether encoding is enabled. By default, the value of `escapeXml` is `true`, so that special characters are encoded. There is no reason to use `<c:out>` with its `escapeXml` attribute set to `false`; use an EL expression instead.

The `test_c_out.jsp` page, shown in Listing 18-1, demonstrates using `<c:out>`.

Listing 18-1   *The test_c_out.jsp Page*

```
<%@ taglib uri="http://java.sun.com/jsp/jstl/core" prefix="c" %>
<%--
  create a request-scoped variable named message and assign a value
--%>
<c:set var="message" value="Use <br/> to change lines"
  scope="request"/>

with encoding: <c:out value="${message}"/>
<br/>
without encoding: ${message}
<br/>
Use specifically for encoding:
<c:out value="Do you know what <br/> means?"/>
<br/>
There is no point setting escapeXml to false:
<c:out escapeXml="false" value="Do you know what <br/> means?"/>
<br/>
<c:out value="${sessionScope.myVar}" default="myVar not found"/>
```

You can invoke the `c_outTest.jsp` page using the following URL:

`http://localhost:8080/JSFCh18/test_c_out.jsp`

The result is shown in Figure 18-1.

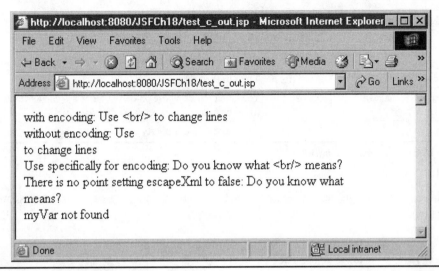

Figure 18-1   *Testing <c:out>*

The <c:set> Tag

You can use the <c:set> tag to assign a value to a scoped variable or to the property of a target object. Its syntax has four forms. The first form is used to set the value of a scoped variable using the value attribute:

```
<c:set value="value"  var="varName"
  [scope="{page|request|session|application}]"/>
```

The second form sets the value of a scoped variable using the body content:

```
<c:set var="varName" [scope="{page|request|session|application}]">
  body content
</c:set>
```

The third form sets the property of a target object using the <u>value</u> attribute:

```
<c:set value="value"  target="target" property="propertyName"/>
```

The fourth form sets the property of a target object using the body content:

```
<c:set target="target" property="propertyName">
  body content
</c:set>
```

The body content is JSP. The attributes are listed in Table 18-3.

Attribute	rtexprvalue	Type	Description
value	true	Object	The expression to be evaluated
var	false	String	The name of the scoped variable to be assigned a value
scope	false	String	The scope of var
target	true	Object	The target object whose property will be assigned a value (must be a JavaBeans instance or a java.util.Map object)
property	true	String	The name of the property to be assigned a value

Table 18-3   *The <c:set> Attributes*

As an example, consider the `<c:set>` actions in the `test_c_set.jsp` page, shown in Listing 18-2.

Listing 18-2   *The test_c_set.jsp Page*

```
<%@ taglib uri="http://java.sun.com/jsp/jstl/core" prefix="c" %>
Assign value to a scoped variable:
<br/>
<c:set var="x" value="${10*12}" scope="request"/>
${x}
<br/>
<c:set var="x" scope="request">Hello World</c:set>
${x}
```

You can invoke the `test_c_set.jsp` page using the following URL:

`http://localhost:8080/JSFCh18/test_c_set.jsp`

The result is shown in Figure 18-2.

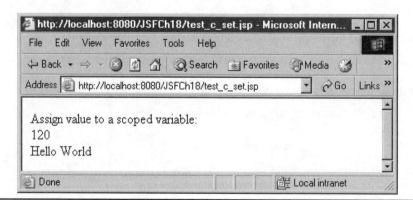

Figure 18-2   *Testing <c:set>*

Why Explicitly Remove a Scoped Variable?

Is it necessary to explicitly remove a scoped variable? Doesn't the JSP container remove a scoped variable automatically when it is out of scope? The answer is yes and no. For those variables having page or request scopes, it is not really important to remove them explicitly, because the `PageContext` or `Request` objects themselves will be destroyed by the JSP container after the current request is served.

For an application-scoped variable, however, it is important to explicitly remove a scoped variable, because otherwise that variable will remain until the application is shut down. Also, for a session-scope variable, removal can be particularly important. For example, if you set a session variable called `loggedIn` when a user logs in successfully, you may want to explicitly remove this variable when the user logs out.

The <c:remove> Tag

You use <c:remove> to remove a scoped variable. The syntax is as follows:

```
<c:remove var="varName"
  [scope="{page|request|session|application}"]/>
```

Table 18-4 shows the <c:remove> attributes.

If the scope attribute is not present, the JSP container will attempt to remove variables having the specified name from all scopes.

As an example, consider the <c:remove> actions in the test_c_remove.jsp page, shown in Listing 18-3.

Listing 18-3   *The test_c_remove.jsp Page*

```
<%@ taglib uri="http://java.sun.com/jsp/jstl/core" prefix="c" %>
Assign value to a scoped variable:
<br/>
<c:set var="x" value="${10*12}" scope="request"/>
${x}
<br/>
Remove the variable:
<c:remove var="x"/>
${x}
```

Attribute	rtexprvalue	Type	Description
var	false	String	The name of the scoped variable to be removed
scope	false	String	The scope for var

Table 18-4   *The <c:remove> Attributes*

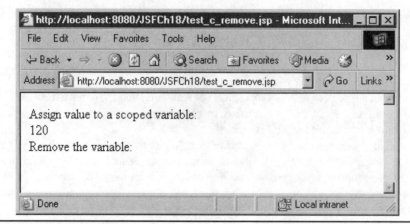

Figure 18-3   *Testing <c:remove>*

You can invoke the `test_c_remove.jsp` page using the following URL:

`http://localhost:8080/JSFCh18/test_c_remove.jsp`

Figure 18-3 shows the result in the browser.

The <c:catch> Tag

You use `<c:catch>` to catch a `java.lang.Throwable` that is thrown by any of the nested actions. The syntax of `<c:catch>` is as follows:

```
<c:catch [var="varName"]>
  nested actions
<c:/catch>
```

The body content is JSP. The var attribute must be a `String` literal and is the name of the scoped variable created when an exception is thrown from a nested action.

As an example, in the `test_c_catch.jsp` page, shown in Listing 18-4, we deliberately cause the JSP container to throw an exception by trying to divide a number by a string.

Listing 18-4   *The test_c_catch.jsp Page*

```
<%@ taglib uri="http://java.sun.com/jsp/jstl/core" prefix="c" %>
<c:set var="s" value="Hello"/>

<c:catch var="errorMessage">
  ${123/s}
```

```
</c:catch>
Error message: ${errorMessage}
```

You can invoke the `test_c_catch.jsp` page using the following URL:

`http://localhost:8080/JSFCh18/test_c_catch.jsp`

You will see the result shown in Figure 18-4.

Executing Conditional Actions

Conditional actions are used to deal with situations where the output of a page depends on the value of certain input. Java processes conditions using the `if`, `if ... else`, and `switch ... case` statements. There are four conditional actions in JSTL: `<c:if>`, `<c:choose>`, `<c:when>`, and `<c:otherwise>`.

The <c:if> Tag

The `<c:if>` tag tests a condition and lets the JSP container process its body content only if the condition evaluates to true. The syntax of `<c:if>` has two forms. The first form has no body content:

```
<c:if test="testCondition"  var="varName"
  [scope="{page|request|session|application}]/>
```

The second form is used with body content:

```
<c:if test="testCondition [var="varName"]
  [scope="{page|request|session|application}]>
  body content
</c:if>
```

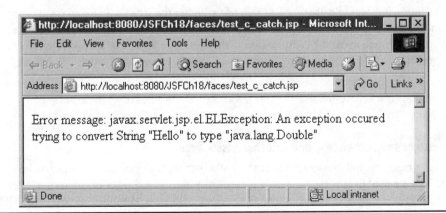

Figure 18-4   *Testing <c:catch>*

Attribute	rtexprvalue	Type	Description
test	true	boolean	The test condition that determines if any existing body content should be processed
var	false	String	The name of the scoped variable to hold the value of the test condition (the type of var is boolean)
scope	false	String	The scope for var

Table 18-5   *The <c:if> Attributes*

The body content is JSP. Table 18-5 lists the <c:if> attributes. If a <c:if> action has a scope attribute, the var attribute must also be present.

For example, the following <c:if> action displays the string "You logged in successfully" if there is a parameter userName with the value of ken and a parameter password with the value of blackcomb.

```
<c:if test="${param.userName=='ken' && param.password=='blackcomb'}">
  You logged in successfully.
</c:if>
```

To simulate an else block, use two <c:if> actions with opposite conditions. For instance, the following snippet displays "You logged in successfully" if the userName and password parameters are ken and blackcomb, respectively. Otherwise, it displays "Login failed."

```
<c:if test="${param.userName=='ken' && param.password=='blackcomb'}">
  You logged in successfully.
</c:if>
<c:if
test="${!(param.userName=='ken' && param.password=='blackcomb')}">
  Login failed.
</c:if>
```

The following example uses <c:if> to test whether the userName and password parameters are ken and blackcomb, and stores the result in the page-scoped variable loggedIn. It then uses an EL expression to display "You logged in successfully" if the loggedIn variable is true, and "Login failed" if the loggedIn variable is false.

```
<c:if var="loggedIn"
  test="${param.userName=='ken' && param.password=='blackcomb'}"/>
${(loggedIn)? "You logged in successfully" : "Login failed"}
```

The <c:choose>, <c:when>, and <c:otherwise> Tags

The <c:choose> and <c:when> tags act similarly to the switch and case keywords in Java. They are used to provide the context for mutually exclusive conditional execution. The <c:choose> tag must have one or more <c:when> tags nested inside it, and each <c:when> represents a case that can be evaluated and processed. The <c:otherwise> tag represents the default conditional block that will be processed if none of the <c:when> action test conditions evaluates to true. If present, <c:otherwise> must appear after the last <c:when>.

The <c:choose> and <c:otherwise> tags do not have any attributes. The <c:when> tag must have a test attribute containing the test condition that determines whether the body content should be processed. The type of the test attribute is boolean, and the value can be assigned dynamically.

As an example, the following block tests the value of a parameter called status. If the value of status is full, it displays "You are a full member." If the value is student, it displays "You are a student member." If the parameter status does not exist or if its value is not full or student, it displays nothing.

```
<c:choose>
  <c:when test="${param.status=='full'}">
    You are a full member
  </c:when>
  <c:when test="${param.status=='student'}">
    You are a student member
  </c:when>
</c:choose>
```

The following example is similar to the previous one, but it uses a <c:otherwise> tag to display "Please register" if the status parameter does not exist or if its value is not full or student.

```
<%@ taglib uri="http://java.sun.com/jsp/jstl/core" prefix="c" %>
<c:choose>
  <c:when test="${param.status=='full'}">
    You are a full member
  </c:when>
  <c:when test="${param.status=='student'}">
    You are a student member
  </c:when>
  <c:otherwise>
    Please register
  </c:otherwise>
</c:choose>
```

Iterating with Iterator Actions

Iterator actions are useful when you need to iterate a number of times or over a collection of objects. The JSTL provides two iterator actions: <c:forEach> and <c:forToken>.

The <c:forEach> Tag

Using <c:forEach>, you can iterate the body content a number of times or iterate a collection of objects. You can iterate over all implementations of java.util.Collection and java.util.Map, as well as arrays of objects or primitive types. You can also iterate over java.util.Iterator and java.util.Enumeration objects, but you should not use the Iterator or Enumeration object in more than one action, because an Iterator or Enumeration object will not be reset.

The syntax for <c:forEach> has two forms. The first one is for repeating the body content a fixed number of times:

```
<c:forEach [var="varName"]
  begin="begin" end="end" step="step">
body content
</c:forEach>
```

The second form is used to iterate over a collection of objects.

```
<c:forEach items="collection" [var="varName"]
  [varStatus="varStatusName"] [begin="begin"] [end="end"]
  [step="step"]>
body content
</c:forEach>
```

The body content is JSP. Table 18-6 lists the c:forEach attributes.

Attribute	rtexprvalue	Type	Description
var	false	String	The name of the scoped variable for the current item of the iteration
items	true	Any of the supported types	Collections of objects to iterate over
varStatus	false	String	The name of the scoped variable that holds the status of the iteration (the value is of type javax.servlet.jsp.jstl.core .LoopTagStatus)
begin	true	int	If items is specified, iteration begins at the item located at the specified index, in which the first item of the collection has an index of 0; if items is not specified, iteration begins with the index set at the value specified; if specified, the value of begin must be equal to or greater than 0
end	true	int	If items is specified, iteration ends at the item located at the specified index (inclusive); if items is not specified, iteration ends when the index reaches the value specified
step	true	int	Iteration will process only every step items of the collection, starting with the first one; if present, the value of step must be equal to or greater than 1

Table 18-6   *The <c:forEach> Attributes*

For example, the following <c:forEach> action displays the numbers 1 through 5.

```
<c:forEach var="x" begin="1" end="5">
${x},
</c:forEach>
```

The next example uses the ShoppingItem class in Listing 18-5 and the ShoppingCartBean class in Listing 18-6.

Listing 18-5   *The ShoppingItem Class*

```
package ch18;
public class ShoppingItem {
  private String productName;
  private String description;
  private int quantity;
  private double price;

  public ShoppingItem() {
  }
  public ShoppingItem(String productName, String description,
    int quantity, double price) {
    this.productName = productName;
    this.description = description;
    this.quantity = quantity;
    this.price = price;
  }

  public String getProductName() {
    return productName;
  }
  public void setProductName(String productName) {
    this.productName = productName;
  }
  public String getDescription() {
    return description;
  }
  public void setDescription(String description) {
    this.description = description;
  }
  public int getQuantity() {
    return quantity;
  }
  public void setQuantity(int quantity) {
```

```
    this.quantity = quantity;
  }
  public double getPrice() {
    return price;
  }
  public void setPrice(double price) {
    this.price = price;
  }
}
```

The ShoppingItem class represents a shopping item, with the properties productName, description, price, and quantity.

Listing 18-6   *The ShoppingCartBean Class*

```
package ch18;

import java.util.Collection;
import java.util.ArrayList;

public class ShoppingCartBean {
  private Collection shoppingItems;
  public ShoppingCartBean() {
    shoppingItems = new ArrayList();
    shoppingItems.add(
      new ShoppingItem("Chocomilk",
        "1 liter chocolate milk",
        2, 1.99));
    shoppingItems.add(
      new ShoppingItem("Mocca Yoghurt",
        "200g authentic yoghurt",
        1, 2.99));
    shoppingItems.add(
      new ShoppingItem("Timtim",
        "200g white chocolate",
        10, 3.99));
  }
  public Collection getShoppingItems() {
    return shoppingItems;
  }
}
```

The ShoppingCartBean class has one property, shoppingItems, which is a collection of ShoppingItem objects. When instantiated, the ShoppingCartBean class adds three ShoppingItem objects into its shoppingItems collection.

The test_c_forEach.jsp page, shown in Listing 18-7 uses two <c:forEach> actions to iterate the shoppingItems collection of a ShoppingCartBean instance.

Listing 18-7   *The test_c_forEach.jsp Page*

```jsp
<%@ taglib uri="http://java.sun.com/jsp/jstl/core" prefix="c" %>
<jsp:useBean id="shoppingCart"
  class="ch18.ShoppingCartBean" scope="page"/>
Shopping Cart:
<br/>
<c:forEach var="item" items="${shoppingCart.shoppingItems}">
  ${item.description} <br/>
</c:forEach>
<hr/>
<br/>
Shopping Cart
<br/>
<table border="1">
<tr>
  <td><b>Product</b></td>
  <td><b>Description</b></td>
  <td><b>Price</b></td>
  <td><b>Quantity</b></td>
</tr>
<c:forEach var="item" items="${shoppingCart.shoppingItems}" varStatus="status">
  <c:choose>
    <c:when test="${status.count%2==0}">
      <tr bgcolor="#eeeeee">
    </c:when>
    <c:otherwise>
      <tr bgcolor="#dddddd">
    </c:otherwise>
  </c:choose>
  <td>${item.productName}</td>
  <td>${item.description}</td>
  <td align="right">\$${item.price}</td>
  <td align="right">${item.quantity}</td>
</tr>
</c:forEach>
</table>
```

The `test_c_forEach.jsp` page starts by creating a JavaBean of type `ch18`
`.ShoppingCartBean` in the page scope. The name for this JavaBean instance is
`shoppingCart`.

```
<jsp:useBean id="shoppingCart" class="ch14.ShoppingCartBean"
  scope="page"/>
```

The first `<c:forEach>` is as follows:

```
<c:forEach var="item" items="${shoppingCart.shoppingItems}">
  ${item.description} <br/>
</c:forEach>
```

Its `items` attribute refers to the `shoppingItems` property of the `shoppingCart`
`ch18.ShoppingCartBean`. The `var` attribute has a value of `item`, which is the name to
identify the element being iterated. The body content that will be iterated is the `description`
property of the `ShoppingItem` object.

The second `<c:forEach>` contains more complex body content, in which each shopping
item is output as a table row. Additionally, the background color of even-numbered rows
is different from that of odd-numbered rows. The color differentiation is achieved using
`<c:choose>`, `<c:when>`, and `<c:otherwise>`.

```
  <c:choose>
    <c:when test="${status.count%2==0}">
      <tr bgcolor="#eeeeee">
    </c:when>
    <c:otherwise>
      <tr bgcolor="#dddddd">
    </c:otherwise>
  </c:choose>
```

The `varStatus` attribute is given the value `status`, which becomes the name of the
`javax.servlet.jsp.jstl.core.LoopTagStatus` object from the tag handler.
The `LoopTagStatus` interface has the `count` property, which returns the count of the
current round of iteration. The value of `status.count` is 1 for the first iteration, 2 for
the second iteration, and so on. By testing the remainder of `status.count%2`, you know
whether the tag is processing an even-numbered or odd-numbered element.

The `test_c_forEach.jsp` page can be invoked using the following URL:

```
http://localhost:8080/JSFCh18/test_c_forEach.jsp
```

You will see the result shown in Figure 18-5.

The <c:forTokens> Tag

You can use `<c:forTokens>` to iterate over tokens, separated by the specified delimiters.
The syntax for this action is as follows:

Figure 18-5   *Testing c_forEach*

```
<c:forTokens items="stringOfTokens" delims="delimiters"
  [var="varName"] [varStatus="varStatusName"]
  [begin="begin"] [end="end"] [step="step"]>
  body content
</c:forTokens>
```

The body content is JSP. Table 18-7 shows the <c:forTokens> attributes.
Here is an example of using <c:forTokens>:

```
<c:forTokens var="item" items="Argentina,Brazil,Columbia" delims=",">
  ${item} <br/>
</c:forTokens>
```

When pasted in a JSP page, this code will result in the following:

```
Argentina
Brazil
Columbia
```

Solving Common JSF Problems with JSTL Tags

A potential problem in JSF applications is the unrestricted accessibility of their JSP pages.
You know that a JSP page represents a component tree of a request, and each JSF request

Attribute	rtexprvalue	Type	Description
var	false	String	The name of the scoped variable for the current item of the iteration
items	true	String	String of tokens to iterate over
varStatus	false	String	The name of the scoped variable that holds the status of the iteration (the value is of type `javax.servlet.jsp.jstl.core.LoopTagStatus`)
begin	true	int	The start index of the iteration, where the index is zero-based; if specified, `begin` must be equal to or greater than 0
end	true	int	The end index of the iteration, where the index is zero-based
step	true	int	Iteration will process only every `step` tokens of the string, starting with the first one; if specified, `step` must be equal to or greater than 1
delims	true	String	The set of delimiters

Table 18-7 *The <c:forTokens> Attributes*

must invoke the `Faces` servlet. Therefore, you must include the pattern `/faces/` in all URLs. For example, here is the URL used to invoke a JSP page called `login.jsp` in JSF:

```
http://localhost:8080/JSFCh18/faces/login.jsp
```

However, the JSP pages reside in the application directory; therefore, they are directly visible. In other words, there is nothing preventing the user from bypassing JSF by entering the following URL to access the `login.jsp` page:

```
http://localhost:8080/JSFCh18/login.jsp
```

If the `login.jsp` page contains JSF UI components, an exception will be thrown. In any case, this is not elegant at all. What we want to happen if the user tries to access a JSP page directly is for that user to be directed to a default page. In other words, we want to restrict access to JSP pages. Any JSP page in a JSF application should be invoked only if the JSP page is a forward destination of the `Faces` servlet.

Servlet 2.4 solves this problem elegantly. A Servlet 2.4-compliant servlet container adds five attributes to the `Request` object forwarded to another resource. These attributes are as follows:

```
javax.servlet.forward.request_uri
javax.servlet.forward.context_path
javax.servlet.forward.servlet_path
javax.servlet.forward.path_info
javax.servlet.forward.query_string
```

If a `Request` object is not forwarded, the values for these attributes are `null`. On the other hand, these attributes in a forwarded resource will have non-`null` values. They are useful, for example, if you want to enforce that a resource can be invoked only from another resource and must not be called directly.

Restricting Access to JSP Pages

Combined with the JSTL <c:if> tag, the new Servlet 2.4 attributes can be used to restrict access to a JSP page. You achieve this by using the following <c:if> action on top of every JSP page in a JSF application:

```
<c:if
test="${requestScope['javax.servlet.forward.servlet_path']==null}">
  <jsp:forward page="defaultPage"/>
</c:if>
```

The <c:if> action checks the value of the javax.servlet.forward.servlet _path attribute in the request object. If it is null, the JSP page is not a forward destination of another resource, so the user must be forwarded to a default page.

A similar approach can also be used to restrict access to certain JSP pages. In many Web applications, it is not uncommon to have resources with limited access, such as pages that can be seen only if the user has successfully logged in.

Improving the Login Application

Let's revisit the login application presented in Chapter 8. Recall that the application consists of two JSP pages: login.jsp and welcome.jsp. The login.jsp page contains a form for the user to log in. If the user logs in successfully (by entering ken and blackcomb as the user name and password), the welcome.jsp page will be displayed. However, there is nothing preventing the user from accessing the welcome.jsp page directly.

Now, we will fix the problem in this application by using the JSTL <c:if> tag with the new Servlet 2.4 attributes. First, we need to modify the LoginBean, as shown in Listing 18-8.

Listing 18-8 *The LoginBean*

```
package ch18;
import javax.faces.application.Action;
import javax.faces.application.Message;
import javax.faces.application.MessageImpl;
import javax.faces.context.ExternalContext;
import javax.faces.context.FacesContext;
import javax.servlet.http.HttpSession;

public class LoginBean {
  private String userName;
  private String password;
  private Action login;
  public String getUserName() {
```

```
      return userName;
  }
  public void setUserName(String userName) {
    this.userName = userName;
  }
  public String getPassword() {
    return password;
  }
  public void setPassword(String password) {
    this.password = password;
  }
  public Action getLogin() {
    if (login==null)
      login = new LoginAction();
    return login;
  }

  class LoginAction extends Action {
    public String invoke() {
      FacesContext facesContext = FacesContext.getCurrentInstance();
      if ("ken".equals(userName) && "blackcomb".equals(password)) {
        ExternalContext externalContext =
          facesContext.getExternalContext();
        HttpSession session =
          (HttpSession) externalContext.getSession(true);
        session.setAttribute("loggedIn", "1");
        return "success";
      }
      else {
        Message loginErrorMessage = new
          MessageImpl(1, "<hr>Login failed", null);
        facesContext.addMessage(null, loginErrorMessage);
        return "failed";
      }
    }
  }
}
```

Pay special attention to the code shown in bold in Listing 18-8. If the user types in the correct user name and password, you obtain the HttpSession object from the ExternalContext object and add an attribute called loggedIn.

Now, let's look at the login.jsp and welcome.jsp pages, shown in Listings 18-9 and 18-10.

Listing 18-9   *The login.jsp Page*

```
<%@ taglib uri="http://java.sun.com/jsf/html" prefix="h" %>
<%@ taglib uri="http://java.sun.com/jsf/core" prefix="f" %>
<%@ taglib uri="http://java.sun.com/jsp/jstl/core" prefix="c" %>
<%--
The following <c:if> makes sure that the current page is not
directly invoked by using http://localhost:8080/JSFCh18/login.jsp
If the user tries to do so, it will forward to /faces/login.jsp.
--%>
<c:if
test="${requestScope['javax.servlet.forward.servlet_path']==null}">
  <jsp:forward page="${initParam.loginPage}"/>
</c:if>
<html>
<head>
<title>Login</title>
</head>
<body>
<f:use_faces>
<h:form   formName="loginForm">
<h2>Please enter your user name and password</h2>
<br>User Name: <h:input_text valueRef="loginBean.userName"/>
<br>Password: <h:input_secret valueRef="loginBean.password"/>
<br><h:command_button commandName="login" label="login"
actionRef="LoginBean.login"/>
<br>
<h:output_errors/>
</h:form>
</f:use_faces>
</body>
</html>
```

The login.jsp page in Listing 18-9 starts with a `<c:if>` that tests whether the attribute javax.servlet.forward.servlet_path in the Request object exists. If this attribute does not exist, that means the user tried to invoke the page directly and the user will be forwarded to the login page specified by the loginPage initial parameter. If the attribute exists, the Login form is displayed.

Listing 18-10   *The welcome.jsp Page*

```
<%@ taglib uri="http://java.sun.com/jsf/html" prefix="h" %>
<%@ taglib uri="http://java.sun.com/jsf/core" prefix="f" %>
<%@ taglib uri="http://java.sun.com/jsp/jstl/core" prefix="c" %>
<%--
```

```
     The following <c:if> makes sure that the user can only see
     this page if there is a session attribute named 'loggedIn'.
     If this attribute is not found, forward to /faces/login.jsp.
--%>
<c:if test="${sessionScope.loggedIn==null}">
  <jsp:forward page="${initParam.loginPage}"/>
</c:if>
<html>
<head>
<title>Welcome</title>
</head>
<body>
You logged in successfully.
</body>
</html>
```

The welcome.jsp page begins with a <c:if> that tests the existence of a session attribute named loggedIn. If the attribute cannot be found, the user will be forwarded to the Login page specified by the loginPage initial parameter. If the attribute exists, the Welcome message is displayed.

Summary

The JSTL is an important library that can help you develop JSF applications more rapidly. Used correctly, it can solve some problems in JSF. This chapter presented a number of useful tags in the JSTL that can help JSF programmers. It also offered some solutions to common JSF problems—specifically, how to restrict access to JSP pages in a JSF application.

This chapter is the last chapter in the book. You have seen how JSF makes it possible to develop Web applications more rapidly by providing features that solve common problems in Web development: input validation, standard user interface component, page navigation, JavaBean management, event-handling, etc. The last two chapters showed how the JSP 2.0 expression language and JSTL can also help you write better JSF applications.

Installing and Configuring Tomcat 5

IN THIS CHAPTER:

Setting the JAVA_HOME Environment Variable

Installing and Running Tomcat

Configuring Tomcat

Finding Tomcat Resources

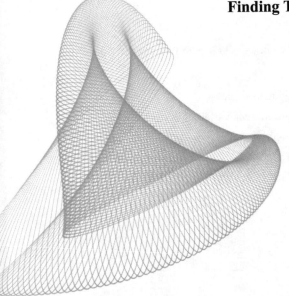

F ree and open-sourced, Tomcat is the most popular Web container for running servlet/JSP applications. Since JSF applications are also servlet applications, you need a Web container such as Tomcat to run them.

At the time this book was published, the latest version of Tomcat is 5, which supports Servlet 2.4 and JSP 2.0. Even though you can run your JSF applications in Tomcat 4, you should always get Tomcat 5 for new installation. If you have an existing deployment of version 4, it is worthwhile to upgrade to Tomcat 5, so that you can enjoy the new features in Servlet 2.4 and JSP 2.0.

This appendix explains the installation and basic configuration of Tomcat 5 in Windows NT/2000/XP and Linux.

NOTE

You need Java Development Kit (JDK) 1.2 or later to run Web applications in Tomcat, because Tomcat is written in Java. You may be able to run Tomcat with a Java Runtime Environment (JRE) only (without a compiler), but this means you will need to precompile JSP pages before deployment. This appendix explains how to run Tomcat with a JDK and assumes that you have installed Java 2, Standard Edition (J2SE) 1.4.

Setting the JAVA_HOME Environment Variable

The key to a successful installation of Tomcat 5 is the setting of the JAVA_HOME environment variable. Tomcat needs this variable so that it can find a Java runtime to run itself. If one of your applications contains JSP pages, Tomcat needs a Java compiler to run them as well.

This section presents instructions on how to set this variable in both Windows and Unix/Linux systems.

Setting JAVA_HOME in Windows

To set the JAVA_HOME environment variable on a Windows NT/2000/XP computer, follow these steps:

1. Open the Control Panel and double-click the System applet.
2. Click the Advanced tab, and then click the Environment Variables button.
3. Click the New button in the System Variables section.
4. In the Variable Name box, type **JAVA_HOME**. In the Variable Value box, type the JDK installation directory. For example, if you installed the JDK in the `C:\jdk1.4` directory, enter `C:\jdk1.4`.
5. Click OK.

Setting JAVA_HOME in Unix/Linux

If you are using the `bash` shell, type the following command:

```
JAVA_HOME=/path/to/jdk
export JAVA_HOME
```

where `/path/to/jdk` is the path to your Java installation.

If you are using `tcsh`, type the following command:

```
setenv JAVA_HOME /path/to/jdk
```

Installing and Running Tomcat

Installing Tomcat 5 is very easy. Just make sure that J2SE 1.4 is already installed and you've set the `JAVA_HOME` environment, as described in the previous section. Then follow these steps.

1. Download the latest version of the Tomcat 5 binary from Apache Software Foundation's Web site at `http://jakarta.apache.org/site/binindex.cgi`. For a Windows installation, you may want to download the zip file. You can extract this file using your favorite zip/unzip program, such as WinZip. However, if you prefer, you can download any other file format.

2. Extract the compressed file into a directory. This directory is referred to as `%CATALINA_HOME%`.

3. On Windows, run the `%CATALINA_HOME%\bin\startup.bat` program. On Linux/Unix, run the `%CATALINA_HOME%/bin/startup.sh` program.

That's all there is to installing Tomcat 5. If Tomcat is installed properly, it will now be running on port 8080. Direct your browser to the following URL:

```
http://machineName:8080/
```

where `machineName` is the name of the computer running Tomcat.

If your browser is on the same computer as the one running Tomcat, the URL is this:

```
http://localhost:8080
```

You'll see a screen similar to the one shown in Figure A-1.

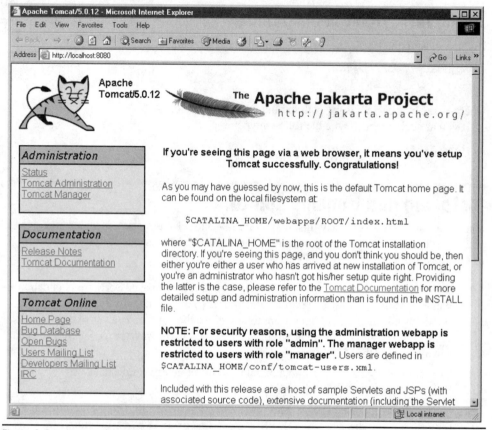

Figure A-1 *Successful Tomcat 5 installation*

Stopping Tomcat

To stop Tomcat 5 on Windows, run the `%CATALINA_HOME%\bin\shutdown.bat` program. On Linux/Unix, run the `%CATALINA_HOME%/bin/shutdown.sh` program.

Alternatively, on Windows, to stop Tomcat you can just close the console window in which Tomcat is running.

Reviewing Tomcat Directories

When you install Tomcat, the installation program creates a number of directories under `%CATALINA_HOME%`, as listed in Table A-1. Understanding the function of each subdirectory is important to configuring Tomcat and deploying your JSF applications.

Directory	Contents
`bin`	Startup, shutdown scripts, and other files
`common`	Tomcat standard APIs
`conf`	Configuration files including `server.xml` (Tomcat's main configuration file), `tomcat-user.xml`, and the global `web.xml` (deployment descriptor) file
`logs`	Tomcat's log files
`server`	Files necessary to run Tomcat
`shared`	Common classes shared by Web applications
`temp`	Directory used by the Java Virtual Machine (JVM) for temporary files (`java.io.tmpdir`)
`webapps`	Servlet and JSP applications
`work`	Temporary working directory for Web applications

Table A-1 *Subdirectories under %CATALINA_HOME%*

Configuring Tomcat

You can configure Tomcat 5 by editing the `server.xml` file in the `%CATALINA_HOME%/conf` directory. The two most common settings you will need to adjust are the port and automatic reloading settings.

Changing the Port

By default, Tomcat runs on port 8080. As a result, your users must always type the port number :8080 after the domain part in the URL. In fact, users must always type the port number unless Tomcat is run on port 80, the default port for HTTP. (This book assumes that your Tomcat runs on port 8080.)

CAUTION

You must not change the Tomcat port to 80 if you are going to run Tomcat with other Web servers because port 80 is the default port used by Web servers.

To change the port, first you need to find the following lines in the Tomcat configuration file, `server.xml`:

```
<!-- Define a non-SSL Coyote HTTP/1.1 Connector on port 8080 -->
<Connector port="8080"
maxThreads="150" minSpareThreads="25" maxSpareThreads="75"
    enableLookups="false" redirectPort="8443" acceptCount="100"
    debug="0" connectionTimeout="20000"
    disableUploadTimeout="true" />
```

You can see that in the second line there is the `port` attribute with a value of `8080`. Change that value to **80** and save the file.

You need to restart Tomcat for this change to take effect. Now, you can call any page without including the port number in the URL.

On the Unix/Linux platform, if you want to run a process using port numbers lower than 1024, you must log in as the super user.

Enabling Automatic Reloading

While you are developing JSF applications, you will repeatedly compile and recompile servlets and other classes needed by your application. When a class is recompiled, this new version of Java class must be loaded into the memory, and you must restart Tomcat. However, Tomcat supports automatic context reloading by creating a thread that continuously checks the timestamp of any class under the `WEB-INF/classes` and `WEB-INF/lib` directories of an application. If any class is modified, the whole context is reloaded.

Enabling Automatic Reloading

By default, automatic reloading is disabled. To enable it, you must configure a `Context` element for your application under a host element and set the reloadable attribute to `true`. For example, add the following to your `server.xml` file to enable automatic reloading for the application `JFSCh01`:

```
<host>
  ...
  <Context path="/JSFCh01" docBase="JSFCh01" reloadable="true"/>
</host>
```

Changing the Check Interval

By default, the check interval is 15 seconds, meaning that your application is checked every 15 seconds. To change the check interval, you must nest a `Loader` element inside the `Context` element and set the following:

▶ The `className` to `org.apache.catalina.loader.WebappLoader`

▶ The `reloadable` attribute to `true`

▶ The `checkInterval` attribute to the number of seconds you want your application to be checked

As an example, the following `Context` element tells Tomcat to check the application every 7 seconds:

```
<Context path="/JSFCh18" docBase="JSFCh18" reloadable="true">
  <Loader className="org.apache.catalina.loader.WebappLoader"
    reloadable="true" checkInterval="7"/>
</Context>
```

NOTE

The application is also reloaded if the `web.xml` *file is changed, but not if the* `faces-config.xml` *file (the JSF application configuration file) is updated.*

Finding Tomcat Resources

Tomcat's official Web site, `http://jakarta.apache.org/tomcat`, provides important information regarding Tomcat configuration. The FAQ is especially useful. Also, if you cannot find the solution to a problem here, you can ask questions in the Tomcat user mailing list. Make sure you check the archive before posting anything, to avoid asking a question that has already been answered. More documentation on Tomcat can be found at `http://jakarta.apache.org/tomcat/tomcat-5.0-doc/index.html`.

If you are interested in Tomcat's history, you may find the following two sites interesting:

▶ On how Tomcat got its name: `http://marc.theaimsgroup.com/?l=tomcat-user&m=104432576828011&w=2`

▶ The biography of James Duncan Davidson, the creator of Tomcat: `http://x180.net/Bio/index.html`

Also, if you are interested in some information about whether or not to package a JSF application into a WAR file, visit `http://marc.theaimsgroup.com/?l=tomcat-user&m=104874913017036&w=2`.

The Web Application Deployment Descriptor

IN THIS CHAPTER:

An Overview of the web.xml File

The web-app Elements in the web.xml File

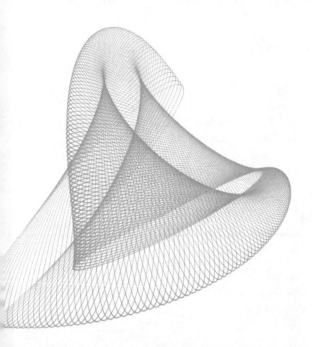

Servlet technology allows you to configure the application via a deployment descriptor, which takes the form of an XML document called `web.xml`. The deployment descriptor always resides in the `WEB-INF` directory of the application.

It is very important that you understand how to configure your deployment descriptor. This appendix starts with a general overview of the `web.xml` file and then discusses each element that it can contain. JSF is based on Servlet 2.3, and this appendix presents the deployment descriptor of Servlet 2.3. Most of the elements in the deployment descriptor discussed here are still valid in Servlet 2.4.

An Overview of the web.xml File

A deployment descriptor is an XML document that contains elements that describe various aspects of a servlet/JSP application such as servlet registration, servlet mapping, and listener registration. A deployment descriptor starts with the following header:

```
<?xml version="1.0" encoding="ISO-8859-1"?>
```

This header specifies the version of XML and the encoding used. The header is followed by the following `DOCTYPE` declaration:

```
<!DOCTYPE web-app
  PUBLIC "-//Sun Microsystems, Inc.//DTD Web Application 2.3//EN"
  "http://java.sun.com/dtd/web-app_2_3.dtd">
```

This code specifies the document type definition (DTD) against which you can check the validity of the XML document. The `<!DOCTYPE>` element shown here has several attributes that tell us a lot about the DTD:

▶ `web-app` defines the root element of this document (the deployment descriptor, not the DTD file).

▶ `PUBLIC` means that the DTD file is intended for public use.

▶ `"-//Sun Microsystems, Inc.//DTD Web Application 2.3//EN"` means that the DTD is maintained by Sun Microsystems, Inc. This information also indicates that the type of the document it describes is DTD Web Application 2.3, and the DTD is written in English.

▶ The URL `"http://java.sun.com/dtd/web-app_2_3.dtd">` represents the location of the DTD file.

NOTE

In a deployment descriptor, you use `<! -- ... -->` for comments.

The root element of a deployment descriptor is `web-app`. The DTD file states that the syntax of the `web-app` element's subelements is as follows:

```
<!ELEMENT web-app (icon?, display-name?, description?,
distributable?, context-param*, filter*, filter-mapping*,
listener*, servlet*, servlet-mapping*, session-config?,
mime-mapping*, welcome-file-list?,
error-page*, taglib*, resource-env-ref*, resource-ref*,
security-constraint*, login-config?, security-role*,env-entry*,
ejb-ref*, ejb-local-ref*)>
```

As you can see, this element can have up to 23 kinds of subelements, all of which are optional. The question mark (?) indicates that a subelement is optional and can appear only once. The asterisk (*) specifies subelements that can appear zero or more times in the deployment descriptor. Some of the subelements can have subelements of their own.

The web-app Elements in the web.xml File

Following the `web-app` element declaration in the `web.xml` file are the declarations of each subelement. The following sections describe all of the subelements a deployment descriptor may contain.

NOTE

In Servlet 2.3, subelements must appear in the order specified in the DTD file syntax description. For example, if the `web-app` element in a deployment descriptor has both `servlet` and `servlet-mapping` subelements, the `servlet` subelement must appear before the `servlet-mapping` subelement. In Servlet 2.4, the order is not important.

The icon Element

The `icon` element is used to specify the filenames for a small (16 by 16) and/or a large (32 by 32) icon in either GIF or JPEG format.

```
<!ELEMENT icon (small-icon?, large-icon?)>
<!ELEMENT small-icon (#PCDATA)>
<!ELEMENT large-icon (#PCDATA)>
```

The `icon` element contains optional `small-icon` and `large-icon` subelements. The filename is a path relative to the root of the web application archive (WAR).

The deployment descriptor does not use the `icon` element. However, if you use an XML tool to edit your deployment descriptor, the XML editor can use the icon.

The display-name Element

The `display-name` element contains a name to be displayed by an XML editor if you use a tool to edit your deployment descriptor.

```
<!ELEMENT display-name (#PCDATA)>
```

The following is a deployment descriptor that has a `display-name` element:

```
<?xml version="1.0" encoding="ISO-8859-1"?>
<!DOCTYPE web-app
    PUBLIC "-//Sun Microsystems, Inc.//DTD Web Application 2.3//EN"
    "http://java.sun.com/dtd/web-app_2_3.dtd">

<web-app>
    <display-name>Online Store Application</display-name>
</web-app>
```

The description Element

You use the `description` element to provide any information about the deployment descriptor. An XML editor can use the value of the `description` element.

```
<!ELEMENT description (#PCDATA)>
```

The distributable Element

You use the `distributable` element to tell the servlet/JSP container that the application is written to be deployed in a distributed Web container.

```
<!ELEMENT distributable EMPTY>
```

For example, the following is a deployment descriptor that contains a `distributable` element:

```
<?xml version="1.0" encoding="ISO-8859-1"?>
<!DOCTYPE web-app
    PUBLIC "-//Sun Microsystems, Inc.//DTD Web Application 2.3//EN"
    "http://java.sun.com/dtd/web-app_2_3.dtd">
<web-app>
    <distributable/>
</web-app>
```

The context-param Element

The `context-param` element contains a pair of parameter names and values used as the application's servlet context initialization parameter. The parameter name must be unique throughout the Web application.

```
<!ELEMENT context-param (param-name, param-value, description?)>
<!ELEMENT param-name (#PCDATA)>
<!ELEMENT param-value (#PCDATA)>
<!ELEMENT description (#PCDATA)>
```

The param-name subelement contains the parameter name, and the param-value subelement contains the parameter value. Optionally, a description subelement can describe the parameter.

The following is a valid deployment descriptor with a context-param element:

```
<?xml version="1.0" encoding="ISO-8859-1"?>
<!DOCTYPE web-app
  PUBLIC "-//Sun Microsystems, Inc.//DTD Web Application 2.3//EN"
  "http://java.sun.com/dtd/web-app_2_3.dtd">
<web-app>
  <context-param>
    <param-name>jdbcDriver</param-name>
    <param-value>com.mysql.jdbc.Driver</param-value>
  </context-param>
</web-app>
```

The filter Element

The filter element specifies a filter in the Web application. You use a filters to manipulate the request and response objects before and after they are processed by the servlet. A filter is mapped either to a servlet or to a URL pattern using the filter-mapping element described in the next section. The filter element and the filter-mapping element for this filter must have the same name.

```
<!ELEMENT filter (icon?, filter-name, display-name?, description?,
  filter-class, init-param*)>
<!ELEMENT filter-name (#PCDATA)>
<!ELEMENT filter-class (#PCDATA)>
```

The icon, display-name, and description elements are the same as those described in previous sections. The init-param element has the same element descriptor as context-param. The filter-name element defines the name of the filter, which must be unique within the application. The filter-class element specifies the fully qualified name for the filter class.

The following is a deployment descriptor that uses a filter element:

```
<?xml version="1.0" encoding="ISO-8859-1"?>
<!DOCTYPE web-app
  PUBLIC "-//Sun Microsystems, Inc.//DTD Web Application 2.3//EN"
  "http://java.sun.com/dtd/web-app_2_3.dtd">
<web-app>
  <filter>
    <filter-name>Encryption Filter</filter-name>
    <filter-class>com.branysoftware.EncryptionFilter</filter-class>
  </filter>
</web-app>
```

The filter-mapping Element

The `filter-mapping` element declares the filter mappings in the Web application. A filter can be mapped either to a servlet or to a URL pattern. Mapping a filter to a servlet causes the filter to work on the servlet. Mapping a filter to a URL pattern applies the filtering to any resource whose URL matches the URL pattern. Filtering is performed in the same order as the appearance of `filter-mapping` elements in the deployment descriptor.

```
<!ELEMENT filter-mapping (filter-name, (url-pattern | servlet-name))>
<!ELEMENT filter-name (#PCDATA)>
<!ELEMENT url-pattern (#PCDATA)>
<!ELEMENT servlet-name (#PCDATA)>
```

The `filter-name` value must match one of the filter names declared in the `filter` elements. The following is a deployment descriptor that contains a `filter-mapping` element:

```
<?xml version="1.0" encoding="ISO-8859-1"?>
<!DOCTYPE web-app
  PUBLIC "-//Sun Microsystems, Inc.//DTD Web Application 2.3//EN"
  "http://java.sun.com/dtd/web-app_2_3.dtd">
<web-app>
  <filter>
    <filter-name>Encryption Filter</filter-name>
    <filter-class>com.brainysoftware.EncryptionFilter</filter-class>
  </filter>
  <filter-mapping>
    <filter-name>Encryption Filter</filter-name>
    <servlet-name>EncryptionFilteredServlet</servlet-name>
  </filter-mapping>
</web-app>
```

The listener Element

The `listener` element is used to register a listener class that you include in a Web application. You can use a listener to get notification of when an event occurs and does something as a response.

```
<!ELEMENT listener (listener-class)>
<!ELEMENT listener-class (#PCDATA)>
```

The following is a valid deployment descriptor containing a `listener` element:

```
<?xml version="1.0" encoding="ISO-8859-1"?>
<!DOCTYPE web-app
  PUBLIC "-//Sun Microsystems, Inc.//DTD Web Application 2.3//EN"
  "http://java.sun.com/dtd/web-app_2_3.dtd">
```

```
<web-app>
  <listener>
    <listener-class>MyAppListener</listener-class>
  </listener>
</web-app>
```

The servlet Element

The `servlet` element is used to declare a servlet.

```
<!ELEMENT servlet (icon?, servlet-name, display-name?, description?,
  (servlet-class|jsp-file), init-param*, load-on-startup?, run-as?,
  security-role-ref*)>
<!ELEMENT servlet-name (#PCDATA)>
<!ELEMENT servlet-class (#PCDATA)>
<!ELEMENT jsp-file (#PCDATA)>
<!ELEMENT init-param (param-name, param-value, description?)>
<!ELEMENT load-on-startup (#PCDATA)>
<!ELEMENT run-as (description?, role-name)>
<!ELEMENT role-name (#PCDATA)>
```

The `icon`, `display-name`, and `description` elements are the same as those described in the previous sections. The `init-param` element descriptor is the same as `context-param`. You use the `init-param` subelement to pass an initial parameter name and value to the servlet.

The servlet-name, servlet-class, and jsp-file Elements

A `servlet` element must contain a `servlet-name` element and a `servlet-class` element, or a `servlet-name` element and a `jsp-file` element. These are described as follows:

▶ The `servlet-name` element defines the name for that servlet and must be unique throughout the application.

▶ The `servlet-class` element specifies the fully qualified class name of the servlet.

▶ The `jsp-file` element specifies the full path to a JSP file within the application. The full path must begin with a /.

The load-on-startup Element

The `load-on-startup` element is used to load the servlet automatically into memory when the Web container starts up. Loading a servlet means instantiating the servlet and calling its `init` method. You use this element to avoid delay in the response for the first request to the servlet, caused by the servlet loading to memory. If this element is present and a `jsp-file` element is specified, the JSP file is precompiled into a servlet, and the resulting servlet is loaded.

The content of a `load-on-startup` value is either empty or an integer number. The value indicates the order of loading into memory by the Web container. For example, if there are two `servlet` elements, and both contain `load-on-startup` subelements, the servlet with a lower number in the `load-on-startup` subelement is loaded first. If the value of the `load-on-startup` is empty or a negative number, it is up to the Web container to decide when to load the servlet. If two servlets have the same value for their `load-on-startup` subelements, the Web container decides which servlet to load first.

The run-as Element

If a `run-as` element is defined, it overrides the security identity used to call an Enterprise JavaBean (EJB) by that servlet in this Web application. The `role-name` is one of the security roles defined for the current Web application.

The security-role-ref Element

The `security-role-ref` element defines a mapping between the name of the role called from a servlet using `isUserInRole(String name)` and the name of a security role defined for the Web application. The `security-role-ref` element is described as follows:

```
<!ELEMENT security-role-ref (description?, role-name, role-link)>
<!ELEMENT description (#PCDATA)>
<!ELEMENT role-name (#PCDATA)>
<!ELEMENT role-link (#PCDATA)>
```

The `role-link` element is used to link a security role reference to a defined security role. The `role-link` element must contain the name of one of the security roles defined in the `security-role` elements.

The servlet Element for the Faces Servlet

In JSF applications, you always define one `servlet` element for the Faces Servlet, such as in the following:

```xml
<?xml version="1.0"?>
<!DOCTYPE web-app PUBLIC
  "-//Sun Microsystems, Inc.//DTD Web Application 2.3//EN"
  "http://java.sun.com/dtd/web-app_2_3.dtd">
<web-app>
  <!-- Faces Servlet -->
  <servlet>
    <servlet-name>Faces Servlet</servlet-name>
    <servlet-class>javax.faces.webapp.FacesServlet</servlet-class>
    <load-on-startup> 1 </load-on-startup>
  </servlet>
  <!-- Faces Servlet Mapping -->
  <servlet-mapping>
    <servlet-name>Faces Servlet</servlet-name>
    <url-pattern>/faces/*</url-pattern>
  </servlet-mapping>
</web-app>
```

The servlet-mapping Element

The `servlet-mapping` element maps a URL pattern to a servlet.

```
<!ELEMENT servlet-mapping (servlet-name, url-pattern)>
<!ELEMENT servlet-name (#PCDATA)>
<!ELEMENT url-pattern (#PCDATA)>
```

An example of using the `servlet-mapping` element is presented in the previous section, "The servlet Element."

The session-config Element

The `session-config` element defines the parameters for the `javax.servlet` `.http.HttpSession` objects in the Web application.

```
<!ELEMENT session-config (session-timeout?)>
<!ELEMENT session-timeout (#PCDATA)>
```

The `session-timeout` element specifies the default session timeout interval in minutes. This value must be an integer. If the value of the `session-timeout` element is zero or a negative number, the session will never time out.

The following is a deployment descriptor that makes the default `HttpSession` object invalid 30 minutes after the last access from the user:

```
<?xml version="1.0" encoding="ISO-8859-1"?>
<!DOCTYPE web-app
  PUBLIC "-//Sun Microsystems, Inc.//DTD Web Application 2.3//EN"
  "http://java.sun.com/dtd/web-app_2_3.dtd">
<web-app>
  <session-config>
    <session-timeout>30</session-timeout>
  </session-config>
</web-app>
```

The mime-mapping Element

The `mime-mapping` element maps a mime type to an extension.

```
<!ELEMENT mime-mapping (extension, mime-type)>
<!ELEMENT extension (#PCDATA)>
<!ELEMENT mime-type (#PCDATA)>
```

The `extension` element describes the extension. The `mime-type` element is the MIME type.

For example, the following deployment descriptor maps the extension `txt` to `text/plain`:

```
<?xml version="1.0" encoding="ISO-8859-1"?>
<!DOCTYPE web-app
    PUBLIC "-//Sun Microsystems, Inc.//DTD Web Application 2.3//EN"
    "http://java.sun.com/dtd/web-app_2_3.dtd">
<web-app>
  <mime-mapping>
    <extension>txt</extension>
    <mime-type>text/plain</mime-type>
  </mime-mapping>
</web-app>
```

The welcome-file-list Element

The `welcome-file-list` element specifies the default file that is displayed when the URL entered by the user in the browser does not contain a servlet name or a JSP page.

```
<!ELEMENT welcome-file-list (welcome-file+)>
<!ELEMENT welcome-file (#PCDATA)>
```

For example, suppose the user enters something like `http://www.mycompany.com/appName/` in the browser's address box. If no `welcome-file-list` element is specified in the deployment descriptor for a Web application, the user sees a permission error message or the list of files and directories in the application directory. With a `welcome-file-list` element defined, the user will see the file specified by that element instead.

The `welcome-file` subelement contains the name of the default file. A `welcome-file-list` element can contain one or more `welcome-file` subelements. If the file specified in the first `welcome-file` element cannot be found, the Web container will try to display the second one, and so on.

The following is a deployment descriptor that contains a `welcome-file-list` element. The element contains two `welcome-file` elements: the first specifies a file in the application directory called `main.html`, and the second defines the `welcome.jsp` file under the `jsp` directory, which is under the application directory.

```
<?xml version="1.0" encoding="ISO-8859-1"?>
<!DOCTYPE web-app
  PUBLIC "-//Sun Microsystems, Inc.//DTD Web Application 2.3//EN"
  "http://java.sun.com/dtd/web-app_2_3.dtd">
<web-app>
  <welcome-file-list>
    <welcome-file>main.html</welcome-file>
    <welcome-file>jsp/welcome.jsp</welcome-file>
  </welcome-file-list>
</web-app>
```

If the `main.html` file is not found in the application directory when a user types a URL that does not contain a servlet name or a JSP page or other resource, the `welcome.jsp` file in the `jsp` directory will be displayed.

The error-page Element

The `error-page` element maps an error code or an exception type to a resource path in the Web application, so that if a particular HTTP error or a specified Java exception occurs, the resource will be displayed instead.

```
<!ELEMENT error-page ((error-code | exception-type), location)>
<!ELEMENT error-code (#PCDATA)>
<!ELEMENT exception-type (#PCDATA)>
<!ELEMENT location (#PCDATA)>
```

The `error-code` element contains an HTTP error code. The `exception-type` element is the fully qualified name of a Java exception type. The `location` element is the path to the resource in the Web application relative to the application directory. The value of `location` must start with a /.

For example, the following deployment descriptor causes the Web container to display the `error404.html` page in the application directory every time the HTTP 404 error code occurs:

```
<?xml version="1.0" encoding="ISO-8859-1"?>
<!DOCTYPE web-app
   PUBLIC "-//Sun Microsystems, Inc.//DTD Web Application 2.3//EN"
   "http://java.sun.com/dtd/web-app_2_3.dtd">
<web-app>
  <error-page>
    <error-code>404</error-code>
    <location>/error404.html</location>
  </error-page>
</web-app>
```

The taglib Element

The `taglib` element describes a JSP custom tag library.

```
<!ELEMENT taglib (taglib-uri, taglib-location)>
<!ELEMENT taglib-uri (#PCDATA)>
<!ELEMENT taglib-location (#PCDATA)>
```

The `taglib-uri` element is the URI of the tag library used in the Web application. The value for `taglib-uri` is relative to the `WEB-INF` directory.

The `taglib-location` element contains the location where the tag library descriptor (TLD) file for the tag library can be found.

The resource-env-ref Element

You use the `resource-env-ref` element to specify a declaration of a servlet's reference to an administered object associated with a resource in the servlet's environment.

```
<!ELEMENT resource-env-ref (description?, resource-env-ref-name,
  resource-env-ref-type)>
<!ELEMENT resource-env-ref-name (#PCDATA)>
<!ELEMENT resource-env-ref-type (#PCDATA)>
```

The `resource-env-ref-name` element is the name of a resource environment reference whose value is the entry name of the environment used in servlet code. The name is a Java Naming and Directory Interface (JNDI) name relative to the `java:comp/env` context and must be unique throughout the Web application.

The `resource-env-ref-type` element defines the type of a resource environment reference. Its value must be the fully qualified name of a Java class or interface.

The resource-ref Element

The `resource-ref` element specifies a declaration of a servlet's reference to an external resource.

```
<!ELEMENT resource-ref (description?, res-ref-name,
res-type, res-auth, res-sharing-scope?)>
<!ELEMENT description (#PCDATA)>
<!ELEMENT res-ref-name (#PCDATA)>
<!ELEMENT res-type (#PCDATA)>
<!ELEMENT res-auth (#PCDATA)>
<!ELEMENT res-sharing-scope (#PCDATA)>
```

The subelements of `resource-ref` are described as follows:

▶ `res-ref-name` is the name of the resource factory reference name. The name is a JNDI name relative to the `java:comp/env` context. The name must be unique throughout the Web application.

▶ `res-auth` indicates whether the servlet code signs on programmatically to the resource manager or the container will sign on to the resource manager on the servlet's behalf. The value of this element must be either `Application` or `Container`.

▶ `res-sharing-scope` indicates whether connections obtained through the given resource manager connection factory reference can be shared. The value of this element must be either `Shareable` (the default) or `Unshareable`.

The security-constraint Element

The `security-constraint` element in the deployment descriptor allows you to restrict access to certain resources without programming.

```
<!ELEMENT security-constraint (display-name?,
  web-resource-collection+,
  auth-constraint?, user-data-constraint?)>
<!ELEMENT display-name (#PCDATA)>
<!ELEMENT web-resource-collection (web-resource-name, description?,
url-pattern*, http-method*)>
<!ELEMENT auth-constraint (description?, role-name*)>
<!ELEMENT user-data-constraint (description?, transport-guarantee)>
```

The web-resource-collection Element

The `web-resource-collection` element identifies a subset of resources to which access needs to be restricted. In `web-resource-collection`, you can define the URL pattern(s) and the HTTP method. If no HTTP method is present, the security constraint applies to all methods.

```
<!ELEMENT web-resource-collection (web-resource-name, description?,
  url-pattern*, http-method*)>
<!ELEMENT web-resource-name (#PCDATA)>
<!ELEMENT description (#PCDATA)>
<!ELEMENT url-pattern (#PCDATA)>
<!ELEMENT http-method (#PCDATA)>
```

The `web-resource-name` is a name associated with the protected resource. The `http-method` element can be assigned one of the HTTP methods, such as GET and POST.

The auth-constraint Element

The `auth-constraint` element specifies the user roles that should have access to this resource collection. If no `auth-constraint` element is specified, the security constraint applies to all roles.

```
<!ELEMENT auth-constraint (description?, role-name*)>
<!ELEMENT description (#PCDATA)>
<!ELEMENT role-name (#PCDATA)>
```

The `role-name` element contains the name of a security role.

The user-data-constraint Element

The `user-data-constraint` element is used to indicate how to protect data transmitted between the client and Web container.

```
<!ELEMENT user-data-constraint (description?, transport-guarantee)>
<!ELEMENT description (#PCDATA)>
<!ELEMENT transport-guarantee (#PCDATA)>
```

The `transport-guarantee` element must have one of the following values:

▶ `NONE` means that the application does not require transport guarantees.

▶ `INTEGRAL` means that the data between the server and the client should be sent in such a way that it cannot be changed in transit.

▶ `CONFIDENTIAL` means that the data transmitted must be encrypted.

In most cases, Secure Sockets Layer (SSL) is used for either `INTEGRAL` or `CONFIDENTIAL`.

The login-config Element

The `login-config` element is used to specify the authentication method used, the realm name, and the attributes needed by the form login mechanism.

```
<!ELEMENT login-config (auth-method?, realm-name?,
  form-login-config?)>
<!ELEMENT auth-method (#PCDATA)>
<!ELEMENT realm-name (#PCDATA)>
<!ELEMENT form-login-config (form-login-page, form-error-page)>
```

The subelements of `login-config` are described as follows:

▶ `auth-method` specifies the authentication method. Its value is one of the following: `BASIC`, `DIGEST`, `FORM`, or `CLIENT-CERT`.

▶ `realm-name` specifies the realm name to use in HTTP Basic authorization.

▶ `form-login-config` specifies the login and error pages that should be used in form-based login. If form-based authentication is not used, these elements are ignored. This element is defined as follows, where `form-login-page` specifies a path to a resource that displays a login page, and `form-error-page` specifies a path to a resource that displays an error page when user login fails. For both pages, the path must start with a / and is relative to the application directory.

```
<!ELEMENT form-login-config (form-login-page, form-error-page)>
<!ELEMENT form-login-page (#PCDATA)>
<!ELEMENT form-error-page (#PCDATA)>
```

The security-role Element

The `security-role` element specifies the declaration of a security role used in the security constraints.

```
<!ELEMENT security-role (description?, role-name)>
<!ELEMENT description (#PCDATA)>
<!ELEMENT role-name (#PCDATA)>
```

The env-entry Element

The env-entry element specifies an application environment entry.

```
<!ELEMENT env-entry (description?, env-entry-name, env-entry-value?,
   env-entry-type)>
<!ELEMENT description (#PCDATA)>
<!ELEMENT env-entry-name (#PCDATA)>
<!ELEMENT env-entry-value (#PCDATA)>
<!ELEMENT env-entry-type (#PCDATA)>
```

The env-entry-name element contains the name of a Web application's environment entry. The name is a JNDI name relative to the java:comp/env context. The name must be unique throughout the application.

The env-entry-value element contains the value of a Web application's environment entry. The value must be a String that is valid for the constructor of the specified type that takes a single String parameter, or for java.lang.Character, a single character.

The env-entry-type element contains the fully qualified Java type of the environment entry value that is expected by the Web application's code. This element must have one of the following values:

```
java.lang.Boolean
java.lang.Byte
java.lang.Character
java.lang.String
java.lang.Short
java.lang.Integer
java.lang.Long
java.lang.Float
java.lang.Double
```

The ejb-ref Element

The ejb-ref element specifies a reference to an EJB's home.

```
<!ELEMENT ejb-ref (description?, ejb-ref-name, ejb-ref-type, home,
   remote, ejb-link?)>
<!ELEMENT description (#PCDATA)>
<!ELEMENT ejb-ref-name (#PCDATA)>
<!ELEMENT ejb-ref-type (#PCDATA)>
<!ELEMENT home (#PCDATA)>
```

```
<!ELEMENT remote (#PCDATA)>
<!ELEMENT ejb-link (#PCDATA)>
```

The `ejb-ref-name` element contains the name of an EJB reference. The EJB reference is an entry in the servlet's environment and is relative to the `java:comp/env` context. The name must be unique within the Web application. It is recommended that its name begin with `ejb/` for consistency.

The `ejb-ref-type` element contains the expected type of the referenced EJB. The value must be either `Entity` or `Session`.

The `home` element contains the fully qualified name of the EJB's home interface. The `remote` element contains the fully qualified name of the EJB's remote interface.

The `ejb-link` element is used in the `ejb-ref` or `ejb-local-ref` elements to specify that an EJB reference is linked to another EJB. The value of the `ejb-link` element must be the `ejb-name` of an EJB in the same J2EE application unit. The name in the `ejb-link` element may be composed of a path name specifying the `ejb-jar` containing the referenced EJB. The name of the target bean is appended and separated from the path name by using a # character. The path name is relative to the WAR containing the Web application that is referencing the EJB. This allows multiple enterprise beans with the same `ejb-name` to be identified uniquely.

The ejb-local-ref Element

The `ejb-local-ref` element is used for the declaration of a reference to an EJB's local home.

```
<!ELEMENT ejb-local-ref (description?, ejb-ref-name, ejb-ref-type,
   local-home, local, ejb-link?)>
<!ELEMENT description (#PCDATA)>
<!ELEMENT ejb-ref-name (#PCDATA)>
<!ELEMENT ejb-ref-type (#PCDATA)>
<!ELEMENT local-home (#PCDATA)>
<!ELEMENT local (#PCDATA)>
<!ELEMENT ejb-link (#PCDATA)>
```

The `local` element contains the fully qualified name of the EJB's local interface. The `local-home` element contains the fully qualified name of the EJB's local home interface.

Index

INTERNATIONAL CONTACT INFORMATION

AUSTRALIA
McGraw-Hill Book Company
Australia Pty. Ltd.
TEL +61-2-9900-1800
FAX +61-2-9878-8881
http://www.mcgraw-hill.com.au
books-it_sydney@mcgraw-hill.com

CANADA
McGraw-Hill Ryerson Ltd.
TEL +905-430-5000
FAX +905-430-5020
http://www.mcgraw-hill.ca

GREECE, MIDDLE EAST, & AFRICA
(Excluding South Africa)
McGraw-Hill Hellas
TEL +30-210-6560-990
TEL +30-210-6560-993
TEL +30-210-6560-994
FAX +30-210-6545-525

MEXICO (Also serving Latin America)
McGraw-Hill Interamericana Editores
S.A. de C.V.
TEL +525-1500-5108
FAX +525-117-1589
http://www.mcgraw-hill.com.mx
carlos_ruiz@mcgraw-hill.com

SINGAPORE (Serving Asia)
McGraw-Hill Book Company
TEL +65-6863-1580
FAX +65-6862-3354
http://www.mcgraw-hill.com.sg
mghasia@mcgraw-hill.com

SOUTH AFRICA
McGraw-Hill South Africa
TEL +27-11-622-7512
FAX +27-11-622-9045
robyn_swanepoel@mcgraw-hill.com

SPAIN
McGraw-Hill/
Interamericana de España, S.A.U.
TEL +34-91-180-3000
FAX +34-91-372-8513
http://www.mcgraw-hill.es
professional@mcgraw-hill.es

UNITED KINGDOM, NORTHERN,
EASTERN, & CENTRAL EUROPE
McGraw-Hill Education Europe
TEL +44-1-628-502500
FAX +44-1-628-770224
http://www.mcgraw-hill.co.uk
emea_queries@mcgraw-hill.com

ALL OTHER INQUIRIES Contact:
McGraw-Hill/Osborne
TEL +1-510-420-7700
FAX +1-510-420-7703
http://www.osborne.com
omg_international@mcgraw-hill.com

Sound Off!

Visit us at **www.osborne.com/bookregistration** and let us know what you thought of this book. While you're online you'll have the opportunity to register for newsletters and special offers from McGraw-Hill/Osborne.

We want to hear from you!

Sneak Peek

Visit us today at **www.betabooks.com** and see what's coming from McGraw-Hill/Osborne tomorrow!

Based on the successful software paradigm, Bet@Books™ allows computing professionals to view partial and sometimes complete text versions of selected titles online. Bet@Books™ viewing is free, invites comments and feedback, and allows you to "test drive" books in progress on the subjects that interest you the most.